Federal Procurement Ethics
THE COMPLETE LEGAL GUIDE

Revised Edition

Federal Procurement Ethics
THE COMPLETE LEGAL GUIDE
Revised Edition

Terrence M. O'Connor

DEFENSE ACQUISITION UNIVERSITY
DAVID D. ACKER LIBRARY
9820 BELVOIR ROAD
FORT BELVOIR, VA 22060-5565

MANAGEMENTCONCEPTS
8230 Leesburg Pike, Suite 800
Vienna, VA 22182
(703) 790-9595
Fax: (703) 790-1371
www.managementconcepts.com

Copyright © 2010 by Management Concepts, Inc.

All rights reserved. No part of this book may be reproduced or utilized in any form or by any means, electronic or mechanical, including photocopying, recording, or by an information storage and retrieval system, without permission in writing from the publisher, except for brief quotations in review articles.

Library of Congress Cataloging-in-Publication Data

O'Connor, Terrence M.
  Federal procurement ethics : the complete legal guide / Terrence M. O'Connor. — Rev. ed.
    p. cm.
  ISBN 978-1-56726-277-3
1. Public contracts—United States. 2. Government purchasing—Law and legislation—United States. 3. Contracts—Moral and ethical aspects—United States. I. Title.
KF850.O256 2010
346.7302'3—dc22

                                                                                   2009038890

Printed in the United States of America

10   9   8   7   6   5   4   3   2   1

About the Author

Terrence M. O'Connor is Special Counsel to the law firm of Albo & Oblon, L.L.P. in Arlington VA for government contract issues. A graduate of Notre Dame Law School, he served as a government attorney from 1971 to 1985. He then went into private practice advising government contractors and litigating government contract cases before the various Boards of Contract Appeals, the Government Accountability Office, the U.S. Court of Federal Claims, and the U.S. Court of Appeals for the Federal Circuit. In 1985, he also began teaching government contract courses for Management Concepts, which continue to today. In 1991, he received his Master of Laws (Government Procurement Law) degree from the George Washington University Law Center.

For more than 25 years, he has written the "Recent Decisions" column for the *Federal Acquisition Report*. He has also authored several books published by Management Concepts, including *Understanding Government Contract Law* and *Federal Contracting Answer Book*.

Contents

Author's Note on the Revised Edition............................ xiii

Preface... xv

Acknowledgments.. xxi

PART I: THE NEW ETHICS REQUIREMENTS 1

CHAPTER 1: The Components of a Contractor's Ethics Program.....3
   Self-disclosure..4
   A Code of Business Ethics 9
   Ethics Training Program 14

CHAPTER 2: Applicability of the New Ethics Regulations 17
   Conditions that Trigger the New Regulations 18
   Exceptions to "Covered Contracts"..............................19
   Flow-down Clauses for Subcontracts 21
      A Purchase Order Is a Subcontract 22
   Compliance 23
   Government Posters..24

PART II: The FAR Rules 27

CHAPTER 3: Ethics Rules for Getting a Contract 29
   Procurement Integrity Regulations. 30
      Protecting Procurement Information. 32
         Who is covered by the anti-leaking laws?...................33
         What is covered by the anti-leaking laws? 34
         When do these prohibitions against leaking information
            kick in? 37
         How must the leaked information have been provided or
            obtained? 38
      Job Offers for Competitive Procurements over $100,000. 38
      The Revolving Door—Contracts over $10 Million. 39
   How the Government Deals with Violations 41
   Conflicts of Interest 44
      Personal Conflicts of Interest 44
      Organizational Conflicts of Interest 46
         Biased Ground Rules 48
         Unequal Access to Information. 48
         Impaired Objectivity 59
   Misrepresentation/Bait and Switch 61
   Status of the Offeror. 64
      Responsibility Determinations 64
      Debarment and Suspension. 69
   Ensuring Compliance with Procurement Integrity Rules 71

CHAPTER 4: Ethical Rules for Administering Contracts 77
   Defective Pricing 78
      Current, Accurate, and Complete Cost or Pricing Data 81
         Cost or Pricing Data 81
         Current, Accurate, and Complete. 82
         Government Reliance on Defective Pricing 86

Claims Involving Fraud. 88
Government's Rights under the Inspection Clause 93
Termination for Default 94
Penalties for Fraud 97
    Program Fraud Civil Remedies Act 97
    Suspension and Debarment. 98
        Suspension 98
        Debarment 103

PART III: FEDERAL STATUTES AND RULES AFFECTING PROCUREMENT 113

CHAPTER 5: Federal Employee Conduct 115
Conflicts of Interest 117
    "Participate personally and substantially". 118
    "Particular matter" 119
    "Negotiating for employment". 120
Bribes and Gratuities 125
Standards of Conduct 128
    Restrictions on Outside Activities. 130
    Restrictions on Seeking Employment 134

Chapter 6: Federal Laws about Contractor Conduct 139
False Statements Act. 139
False Claims Act 142
    Criminal False Claims 142
    Civil False Claims 142
    Criminal Conviction Does Not Bar Civil Fines for Fraud 144
    Implied Certifications 153
Qui Tam Suits 157
Mail Fraud and Wire Fraud 159
Major Procurement Fraud. 161
Obstruction of Agency Proceedings. 162

Miscellaneous Laws..163
    Trade Secrets Act 164
    Conspiracy 164
    Theft of Government Property 164
    Restrictions on Lobbying and Consultants...................165
    Covenant against Contingent Fees 165
    The Byrd Amendment..167

PART IV: PREVENTING AND UNCOVERING FRAUD 173

CHAPTER 7: Fighting Fraud: Common Fraudulent Activities 175
    Defective Pricing..176
    Antitrust Violations 177
        Indicators of Collusive Bidding and Price Fixing...............178
        Examples of Collusive Bidding and Price Fixing 180
    Cost Mischarging...182
        Allowable Costs 183
        Accounting Mischarges..................................185
        Material Cost Mischarges...............................185
        Labor Mischarges.......................................186
        Examples of Cost Mischarging 190
    Product Substitution 190
        Indicators of Product Substitution Fraud...............192
        Examples of Product Substitution Fraud.................193
    Progress Payment Fraud 194
        Indicators of Progress Payment Fraud 195
        Examples of Progress Payment Fraud 195
    Fast Pay Fraud 196
        Indicators of Fast Pay Fraud 197
        Example of Fast Pay Fraud 197
    Summary of Potential Areas for Fraud in the
        Government Procurement Process 198

Contract Formation 198
    Fraud in Identifying the Government's Need for Goods
    and Services 198
    Fraud in the Pre-Solicitation Phase 199
    Fraud in the Solicitation Phase 199
    Fraud in the Award of the Contract....................... 200
    Fraud in the Negotiation of a Contract 201
Contract Administration 201
    Fraud in Defective Pricing.................................201
    Fraud in Cost Mischarging 202
    Fraud in Product Substitution 202
    Fraud in Progress Payments 203
    Fraud in Fast Pay Procedure 203

APPENDIX A: Final Rules: Federal Acquisition Regulation and FAR Case 2006-007, Contractor Code of Business Ethics and Conduct 205

APPENDIX B: Proposed Rules: Federal Acquisition Regulation and FAR Case 2006-007, Contractor Compliance Program and Integrity Reporting.. 233

APPENDIX C: Code of Ethics Guide............................307

APPENDIX D: Advisory Opinion of the Office of Government Ethics 331

APPENDIX E: Office of Government Ethics, Ethics and Working with Contractors...................................... 343

Index 373

Author's Note on the Revised Edition

Shortly after *Federal Procurement Ethics: The Complete Legal Guide* went to the printer, the government made several significant additions to its procurement ethics rules. The full text of these additional rules can be found in the *Federal Register* at 73 FR 67064 (published November 12, 2008) and also reprinted in Appendix B. In May 2009, Congress added more rules that made significant changes to the False Claims Act—changes that all government contractors need to know not only to comply with the anti-fraud laws, but to comply with the recently added training requirements that make training in the False Claims Act an essential element of corporate ethics training programs.

This latest addition to the procurement ethics rules made it clear that is was now time to update this book to incorporate the government's additions to its procurement ethics rules as well as the revisions to the False Claims Act.

The important 2008 changes affected five key areas:

▶ All government contractors and subcontractors now have a "self-disclosure" duty.

- A business ethics awareness and compliance program and an internal control system must now include certain required components.
- Commercial item contracts or subcontracts over $5 million with a period of performance of over 120 days now impose a requirement that the contractors and subcontractors have a code of business ethics but not a business ethics awareness and compliance program and an internal control system.
- Contracts and subcontracts over $5 million with a period of performance of over 120 days performed outside the United States are now subject to the ethics requirements.
- Flowdown requirements are now imposed on contracts and subcontracts that are for commercial items or that will be performed outside the United States.

Congress also made changes to the False Claims Act:

- Subcontractors now can violate the False Claims Act.
- A contractor failing to report overpayments can violate the False Claims Act.

We hope this revision gives you plain-English explanations of these complex rules and that this book continues to be the complete legal guide to procurement ethics.

Preface

How Contractors and Contracting Officers Can Profit from the New Ethics Rules was my preferred title for this book. Obviously, my editors did not agree.

Make no mistake, however: Both contractors and contracting officers can benefit immensely from aggressively adopting and carrying out codes of business ethics, establishing internal control systems, and conducting training programs encouraged by recent changes in the Federal Acquisition Regulation (FAR), see Appendix A (2007 changes, 72 FR 65873) and Appendix B (2008 changes, 73 FR 67064).

One important way that both can profit from vigorous ethics compliance is through the increase in trust engendered by a contractor aggressively championing ethics. At the risk of generalizing, my experience has been that there are often bad feelings between contracting officers and contractors.

This has been true for centuries. In the 19th century, Calendar Irving, the person in charge of government contracting for the War of 1812, stated that "contractors are all crooked and greedy, paying low wages to produce inferior goods and increase profits at the public's expense." In the 20th century, Harry Truman said "I have never yet found a contractor who, if not watched, would not leave the government holding the bag." And in the 21st century, a retired contracting officer who went to work for a contractor left contracting completely because "contracting officers consider contractors crooks who have not yet been indicted."[1]

Let's not debate whether these incendiary quotes are accurate or are stereotypes. Instead, let's look at the flipside, "the good contractor." I base my ideas on the more than 24 years I have spent teaching government contract law to contract specialists and contracting officers. In my classes, when discussing whether a contracting officer is willing to give the contractor the benefit of the doubt in calculating an equitable adjustment, I often hear, "Well, if they're a good contractor. . . ." Once I hear that, I know where the contracting officer is going. Just as a teacher is willing to give a proven good student a break, a contracting officer is much more willing to be fair to a proven "good" contractor.

Being a good contractor provides important advantages in today's competitive government contract marketplace. Regardless of whether you believe that contractors and contracting officers generally do not trust each other, the new ethics rules give both sides a chance to improve a relationship that all would agree can benefit from improvement.

I view the new ethics rules as an opportunity for contracting officers and contractors to develop a relationship built on trust—a chance for contractors to demonstrate that they are good contractors and to be regarded as such. But this increase in trust between contractors and contracting officers is not the only result I anticipate from contractors aggressively championing the new ethics rules. I also see dollar signs.

Some interesting research shows that there's profit in ethics compliance. A Deloitte website notes:

> Companies that are explicit about their business ethics in their annual reports outperform (in financial and other indicators) those companies that don't have a code of ethics. Other studies reveal a robust relationship between a company's ethical climate and employee job satisfaction. . . . those with low job satisfaction and little company commitment are more likely to be latent, absent or resign.[2]

Finally, in addition to increasing trust and profits, a contractor that aggressively champions ethics can benefit in other ways. When acting as a subcontractor, that contractor will be easier for the prime contractor to work with because the contractor-turned-subcontractor has already adopted whatever flow down provisions the prime must impose on a subcontractor. Moreover, when submitting offers for future contracts, a contractor able to brag about its "Cadillac" ethics compliance program may have an advantage.

To me, it all boils down to: How much effort should a vendor put into complying with the new rules? I look at the "effort" issue as giving contractors two alternatives:

1. Do only what the FAR requires -- do the "shall" but not the "should"

2. Go beyond the "shall" and do the "should"

I advocate contractors aggressively championing ethics compliance. I advise my clients that they should pick alternative 2, go beyond the "shall" and do the "should."

My recommendation especially applies to the "should" requirements of an internal control system. Not all contractors are required to have an internal control system. As we will see, small businesses are not required to adopt an internal control system. But there is an advantage to a small business that voluntarily adopts one: if the small business should be convicted of a felony or Class A misdemeanor, whether or not the crime arises from a procurement situation, the small business will have complied with the guidelines issued by the U.S. Sentencing Commission and accordingly would be treated more leniently because it had adopted an internal control system.

For the more than 35 years I have been a lawyer in government contracts, I have seen time and again the truth of the statement, "It is cheaper to stay out of trouble than to get out of trouble." It takes little additional effort on a contractor's part to adopt an aggressive ethics compliance program. But let's be clear about this: Passive compliance is probably enough to get by. The regulations do not require that a contractor submit its code of business ethics, internal control system, or training program to the government for approval. As long as a company has no ethical problems in its government contracts, the government will not get too involved in the fine points:

> The contracting officer is not required to verify compliance, but may inquire at his or her discretion as part of contract administrative duties. . . . The Government will not be routinely reviewing plans unless a problem arises. The Government does not need the code of ethics as a deliverable. 72 FR 65878, Appendix A.

On the other hand, what I am arguing for is what I call "110 percent compliance." To me, it means aggressively teaching, advocating, and enforcing ethics, personal integrity, and company values.

One example might show the difference in approach. Clearly, every company appoints someone to be an ethics or integrity czar. Passive compliance means that a currently overloaded employee gets ethics added to his or her duties. In contrast, with "110 percent compliance," the company makes serving as the "integrity czar" the sole function of one person.

Admittedly, in many small companies, this would be cost-prohibitive. But let's look at another example: training.

A company that does ethics training one time for all employees, except for new hires, is passively compliant. On the other hand, a company that does quarterly ethics training or refreshers is demonstrating "110 percent compliance." Throughout this book, I advocate that contractors take the most aggressive approach possible. Clearly, this is the best way to stay out of trouble.

The book is organized in four parts.

Part I presents the new ethics requirements, focusing on the duty contractors have to disclose to the government certain law violations associated with their government contracts, the components of a contractor's ethics program (Chapter 1) and the applicability of those requirements for different types and sizes of contracts (Chapter 2).

Part II focuses on the FAR rules that procurement personnel, contract specialists, and contractor employees must observe in the contract solicitation process (Chapter 3) and the contract administration process (Chapter 4).

But those involved in the procurement process must comply with more than the FAR. Contractor employees and contract specialists/contracting officers involved in the procurement process must also observe a wide range of federal laws and regulations other than the FAR, including statutes like the False Statements Act that are imposed on personnel regardless of their involvement in the procurement process.

Part III discusses the federal statutes and regulations that all government employees and contractor personnel must comply with, such as rules against bribery. Chapter 5 focuses on federal employee conduct, and Chapter 6 focuses on federal contractor conduct. These two chapters are especially important because they describe the four federal criminal statutes (conflict of interest, bribery, gratuities, criminal False Claims Act) and the civil False Claims Act to which the self disclosure FAR requirements adopted in late 2008 apply. In addition, Chapter 6 includes a discussion of the 2009 amendments to the False Claims Act.

Part IV, Preventing and Uncovering Fraud, should be at the heart of any ethics training program, whether for contractors or government personnel. Chapter 7 discusses indicators of fraud and contains a wealth of information on what procurement personnel should be on the lookout for in their fraud prevention efforts.

Throughout, I have included relevant cases that have been decided by the Government Accountability Office and the courts. In some areas, no cases have been decided within the past 10 years. Some topics and ethics simply do not get litigated often. Regardless, the existing case law remains relevant and important.

Terry O'Connor
Alexandria, Virginia

NOTES

1. National Contract Management Association, "Speaking Out," *Contract Management*, January 2008, 12.
2. http://www.deloitte.com/dtt/cda/doc/content/us_consulting_strategichrreview_070806.pdf (accessed May 2008).

Acknowledgments

Not well schooled in the publishing business, I would have thought that publishing what in reality is a 5th Edition of my procurement ethics book would be easy: I would just update the text with recent cases. My faithful editor, Myra Strauss, had a better idea: do a complete revision, make it more readable, overhaul major parts of the book, and update the text with recent cases. As a result of her vision, my name ends up on a significantly more useful guide on a very difficult topic. I also have to acknowledge her skillful colleague, Lena Johnson. Her day-to-day shepherding of the numerous drafts and revisions showed her attention to detail that every writer counts on to make sure a book is accurate. Finally, I know that Jared Stearns has and will continue to help get the book to a wide audience. I never could have done it without them. Thank you Myra, Lena, and Jared.

Finally, I have been remiss in not earlier acknowledging the significant role that Barbara Beach of Management Concepts has played in my writing career. Her request decades ago that I write the "Recent Decisions" column for the *Federal Acquisition Report* gave me my start in writing about government contracts and I want her to know how much I appreciate her obvious "good judgment."

Terry O'Connor
Alexandria, Virginia

PART I
The New Ethics Requirements

After getting little attention for over a decade, procurement ethics received a double-dose of attention in 2007 and 2008.

In late 2007, new ethics rules and policies for contractors were added to the Federal Acquisition Regulation (FAR). Although new to the FAR, the policies are almost identical to the ethics policies that have been included in the Defense Federal Acquisition Regulation Supplement (DFARS) for nearly 10 years.

Boiling down all 10,000+ words the government used to describe the new rules in the *Federal Register,* the revisions basically deal with three components of a contractor ethics program:

- A written code of business ethics
- An internal control system to help contractors and their employees comply with the code
- An ethics training program (also referred to as an ethics awareness program).

The revisions urged, but did not require, all government contractors to adopt all three components. In addition, they required some government contractors to adopt all three components. Finally, they required a small business awarded a contract over $5 million with a period of performance of 120 days or more to have a code of business ethics but not an internal control system or a training program.

In late 2008, FAR imposed additional ethics regulations on government contractors. The 2008 changes added an ethics "self-disclosure" requirement and more "internal control" requirements.

Chapter 1 describes the FAR requirements for self-disclosure as well as the FAR requirements for the three components of a contractor's ethics program, namely, a code of business ethics, an internal control system, and ethics training. Since not all contracts trigger a contractor's setting up all three components, in Chapter 2 we consider the applicability of these components and then turn to the contracts excluded from these rules. In Chapter 2, we also discuss related and important aspects of the applicability of ethics rules: a contractor's responsibility to flow the ethics requirements down to subcontractors, compliance-checking, and the role that a hotline poster plays in all of this.

1 The Components of a Contractor's Ethics Program

The new ethics rules added to the Federal Acquisition Regulation (FAR) in late 2007 (see Appendix A) cover three components of a contractor's ethics program:

- A written code of business ethics
- An internal control system to help contractors and their employees comply with the code
- An ethics training program (also referred to as an ethics awareness program).

The changes made in late 2008 (see Appendix B) converted the "suggested" components of an internal control system to "required" components, described in more detail what a company's ethics training program should involve, and imposed a self-disclosure requirement on contractors.

A contractor can take two different approaches to implementing these rules:

1. Do only what the FAR requires—do the "shall" but not the "should"
2. Go beyond the "shall" and do the "should"

This chapter describes the self-disclosure requirements FAR imposes on all contractors as well as the three components of a contractor's ethics program that apply to some but not all contractors. In doing so, we take the aggressive approach and assume that any contractor would want the benefits of being seen as "a good contractor" (see Preface, p. xiv) in the eyes of a contracting officer and therefore would want to adopt not only those ethics provisions required of the contractor but also those that FAR encourages a contractor to voluntarily adopt, the "shoulds." Chapter 2 focuses on the applicability of the components of an ethics program to different types and sizes of contracts.

SELF-DISCLOSURE

The basic rule regarding self-disclosure is this: Generally stated, all contractors and subcontractors face debarment or suspension for failure to disclose illegal contract activities they know about. This general rule has a number of details that have to be mastered but, contrary to the cliché, the devil is *not* in the details here. The details, according to the FAR Council, are designed to make compliance easier on contractors. Many of these important details are described only in the 30,000 words of the Federal Register publication of the rules, therefore we have included the commentary that accompanies the FAR rules in Appendixes A and B.

A contractor looking only at the new FAR language will miss many of the important fine points of the FAR provisions. The FAR is only the "letter of the law." Additional guidance and explanations of the new regulations—the spirit of the law—can be found in the "Responses" accompanying the new regulations in the *Federal Register*. These responses, prepared by the FAR Council, address comments made by the public on the proposed regulations. They contain important information that is missing from the new rules themselves.

So in describing these new rules, you will see references to the *Federal Register* pages featuring the "Responses" for December 2007 rules, which start at 72 FR 65873 (published November 23, 2007), and the December 2008 rules, which start at 73 FR 67064 (published November 12, 2008).

The starting point of the self-disclosure rules is the text of the FAR clause, FAR 3.1003(a)(2):

> [A] contractor may be suspended and/or debarred for knowing failure by a principal to timely disclose to the Government, in connection with the award, performance, or closeout of a Government contract performed by the contractor or a subcontract awarded thereunder, credible evidence of a violation of Federal criminal law involving fraud, conflict of interest, bribery, or gratuity violations found in Title 18 of the United States Code or a violation of the civil False Claims Act. Knowing failure to timely disclose credible evidence of any of the above violations remains a cause for suspension and/or debarment until 3 years after final payment on a contract (see 9.406-2(b)(1)(vi) and 9.407-2(a)(8)).

To some extent, this clause makes government contractors and subcontractors responsible for blowing the whistle on illegal conduct in their own contracts—or risk being debarred or suspended if they don't. But the following five details are critical.

1. The self-disclosure rule applies only to a "principal" in a company. It is not the employees of a company that must report possible wrongdoing. It is only a company "principal," defined by FAR 2.101 as: "an officer, director, owner, partner, or a person having primary management or supervisory responsibilities within a business entity (*e.g.*, general manager; plant manager; head of a subsidiary, division, or business segment; and similar positions)." The effect of this "princi-

pal principle" is that a company cannot be debarred if an employee knows of illegal conduct on a company contract but fails to report it to top management.

2. The self-disclosure duty applies only if the company principal "knows" about the illegal conduct—*not* what the principal "should have known." This "knowing" requirement protects the principal: "[r]equiring a 'knowledge' element to the cause of action actually provides more protection for contractors. The Councils do not agree with adding 'or should have known.' The principals are only required to disclose what they know." 73 FR 67069.

3. A principal only has to disclose illegal conduct he or she knows about if there is "credible evidence" of illegal activity. The FAR does not define this critical term, but the FAR Council does give some guidance on what it means in discussing why it changed the operative phrase from "reasonable grounds to believe" to "credible evidence" at the request of the Justice Department:

> [Credible evidence] indicates a higher standard, implying that the contractor will have the opportunity to take some time for preliminary examination of the evidence to determine its credibility before [disclosing it] to the Government. . . . In addition, adding to the standard of "credible evidence" the requirement to make a "timely" report implies that the contractor will have the opportunity to take some time for preliminary examination of the evidence to determine its credibility before deciding to disclose to the Government. . . . This does not impose upon the contractor an obligation to carry out a complex investigation, but only to take reasonable steps that the contractor considers sufficient to determine that the evidence is credible. 73 FR 67073.

4. A company "principal" does not have to be an expert on the entire U.S. criminal code. The self-disclosure duty applies only to known violations of four federal criminal laws or the civil False Claims Act. The disclosure duty applies to federal criminal laws on fraud, conflicts of interest, bribery and gratuities, but not antitrust violations like bid rigging.

It's important to make special mention of the conflict of interest laws. Conflicts of interest are prohibited by federal laws, and by federal and agency regulations. The only conflicts of interest subject to the self-disclosure duty are those covered by title 18 of the U.S. Code, the federal criminal code. The FAR Procurement Integrity provisions at 3.104-2(b) are helpful:

Government officers and employees (employees) are prohibited by 18 U.S.C. 208 and 5 CFR Part 2635 from participating personally and substantially in any particular matter that would affect the financial interests of any person with whom the employee is seeking employment. An employee who engages in negotiations or is otherwise seeking employment with an offeror or who has an arrangement concerning future employment with an offeror must comply with the applicable disqualification requirements of 5 CFR 2635.604 and 2635.606. The statutory prohibition in 18 U.S.C. 208 also may require an employee's disqualification from participation in the acquisition even if the employee's duties may not be considered 'participating personally and substantially,' as this term is defined in 3.104-1. . . . Post-employment restrictions are covered by 18 U.S.C. 207 and 5 CFR parts 2637 and 2641, that prohibit certain activities by former Government employees, including representation of a contractor before the Government in relation to any contract or other particular matter involving specific parties on which the former employee participated personally and substantially while employed by the Government. Additional restrictions apply to certain senior Government employees and for particular matters under an employee's official responsibility[.]

5. The self-disclosure duty has, in a sense, a statute of limitations. It starts from the beginning of the solicitation process and lasts until three years after contract closeout. The FAR Councils initially considered using contract closeout as the end point for the requirement to disclose fraud, but:

> [A]ccording to the Justice Department, contract fraud often occurs at the time of closeout, and cutting off the obligation to disclose at that point would exempt many of these violations from the obligation to disclose. Three years after final payment is consistent with most of the contractor record retention requirements (see Audit and Records clauses at FAR 52.214-26 and 52.215-2). Therefore, the Councils concur with Justice's recommendation that the mandatory disclosure of violations should be limited to a period of three years after contract completion, using final payment as the event to mark contract completion. 73 FR 67073.

It's important to remember that this duty of self-disclosure that every contractor has is also a required part of a code of business ethics and conduct that only some contractors must have. For example, although a small business does not have to have an internal control system designed to encourage self-disclosure, the small business still has the same self-disclosure duty imposed on all government contractors. Later in this chapter, we will focus more specifically on the FAR requirements for business ethics awareness and the compliance program and internal control system that, as mentioned above, are required only of some contractors but not required of a small business nor all contracts for the acquisition of a commercial item. Before doing so, we will discuss a requirement that, like the duty of self-disclosure, all contractors have: the requirement of adopting a Code of Business Ethics.

A CODE OF BUSINESS ETHICS

Developing and adopting a code of business ethics is generally not burdensome for a contractor. Codes can be drafted using numerous models found on the Internet (see Appendix C for an example). The code of business ethics developed by the U.S. Department of Transportation Suspension and Debarment Work Group[1] offers this definition:

> A Code of Business Ethics is an open disclosure of the way an organization operates and provides visible guidelines for behavior. It serves as an important communication vehicle to the company's employees, customers, subcontractors, and the community at large that the organization is committed to the highest ethical standards of conduct in its operations.
>
> Additionally, a Code of Business Ethics is intended to promote ethical and law-abiding conduct within an organization and clearly communicate to employees what is expected of them and the consequences for violations.
>
> The following are a few of the elements an effective Code of Business Ethics should have:
>
> - Commitment by the organization's directors and top management to abiding by the Code and also ensuring that all employees are aware of and abide by the Code
> - Applicability to all levels of the organization
> - A letter from the President or Chief Executive of the organization communicating what the Code is and the organization's commitment to following the Code

- A table of contents so that employees will be able to easily find the organization's policy for a specific issue

- A statement of policy concerning the Code and the general rules that apply to the Code

- Standards of Conduct that communicate what issues employees should be aware of and what to do whenever confronted with any such issue

- A statement requiring employees to report suspected violations and to cooperate with the implementation of the code.

Since these templates are available for contractors to use, drafting a code of business ethics should not be difficult. To summarize, all contractors "should" have a code of business ethics. As we will see in Chapter 2, only some contractors must have a code of business ethics.

Required Components of a Business Ethics Awareness and Compliance Program and an Internal Control System

The 2007 FAR requirements in Appendix A for codes of business ethics, training, and internal controls, were a good start for ethics reform, but unfortunately contained a huge landmine: They left contractors thinking that 100 percent compliance provided complete protection if their company somehow got involved in criminal activity. According to the FAR Councils, faithfully following the 2007 FAR requirements created "a false sense of security" in contractors.

> Businesses (especially small businesses) may believe they have met all the compliance requirements of the U.S. Government by following the FAR; this will create a false sense of security.
> 72 FR 64020.

To the FAR Councils, this false sense of security arose from the fact that the 2007 FAR changes failed to alert contractors to the U.S. Sentencing Commission's guidelines used in sentencing contractors convicted of a felony or Class A misdemeanor, whether or not the crime arose from a procurement situation.

> The U.S. Sentencing Guidelines provide guidance on what the U.S. Sentencing Commission expects in the way of an effective compliance and ethics program from organizations convicted of a felony or Class A misdemeanor. The Department of Justice and other respondents to the FAR Case 2006–007 proposed rule [now adopted] considered that that proposed rule left out important elements that are covered in the U.S. Sentencing Guidelines and that this can create confusion. 72 FR 94019-20.

This defect in the 2007 ethics rules was corrected by the 2008 FAR rules in Appendix B. Now, the FAR's description of an internal control system satisfies the U.S. Sentencing Commission's guidelines. In addition, while the 2007 FAR changes provided only vague guidelines for developing an ethics awareness and compliance program and an internal control system, the 2008 FAR changes give a much more detailed and helpful description of them.

Required Components of a Business Ethics Awareness and Compliance Program

The FAR now describes this program in 52.203-13(c)(1):

> (i) This program shall include reasonable steps to communicate periodically and in a practical manner the Contractor's standards and procedures and other aspects of the Contractor's business ethics awareness and compliance program and internal control system, by conducting effective training programs and otherwise disseminating information appropriate to an individual's respective roles and responsibilities.

(ii) The training conducted under this program shall be provided to the Contractor's principals and employees, and as appropriate, the Contractor's agents and subcontractors.

We will look at each of these in turn.

Required Components of an Internal Control System

FAR 52.203-13 (c)(2)(i), adopted as part of the 2008 ethics changes, provides an outline of the internal control system:

(i) The Contractor's internal control system shall—

(A) Establish standards and procedures to facilitate timely discovery of improper conduct in connection with Government contracts; and

(B) Ensure corrective measures are promptly instituted and carried out.

FAR 52.203-13(c)(2)(ii) describes the specific components of an internal control system:

At a minimum, the Contractor's internal control system shall provide for the following:

(A) Assignment of responsibility at a sufficiently high level and adequate resources to ensure effectiveness of the business ethics awareness and compliance program and internal control system.

(B) Reasonable efforts not to include an individual as a principal, whom due diligence would have exposed as having engaged in conduct that is in conflict with the Contractor's code of business ethics and conduct.

(C) Periodic reviews of company business practices, procedures, policies, and internal controls for compliance with the Contractor's code of business ethics and conduct and the special requirements of Government contracting, including—

1) Monitoring and auditing to detect criminal conduct;

2) Periodic evaluation of the effectiveness of the business ethics awareness and compliance program and internal control system, especially if criminal conduct has been detected; and

3) Periodic assessment of the risk of criminal conduct, with appropriate steps to design, implement, or modify the business ethics awareness and compliance program and the internal control system as necessary to reduce the risk of criminal conduct identified through this process.

(D) An internal reporting mechanism, such as a hotline, which allows for anonymity or confidentiality, by which employees may report suspected instances of improper conduct, and instructions that encourage employees to make such reports.

(E) Disciplinary action for improper conduct or for failing to take reasonable steps to prevent or detect improper conduct.

(F) Timely disclosure, in writing, to the agency OIG, with a copy to the Contracting Officer, whenever, in connection with the award, performance, or closeout of any Government contract performed by the Contractor or a subcontract thereunder, the Contractor has credible evidence that a principal, employee, agent, or subcontractor of the Contractor has committed a violation of Federal criminal law involving fraud, conflict of interest, bribery, or gratuity violations found in Title 18 U.S.C. or a violation of the civil False Claims Act (31 U.S.C. 3729-3733).

(G) Full cooperation with any Government agencies responsible for audits, investigations, or corrective actions.

Notice, as mentioned earlier, that the self-disclosure requirement to avoid a debarment or suspension is also part of a contractor's code of business ethics and conduct required by FAR 52.203-13.

ETHICS TRAINING PROGRAM

Of the three components of a contractor ethics program, the training program is the least defined in the FAR. It is not required for small businesses nor for commercial item contracts as we shall see in Chapter 2.

FAR does not describe what topics must be included in the training. Obviously, the training program would inform employees about the code of business ethics and how to comply with it.

Although the FAR says little about what such a program should look like, FAR gives some details as to who should receive training:

> The training conducted under this program shall be provided to the Contractor's principals and employees, and as appropriate, the Contractor's agents and subcontractors. FAR 52.203-13(c)(1)(ii).

That same FAR clause defines two of these terms:

> Agent means any individual, including a director, an officer, an employee, or an independent contractor, authorized to act on behalf of the organization.

> Principal means an officer, director, owner, partner, or a person having primary management or supervisory responsibilities within a business entity (e.g., general manager; plant manager; head of a subsidiary, division, or business segment, and similar positions). FAR 52.203-13(a).

The training program component is somewhat vague. Although the FAR Councils' comments in the 2008 changes provide helpful information on other topics, they provide little elaboration on what this training program should look like. One comment to the FAR Councils complained that:

> . . . the requirements for training could take substantial time away from performing on their contracts to train staff on an unknown scope of Federal criminal law. The Government would incur costs from this activity through delays in the fulfillment of contracts and increased contractor expenses that will be passed along to customers.

In its response, the FAR Councils asserted that enough guidance had been given:

> By identifying the scope of violations of the Federal criminal law as those involving fraud, conflict of interest, bribery, or gratuity violations found in Title 18 of the United States Code, the Councils believe that the training requirements have been more clearly defined and the contractor's training requirement has been reduced. 73 FR 67067.

In another response, the FAR Councils stated:

> The Councils do not agree that it is necessary under this case to dictate to contractors what they need to cover in business ethics training. If we highlight education on the civil FCA, or other specific areas, the contractors may place undue emphasis only on those areas mentioned in the regulations. The business ethics training courses may cover appropriate education on the civil FCA, as well as many other areas such as conflict of interest and procurement integrity and other areas determined to be appropriate by the contractor, considering the relevant risks and controls. 73 FR 67067.

Bottom line: Companies are on their own in designing the training program that must cover the four criminal laws mentioned above plus the civil False Claims Act. These laws are discussed in detail in Chapters 5 and 6.

NOTE

1. Department of Transportation Suspension and Debarment Work Group. Online at www.fhwa.dot.gov/construction/cqit/ethcguid.cfm (accessed May 2008).

2 Applicability of the New Ethics Regulations

We urge contractors to take an aggressive approach to ethics compliance for several reasons:

1. It is cheaper to stay out of trouble than to get out of trouble.

2. A company championing an aggressive ethics program has happier employees and makes more money.

3. A contracting officer will be more willing to work with a contractor he or she trusts than one that fits the contracting officer stereotype of the "contractor-crook."

Accordingly, we encourage a contractor to adopt:

- Not simply what the FAR says a contractor *shall* adopt
- But instead, what the FAR says a contractor *should* adopt.

As a basis for designing and implementing an effective, compliant ethics program, a contractor needs to understand the rules set forth in the FAR. In trying to understand the newly adopted rules, a contractor must also consider the important guidance found in the *Federal Register* Responses that accompany the new regulations. These observations, prepared by the authors of the new regulations (the FAR Councils) address comments made by the public on the proposed regulations. The *Federal Register* Responses can contain important information missing from the new rules themselves. For example, in responding to public concern about how the government would monitor contractor compliance with these new regulations—an issue not addressed in the adopted FAR revisions—the FAR Councils' Response advises that the government is to simply check *whether* companies have taken these measures and *not* to debate the words a contractor used in attempting to comply with the new regulations. (These helpful observations are found in the *Federal Register* publication of the finalized regulations and included in Appendixes A and B.)

CONDITIONS THAT TRIGGER THE NEW REGULATIONS

The new regulations first establish the policy that the FAR Councils want all contractors to adopt. The regulations use *should* rather than *shall*. In plain English, here is a three-rule summary.

Rule 1. All government contractors *should* have a code of business ethics, supported by an internal control system and an ethics training program:

> (b) Contractors should have a written code of business ethics and conduct. To promote compliance with such code of business ethics and conduct, contractors should have an employee business ethics and compliance training program and an internal control system that—
>
> > (1) Are suitable to the size of the company and extent of its involvement in Government contracting;
> >
> > (2) Facilitate timely discovery and disclosure of improper conduct in connection with Government contracts; and

(3) Ensure corrective measures are promptly instituted and carried out.

FAR 3.1002(b).

In addition to the *should* regulations, other regulations require *some* contractors to do more.

Rule 2. Any "large business" government contractor awarded a "covered contract" for over $5 million with a period of performance of 120 days or more (that is not exempt from the new regulations) *must* have all three components of a company ethics program: a code of business ethics, an internal control system, and an ethics training program.

Rule 3. A "small business" having a "covered contract" of over $5 million with a period of performance of 120 days or more must comply with only one of the new provisions, the requirement for a code of business ethics. The small business is not required to have an ethics training program or an internal control system:

> (c) Business ethics awareness and compliance program and internal control system. This paragraph (c) does not apply if the Contractor has represented itself as a small business concern pursuant to the award of this contract…

FAR 52.203-13(c).

EXCEPTIONS TO "COVERED CONTRACTS"

Rules 2 and 3 mention contractors winning a contract valued at over $5 million with a period of performance of more than 120 days. Such contracts are called "covered contracts."

What about contracts for commercial items? According to FAR 3.1004(a), any contract over $5 million with a period of performance of more than 120 days must include FAR 52.203 – 13, Contractor Code of Business Ethics and Conduct. As a result, a commercial item contract over $5 million with a period of performance of more than 120 days must include that FAR clause in it and accordingly contractors with commercial item "covered contract" must have a code of business ethics as required by FAR 52.203-13(b) and must disclose improper contract conduct (the duty of self-disclosure) However, FAR 52.203-13 (c) exempts commercial item contracts from the requirement of the business ethics awareness and compliance program and internal control system. The end result is that commercial item contracts, like all contracts, include the requirement of contractor self-disclosure of improper contract conduct but like contracts with a small business, exclude the requirement of a business ethics awareness and compliance program and internal control systems.

What about Federal Supply Schedule contracts? According to the FAR Council, "if it is anticipated that the dollar value of orders on an FSS contract will exceed $5 million, then this clause [FAR 52.203-13] is included in the basic contract against which orders are placed." 73 FR 67085.

What about contracts performed outside the United States? Prior to the 2008 FAR changes, contracts performed outside the United States were treated like commercial item contracts, so none of the 2007 changes applied. Like those for commercial item contracts, the regulations changed in 2008. But the changes for contracts performed outside the United States are much broader than the changes for commercial item contracts.

Now, contractors holding contracts to be performed outside the United States over $5 million with a period of performance of over 120 days must have a code of business ethics, a business ethics awareness and compliance program (including a training program), and an internal control system. In addition, the contracts must contain a provision that flows the ethics requirements down to large subcontracts. The result is that subcontracts performed outside the United States over $5 million with a period of performance of more than 120 days now carry a requirement that the large business subcontractor have a code of business ethics, a business ethics awareness and compliance program (including a training program), and an internal control system.

As mentioned earlier, these contracts are also covered by the self-disclosure requirements.

FLOW-DOWN CLAUSES FOR SUBCONTRACTS

The 2008 amendments make a significant change from the 2007 amendments regarding subcontracts for the acquisition of commercial items and subcontract performed entirely outside the United States. As revised in 2008, these subcontracts are not excluded. Thus, subcontracts for commercial items and subcontracts performed entirely outside the United States must include FAR 52.203-13.

> (d) Subcontracts. (1) The Contractor shall include the substance of this clause, including this paragraph (d), in subcontracts that have a value in excess of $5 million and a performance period of more than 120 days.
>
> FAR 52.203-13(d).

Once flowed-down to that subcontract, the rules of 52.203-13 apply. For example, a small business with a subcontract in excess of $5 million and a performance period of more than 120 days must have only a code of business ethics and not the compliance or training program.

In addition, it's important to remember that any government contractor or subcontractor has the duty of disclosing improper contract conduct or face debarment and suspension.

> Regarding subcontractors, the new provisions apply to any subcontract over $5 million with a period of performance of 120 days or more, for the same reasons that they apply to prime contracts. "The same reasonable efforts the contractor may take to exclude from its organizational structure principals whom due diligence would have exposed as engaging in illegal acts are the same reasonable efforts the contractor should take in selecting its subcontractors." Subcontractors should also use those same reasonable efforts in employment and subcontracting efforts.
>
> 73 FR 67084.

A Purchase Order Is a Subcontract

When government contract provisions are supposed to "flowdown" the supply chain, a recurring issue is whether a purchase order from a supplier is a subcontract. For purposes of the flowdown of these ethics rules, a purchase order is a subcontract, according to the FAR Councils:

> Sometimes construction firms think that "subcontract" does not include purchase orders.
>
> The FAR does not make this distinction. The intent is that the flowdown applies to all subcontracts, including purchase orders.
>
> 72 FR 65880, Appendix A.

A large business subcontractor might have to adopt the internal control system and training program. Here's an example of the complications of federal contracting. A small business with a contract over $5 million having a period of performance over 120 days does not have to have an internal control system or ethics training program. But a large business subcontractor might have to:

> Because the clause 52.203-13 is still included in the contract with small businesses, the requirements for formal training program and internal control systems will flow down to large business subcontractors, but not apply to small businesses.
>
> 72 FR 65881, Appendix A.

A prime need only check that the sub has an internal control system and training program. Nobody wants to see a small business being responsible for checking out the internal control system of, say, Boeing or Microsoft:

> The contractor is not required to judge or monitor the ethics awareness program and internal control systems of the subcontractors—just check for existence.
>
> 72 FR 65880, Appendix A.

COMPLIANCE

How will the government check if contractors are complying with the FAR ethics regulations?

Note that the regulations do not require that a contractor submit its code of business ethics, training program, or internal control system to the government for approval. As long as a company has no ethical problems in its government contracts, the government will not get too involved in the fine points.

The contracting officer is not required to verify compliance, but may inquire at his or her discretion as part of contract administrative duties. Review of contractors' compliance would be incorporated into normal contract administration. The Government will not be routinely reviewing plans unless a problem arises. The Government does not need the code of ethics as a deliverable. What is important is that the Contractor develops the code and promotes compliance of its employees.

72 FR 65878, Appendix A.

GOVERNMENT POSTERS

The regulations require display of a government fraud hotline poster after the award of some contracts. The poster threshold is similar to the mandatory code of business ethics threshold, minus the "120 days or more" language. Also, the new regulations deal with company websites. FAR 3.1004(b) requires a hotline poster for contracts over $5 million (or lesser amount as determined by the agency) regardless of the length of the period of performance. Excluded are contracts for commercial items under FAR Part 12 and contracts that will be performed outside the United States.

FAR 52.203-14, Display of Hotline Poster(s) (Dec 2007), requires a contractor to display fraud hotline poster(s):

> (1) During contract performance in the United States, the Contractor shall prominently display in common work areas within business segments performing work under this contract and at contract work sites—
>
> > (i) Any agency fraud hotline poster or Department of Homeland Security (DHS) fraud hotline poster identified in paragraph (b)(3) of this clause; and

> (ii) Any DHS fraud hotline poster subsequently identified by the Contracting Officer.
>
> (2) Additionally, if the Contractor maintains a company website as a method of providing information to employees, the Contractor shall display an electronic version of the poster(s) at the website.
>
> FAR 52.203-14.

The clause makes contractor access to the poster easy. FAR 52.203-14(b)(3) requires the contracting officer to identify where any required posters can be obtained.

There is also a poster exception for a contractor that has an ethics awareness program:

> (c) If the Contractor has implemented a business ethics and conduct awareness program, including a reporting mechanism, such as a hotline poster, then the Contractor need not display any agency fraud hotline posters as required in paragraph (b) of this clause, other than any required DHS posters.
>
> FAR 52.203-14(c).

Contractors should especially note the subtle advantage these rules provide for contractors posting anti-fraud posters on their website: The first phone calls about suspected fraud can come to the company and not to the government.

Like the flowdown provisions for the code of business ethics, etc., the hotline poster requirement has a flowdown provision:

> Subcontracts. The Contractor shall include the substance of this clause, including this paragraph (d), in all subcontracts that exceed $5 million, except when the subcontract—

(1) Is for the acquisition of a commercial item; or

(2) Is performed entirely outside the United States.

FAR 52.203-14(d).

These triggers and conditions notwithstanding, we reiterate that an aggressive approach to ethics—one that not only converts *should* into *shall* but also complies with the U.S. Sentencing Commission's guidelines—offers contractors many dividends.

PART II
The FAR Rules

Having looked, in Part I, at the components and applicability of a procurement ethics compliance program for a contractor, the next question becomes: With what rules and regulations must the contractor's program comply? The answer requires procurement personnel to look at all the laws that apply not only to procurement activities but also to everything else federal employees and contractor personnel do in the course of conducting business.

In breaking down this mass of rules and regulations, we start with the rules that apply to the procurement process, which are found in the FAR. Chapter 3 focuses on the FAR provisions applicable to the solicitation process—getting a contract. Chapter 4 then turns to the FAR provisions applicable to administering contracts.

3 Ethics Rules for Getting a Contract

The biggest problem in understanding the ethics rules for getting a government contract is not that there are so many rules—that's probably the second biggest problem. The biggest problem is that these rules are spread out over so many pages of laws, regulations, and decisions and are found in so many locations: the FAR, agency FAR supplements, decisions of the Government Accountability Office (GAO) and the Court of Federal Claims (CFC), and opinions of agency ethics offices, just to name a few.

This chapter deals with the most common ethics problems in the contract formation stage. First, it addresses the Procurement Integrity Act and implementing the FAR regulations. These regulations cover such common problems as protecting procurement information from being leaked to unauthorized personnel, job offers made to government employees during the course of a procurement, and the revolving-door issue, which walks the difficult line between keeping government employees employable in the private market and making sure that former government employees do not use insider information to harm the government. We also explore the unique rules dealing with violations of the procurement integrity rules.

Next is a discussion of two kinds of conflicts of interest: personal conflicts of interest, which stem from the undue influence of a particular person, and organizational conflicts of interest, which are the result of some other activities. For example, a contractor could get an unfair competitive advantage or be put in the position of performing different jobs that might bias the contractor's judgment. From here, we move on to a discussion of misrepresentation, or "bait and switch," where an offeror promises to provide the government certain personnel if it wins the contract but provides different personnel after it wins the contract. We then turn to the status of the offeror: Is the offeror a responsible vendor, and has the offeror been suspended or debarred?

The chapter ends with a discussion of how the government seeks to ensure compliance with the rules governing the procurement process and the remedies it can impose when the rules are violated, including voiding or rescinding a contract.

▎ PROCUREMENT INTEGRITY REGULATIONS

The most important rules for ethically getting a government contract are in the Procurement Integrity Act (41 U.S.C. 423). First enacted in October 1980 (during an election year and with no congressional hearings), this law has engendered continued controversy and has been amended several times over the years.

In 1996, Congress passed a significant overhaul of the law. These revisions greatly streamlined the procurement integrity rules. Gone are difficult-to-work-with terms like "procurement official" and "competing contractor"; also gone are overlapping anti-gratuity measures and procurement integrity certifications. In their place are more refined provisions dealing with the following:

- ▶ Protecting government source selection information and contractor proprietary information from getting into the wrong hands

CHAPTER 3 | Ethics Rules for Getting a Contract

- Preventing a job offer to a government procurement official from being used as an enticement for getting a contract
- A one-year revolving door prohibition for those involved in procurements over $10 million.

In addition, the government has made understanding the procurement integrity rules much easier by including in the FAR helpful plain English descriptions of what's required. Therefore, instead of describing procurement integrity by going through the statute section by section, we will use the FAR provisions to describe the procurement integrity rules.

It's important to remember that not all these rules apply to *all* contracts. Rather, the rules apply based on size of contract. The anti-leaking restrictions apply to *all* competitive procurements. The restrictions on job offers apply to procurements over the simplified acquisition threshold, generally $100,000. The revolving-door provisions apply to contracts over $10 million.

Before looking more specifically at the procurement integrity rules in FAR 3.104, it's important to know that some violations of these FAR regulations can also be violations of federal criminal law. Specifically:

- *Gifts, gratuities, and bribes.* FAR 3.101-2 (Solicitation and Acceptance of Gratuities by Government Personnel) prohibits a government employee from asking for or accepting "directly or indirectly, any gratuity, gift, favor, entertainment, loan, or anything of monetary value from anyone who (a) has or is seeking to obtain Government business with the employee's agency. . . ." In addition, offering or accepting a bribe or gratuity is a federal crime (18 U.S.C. 201 and 10 U.S.C. 2207).

- *Personal conflicts of interest.* Government employees who participate personally and substantially in any particular matter that would affect the financial interests of any person with whom the employee is seeking employment also may violate federal criminal law (18 U.S.C. 208).

- *Job offers.* Federal employees are reminded in FAR 3.104-2(b)(2) that "The statutory prohibition in 18 U.S.C. 208 also may require an employee's disqualification from participation in the acquisition even if the employee's duties may not be considered 'participating personally and substantially,' as this term is defined in 3.104-1."

- *Private employment after federal service.* Federal criminal laws address the "revolving door" restrictions in 18 U.S.C. 207.

- *Release of "protected" information.* FAR parts 14 and 15 restrict the release of information. For example, dealing with unsolicited proposals, FAR 15.608 warns that "Government personnel shall not disclose restrictively marked information (see FAR 3.104 and 15.609) included in an unsolicited proposal. The disclosure of such information concerning trade secrets, processes, operations, style of work, apparatus, and other matters, except as authorized by law, may result in criminal penalties under the Trade Secrets Act (18 U.S.C. 1905)."

Protecting Procurement Information

These restrictions apply to all *competitive* procurements; therefore, they do not apply to a sole-source procurement.

It is a crime punishable by up to five years in jail for unauthorized persons to disclose or receive procurement information. Civil fines are also imposed for these violations.

A lot of fine print, however, surrounds this general rule. In describing who can and cannot *legally* get procurement information during the solicitation process, Congress had to draw a number of fine lines. One way to make sense of what is allowed and what is not is to consider the "anti-leaking" laws in terms of *who, what, when,* and *how.*

▓▓ "Who" is covered by the anti-leaking laws?

It would have been helpful if Congress had defined the giver and taker of leaked information in the same way, or if Congress had made anybody in the world a potential giver or taker of procurement-sensitive information. But that's not the case. There can be more takers than givers, and when you think about it, that makes sense. The only people who could possibly give out source selection information must have some connection with government procurement. On the other hand, no one in the entire world should be able to improperly receive procurement-sensitive information.

The FAR prohibits certain individuals from giving out procurement-sensitive information, specifically anyone who:

> ► Is a present or former official of the United States, or a person who is acting or has acted for or on behalf of, or who is advising or has advised the United States with respect to, a federal agency procurement and

> ► By virtue of that office, employment, or relationship, has or had access to contractor bid or proposal information or source selection information.

FAR 3.104-3(a)(2).

The FAR also prohibits anyone from receiving procurement-sensitive information. The only exceptions are people "authorized, in accordance with applicable agency regulations or procedures, by the agency head or the contracting officer to receive such information." FAR 3.104-4(a). Presumably, this would include consultants hired to help the government through different parts of the solicitation process, such as experts to help in the evaluation process.

▌▌▌ *"What" is covered by the anti-leaking laws?*

How can someone tell whether a specific piece of information is protected from disclosure? The easy way is if the information is marked as being protected information. The hard way is if the protected information is not marked as protected but by regulation is made protected.

The FAR takes the hard way. Although it requires that certain kinds of solicitation information be specially marked to be protected, other kinds of solicitation information have to be protected even if they are not specially marked as protected.

The information covered by the anti-leaking laws falls into two categories: information the government provides, such as an internal source selection plan; and information a bidder provides, such as its price.

The FAR defines source selection information—the information the government provides—as:

> Any of the following information that is prepared for use by an agency for the purpose of evaluating a bid or proposal to enter into an agency procurement contract, if that information has not been previously made available to the public or disclosed publicly:
>
> (1) Bid prices submitted in response to an agency invitation for bids, or lists of those bid prices before bid opening.
>
> (2) Proposed costs or prices submitted in response to an agency solicitation, or lists of those proposed costs or prices.
>
> (3) Source selection plans.

(4) Technical evaluation plans.

(5) Technical evaluations of proposals.

(6) Cost or price evaluations of proposals.

(7) Competitive range determinations that identify proposals that have a reasonable chance of being selected for award of a contract.

(8) Rankings of bids, proposals, or competitors.

(9) Reports and evaluations of source selection panels, boards, or advisory councils.

(10) Other information marked as "Source Selection Information--See FAR 2.101 and 3.104" based on a case-by-case determination by the head of the agency or the contracting officer, that its disclosure would jeopardize the integrity or successful completion of the Federal agency procurement to which the information relates.

FAR 2.101.

Significantly, and unfortunately, the information identified in paragraphs (1) through (9) is considered source selection information whether or not it is marked as "protected." Although agencies are encouraged to mark as much of this information as possible as source selection information, items (1) through (9) are protected regardless.

Bidder-produced information is also defined in the FAR:

"Contractor bid or proposal information" means any of the following information submitted to a federal agency as part of or in connection with a bid or proposal to enter into a federal agency procurement contract, if that information has not been previously made available to the public or disclosed publicly:

(1) Cost or pricing data (as defined by 10 U.S.C. 2306a(h)) with respect to procurements subject to that section, and section 304A(h) of the Federal Property and Administrative Services Act of 1949 (41 U.S.C. 254b(h)), with respect to procurements subject to that section.

(2) Indirect costs and direct labor rates.

(3) Proprietary information about manufacturing processes, operations, or techniques marked by the contractor in accordance with applicable law or regulation.

(4) Information marked by the contractor as "contractor bid or proposal information" in accordance with applicable law or regulation.

(5) Information marked in accordance with 52.215-1(e).

FAR 3.104-1.

This last category of information, with its reference to a FAR solicitation provision, FAR 52.215-1(e), gives vendors a chance to protect material they submit during the solicitation process:

(e) Restriction on disclosure and use of data. Offerors that include in their proposals data that they do not want disclosed to the public for any purpose, or used by the Government except for evaluation purposes, shall—

(1) Mark the title page with the following legend:

This proposal includes data that shall not be disclosed outside the Government and shall not be duplicated, used, or disclosed—in whole or in part—for any purpose other than to evaluate this proposal. If, however, a contract is awarded to this offeror as a result of—or in connection with—the submission of this data, the Government shall have the right to duplicate, use, or disclose the data to the extent provided in the resulting contract. This restriction does not limit the Government's right to use information contained in this data if it is obtained from another source without restriction. The data subject to this restriction are contained in sheets [insert numbers or other identification of sheets]; and

(2) Mark each sheet of data it wishes to restrict with the following legend:

Use or disclosure of data contained on this sheet is subject to the restriction on the title page of this proposal.

FAR 52.215-1(e)

In practice, vendors tend to be overly broad in their designation of the material they want protected. The FAR deals with this by providing a process by which the contracting officer can limit these overly broad categorizations of contractor bid and proposal information. FAR 3.104-4(d).

▮▮▮ "When" do these prohibitions against leaking information kick in?

The procurement integrity regulations in the FAR apply only up to the time of award of a contract; or as the regulations say, the improper leaking of information must have occurred "before the award of a federal agency procurement contract to which the information relates." A person must not, other than as provided by law, knowingly obtain contractor bid or proposal information or source selection information before the award of a federal agency procurement contract to which the information relates.

So, in a sense, these procurement integrity regulations prohibiting the disclosure of protected information seem to go away once the contract is awarded.

That doesn't mean, however, that there are no rules against disclosing certain solicitation information once the ink dries on the award document. For example, the Privacy Act (5 U.S.C. 552a), the Trade Secrets Act (18 U.S.C. 1905), and the Freedom of Information Act (5 U.S.C. 552) also deal with protecting government information.

"How" must the leaked information have been provided or obtained?

Fortunately, for people trying to understand these restrictions, both givers and takers of procurement information must *knowingly* give up or take the protected information.

Job Offers for Competitive Procurements over $100,000

A second major part of the procurement integrity rules covers job offers a government employee gets from a potential government contractor during the solicitation process. Dangling a job offer before a government employee while the solicitation process is going on is not a good idea. Generally, the government employee must disclose the offer and get out of the procurement. Like the anti-leaking rules, the job offer rules do not apply to sole-source procurements.

Job offer restrictions apply to a government employee in a solicitation *over* the $100,000 simplified acquisition threshold. (The FAR does set higher dollar limits for some rare situations.)

But not everyone in the solicitation process is covered; only those "participating personally and substantially" in the solicitation process are covered. For example, the contracting officer awarding the contract is covered, but a mailroom clerk is not.

After getting a job offer contact from a potential contractor, the government employee must:

1. *Report* the contact to his or her boss and to the agency ethics official and

2. Either *reject* the offer or *recuse* himself or herself.

An employee "contact" is broadly defined. Unsolicited communications from offerors regarding possible employment are considered "contacts."

The FAR also broadly defines who can make contacts to the federal employee:

> Employment contacts between the employee and the offeror, that are conducted through agents, or other intermediaries, may require disqualification under 3.104-3(c)(1).
>
> FAR 3.104-5(a).

The Revolving Door—Contracts over $10 Million

The phrase "revolving door" refers to the problem of people coming into government service for a while and going back into the private market for a while and then perhaps coming back into government service.

The revolving door is probably the hardest issue to deal with fairly, not just for government employees involved in the procurement process but also for government employees involved in any aspect of government service, procurement or otherwise.

It's a difficult issue. The rules must walk a complicated line between protecting the government process from improper influences from government employees formerly in the private market and making sure that government employees do not become unemployable in the private market as a result of their government service.

Revolving-door rules cover government employees in the procurement process as well as government employees in general. Here we deal with only the revolving-door prohibitions on those involved in the procurement process. Unlike the anti-leaking and job offer rules, the revolving-door rules apply to both competitive procurements and sole-source procurements.

It's easy to summarize the procurement integrity revolving-door provisions. FAR 3.104-3(d) specifies that the revolving-door prohibition is for one year and applies only to government employees involved in contracts over $10 million. Those include the procuring contracting officer; the source selection authority; a member of a source selection evaluation board or the chief of a financial or technical evaluation team; a program manager, deputy program manager, or administrative contracting officer; and someone who personally made a decision to award a contract, subcontract, modification of a contract or subcontract, or task order or delivery order.

Also included are government employees who established overhead or other rates applicable to a contract, approved issuance of a contract payment or payments, or paid or settled a claim.

The former government employee cannot be an employee, officer, director or consultant of the contractor with a contract over $10 million for one year after the government employee made a decision relating to that contract. But in restricting these former government employees, Congress provided a big loophole to make sure that former government employees would not be unemployable. Although Congress limited the right of these government employees to work for the company that had a contract over $10 million, the FAR allows these employees to work for an affiliate of this company:

> Nothing . . . may be construed to prohibit a former official of a federal agency from accepting compensation from any division or affiliate of a contractor that does not produce the same or similar products or services as the entity of the contractor that is responsible for the contract. . . .
>
> FAR 3.104-3(d)(3).

This loophole makes sense because it puts a one-year prohibition on the employee's working on the same product or service but not on the employee's working on other products or services the company provides.

Another provision that makes sense is FAR 3.104-6, which requires agencies to have ethics advisors to help government employees decide the propriety of working for a company and therefore follow the revolving-door provisions. The regulations provide a list of required information that must be sent to the agency ethics official. The official must provide an answer within 30 days (or as soon thereafter as practicable).

These opinions provide a "safe harbor." Employees and contractors who rely in good faith on these opinions cannot be convicted of a *knowing* violation of the procurement integrity regulations.

HOW THE GOVERNMENT DEALS WITH VIOLATIONS

FAR 3.104-7 describes the processing of violations or possible violations of these procurement integrity rules that come to the contracting officer's attention.

The general test is one of impact. If the contracting officer determines that the reported violation or possible violation has no impact on the pending contract award, the contracting officer is to report that conclusion to the appropriate agency official. With that official's concurrence, the contracting officer may proceed to award. If that official does not concur, the award of the contract is withheld and the head of the contracting agency (HCA) makes the final decision.

If, on the other hand, the information would impact the award, the contracting officer must promptly advise the HCA of the information disclosed and let the HCA make the final decision.

FAR 3.104-7(f) creates a loophole. If the HCA or designee receiving information concerning a possible violation finds that award is justified by urgent and compelling circumstances or is otherwise in the interest of the government, the HCA may let the contracting officer award the contract after notification of the head of the agency in accordance with agency procedures.

The following GAO decisions show how an agency properly handled alleged violations.

> The Loral Western Development Lab lost a National Security Agency (NSA) contract for the agency's worldwide Capital Software Lifecycle Support program to HRB Systems. Loral protested, arguing that the agency had failed to consider that HRB violated the procurement integrity regulations because HRB allegedly had improper insider information: after the first round of best and final offers (BAFOs) a Loral employee told Loral management that an HRB employee told him that Loral's proposal was approximately $8 million lower than HRB's and that a second round of BAFOs would be requested. Loral told the agency about this rumor and was told that the alleged violation was being investigated by the agency's inspector general. Loral argued that the agency improperly awarded the contract to HRB before completion of the investigation. Loral noted that its proposal was in fact about $8 million lower than HRB's and also that there was a second round of BAFOs.

GAO denied the protest. There was no requirement that a contracting officer stop the procurement to investigate a procurement integrity violation. Nonetheless, NSA had investigated the matter and had asked both offerors to execute a special Procurement Integrity Certificate saying they were not aware of any violations of the act. In addition, GAO said these violations were only rumors. Moreover, the contracting officer continued the procurement only after being told, by higher level officials, to do so. Finally, and significant to GAO, HRB did not in fact raise its price even though it allegedly knew it was $8 million lower than Loral's.

Loral Western Development Labs, B-525606, May 5, 1994.

Computer Technology Associates, Inc. (CTA), Unisys Corp., and Science Applications International Corp. (SAIC) submitted quotations for a General Services Administration (GSA) contract. Someone at CTA apparently hacked into the GSA email system and got the transcripts of the oral presentations that Unisys and SAIC made to GSA as part of the solicitation process. After the transcripts were downloaded and copied, they were given to the CTA project manager and deputy project manager. Each reviewed at least one of the transcripts and highlighted some passages. The SAIC transcript had, according to GAO, more than 30 of its 148 pages marked. (At the time of the protest, these employees and the "hacker" had been fired.) To its credit, the head of CTA told GSA about the transcripts. The employees who marked up the transcripts, in the words of GAO, "deny using or revealing any information from the transcripts" in the CTA proposal. In addition, CTA management directed the employee responsible for submitting the company's proposal revisions to GSA to exclude any input received from the project manager or deputy project manager. Nevertheless, GSA disqualified CTA from the competition. CTA protested to GAO, arguing that having the transcripts had no impact on the solicitation process because CTA made sure that the information in them was not used in its proposal revisions.

GAO had no doubt that the Procurement Integrity Act had been violated. The issue was "impact": Did the violations have any impact on the solicitation? According to GAO, they did. "[E]ven without proof of actual use of the information, the actions of CTA's employees had a significant, negative impact on the integrity of the procurement system, and we find reasonable the judgment of the agency that the competition has been tainted by those actions."

Computer Technology Associates, Inc., B-288622, November 7, 2001.

CONFLICTS OF INTEREST

Two types of conflicts of interest are relevant to procurement integrity:

- Personal: an individual person's objectivity is impaired.
- Organizational: an entity's objectivity is impaired.

One difference between the two is what a reviewing forum, such as GAO, looks at to prove one or the other. Another distinction is whether an appearance of a conflict is relevant:

> Where organizational affiliation creates the appearance of a conflict of interest, we have recognized the importance of addressing even apparent conflicts. . . . Where, however, it is an individual's alleged actions (rather than an organizational affiliation) that creates the asserted impropriety, we focus our review on the record's support for the alleged actions. Specifically, here, we reviewed whether the record showed that the awardee may have obtained an unfair competitive advantage in the procurement by virtue of its employment of a former government employee; that is, whether the actions of the former government employee may have resulted in prejudice in favor of the awardee. *Perin/Jones, Joint Venture*, B-285906, November 1, 2000.

Personal Conflicts of Interest

The most notorious example of a personal conflict of interest involved Darleen Druyun, who in 2004 pled guilty to violating 18 U.S.C. 208(a). That law prohibits a government employee from "participating personally and substantially as a Government officer or employee . . . in a . . . contract . . . in which, to his knowledge . . . an organization with whom he is negotiating or has any arrangement concerning prospective employment, has a financial interest." Druyun was negotiating for a job with Boeing while she was also negotiating with Boeing on behalf of the Air Force for the lease of 100 Boeing KC 767A tanker aircraft. *Lockheed Martin Corporation,* B-295402, February 18, 2005.

The U.S. Court of Appeals for the Federal Circuit has given helpful advice on what a personal conflict of interest looks like in the solicitation process, specifically, whether an individual identified as a reference for an offeror may properly sit on an evaluation panel considering that offeror's bid:

> In order to prevail on its conflict of interest claim, Galen must establish a violation of statutory or regulatory conflict of interest provisions. The mere presence of one of Downing's past performance references on each evaluation panel alone does not constitute proof of a conflict of interest. . . . Indeed, our precedent points to the contrary. For example, in CACI, Inc.- Federal, we discussed whether a conflict of interest existed when four of the five members of the proposal evaluation board were alleged to have prior professional and social relationships with the vice president of the successful bidder. . . . This court reversed the trial court's decision . . . rejecting the argument that discussions of employment between two evaluators and the successful bidder supported reversal of the contract award, and noting that the discussions were "only preliminary exploratory talks, directed to possibilities that never materialized, not negotiations," and occurred long before the Department issued the request for proposals.
>
> In contrast to the facts in CACI, the Department of Veterans Affairs (VA) evaluation panel in the present case had only one evaluator out of four with alleged ties to Downing. During the pre-corrective action evaluation, one of Downing's three past-performance references was on a panel of six technical evaluators. During the

post-corrective action evaluation, one past-performance reference was on a panel of four technical evaluators. Moreover, there is no evidence that either [the challenged evaluator-references] had been contacted and agreed to serve as a past-performance reference for Downing, and thus no evidence that they were interested in her success as opposed to simply more knowledgeable about her.... Here, Galen has not shown any active close or pecuniary relationship between Downing and either evaluator at any time. Therefore, the mere fact that Downing listed an evaluator as a past performance reference does not constitute a conflict of interest.

For even an appearance of a conflict of interest to exist, a government official must at least appear to have some stake in the outcome of government action influenced by that individual. Galen has shown no such connection here. As required by the solicitation, Downing listed past performance references to validate Downing's "past experience and any current contracts providing services of this type." The mere presence of an individual's name on list of past performance references does not indicate any "interest" on the part of that individual in the final outcome of the evaluation.

Galen Medical Associates, Inc. v. United States, 369 F.3d 1324 (Fed. Cir. 2004).

Organizational Conflicts of Interest

A personal conflict of interest is usually not difficult to spot. For example, a contracting officer faced with the possibility of awarding a contract to a company run by the contracting officer's spouse faces a conflict between loyalty to the government and loyalty to the spouse. The conflict is quite obvious.

An organizational conflict of interest (OCI) is harder to spot. The FAR defines an OCI this way:

> ... when because of other activities or relationships with other persons, a person is unable or potentially unable to render impartial assistance or advice to the government, or the person's objectivity in performing the contract work is or might be otherwise impaired, or a person has an unfair competitive advantage.
>
> FAR 2.101.

The FAR also gives the contracting officer the job of identifying and dealing with OCIs:

> (a) Using the general rules, procedures, and examples in this subpart, contracting officers shall analyze planned acquisitions in order to—
>
> (1) Identify and evaluate potential organizational conflicts of interest as early in the acquisition process as possible; and
>
> (2) Avoid, neutralize, or mitigate significant potential conflicts before contract award.
>
> FAR 9.504.

GAO adds a good point:

> Because conflicts may arise in factual situations not expressly described in the relevant FAR sections, the regulation advises contracting officers to examine each situation individually and to exercise "common sense, good judgment, and sound discretion" in assessing whether a significant potential conflict exists and in developing an appropriate way to resolve it.
>
> *American Management Systems, Inc.,* B-285645, September 8, 2000.

GAO has grouped organizational conflicts of interest into three general categories depending on their impact:

- Biased ground rules
- Unequal access to information
- Impaired objectivity.

Computers Universal, Inc., B-292794, November 18, 2003.

Biased Ground Rules

The most obvious conflict of interest is biased ground rules. The most common example is a contractor writing a specification and then being able to bid on that specification. For example:

> Here, the primary concern is that the firm could skew the competition, whether intentionally or not, in favor of itself. . . . These situations may also involve a concern that the firm, by virtue of its special knowledge of the agency's future requirements, would have an unfair advantage in the competition for those requirements.

The Leads Corp., B-292465, September 26, 2003.

The other two OCIs—unequal access to information and impaired objectivity—are more difficult to spot.

Unequal Access to Information

A common OCI argument is that a competitor has an "unequal access to information" or an "unfair competitive advantage." This alleged inequality can arise from something the government has done or something a competitor has done.

Protecting the solicitation process from this inequality is the contracting officer's job. The contracting officer has the authority, indeed the responsibility, to ensure that the solicitation process is fair. This authority is based on FAR 1.602-2, which gives a contracting officer wide latitude to exercise business judgment when "safeguarding the interests of the United States in its contractual relationships."

The CFC in a 2007 case described what the contracting officer should look for. Courts consider:

> (1) whether an offeror had access to nonpublic information that was unavailable to the protester; (2) whether that nonpublic information was competitively useful in responding to the solicitation; (3) whether, by having unequal access to that information, the awardee was afforded an advantage that was unfair; and (4) whether not having equal access to that information prejudiced the protester.
>
> *Arinc Engineering Servs., L.L.C. v. United States,*
> 77 Fed. Cl. 196, 202 (2007).

The same decision agrees with the FAR that the contracting officer is in charge: "The responsibility for determining whether such unequal access exists and what steps should be taken in response thereto rests squarely with the contracting officer."

In making this decision, the contracting officer must have a "rational basis"—a good reason for finding an OCI.

> The Army had developed a computer system for handling medical logistics information called the Theater Wide Enterprise Logistics System. Now the system needed operations and maintenance support. The problem, from the protester's viewpoint, was that vendors involved in the development work were unfairly awarded the contracts for the maintenance and operations work. One argument the protester raised was that the winner had an organizational conflict of interest because the subcontractors the winner intended to use on the contract had worked on the earlier Army contract and therefore gave the winner unequal access to information that helped it win the new contract. The primary conclusion of the court in finding that there was no OCI was that the contracting officer had done a thorough and exhaustive analysis of whether there was any OCI. "The record shows that the contracting officer performed two thorough and comprehensive investigations and carefully documented his conclusion that no OCI existed." The contracting officer had analyzed the work that would be required under the current contract, had interviewed government personnel who worked on the development contract, and then had looked at the work done by the winner and its proposed subcontractors had done on the prior contract. The contracting officer concluded that none had a role in developing the requirements for the solicitation at issue; that none had any access to underlying software code configuration for the system; that none gave technical direction to the system; and that none had discussions where contracts sensitive information had been discussed. The court denied the protest.
>
> *MASAI Technologies Corp. v. United States*,
> U.S. Court of Federal Claims No. 07-714C, November 14, 2007.

The fact that an agency impropriety was committed does not, however, mean that the protester automatically wins on the basis of an OCI. The protester must also show that the impropriety actually harmed the protester. Moreover, the agency's decision must be based on facts and not mere innuendo or suspicions. We will look next at "rational basis" cases, then "harm," and then the "hard proof" required.

One good example of a "rational basis" is the Compliance Corporation case, which involved industrial espionage.

CHAPTER 3 | Ethics Rules for Getting a Contract 51

> The Naval Investigative Service (NIS) conducted an investigation and reported the following to a Navy contracting officer: the director in charge of contracts for Compliance Corporation had contacted an employee at Eagan, McAllister Associates (EMA), a competitor for a pending solicitation. The Compliance Corporation director sought certain information (including proprietary salary information) on the current contract held by EMA. The day after the two met, EMA found on the desk of the contacted EMA employee a pile of EMA documents relating to the solicitation, handwritten notes of the EMA employee's meeting the previous day with the Compliance Corporation director, and copies of handwritten notes from another Compliance employee. The EMA employee denied that she was going to give them to the Compliance director; when asked about the suspicious presence of all these documents on her desk, she said, "All the items and paper just fell in together." She admitted giving the Compliance director an estimation of EMA salary scales from several years back (which would have covered the period from the start of the current contract and two option years). There was some indication that the Compliance director had offered the EMA employee a job if she obtained the information. Both the Compliance director and the EMA employee denied that information on the current EMA contract and proposal was requested or that the EMA employee was offered a job in exchange.
>
> Based on the NIS investigation, the contracting officer excluded Compliance from the competition. Compliance protested to GAO, arguing that the contracting officer had no authority to disqualify competitors. GAO disagreed. It said that a contracting officer may disqualify a competitor where it reasonably appears that a firm may have obtained an unfair competitive advantage. GAO found that the contracting officer in this instance had a reasonable basis for so concluding and dismissed the protest.
>
> *Compliance Corporation,* B-239252, August 15, 1990.
See also *Compliance Corp. v. United States,* 22 Cl.Ct. 193 (1990), aff'd. 960 F.2d 157 (Fed. Cir.1992) (table).

Another good example of an agency having a "rational basis" for its actions is found in a protest of an Air Force solicitation.

> The Air Force wanted to establish a new agency for doing scheduling associated with the re-engineering of its Air Combat Command. It began its efforts in 1999 when it awarded an indefinite delivery/indefinite quantity contract for consultant services and awarded some preliminary work to B3H which subbed the work out to DSD Laboratories during both 1999 and 2000. Specifically, the preliminary work involved the design and organization of the new agency and then actually working with the Air Force for a 15 month period as the service started to use the new agency. Later, the Air Force wanted to award a contract for further work on the re-engineering effort. This work was scheduled as contract support for the 1999 and 2000 task orders. The Air Force excluded DSD from the solicitation.
>
> The Air Force believed that DSD had, as part of its task order work, "played a role in making recommendations to the Air Force regarding the composition of the very organization that the Request for Quotations (RFQ) now seeks to fill. As the recommendations made by B3H and DSD formed the basis of the Statement of Work for the RFQ, the contracting officer had a legitimate concern that DSD might have, intentionally or not, skewed the competition in favor of itself for the RFQ." The court found that the contracting officer's exclusion of DSD was reasonable, and as a result, denied DSD's request to stop the contract award.
>
> As the court put it, "given the nature of the work performed on the 1999 task order, the contracting officer had a reasonable basis for excluding DSD from the year 2000 solicitation on organizational conflict of interest grounds. Furthermore, the year 2000 task order requires DSD to assist in the stand up of the new organization, to `continue to refine the written stand up plan, which recommends what is required to organize, establish and man such an organization,' and to 'trouble shoot and fix process oversights, errors or needed revisions.' Thus, if DSD were the contractor, for the new organization, it could help 'stand itself up,' help establish its own manning, and trouble shoot itself under the description of work contained in the 2000 task order."
>
> *DSD Laboratories, Inc. v. United States,* 46 Fed. Cl. 467 (2000).

Assuming that a protester can establish that an agency's decision lacked a rational basis, the protester must also prove that it was harmed by the unfair competitive advantage. A protester suffers no harm if it would have lost the procurement anyway, despite the unfair competitive advantage. Moreover, proof of harm must be established with facts and not mere suspicions or innuendos.

CHAPTER 3 | Ethics Rules for Getting a Contract   53

> NASA told NSI Technology Services Corporation (NSI) that its proposal would not be further considered based on technical grounds. NSI protested to GAO. On each page of its protest, NSI put the legend "This document contains material which should not be disclosed except to appropriate officials of NASA." Despite this restrictive legend, NASA disclosed its contents by giving Serv-Air a copy of the entire NSI protest. GAO denied the protest. It said that NSI had suffered no harm as a result of the release of the NSI proprietary information to Serv-Air. NSI was officially out of the competition and thus there was no way under NASA procedures that NSI could win the contract at that point. NASA had already debriefed NSI and had indicated that it had no intention of giving any further thought to awarding the contract to NSI. NSI could contact the U.S. Department of Justice since the release of proprietary information violated The Trade Secrets Act. The protest, however, was dismissed.
>
> *NSI Technology Services Corporation,* B-253797.4, December 29, 1993.

Harm can be shown where only one vendor gets information that should have been given to all competitors. The following two cases show the type of information that must be shared and the type that need not be shared.

Critical new information must be shared with all vendors.

> After the Army issued a solicitation for telephone cable and related supplies, GS Elektro-ScheweGmbH (Schewe) asked the government for additional information. The Army gave Schewe a document which stated that the cable must be manufactured in Germany. The IFB did not itself include such a requirement. Schewe ended up winning the contract. When the Army found out that only Schewe had that information, it canceled the contract and re-solicited. Schewe protested the re-solicitation.
>
> GAO said that the government can terminate a contract where there is a defect in the procurement process which resulted in "actual or potential bidders not being treated fairly." Here the IFB did not say that the cable had to be made in Germany. One bidder, however, got a document showing that the agency wanted precisely that. Because one vendor got information that should have been properly given to all, GAO concluded that the Army properly terminated the contract and re-solicited.
>
> *GS Elektro-ScheweGmbH,* B-259103.2, April 13, 1995.

On the other hand, information that is not new or critical need not be shared.

> Continental Service Company (CSC) lost the contract for maintenance and repair of 17 U.S. Army Reserve Facilities. CSC protested, claiming that the winner, Climate Masters, got an unfair competitive advantage because the agency gave Climate Masters information about the solicitations which was not provided to other bidders. GAO acknowledged that information was given solely to Climate Masters. However, the information was information that reflected the only reasonable interpretation of the solicitation that would be possible. Such answers need not be disseminated to other bidders under FAR 14.208(c). Since no new information was provided, the agency did not have to give the information to all the other bidders. Continental's protest was denied.
> *Continental Service Company*, B-258807.2, April 11, 1995.

Information to one vendor, however, might not be critical.

> The Coast Guard needed turbine engine repairs. It had Energy Maintenance Co. (EMC) inspect the engine and report on what repairs were necessary. It then gave the report to the original equipment manufacturer (Turbo Power and Marine Systems) who compared the report with the conditions of the turbine and concluded that the report was accurate. The Coast Guard used the report as the basis for the repair work specification. It excluded from the competition EMC because EMC did the initial report that led to the specification. Turbo, however, was allowed to compete. Gas Turbine Corp. (GTS) asked for a copy of the report but was refused. When GTC lost the procurement to Turbo, it protested arguing that Turbo had an unfair competitive advantage since it had seen the report. GAO admitted that the report gave Turbo advance knowledge of the agency's requirement but said that this advance knowledge did not give Turbo any unfair advantage. Since Turbo was the original equipment manufacturer, it was familiar with the parts to be repaired.
> *Gas Turbine Corp.*, B-251265.2, May 24, 1993.

One reason vendors lose OCI protests is that they do not have "hard proof" that they suffered any harm as a result of, for example, a former government employee moving to the competitor. The mere fact that a former

CHAPTER 3 | Ethics Rules for Getting a Contract   55

government employee ends up working for the winner of a procurement is not "hard proof." Agencies often win these protests because the former government employee had little or no involvement in the procurement itself.

> NASA needed technical support services at Lewis Research Center, Cleveland, Ohio. NASA awarded the contract to Gilcrest Electric and Supply Company. A protest was filed by Cleveland Telecommunications Corp. Cleveland argued that the former NASA employees who now worked for Gilcrest had passed information to Gilcrest with regard to a Cleveland proposed subcontract and that this tainted the solicitation process. NASA acknowledged that two NASA employees had signed letters of intent to work for Gilcrest if Gilcrest got the contract. It argued, however, that the former NASA employees were not procurement officials since they were not involved in the drafting, reviewing or approving of specifications in the RFP, nor did they evaluate proposals, select sources, conduct negotiations or approve the award to Gilcrest. In addition, there was no evidence that these NASA employees participated on behalf of NASA in any way in the procurement or participated on behalf of Gilcrest. In addition, the two NASA employees were recused from the procurement after Gilcrest approached them concerning employment. GAO denied the protest. It found there was nothing wrong with these employees conditionally accepting employment with Gilcrest while they were agency employees since these employees did not participate in any way in the procurement on behalf of NASA or Gilcrest.
> *Cleveland Telecommunications Corp.*, B-257294, September 19, 1994.

> AIT and Associates won a contract with the Air Force for technical engineering services. Its proposed project manager was the contracting officer's technical representative (COTR) who served under the predecessor contract until he retired one day after the current contract was awarded. GAO found nothing improper. The COTR was not a procurement official, he had no involvement with drafting, reviewing or approving the RFP's specifications or evaluating the proposals, selecting the sources, conducting negotiations or approving the award. In addition, there was no evidence that he participated in any way in the procurement on behalf of the Air Force or AIT. In fact, the COTR never participated in the predecessor solicitation process.
> *Creative Management Technology, Inc.*, B-266299, February 9, 1996.

> Ms. E. Hawthorne was awarded a contract with the Department of Agriculture, Forest Service, to do cultural resource documentation of various sites within the Cloudcroft Ranger District, Lincoln National Forest, New Mexico. A newly appointed contracting officer reviewed Hawthorne's contract and decided that the contract award to Hawthorne created the appearance of a conflict of interest and should be terminated because Hawthorne was a former Forest Service employee who had, the agency believed, worked on the design of the project which became the basis for the contract. Hawthorne's involvement on the project was minimal, however, and was limited to preliminary activity not directly related to work subsequently called for under the project. GAO held that there was no actual or apparent conflict of interest here that would justify the Forest Service's termination for convenience. Ms. Hawthorne demonstrated that her involvement was so minimal that her involvement could not reasonably be seen as a conflict of interest.
>
> *E. Hawthorne,* B-250912, January 25, 1993.

In addition, the "natural advantages of incumbency" do not necessarily provide unfair advantages in the procurement process. One reason is that agencies limit these advantages to the extent possible. In the first GAO decision below, an agency limited the advantages an incumbent could take out of a current contract. GAO sanctioned these limits and in fact found that these limits prevented unfair competitive advantage.

> A military handbook put out by the Army had to be updated. One part of the updating process was an industry-government conference on topics covered by the handbook The conference was held twice a year and was open to all. The Army had a contract with Materials Science Corporation (MSC) that included tasks such as coordinating the meeting and providing administrative support to the meeting. That contract was about to end so a new procurement was begun. MSC was one of the offerors as was A-Enterprises, Inc. While the Army was considering the offers, the conference was held. The Army made MSC attend to provide information gathered in the course of carrying out the incumbent contract. The Army, however, had modified the contract it had with MSC to prevent the company from organizing or administering the meeting since the

CHAPTER 3 | Ethics Rules for Getting a Contract   57

> Army was involved in an ongoing procurement. A-Enterprises was eligible to attend the meeting. After MSC won the new contract, A-Enterprises protested, arguing that MSC had an unfair competitive advantage as a result of being the incumbent. It claimed that MSC had been paid to be at the conference, had access to agency evaluators, and was able to tailor its proposal to what it learned at the conference. It also claimed that MSC controlled the invitation list for the conference and prevented A-Enterprises from attending. GAO denied the protest. MSC's participation in the conference was limited to providing two experts to discuss the current contract efforts. In addition, no discussion was held on the pending proposals of either offeror, nor were any discussions held on the pending solicitation itself. GAO concluded that MSC had no unfair competitive advantage and denied the protest.
>
> *A-Enterprises, Inc.*, B-255318, February 18, 1994.

> The Army put out a proposal for food service. The offerors wanted additional information from the government that the incumbent contractor had; for example, they wanted pest control reports, equipment repair tickets, and employee's work schedule used in the current contract The incumbent contractor, Good Food Service, Inc. (GFS), was required to provide the government this information which was then given to all the other offerors. When GFS lost the follow-on contract, it protested arguing that it was put at a competitive disadvantage by disclosure of the alleged proprietary GFS data on the incumbent contract. GAO did not agree. Information such as the pest control report, equipment repair tickets, etc. was information that is "otherwise available to the public without restriction" and therefore, not "proprietary." With regard to the incumbent contractor's weekly and monthly reports which are arguably proprietary, those GFS documents did not contain a restricted legend or any other printed statement indicating that the reports were regarded by GFS as proprietary or confidential. GAO denied the protest, finding that there could be no competitive harm from the release of this information.
>
> *Good Food Service, Inc.*, B-260728, June 20, 1995.

Subcontractors must always be included in the conflict of interest equation. Work that a subcontractor did on prior contracts could disqualify the prime contractor on the basis of conflict of interest. But the fact that the subcontractor simply had prior experience under a contract is no basis for disqualification.

The Defense Information Systems Agency (DISA) had a contract with I-Net for work at the DISA Columbus Regional Control Center. One of the task orders under that contract was partially performed but eventually terminated for convenience. DISA issued another solicitation to do some of the very same work under a separate contract. The contract was awarded to Excel Management, Inc. I-Net was a subcontractor to Excel under the new contract award. Optimum Technology protested, arguing that I-Net's participation in the previous contract gave Excel an unfair competitive advantage. GAO disagreed. The mere existence of a prior or current contract between the contracting agency and the winner does not create an unfair competitive advantage. Nor must an agency compensate for every competitive advantage "inherently gleaned by a potential offeror's prior performance of a particular requirement." There is no basis to object to an offeror's advantage as incumbent unless the advantage was created by an improper preference or other unfair action by the procuring agency. In fact, as GAO pointed out, incumbent contractors with good performance records "can offer real advantages to the Government and proposal strengths flowing from a firm's prior experience." Here, GAO concluded there was no basis to require the exclusion of Excel from competition because of its proposed use of I -Net as a subcontractor.

Optimum Technology, Inc., B-266339.2, April 16, 1996.

The Army did an A-76 study in connection with its installation support services requirements at Fort Benning. The contract would cover buildings maintenance, family housing maintenance, utility systems operations and maintenance, heating etc. The apparent winner, IT had a teaming arrangement with INNOLOG. INNOLOG was performing an integrated sustainment maintenance (ISM) contract. Under the ISM contract, INNOLOG maintained the Executive Management Information System (EIVIIS) database which had data on maintenance activities performed at various Army installations worldwide (including Fort Benning). In GAO's eyes, "using the EMIS, it is possible to obtain relatively in-depth, comprehensive historical information relating to maintenance activities performed at Fort Benning." GAO found that IT had an unfair competitive advantage from its relationship with INNOLOG because it could get information "presumably obtained with proper authorization and not in the course of the source selection process" that was competitively useful. It would let an offeror prepare a more refined proposal that would result solely from information in the RFP. "Such enhanced detail regarding the actual work performed could provide an offeror the

CHAPTER 3 | Ethics Rules for Getting a Contract   59

> opportunity to formulate a better staffing profile in the sense that the firm could propose a smaller number of employees (at a lower skill level) in arriving at its proposed staffing mix." Because the agency had not successfully mitigated the conflict of interest, GAO sustained the protest of a competitor.
> *Johnson Controls World Services, Inc.*, B-286714.2, February 13, 2001.

Also, a contractor carrying out one government contract can get access to non-public information that gives it an unfair advantage in a later contract.

> A subcontractor of a winning contractor had the opportunity to monitor a protesting competitor's performance under an earlier contract. During the earlier contract, the sub had an opportunity to make detailed observations of virtually every aspect of Ktech's [the protester's] work in connection with the prior program, including seeing how the hardware and instrumentation system were being assembled and how the grounding and shielding system was being fabricated. The record thus clearly shows that [the sub] through its prior work as a government contractor, had an opportunity to obtain Ktech's proprietary information during the performance of Ktech's prior contract. GAO found an OCI. Significant here was the fact that neither the government nor the winning contractor refuted the protester's arguments on this point.
> *Ktech Corporation,* B-285330, B-285330.2, August 17, 2002.

▌ *Impaired Objectivity*

Impaired objectivity is a little like the old joke about asking a barber if you need a haircut. According to GAO, there's impaired objectivity when a firm's work under one government contract could entail its evaluating itself, through either an assessment of performance under another contract or an evaluation of a proposal submitted to obtain another contract. The concern in such situations is that the firm's ability to render impartial advice to the government could appear to be undermined by its relationship with the entity whose work product is being evaluated. *Computers Universal, Inc.*, B-292794, November 18, 2003.

The classic case of impaired objectivity is when a contractor will be evaluating something it is also producing. For example, the Navy issued a solicitation for the manufacture of an underwater warfare system that would require the manufacturer to evaluate the performance of its own system. GAO found this to be a "biased objectivity" OCI:

> . . . where, as here, a company is responsible for assessing the performance of systems it has manufactured [is] a classic example of an impaired objectivity OCI. . . . In such situations, the firm risks having its objectivity impaired by a bias in favor of its own systems performance. Similarly, a company manufacturing systems that are, as a practical matter, competing with similar systems produced by other manufacturers, risks having a negative bias regarding the performance of the competing systems. This is particularly true where, as here, the contract requirements clearly anticipate comparisons between the performance of similar systems manufactured by competing firms.

PURVIS Systems, Inc., B-293807.3, August 16, 2004.

But there was no impaired objectivity where one company monitored but did not evaluate a contract performed in part by the same company.

> When the Department of Defense tracks its vehicles in South Korea, the tracking system uses global positioning systems (GPS) equipment. When DoD wanted to get an information management specialist (IMS) to help with the overall tracking system, it hired someone from Critel. But that company already ran the GPS part of the tracking system. An unsuccessful competitor for the IMS contract protested, arguing that Critel had a prohibited OCI. To the protester, there was an OCI because the IMS contracted with Critel but the Critel employee would be monitoring Critel's work as a GPS equipment supplier. GAO didn't think there was an OCI. It distinguished between monitoring the system which was not an OCI and evaluating it which could be an OCI. We find no prohibited OCI here. Under its equipment contract, Critel is required to provide preventative and corrective maintenance and an inspection system covering the

> required services, and also must maintain and make available to the government records of all inspection work performed. While the IMS contractor is required to develop a quality assurance program to provide surveillance of—that is, to monitor—the required scheduled maintenance, it is not responsible for making judgments as to what maintenance is required or how well the maintenance is being performed. GAO distinguished this case from one where a subcontractor was to establish requirements for tests it or its prime contractor would perform. That would be an OCI.
>
> *Computers Universal, Inc.*, B-292794, November 18, 2003.

MISREPRESENTATION/BAIT AND SWITCH

The solicitation process relies heavily on information provided by offerors. A company may win a contract on information it provided the government that is not 100 percent accurate. When do misrepresentations in the solicitation process make the contract void? GAO requires an intentional (as opposed to an unintentional) misrepresentation before it finds the contract improperly awarded.

> The Air Force needed land mobile radio maintenance services. The solicitation that was issued required that a lead technician have a specified minimum level of experience. The winning bidder was ENC which proposed as the lead technician someone employed by the current incumbent, Tucson MobilePhone. When Tucson learned that ENC had proposed its employee as the lead technician, Tucson filed a protest with GAO. The protest was accompanied by an affidavit from the technician stating, first, that he had not authorized, and indeed had forbidden, ENC from utilizing his qualifications to obtain the contract; and second, that he told the Air Force this prior to award. On the basis of these facts, Tucson said that there was misrepresentation of qualifications and asked GAO to terminate the contract. GAO did not. It looked for evidence on whether or not the contracting officer could reasonably conclude that the criteria had been met. While GAO conceded that the technician may not have granted ENC permission to use his credentials, it could not say that ENC intentionally misrepresented to the agency its authority to propose him as lead technician. GAO concluded that the Air Force was not unreasonable in considering his credentials and denied the protest.
>
> *Tucson MobilePhone, Inc.*, B-258408.3, June 5, 1995.

If an intended hire goes elsewhere after a contractor gets a new contract, that is not necessarily a bait and switch. Whether a bidder engaged in a bait and switch depends on whether the bidder was responsive to what the solicitation asked for and whether the bidder told the government the truth about the hiring situation. This reflects the understandable fact that "things change." So it should not be surprising that a bidder can win a contract offering to provide the government with certain individuals who end up not working on the contract after it's awarded.

Drawing the line between "things change" and "bait and switch" can be difficult. However, GAO gave an excellent summary of precisely what a prohibited bait and switch looks like:

> To demonstrate a "bait and switch," a protester must show not only that personnel other than those proposed are performing the services—i.e., the "switch"—but also that: (1) the awardee represented in its proposal that it would rely on certain specified personnel in performing the services; (2) the agency relied on this representation in evaluating the proposal; and (3) it was foreseeable that the individuals named in the proposal would not be available to perform the contract work.
>
> *Ann Riley & Assoc., Ltd. – Reconsideration,* B-271741.3, March 10, 1997, 97-1 CPD ¶ 122 at 2-3.

A decision of the CFC also gave some good examples of what does, and does not, constitute a prohibited bait and switch:

The Army issued a solicitation for personnel to run the Center for Counter Measures at the White Sands Missile Range, New Mexico. The incumbent contractor, Orion International Technologies, had its employees sign a "no compete" agreement preventing them from helping other bidders win the contract. This included not letting other bidders use their resumes on those bids. But the no-compete agreement ended when the contract was awarded—the incumbent's employees were free to work for whoever won the contract. The president of Fiore Industries, Mr. Sanchez, talked to Mr. Zucconi, one of the incumbent's employees, before he signed the no-compete argument. Zucconi agreed to work for Fiore Industries if Fiore won. He didn't know that Fiore ultimately proposed him as project manager even though he never gave Fiore permission to do so. During Fiore's oral presentation that was part of the solicitation process, Zucconi was mentioned, but only once. Sanchez told the government that Zucconi had agreed to work for Fiore if Fiore won the contract. Fiore won, but in the one week between the award and the protest that stopped all work on the contract, Fiore did not hire Zucconi or offer him a job. Zucconi later went to work for the government. Orion protested, arguing bait-and-switch. To the losing incumbent, the winner had misrepresented the qualifications of the winner's proposed staff during its oral proposal to the government. Although the CFC found no bait-and-switch, it described other situations where a bait-and-switch had been found. For example, other bidders proposing people who: "Expressed no willingness to be employees of the bidder submitting their names, were unwilling or unable to show the level of commitment that the solicitation required of potential employees, were unable to be the bidder's employees; or were not directly asked whether they would accept employment. But among all the previous bait-and-switch cases the court considered, it could not find any decision saying that "a bidder may not include the name of a potential employee with its bid if the person is willing to work for the bidder upon award of the contract;" or "That a non-incumbent bidder must abide by an employment agreement between the incumbent and one of its incumbent employees, when that bidder wishes to hire the employee and the employee's inclusion in a proposal accurately reflects the availability of the employee if bidder is awarded the contract." The court denied the protest.

Orion International Technologies v. United States, and Fiore Industries, Inc., 66 Fed.Cl. 569 (2005).

STATUS OF THE OFFEROR

The contracting officer must make an affirmative determination of "responsibility" before awarding a contract to a contractor. The contracting officer must also ascertain that the contractor has not been suspended or debarred from performing government work.

Responsibility Determinations

The provisions of the FAR at Subpart 9.1 state that contracts may be awarded only to responsible contractors. A contractor is required to affirmatively establish that it is a responsible vendor. This includes having a satisfactory record of integrity and business ethics.

The 2008 FAR changes discussed in Part 1 also made changes in what the government may consider in determining whether a contractor is responsible. Specifically, these changes in two ways tied "responsibility" to past performance reports contractors receive under FAR Subpart 42.15. First, according to FAR 9.104-1(d), contractors must "(d) Have a satisfactory record of integrity and business ethics (for example, see Subpart 42.15)." Subpart 42.15 deals with the government evaluating a contractor's past performance. Second, FAR 42.1501 was changed by adding the following language to the FAR's description of what the government should consider in evaluating a contractor's past performance:

> . . . for example, the contractor's record of conforming to contract requirements and to standards of good workmanship; the contractor's record of forecasting and controlling costs; the contractor's adherence to contract schedules, including the administrative aspects of performance; the contractor's history of reasonable and cooperative behavior and commitment to customer satisfaction; the contractor's record of integrity and business ethics,

and generally, the contractor's business-like concern for the interest of the customer. 42.1501 General.

What kind of information does the contracting officer need to make an affirmative determination of responsibility? GAO opinions have provided some guidance on the question:

> The burden is on the bidder to establish responsibility; the contracting officer has a wide degree of discretion and business judgment on this matter; a finding of non-responsibility will be overturned only if the contracting officer decision is shown to have been made in bad faith or without a reasonable basis; the determination to be reasonable should be based upon current information; a pre-award survey which includes a criminal investigating agency's report of bidder misconduct on recent contracts satisfies this requirement; and there is no requirement on the contracting officer's part to conduct an independent inquiry to substantiate the accuracy of the information.
>
> *Becker and Schwindenhammer, GmbH,* B-225396, March 2, 1987, 87-1 CPD ¶ 235.

Further, with regard to the contracting officer's decision on responsibility, a protester must submit virtually irrefutable proof that contracting officials had a specific and malicious intent to harm the party deemed nonresponsible; a contracting officer's failure to examine all pertinent data before making the determination constitutes negligence and not bad faith and therefore does not constitute a basis for overturning the contracting officer's determination of nonresponsibility. *Canadian General Electric, Ltd.,* B-223934.2, July 10, 1987, 87-2 CPD ¶ 29.

If a procurement has problems, not all of them are ones GAO will handle. One situation GAO shies away from is protests that the winner should not have been found responsible. But when it does handles these cases, it looks to see how carefully the contracting officer considered information adverse to the protester.

> The General Services Administration (GSA) issued a solicitation for office space for the Social Security Administration in Roanoke, Virginia. The solicitation made offerors submit "evidence of compliance with local zoning laws or evidence of variances, if any, approved by the proper local authority." In its offer, the eventual winner, Damon Harwood Co., told the contracting officer that it did not currently have the required zoning but that it intended to get it if it won. The contracting officer thought this was good enough, found Harwood responsible, and awarded Harwood the lease. After winning, however, Harwood did not get the required zoning from the city. Unsuccessful offerors protested that GSA made a bad responsibility decision as well as a bad award decision.
>
> GAO saw the protesters' arguments as a challenge to the contracting officer's affirmative determination of responsibility—that, in GAO's words, the government's zoning-compliance provision "established a definitive responsibility criterion that required each offeror to have obtained the necessary approval prior to award so as to ensure that zoning would not be an impediment to contractor compliance" with the contract. GAO said that second-guessing a contracting officer's responsibility decision was something it did only in limited, specified exceptions. And this was one of them. "One specific exception is where a protest identifies 'evidence raising serious concerns that, in reaching a particular responsibility determination, the contracting officer unreasonably failed to consider available relevant information or otherwise violated statute or regulation.' This includes protests where, for example, the protest includes specific evidence that the contracting officer may have ignored information that, by its nature, would be expected to have a strong bearing on whether the awardee should be found responsible." GAO believed that this "evidence of serious concerns" test was met here so it went on to consider the issue. It concluded that the contracting officer sufficiently considered Harwood's zoning problem. The evidence showed that "the contracting officer did consider the available information furnished in Harwood's offer and reasonably determined Harwood's capability to perform . . . the contracting officer was aware of, and specifically considered, the fact that, although Harwood's offered site currently was zoned for light manufacturing permitting office space no greater than 20,000 square feet, local zoning laws permitted use of the site for the proposed SSA building with special exception. . . . The contracting officer reports that he con-

> sidered the likelihood of Harwood obtaining the special exception approval in the context of Harwood's representations of a probable rezoning by the city. . . . The contracting officer therefore concluded that Harwood had submitted acceptable evidence of its capability to perform." So the contracting officer's responsibility decision was reasonable.
>
> Public Facility Consortium I, LLC; JDL Castle Corporation,
B-295911; B-295911.2, May 4, 2005

Two issues keep recurring in the responsibility area: business integrity issues and de facto debarment.

Courts require the contracting officer to provide contractors due process any time a contracting officer is about to find a contractor nonresponsible because of a lack of business integrity. Contracting officers do not have to provide due process where other factors, like the perceived lack of capability, make the offeror nonresponsible.

In *Old Dominion Dairy Products, Inc. v. Secretary of Defense*, 631 F.2d 953 (D.C. Cir. 1980), the court held that where the contracting officer makes a nonresponsibility determination on the basis of the offeror's integrity, the company must be notified of that and must be given an opportunity to respond. In this case, the contracting officer found the company nonresponsible on the basis of an audit report that raised questions about the billing practices of Old Dominion on prior contracts. The court said that due process attached to this decision because a "liberty interest" was at stake.

In *Delta Data Systems Corp. v. United States*, 744 F.2d 197 (D.C. Cir. 1984), the court said that the contracting officer was wrong in not giving an offeror considered nonresponsible an opportunity to respond to new information on which that determination was based where the new information was "of uncertain import, . . . likely to determine the award, and . . . of such a nature that the offeror [was] likely to be able to make a significant contribution to its interpretation."

The issue of what is an integrity matter is an important one because due process accompanies integrity matters but not non-integrity matters. The rationale used for the distinction is that nonresponsibility determinations are administrative in nature, not judicial, and therefore no opportunity to rebut or confront information in the hands of the contracting officer is required as long as integrity of the offeror is not involved.

The second issue is de facto debarment. Agencies may try to do informally what they really should do formally. It clearly is proper for the government to refuse to give a company a contract because the government finds the company to be nonresponsible. But what if an agency makes a series of nonresponsibility determinations against the same company? Hasn't the government in effect debarred the company without going through the formal debarment proceedings? One claim a company can make after it has experienced a series of nonresponsibility determinations is that the string of determinations is a de facto debarment. It's called that because it is not a formal legal debarment involving the paperwork and due process associated with formal debarment proceedings. The end result, however, is still the same: the bidder cannot do business with the government. The injustice of the process is that the government avoids the debarment process.

One issue with a de facto debarment is what constitutes one. Typically, a company that has run into a string of nonresponsibility determinations from government agencies claims that the government has done a de facto debarment when in reality the nonresponsibility determinations have been made independently. At what point does this string of nonresponsibility determinations become a de facto debarment? The critical issue is whether there is evidence that the determination of nonresponsibility is part of a long-term disqualification attempt by the agency.

> Government Contract Advisory Services, Inc. (GCAS) tried to get two contracts with the National Guard but was found to be nonresponsible on both. It protested this to GAO, arguing that these two nonresponsibility determinations, along with a third one under another contract, constituted a de facto debarment. GAO disagreed. It said that there was no evidence of a long-term disqualification attempt. In fact, the nonresponsibility determinations were made at the same time so there was no evidence of "long-term." In addition, different contracting officers reached the same conclusion as to nonresponsibility. Accordingly, there was no de facto debarment and GAO dismissed the protest.
> *Government Contract Advisory Services, Inc.,*
> B-255918, B-255919, March 8, 1994.

Debarment and Suspension

A debarment is the most serious sanction a government contractor can suffer short of a criminal conviction. A debarred contractor is ineligible for government work for a specified period.

Related to debarment is "suspension," which makes a contractor temporarily ineligible for government work so that the government has time to decide whether the more serious sanction of debarment should be imposed. The government can suspend contractors from being eligible for award of a government contract. Suspensions are designed to give the government time in which to investigate possible wrongdoing by a government contractor. The grounds for debarment are broader than those for suspension, which focuses solely on the lack of business integrity. Suspensions are to be based upon "adequate evidence" of violation of any one of a number of specified criminal acts.

We will discuss debarment and suspension in greater detail in Chapter 4. This topic, however, is appropriately discussed here among the ethics rules involving the procurement process since whether an apparent winning vendor is debarred or suspended is a critical inquiry the contracting officer must make before awarding any contract.

Chapter 4 also discusses the 2008 FAR changes that expose a contractor to debarment and suspension for a contractor's failure to timely disclose to the government credible evidence of a violation of federal criminal law involving fraud, conflict of interest, bribery, or gratuity violations; violation of the civil False Claims Act (31 U.S.C. 3729-3733); or significant overpayment(s) on the contract.

A contracting officer's duty at this point in the contract solicitation process is generally to check the "debarred list," i.e., the List of Parties Excluded from Federal Procurement and Nonprocurement Programs, to make sure the apparent winner is not on the list and is ineligible for the contract.

It is commonly thought that a debarred contractor cannot under any circumstances get a government contract while it is debarred. That is not true. The FAR provides a loophole: An agency can contract with a debarred contractor if the agency finds there is a compelling need to do so. A GAO decision shows how small a loophole this is.

> J.B. Kies Construction Co. was debarred for three years (until September 26, 1992) due to violations of the Davis-Bacon Act. In 1992, Kies bid on three construction jobs and was the low bidder on each. Kies, however, received a letter from the contracting officer for each project on September 24, 1992, two days before the debarment would be up, telling Kies that it was ineligible for the contracts because Kies was still debarred. Kies protested to GAO claiming that there was a compelling reason to give it the contracts. First, Kies argued that its debarment began in February 1987 and therefore should have ended in 1990. An "administrative oversight" on the government's part resulted in Kies not being debarred until September 1989. Kies' first argument, therefore, was that since it had been debarred 5 years, the government had a compelling reason

> to give it the contracts. Kies also argued that its debarment was about to end. In fact, Kies was off the debarred list when the government awarded the contracts to other bidders after September 26th. GAO could find no compelling reason to give Kies the contracts. The DoD FAR supplement gives only four instances (such as urgency) that constitute a compelling reason for giving a debarred contractor a contract. GAO said that these four situations show that the intent of the exception is that it be used infrequently. Basically, the government must show that there is no realistic alternative to contracting with the debarred contractor to make the case for a "compelling reason." GAO said that it would only look at the reasonableness of the agency's decision to not use the exception and found the agency's action here to be reasonable. It denied the protest.
>
> *J.B. Kies Construction Co.*, B-250797, February 11, 1993.

ENSURING COMPLIANCE WITH PROCUREMENT INTEGRITY RULES

To ensure compliance with the procurement integrity rules, the regulations require that two clauses be added to any solicitation and contract for other than commercial items that are over the simplified acquisition threshold.

FAR 52.203-8, Cancellation, Rescission, and Recovery of Funds for Illegal or Improper Activity, provides a remedy for violation of the procurement integrity laws. It allows the government to either:

- Cancel the solicitation if the contract has not yet been awarded
- Rescind the contract and recover any money paid under the contract.

Rescinding a contract is a drastic remedy, so safeguards have been imposed on the process. Rescission is allowed where a contractor has been convicted of either:

- Exchanging for value information protected by the Procurement Integrity laws
- Getting or giving a competitive advantage.

Rescission is also authorized where there has been no conviction but the head of the contracting activity concludes on the basis of the preponderance of the evidence that there has been a violation of the procurement integrity laws.

The FAR states:

> (a) If the Government receives information that a contractor or a person has engaged in conduct constituting a violation of subsection (a),(b), (c), or (d) of Section 27 of the Office of Federal Procurement Policy Act (41 U.S.C. 423) (the Act), as amended by section 4304 of the 1996 National Defense Authorization Act (Public Law 104-106), the Government may:
>
> (1) Cancel the solicitation, if the contract has not yet been awarded or issued; or
>
> (2) Rescind the contract with respect to which—
>
> (i) The Contractor or someone acting for the Contractor has been convicted for an offense where the conduct constitutes a violation of subsection 27 (a) or (b) of the Act for the purpose of either—
>
> (A) Exchanging the information covered by such subsection for anything of value; or
>
> (B) Obtaining or giving anyone a competitive advantage in the award of a Federal agency procurement contract; or
>
> (ii) The head of the contracting activity has determined, based upon a preponderance of the evidence, that the

Contractor or someone acting for the Contractor has engaged in conduct constituting an offense punishable under subsections 27(e)(1) of the Act.

(b) If the Government rescinds the contract under paragraph (a) of this clause, the Government is entitled to recover, in addition to any penalty prescribed by law, the amount expended under the contract.

(c) The rights and remedies of the Government specified herein are not exclusive, and are in addition to any other rights and remedies provided by law, regulation, or under this contract.

FAR 52.203-8.

The second clause to be added to solicitation and contract for other than commercial items that exceed the simplified acquisition threshold is FAR 52.203-10. That provision allows the government to reduce the profit on a contract where the government concludes that there has been a violation of the procurement integrity provisions against leaking information or employment contacts during a solicitation.

Of course, if a contractor wins a contract through the use of a wide range of illegal or fraudulent means, the contractor stands not only to lose the contract but also to forfeit all the money it has received from the government under the contract.

The FAR allows the government to void or rescind a contract for:

(1) A final conviction for bribery, conflict of interest, disclosing or obtaining contractor bid or proposal information or source selection information in exchange for a thing of value or to give anyone a competitive advantage in the award of a Federal agency procurement contract, or similar misconduct; or

(2) An agency head determination that contractor bid or proposal information or source selection information has been disclosed or obtained in exchange for a thing of value, or for the purpose of obtaining or giving anyone a competitive advantage in the award of a Federal agency procurement contract.

FAR 3.701.

The regulations let the government rescind a contract based on a final conviction but also upon proof under a much lower standard, a preponderance of the evidence.

FAR 3.705 specifies the due process procedure to be followed in rescissions, calling for, at a minimum, notice to the contractor of the proposed action, a 30-day period for the contractor's submission of any pertinent information, a hearing upon request of the contractor, and a written decision. The regulations expressly state that rescissions under this FAR procedure are not subject to the Contract Disputes Act or to Part 33 of the FAR dealing with disputes:

> [T]herefore, the procedures required by the CDA and the FAR for the issuance of a final contracting officer's decision are not applicable to final agency decisions under this subpart and shall not be followed.
>
> FAR 3.705(e).

Rescinding a contract is a drastic remedy because in declaring a contract void, the government is entitled to a return of any payments made under the contract; *K & R Engineering Co. v. United States*, 616 F.2d 469 (Ct.Cl.1980). A contractor also forfeits any equitable adjustment to which it was entitled. *Greg Pellant Construction*, ASBCA No. 31128, 87-1 BCA ¶19,298 (1987).

CHAPTER 3 | Ethics Rules for Getting a Contract   75

In addition, if the Board has previously held that a contractor was entitled to an equitable adjustment and quantum is subsequently disputed before the Board, the Board may at that later stage deny the contractor an equitable adjustment upon discovery of fraud in the initial award of the contract. *J.E.T.S.*, ASBCA No. 28642, 87-1 BCA ¶19,569 (1987), affirmed 838 F.2d 1196 (Fed. Cir. 1988). The contractor will get nothing for its work, not even under a quantum meruit or quantum valebant theory. *United States v. Amdahl Corp.*, 786 F.2d 387 (Fed. Cir. 1986).

> A bank filed a $435 million claim against the government which arose out of the savings and loan crisis in the 1980s. To help bail out failing savings and loans, the government promised investors attractive tax incentives to encourage them to purchased one of the failing entities. But the promises were so attractive that over time the government lost a lot of tax money. Eventually the government stopped the investors from using the tax breaks. Legally, the government breached the contracts it had with the investors. When the investors sued the government, the government fought back. It learned that, before these investors took the government up on the deal originally, the bank's chief executive officer certified to the government that the bank was complying with all laws and regulations. That wasn't true. In fact, the CEO was breaking New York State conflict of interest laws. That lie—technically, a false certification—cost the bank its government contract and its claim. The U.S. Court of Appeals for the Federal Circuit (CAFC) cited the general rule is that a government contract tainted by fraud or wrongdoing is void ab initio—or from the very start. To prove the contract was tainted by fraud the government had to prove that the contractor (a) obtained the contract by (b) knowingly making (c) a false statement. In this case, the false statement was the CEO's statement that he was following all the laws when in fact he was breaking New York State conflict of interest laws. The statement was knowingly made because even though other bank officers did not in fact know that the CEO was breaking New York State law, the fact that the CEO knew was imputed to the bank itself. Finally, the bank's contract was linked to the CEO's false statement. If the government knew the CEO was breaking the law, the government would not have gone through with the deal.
>
> *The Long Island Savings Bank et al. v. United States*,
> 503 F.3d 1234 (Fed. Cir. 2007).

A good summary of the ethical rules for getting a contract is that "It's cheaper to stay out of trouble than to get out of trouble!"

4 Ethical Rules for Administering Contracts

Performing and administering a government contract presents a number of unique ethical issues. Although the rules that apply to any contract a vendor has with a commercial customer obviously also apply to a contract the vendor has with a government customer, government contractors have additional rules when carrying out a government contract. Not only are the rules different, but who can enforce them is different. In government contracting, fraud can be handled by the Department of Justice and the local U.S. Attorney; more often, though, fraud is handled by the contracting officer administering the contract.

The Justice Department is interested primarily in large-dollar fraud and generally does not get involved in the types of fraud that typically arise from a government contract. The contracting officer and the agency itself have an arsenal of "weapons" at their disposal in the face of contractor fraud. In a sense, government contracts are distinct from commercial contracts in that not only does the judicial system have remedies available for dealing with fraud, but the "customer"—the contracting officer—does as well.

One example of the uniqueness of government contract performance is negotiating with the government. In the private market, negotiation over changes in the work still has "buyer beware" overtones. When negotiating with the government, however, contractors must honestly negotiate on the basis of actual costs. What could be considered "negotiating fat" in private negotiations can become "defective pricing"—our first topic—in government negotiations.

Next we consider claims contractors assert against the government that have fraudulent aspects to them. We then move into the government's rights under the inspection clause and explore how fraud or gross mistakes amounting to fraud can invalidate the finality of the government's acceptance of the contract work. Another remedy for fraud in the performance of a contract, and indeed in the award of a contract, is that the government can terminate the contract for default. Finally, we discuss the penalties agencies can impose for fraud, including suspension and debarment.

DEFECTIVE PRICING

A government contractor has an obligation to price the work it does for the government fairly and honestly. If the contractor overcharges the government, the government has remedies. When the government thinks it has paid too much, instead of accusing the contractor of "overcharging" or "gouging," it accuses the contractor of "defective pricing." Defective pricing can be difficult to establish, however, because the rules the government must abide by are very complex. These rules are laid out in FAR 52.215-10, Price Reduction for Defective Cost or Pricing Data, and FAR 52.215-11, Price Reduction for Defective Cost or Pricing Data-Modifications.

> FAR 52.215-10, Price Reduction for Defective Cost or Pricing Data (Oct 1997)

(a) If any price, including profit or fee, negotiated in connection with this contract, or any cost reimbursable under this contract, was increased by any significant amount because—

(1) The Contractor or a subcontractor furnished cost or pricing data that were not complete, accurate, and current as certified in its Certificate of Current Cost or Pricing Data;

(2) A subcontractor or prospective subcontractor furnished the Contractor cost or pricing data that were not complete, accurate, and current as certified in the Contractor's Certificate of Current Cost or Pricing Data; or

(3) Any of these parties furnished data of any description that were not accurate, the price or cost shall be reduced accordingly and the contract shall be modified to reflect the reduction.

Comparable provisions apply to modifications to contracts, including contracts issued through the sealed bid process. Thus, while a vendor submitting a sealed bid will not have to provide certified cost and pricing data prior to getting the contract, the contractor may have to provide such data as part of a modification to that contract.

But a lot of procurements are *not* subject to the cost and pricing rules. For example, when the government is buying commercial items, cost and pricing data are not an issue because those items generally are exempt from the cost and pricing rules. As stated in the FAR:

► Simplified acquisitions: When the government buys items at or below the simplified acquisition threshold of $100,000, generally, cost and pricing requirements do not apply. FAR 15.403-1(a).

► Contracts and modifications under $650,000 are not subject to cost and pricing requirements. FAR 15.403-4(a)(1)(iii).

Defective pricing can be especially problematic when negotiating a sole-source contract or contract modifications to either sealed bid or negotiated contracts because the government is at a real disadvantage: It cannot rely on competition to keep prices reasonable. In these noncompetitive situations, whether they involve a contract or a modification to a contract, the government needs the defective pricing protections set up by the Truth in Negotiations Act (TINA).

TINA is intended to be a great equalizer by requiring a government contractor to disclose certain cost information so that the government will know what kind of numbers a contractor is working with in any non-competitive negotiations with the government. One method is to require a contractor in certain types of contracting situations to certify that the cost and pricing data it is providing to the government are "current, accurate, and complete." If the data turn out otherwise, the government can get part of the overcharge back.

In a defective pricing case, the government must prove that:

1. The information at issue is "cost or pricing data" as defined by TINA.

2. Such cost or pricing data were not disclosed, or not meaningfully disclosed, to a proper Government representative.

3. The Government relied on the defective data and shows by some reasonable method the amount by which the final negotiated price was overstated.

Sylvania Electric Products, Inc. v. United States, 479 F.2d 1342, 1349, 202 Ct Cl. 16, 22 (1973); *Rosemount, Inc.*, ASBCA No. 37520, 95-2 BCA ¶ 27,770 at 138,454.

Once the government proves (1) and (2) above, it has an advantage because a court assumes that (3) has been met:

> Upon proof of nondisclosure, or the use of inaccurate cost or pricing data, the Government is aided in meeting its burden of establishing that there was a significant overstatement in the contract price by a rebuttable presumption that the natural and probable consequence of the nondisclosure or use of noncurrent or inaccurate cost or pricing data is an increase in the contract price. The contractor must then show that the defective data was not relied upon or that the undisclosed data would not have been relied upon even if there were complete disclosure.

> *Viacom, Inc.—Successor in Interest to Westinghouse Furniture Systems, v. General Services Administration,* GSBCA No. 15871, 05-2 BCA ¶ 33080, September 21, 2005.

Current, Accurate, and Complete Cost or Pricing Data

Typically, controversy surrounds the starting points of a defective pricing analysis: What is "cost or pricing data" and what does "current, accurate, and complete" mean? Further, did the government rely on the defective pricing in making a decision about that contract?

Cost or Pricing Data

The FAR defines "cost or pricing data" as follows:

> "Cost or pricing data" (10 U.S.C. 2306a(h)(1) and 41 U.S.C. 254b) means all facts that, as of the date of price agreement or, if applicable, an earlier date agreed upon between the parties that is as close as practicable to the date of agreement on price, prudent buyers and sellers would reasonably expect to affect price negotiations significantly. Cost or pricing data are data requiring

certification in accordance with 15.406-2. Cost or pricing data are factual, not judgmental; and are verifiable. While they do not indicate the accuracy of the prospective contractor's judgment about estimated future costs or projections, they do include the data forming the basis for that judgment. Cost or pricing data are more than historical accounting data; they are all the facts that can be reasonably expected to contribute to the soundness of estimates of future costs and to the validity of determinations of costs already incurred. They also include such factors as—

(1) Vendor quotations;

(2) Nonrecurring costs;

(3) Information on changes in production methods and in production or purchasing volume;

(4) Data supporting projections of business prospects and objectives and related operations costs;

(5) Unit-cost trends such as those associated with labor efficiency;

(6) Make-or-buy decisions;

(7) Estimated resources to attain business goals; and

(8) Information on management decisions that could have a significant bearing on costs.

FAR 2.101.

Current, Accurate, and Complete

When a vendor submits cost or pricing data, the vendor must sign the government's Certificate of Current Cost and Pricing attesting that its prices are "current, accurate, and complete." FAR 15.403-4(b).

CHAPTER 4 | Ethical Rules for Administering Contracts 83

A continuing controversy in this area is to what lengths the contractor must go to ensure that its data are current. For example, if lower, cheaper supplier quotes are lying in a vendor's sealed-bid box, should a contractor have opened those sealed bids, counter to company policy, and disclosed the lower quotes to the government? At the very least, it seems, the contractor should have disclosed that additional quotes were in its bid box.

> Aerojet Solid Propulsion Company was the only maker of nitroplasticizer, an ingredient for explosives, in early 1989. That year, the government bought some from Aerojet under a negotiated contract. Because it was a negotiated contract, Aerojet had to give the government cost and pricing information on this product. One of the ingredients, nitroethane, was hard to price because it had wild price swings. While Aerojet was negotiating with the government, the parties assumed a price of 1.98/lb for nitroethane. While the negotiations proceeded, Aerojet kept getting bids from suppliers. The government knew about some of these bids, but Aerojet kept two of the bids it received toward the end of negotiations secret and unopened. On June 20, 1990, the parties signed a contract and Aerojet signed a certificate of current cost and pricing. The next day, Aerojet opened the secret sealed bids and saw prices went down about 25 percent. The appeals court concluded that Aerojet should have told the government about the unopened sealed bids: "with chemical prices fluctuating wildly, a reasonable buyer or seller would recognize that mere knowledge of the undisclosed sealed nitroethane bids might give one negotiator an advantage during contract price negotiations. . .any significant variation in the cost of nitroethane significantly affects the cost of nitroplasticizer. The market volatility exposed both parties to increased price risk. The mere existence of more recent nitroethane bids due to be opened imminently would potentially alter the expectations during the May 2 to June 20 negotiations."
>
> *Aerojet Solid Propulsion Company v. Thomas E. White,*
> 291 F.3d 1328 (Fed.Cir. 2002).

"Current" means current as of the end of negotiations:

> The relevant cost or pricing data is that data in existence at the time of price negotiations . . . contractor has no duty to supply accurate

and complete subcontractor cost data created after prime and subcontractor have reached agreement on price . . . data created between cost and pricing data certification and award date [is] not cost or pricing data that was required to be submitted; in TINA context, duty to disclose complete, accurate and current data extends only to the date of price negotiations.

Viacom, Inc.—Successor in Interest to Westinghouse Furniture Systems, v. General Services Administration, GSBCA No. 15871, 05-2 BCA ¶ 33080, September 21, 2005.

Since the government is trying to recoup money, it has the burden of proving its case. This requires valid data analysis, which is sometimes missing.

> Baker School Specialty Co. was negotiating with the government to have seven of its products on the Federal Supply Schedule. Before getting the contract, Baker certified that the government was getting its lowest price. In fact, the government was not getting its lowest price. On several minor sales to commercial customers, the commercial customers received a lower price. The government audited Baker's sales and discovered the lower prices. The auditors, however, looked at only four of the seven items and based a defective pricing claim on the discounts provided to the commercial customers. The audit report disclosed limited detail on the shipments to which the undisclosed discounts were applied. It provided no information on which of the four items the undisclosed discounts were applied. It concluded that the government was entitled to over $36,000 for defective pricing. The board refused to award the government all the money it sought. The government used poor data as the basis of its claim. The audit studied sales of the items that were the largest sellers, not necessarily the items that were affected by the discounts. The government audit did not establish that the discounts were applied to these items or the extent to which the discounts applied. The government had "painted its claim with too broad a brush" the board concluded and denied the government's claim, leaving the door open to a government claim that was better justified.
>
> *Baker School Specialty Co. Inc.,* GSBCA No. 13101, August 7, 1995.

Like buyers anywhere, the government wants to get a price cut if it pays for an item sooner than the vendor expects. If a vendor expects payment in 30 days, for example, it might give the government a two percent discount if the government pays in 10 days. As part of the commercial items program, vendors have to promise that all prices offered to the government are as advantageous as the prices they offer their most favorable customers. To see if a vendor has violated the price warranty clause, the government compares "the average price paid by the government vs. commercial customers for the same item during the offeror's latest fiscal year." The comparison involves a number of specific costs such as base price, transportation charges, allowances, rebates, and billing advantage.

> The government discovered that some vendors were not giving other customers the identical prompt payment discounts given to the government. The government argued that this special treatment violated the price warranty provision. The Armed Services Board of Contract Appeals (ASBCA) said that wasn't true. What the government was supposed to do was to compare the average prices, which would include billing advantage, not compare individual parts of the price. As the board saw it, the government was splitting out billing advantage as a separate issue. The board said that was wrong.
>
> "There's nothing in the clause that permits the government to base a separate overpricing claim solely on a comparison of the discount terms offered the government versus those offered commercially. Any overpricing claim should consider all warranted factors in the aggregate. It cannot single out one of the factors for special scrutiny and treatment. There could be numerous legitimate reasons why the government has not been extended the best possible terms for each and every factor and still has been given the best 'average price' and afforded 'most favored' customer status. For example, here there is no evidence that the base price for computation of discounts for the most favored commercial customers was as low as that offered the government. It is patently unfair to focus solely on one factor that may represent more favorable treatment to a commercial customer while ignoring other factors when the government may have been afforded more favorable treatment. There is no separate and distinct warranty for prompt payment discounts or billing advantage."
>
> *Tropicana Product Sales Inc.*, ASBCA No. 52515, October 29, 2002.

Government Reliance on Defective Pricing

Of the three elements of defective pricing, the third element—whether the government relied on the defective pricing—is often the critical one.

There really should not be any question about it: A proposal from a contractor that doesn't contain accurate pricing information should clearly be against the law. But that's not the way TINA was set up. The act requires a contractor to submit to the government "current, accurate, and complete" prices. But if a contractor does not submit current, accurate, and complete prices, the contractor is not automatically penalized. Bad numbers from a contractor are considered truly bad only if the government relied on them. One of the critical issues in TINA cases is proving that the government relied on those bad numbers.

> When United Technologies Corporation (UTech) submitted a proposal to the Air Force, the contractor's proposal had a number of undisclosed mistakes that were ultimately found to be defective cost or pricing data by the Armed Services Board of Contract Appeals (ASBCA). Interestingly, the defective data had caused an increase in the contract price in some instances, but a decrease in others. Since the data was defective, the next issue was whether the government had relied on it.
>
> Two points in time were relevant: the time that the contract was awarded, and the time that the five option years under that contract were awarded. With regard to the contract award, nobody—not the Defense Contract Audit Agency, the Air Force's price analyst, the contracting officer, or government cost panel— had reviewed the best and final offer (BAFO) cost or pricing data before awarding UTech the contract. And the Record of Acquisition Action (RAA), the paperwork that allegedly showed government reliance, was, in the opinion of the board, "seriously undercut" when its author admitted that he did not recall reviewing any of the cost or pricing data in the contractor's BAFO. Even when it came time to exercise the options, the defective data had not been relied on by the government. Instead of reviewing the cost or pricing data in the contract before exercising the options, the government found the option prices to be fair and reasonable

> based on a market test between the competitors. In other words, the government ignored the underlying contract. In addition, a new contracting officer had become responsible for exercising the options, and he relied on the previous contracting officer's "seriously undercut" RAA.
>
> After the board concluded that the government had not relied on the defective pricing, the government appealed to the CAFC. But the appeals court also found no government reliance and therefore no TINA violation. The appeals court said, "reliance on defective data is a necessary element of a TINA claim." The court gave several examples of previous cases in which bad numbers had not been relied upon. In one case, there was no government reliance because "the contractor demonstrated that it would not have accepted a lower contract price than the price calculated using the defective data." In addition, the appeals court noted that Congress had mandated the reliance element of a TINA claim. In 1986 amendments to TINA, Congress said that contractors could defend a TINA claim by arguing that the government had not relied on the defective data. Since the Air Force here had not relied on the defective pricing in awarding the contract nor in awarding options under that contract, the government had not proved it had relied on the defective pricing.
>
> Michael W. Wynne v. United Technologies Corp.,
463 F.3d 1261 (Fed.Cir. 2006).

Out of fairness, the government does offer some leniency in defective pricing claims. One break contractors have in overpricing claims is that the contractor can take advantage of mistakes it made in pricing the items. The contractor can "offset" unintended errors it committed against overstatements made in negotiations. For example, in one case, a contractor inadvertently failed to include one element of the cost of rewarehousing to be performed by someone other than the named prospective subcontractor. But the error must be unintended. If a contractor intentionally understates a price, there's no leniency.

> Motorola had a government contract with Aydin as a subcontractor. When the government made a defective pricing claim on the contract, the sub argued that it understated the general and administrative (G&A) rate by seven percent and tried to use this mistake to offset the overcharge. But to the board, this wasn't a mistake—it was a bad management decision. The sub was hoping to restructure the company based on another contract and bring the G&A rate on the Motorola contract up to 45 percent. But this was not an unintended error to the board. "Such an erroneous management belief was not defective cost or pricing data, but rather was a judgment that cannot offset overstated cost or pricing data."
>
> *Motorola Inc.*, ASBCA No. 51789, October 11, 2002.

CLAIMS INVOLVING FRAUD

The FAR discusses the contracting officer's role in a claim that might have fraud in it: Refer it to investigators and do not pay it.

> If the contractor is unable to support any part of the claim and there is evidence that the inability is attributable to misrepresentation of fact or to fraud on the part of the contractor, the contracting officer shall refer the matter to the agency official responsible for investigating fraud.
>
> FAR 33.209.

Another FAR provision addresses the contracting officer's role in fraud:

> The authority to decide or resolve claims does not extend to—
>
> (a) A claim or dispute for penalties or forfeitures prescribed by statute or regulation that another Federal agency is specifically authorized to administer, settle, or determine; or
>
> (b) The settlement, compromise, payment, or adjustment of any claim involving fraud.
>
> FAR 33.210.

CHAPTER 4 | Ethical Rules for Administering Contracts   89

If a contracting officer does issue a contracting officer's final decision on a claim involving fraud, any appeal of it to a board or the CFC will be dismissed.

> Medina Construction, a Canadian company, had a contract with the government to repair a hangar in the Azores. Problems arose with the progress payments made to Medina. The government claimed that five of them were forgeries resulting in overpayments of over $200,000. OSI investigated and concluded that these allegations alone did not justify a termination for default. Later, however, the government terminated the contract for convenience. Medina submitted a termination settlement proposal, which for years was not settled. Meanwhile OSI declined to prosecute Medina for procedural reasons (e.g., the Portuguese legal system, which had jurisdiction over the Azores, declined to prosecute the alleged fraud). Medina asked the contracting officer for a contracting officer's final decision on the settlement proposal. The contracting officer obliged, issuing a decision denying Medina any money for the termination for convenience due to the "apparently fraudulent invoices" in the words of the contracting officer. Medina appealed to the court. The court concluded that the contracting officer was not authorized to issue a contracting officer final decision. The Contract Disputes Act, 41 U.S.C. Sec. 605(a) "specifically removes issue of fraud from administration consideration." Regardless of what OSI thought, the contracting officer "persisted in his belief that Medina had committed fraud in the submission of certain payment vouchers." The contracting officer's final decision issued was "unauthorized and invalid." Without a valid contracting officer's final decision before it, the court had no jurisdiction.
> *Medina Construction Ltd. v. United States,* 43 Fed.Cl. 537 (1999).

Curiously, although contractor fraud may be the basis for dismissal of a claim, the fraud committed on one contract cannot be attributed to another contract held by the same contractor.

> In 1996, Giuliani Associates Inc. had a contract with NASA to upgrade the sewage treatment plant at Goddard Space Flight Center, Wallops Island, VA. Like most construction contracts, the contract conditioned progress payments from the government on contractor certifications to the government that subcontractors and suppliers had been paid and would be paid out of proceeds of the

> progress payments. In 1997, Giuliani won another contract at the same location for construction and repair of a water restoration project. The same payment certification provisions were in that contract. In December 2001, Joseph A. Giuliani pled guilty to making a false statement and falsely certifying under the 1997 NASA contract that subcontractors and suppliers had been paid and would be paid when he knew that wasn't true. After the plea agreement was entered into, NASA asked the board to dismiss the claim Giuliani Associates Inc. filed under the 1996 contract based on the fraud conviction under the 1997 contract.
>
> The board refused to let fraud under one contract taint another contract. The board acknowledged numerous cases in which a conviction of fraud or false claims under the same contract justified dismissal of claims under the contract. But that was the extent of the fraud's reach. "The government has not cited, and our research has not uncovered, any decision dismissing an appeal or suit, or sustaining a default termination, on the basis of a fraud tainted contract other than the contract in issue in the pending appeal or suit." The board refused to dismiss the claim and considered the claim on its merits.
>
> *Giuliani Associates, Inc.*, ASBCA No. 51672, 52538, September 9, 2003.

A question arises regarding what the government may do when the contractor submits several claims and not all of them create a reasonable suspicion of fraud in the contracting officer.

Although the FAR seems to imply that the entire "matter" must be referred to investigating authorities, the legislative history of the Contract Disputes Act (CDA) and Board of Contract Appeals (BCA) practice call for BCAs to bifurcate (i.e., separate) claims, considering those not tainted by fraud and referring tainted claims to investigating authorities.

With regard to fraudulent claims that are referred to the Department of Justice and the courts, the legislative history of the CDA states:

> If such cases do arise and are thus handled in the courts, other parts of the claim not associated with possible fraud or misrepresentation of fact will continue on in the agency board or in the Court of Claims where the claim originated.

S. Rept. 1118, 95th Congress, page 20, reprinted in 1978 U.S. Code, *Cong. and Ad News,* pages 5253–5254.

While this language does not expressly mention the contracting officer, the fair implication was that if the board is to consider the claim, it must first have been considered by the contracting officer. This in fact was held to be required in *Joseph Morton Co., Inc. v. United States,* 757 F.2d 1273 (Fed. Cir. 1985).

Claims often involve prime contractors and subcontractors. Subcontractors play an important part in performing government contracts. But sometimes subcontractors get into legal trouble during performance of their work on the prime contract. If a subcontractor is convicted of fraud while performing the prime contract, the sub loses its right to file claims. A tougher question is whether the prime contractor is also prevented from filing claims. Generally, the answer is no. A prime contractor cannot be blamed for the fraud of a subcontractor unless the prime contractor knows of the subcontractor's fraud.

> N.R. Acquisition Corp. had a contract with the Navy to reduce an old aircraft carrier to scrap. The ship contained asbestos so the prime contractor hired a subcontractor to remove this hazardous material. But in the course of removing it, the subcontractor violated a number of environmental laws. The subcontractor company and its president were convicted of violating these criminal laws. In the meantime, the prime contractor filed various claims against the government alleging, for example, that the government had cost the prime contractor more money by the way it limited how the prime could dispose of the ship.
>
> The government asked the court to throw out the entire claim on various grounds, including the argument that the subcontractor's criminal violations prevented the prime contractor from filing the claims from the very beginning. It raised the valid argument that fraud on one contractor claim taints all contractor claims under the contract. In addition, the government argued that the fraud of the subcontractor could be imputed to the prime. The court was not willing to throw the case out at this point.

> At the early stage of the litigation, it wasn't clear what the prime knew and when did it know it. Fraud by a prime contractor taints all prime contractor claims. But that doesn't necessarily hold for subcontractor claims. According to the court, "the case law does not support imputing liability from a subcontractor to a prime contractor and thereby barring its claims with no inquiry as to the knowledge/involvement of the prime contractor."
>
> On the other hand, if the prime's claims include any claims by the defrauding subcontractor, those pass-through claims can be forfeited. The court therefore required the parties to give further consideration to two issues: whether during performance the prime was aware of the sub's activities that "were the subject of the criminal conviction" and "whether and to what extent plaintiff's claims are pass-through claims" on behalf of the sub.
>
> *N. R. Acquisition Co. Inc. v. United States*, 54 Fed.Cl. 490 (2002).

A contractor's fraud can be costly. Its misrepresentation of costs in a claim can result in forfeiture of the claim, civil penalties, and damages equal to the amount of the misrepresentation (loaded with freight costs and overhead), plus the government's cost of reviewing the claim.

> UMC Electronics Company had a contract with the Air Force for floodlight sets. It submitted an almost $4 million claim based on government delay for "incurred costs." UMC, however, had a unique interpretation of the phrase "incurred costs." It submitted as incurred costs material costs, which had never been invoiced, and in some cases for material that had never been received. UMC even conceded that its material costs were not amounts actually paid vendors or reflected on invoices. For example, UMC considered as an incurred cost "unbilled escalation" which, as described by the court "occurred when a vendor did not bill or invoice UMC for an increase in material costs, despite the fact that [UMC's] purchase orders contained escalation clauses that typically triggered a price increase on a certain date." UMC felt that the escalation price increase was an "actual cost" because it believed it would eventually owe it to its vendors.

> The court came down hard on UMC. Federal remedies for fraud, the court noted, are "cumulative and not in the alternative." The court found UMC liable under several statutes. The court found that UMC's actions forfeited the almost $4 million claim, imposed a $10,000 civil penalty, made UMC pay to the government the unsupported portion of the claim, $223,500, and made UMC pay the government's costs of review.
>
> *UMC Electronics Co. v. United States,* 43 Fed.Cl. 776 (1999).

GOVERNMENT'S RIGHTS UNDER THE INSPECTION CLAUSE

The typical FAR inspection clause, like FAR 52.246-2, Inspection of Supplies—Fixed Price, gives the government the right, after the government has accepted the supplies, to change its mind and revoke acceptance if it finds "fraud or gross mistake amounting to fraud." The government must prove the elements of fraud before it can avail itself of the remedies. These elements are different from those for fraud in federal statutes. Board of Contract Appeals decisions reflect the difficulty of proving fraud within the meaning of the Inspection clause.

> In *Dale Ingram, Inc.,* the Board held that the government did not prove the element of reliance, i.e., the government had not proved it relied on the contractor's representation that the roof sheathing he used was all mahogany. Although the inspection certificate had said it was, the government had known that it was not.
>
> ASBCA No. 12152, 74-1 BCA ¶ 10,436 (1974).
>
> In *Solar Construction Co.,* the Board found that the government had failed to carry its burden of proof on the "intent to defraud" element. The Board found in fact that the contractor had been acting in good faith.
>
> HUD BCA No. 79-375-C13, 80-2 BCA ¶ 14,721 (1980).

In *Henry Angelo & Co.*, the Board found that the government had not proved that it had relied on the contractor's certificate of compliance with contract requirements which in fact was misrepresented by the contractor. The contractor said that he had applied the required number of coats of paint when he in fact had not. The Board held that, since the government inspector has signed on a weekly basis a certificate of inspection with language similar to that of the contractor's certificate, the government could not claim that it had relied on the contractor's certificate.

ASBCA No. 30502, 87-1 BCA ¶ 19,619 (1987).

One additional problem with the Inspection clause is that, after fraud is proven, the only remedies available are those under the clause itself; only the finality of acceptance is overcome. That is, although all contract remedies the government had prior to acceptance of the goods are resurrected, no criminal penalties flow from invocation of the clause itself.

The infrequent use of the "fraud" escape clause of the Inspection provision is suggested by the relative absence of reported Board cases on fraud in inspections.

▍ TERMINATION FOR DEFAULT

A government contractor that commits fraud in the course of the contract breaches its contract. This justifies termination of the contract for default.

> Morton had a contract to construct animal disease research facilities. During the course of the contract, Change Order No. 2 was issued; subsequently, Morton was convicted in Federal District Court under the False Statements Act of submitting false and fraudulent cost statements to the government in support of this change order. The contract ultimately was terminated for default for performance reasons. Morton contested the termination for default and sought to have it converted to a termination for convenience. The government sought to justify the termination for default solely upon the prior criminal conviction.

> Morton argued that it was unfair to default terminate a contract with numerous change orders when only one change order had been supported with fraudulent data; the entire contract, Morton argued, was not tainted by this one criminal violation. The government argued that although there was a conviction on only one fraud count, the aspect of the contract to which the change order related was fundamental to the contract and therefore the impact of fraud on this procurement was fundamental. The Court agreed with the government and held that the submission of false documentation for only one change order would justify the termination.
>
> *Joseph Morton Co. v. United States*, 757 F.2d. 1273 (Fed.Cir. 1985).

In the *Morton* decision, although the Federal Circuit did not expressly hold that any fraud would justify a termination for default, it did observe that "there is [legal] support for the argument that any fraud warrants termination for default as a matter of law." *Morton, supra,* 757 F.2d at 1279.

In this case, evidence of a prior criminal conviction supported the default. A question arises regarding whether fraudulent acts that have not (yet) been adjudicated as criminal may be the basis of a termination for default.

The Federal Circuit appears to have concluded that nonadjudicated fraudulent acts may properly be the basis for a termination for default. In one case, the court upheld a termination for default made on the basis of the contractor's false certification of expenditures.

> The cost-reimbursement contract provided for reimbursement to Human Resources Management for expenditures, which were actually paid out the previous month. Resources fraudulently certified that payment of certain reimbursable amounts was "proper and due" when in fact it was not because Resources had not actually paid out these amounts to the subcontractor. The Court concluded, without discussion or citation to authority, that "[b]y filing such false vouchers, Resources breached [the] contract. That breach justified the contracting officer's termination of the contract for default."
>
> *United States v. Human Resources Management, Inc.,*
> 745 F.2d 642, 646 (Fed.Cir. 1984).

The Boards also have upheld the contracting officer's use of a termination for default when there has been a false certification.

> Spread Information Sciences did not deliver products to the government on time. The government terminated the contract for default. Spread then challenged the validity of the termination for default before the Armed Services Board of Contract Appeals (ASBCA). After the appeal had been made, the government learned that Spread had been terminated for default previously and had failed to disclose to the government this previous default. The government then argued that regardless of the validity of the termination for default based on failure to deliver, the government was justified in terminating the contract for default for the improper certification. The Board agreed with the government.
> *Spread Information Sciences, Inc.,*
> ASBCA No. 48438, September 29, 1995.

> The Army needed work done at the Walter Reed Army Medical Center. In September of 1992, American Construction Services (ACS) submitted an offer. The offer certified that the company had not had any contract terminated for default by any Federal Agency within the preceding three years. ACS's "no default" certification was inaccurate, however. ACS had a contract at Aberdeen Proving Grounds terminated for default in September of 1990. The head of ACS knew about the default, but based on the advice of her lawyer that the termination did not have to be disclosed because it was being appealed, she certified that there had been no defaults. At the time she received this advice, however, there had been no appeal of the termination filed at the Board. The Walter Reed contract was terminated because the contractor didn't complete the project on time. The termination was appealed to the board. The government then learned of the false representation as to no prior defaults and asked that the appeal be denied on the basis of the false certification.
>
> The Board agreed with the government and dismissed the appeal. ACS knew that there was a contract terminated for default and it knew that the certification was wrong. The fact that ACS relied on an attorney's advice was no excuse for miscertifying. The question was, simply, whether ACS knew about the default termination (and it did) and miscertified. The board refused to consider ACS's appeal of the termination for default.
> *American Construction Services, Inc.,* ASBCA No. 47769, July 8, 1996.

PENALTIES FOR FRAUD

Penalties for fraud can also include administrative penalties under the Program Fraud Civil Remedies Act and suspension and debarments.

Program Fraud Civil Remedies Act

Fraud in government procurement is only one kind of fraud the government deals with. Government programs like Medicare and Social Security also experience fraud. But often the amounts of fraud involved are too small to justify the involvement of the Justice Department. So in 1986, Congress passed the Program Fraud Civil Remedies Act (31 U.S.C. 3801). Under this act, an agency does not have to uncover big dollar fraud and rely on the Justice Department's criminal or civil processes to deal with it. The agency can deal with small dollar fraud itself through an administrative process.

The Program Fraud Civil Remedies Act is a small-claims-type fraud remedy that can be administered by a contracting officer. The Act allows federal agencies to impose penalties and damages for all false claims where the damages are under $150,000, as well as for all false statements. Government agencies have adopted administrative procedures to implement the provisions of this law. The procedures are designed to protect the interests and rights of both the contractors and the government in the process of establishing liability and determining the amount of any penalties and damages assessed against a contractor.

The Act provides for a penalty of $5,000 per false claim or false statement. Damages for false claims are double the amount of the provable loss (rather than the treble damages of the Civil False Claims Act, for which judicial action is required). The standard of proof the government must meet in establishing the contractor's liability is the same as that under the Civil False Claims Act: a knowing submission of the false claim or statement.

One of the few reported cases involved a woman who improperly cashed her mother's Social Security checks for 18 years, including after her mother died. The Department of Health and Human Services imposed a $170,000 fine, which the courts upheld. *Orfanos v. The Department of Health and Human Services*, 896 F.Supp 23 (D.D.C. 1995).

Suspension and Debarment

As mentioned in Chapter 3, a debarment is the most serious sanction a government contractor can suffer short of a criminal conviction. A debarred contractor is ineligible for government work for a specified period of time. Related to debarment is "suspension," which makes a contractor temporarily ineligible for government work while the government determines whether the more serious sanction of debarment should be imposed.

The reasons to suspend or debar changed in 2008 when the FAR added contractors failure to disclose to the government credible evidence of (i) Violation of Federal criminal law involving fraud, conflict of interest, bribery, or gratuity violations found in Title 18 of the United States Code; (ii) Violation of the civil False Claims Act (31 U.S.C. 3729-3733); or (iii) Significant overpayment(s) on the contract.

Suspension

The government can suspend contractors from being eligible for award of a government contract. Suspensions are designed to give the government time to investigate possible wrongdoing by a government contractor. The grounds for debarment are broader than those for suspension, which focuses solely on the contractor's lack of business integrity. Suspensions

CHAPTER 4 | Ethical Rules for Administering Contracts

are to be based on "adequate evidence" of violation of any one of a number of specified criminal acts. In determining the adequacy of the evidence, FAR 9.407-1(b) directs agencies to consider how much information is available, how credible that information is given the circumstances, whether important allegations are corroborated, and what inferences can reasonably be drawn.

> Statements made to the German police indicated that the president of a company paid bribes to various U.S. government employees to get government contracts. The Army suspended the company on the basis of these statements. The company challenged the suspension, arguing that the president was no longer part of the company, that the company was owned not by the former president but by his sons, and that no other officials of the company participated in or knew of the bribes.
>
> GAO said that the Army had adequate evidence to suspend the company. The company did not deny that bribes had been paid; its main argument was that the president had been walled off from further participation in the company. GAO said that the Army was correct in suspending the company because the president was in office when bribes were paid and there was a father-son relationship with the owners of the company.
>
> *Howema Bau-GmbH*, B-245386, September 4, 1991.

One study of the suspension and debarment process led to the conclusion that:

> Based on interviews with a number of agency officials responsible for debarment and suspension, [the author] concludes that they do not generally concern themselves with precise-evidentiary standards, rather the actual standard appears to be that they are certain in their own minds that the offense occurred.
>
> Note, Graylisting of Federal Contractors, 31 Catholic U. Law Rev. 731 at 733, nt. 14 citing A. Lahendro, The Debarment and Suspension of Government Contractors (1975) (unpublished thesis on file at The George Washington University, Washington, DC).

The FAR specifies the violations that merit suspension as follows:

(a) The suspending official may suspend a contractor suspected, upon adequate evidence, of—

(1) Commission of fraud or a criminal offense in connection with

(i) obtaining,

(ii) attempting to obtain, or

(iii) performing a public contract or subcontract;

(2) Violation of Federal or State antitrust statutes relating to the submission of offers;

(3) Commission of embezzlement, theft, forgery, bribery, falsification or destruction of records, making false statements, tax evasion, or receiving stolen property;

(4) Violations of the Drug-Free Workplace Act of 1988 (Public Law 100-690), as indicated by—

(i) Failure to comply with the requirements of the clause at 52.223-6, Drug-Free Workplace; or

(ii) Such a number of contractor employees convicted of violations of criminal drug statutes occurring in the workplace as to indicate that the contractor has failed to make a good faith effort to provide a drug-free workplace (see 23.504);

(5) Intentionally affixing a label bearing a "Made in America" inscription (or any inscription having the same meaning) to a product sold in or shipped to the United States or its outlying areas, when the product was not made in the United States or its outlying areas (see Section 202 of the Defense Production Act (Public Law 102-558));

(6) Commission of an unfair trade practice as defined in 9.403 (see section 201 of the Defense Production Act (Public Law 102-558));

(7) Delinquent Federal taxes in an amount that exceeds $3,000;

(8) Knowing failure by a principal, until 3 years after final payment on any Government contract awarded to the contractor, to timely disclose to the Government, in connection with the award, performance, or closeout of the contract or a subcontract thereunder, credible evidence of--

> (i) Violation of Federal criminal law involving fraud, conflict of interest, bribery, or gratuity violations found in Title 18 of the United States Code;
> (ii) Violation of the civil False Claims Act (31 U.S.C. 3729-3733); or
> (iii) Significant overpayment(s) on the contract, other than overpayments resulting from contract financing payments as defined in 32.001; or

(9) Commission of any other offense indicating a lack of business integrity or business honesty that seriously and directly affects the present responsibility of a Government contractor or subcontractor.

FAR 9.407-2.

An indictment can be a basis for a suspension.

> GSA needed protection and patrol services at various federal buildings in Florida. The apparent low bidder, BASIX, was in line for award but the contract specialist found that the Department of Veteran Affairs had suspended the former president of BASIX and the firm itself from federal contracting. The letter informing the former president of the suspension was not clear, however. First, it said "This is to notify you that the Department of Veteran Affairs is proposing to suspend you...." Later, the letter stated "You are hereby excluded from receiving contracts from federal government agencies." The letter explained that the suspension was based on the indictment of the president for conspiracy to defraud the Securities and Exchange Commission, and for securities fraud, bank fraud, and mail fraud.
>
> After GSA notified BASIX that it was ineligible for award because of the suspension, BASIX protested the denial of the contract to GAO. BASIX argued that it was not suspended at the time of bid opening and quoted the paragraph included in the letter from the Veterans Affairs that the agency was "proposing to suspend you." The protester argued that it had been informed that it was proposed for suspension but not actually suspended.
>
> GAO disagreed with the protester. Under FAR Section 14.404-2(h), bids received from suspended parties must be rejected unless a "compelling reason" determination is made. GAO said that the VA letter clearly indicated that BASIX was suspended though the introductory language "proposing to suspend" was included in the language. GAO concluded that the protester was clearly on notice that it had been suspended and denied the protest.
>
> *BASIX, Inc.*, B-255613, March 15, 1994.

The *BASIX* case is an example of an indictment serving as a basis for a suspension. A suspension may also be based on the indictment of another person where the person suspended was an unindicted coconspirator.

> Leslie G. Range was doing business as Pro-Mark, Inc. trying to get contracts from the Department of Housing and Urban Development (HUD). After being notified that Pro-Mark would get a HUD contract to provide technical assistance to grantees, Pro-Mark was suspended from further consideration for the contract. This occurred after HUD learned that Range was named as an unindicted co-conspirator in a scheme to bribe a HUD official. The HUD official pled guilty to criminal conduct and admitted that he had received $400 in cash and in hotel gratuities from Range.
>
> Pro-Mark challenged the suspension in federal court, claiming that its due process rights were violated. Pro-Mark claimed it was entitled to notice and an opportunity to be heard in its defense before HUD could suspend it from consideration for the contract. The court disagreed and upheld the suspension.
>
> *Pro-Mark, Inc. v. The Department of Housing and Urban Development,*
> U.S. District Court for the Southern District of Mississippi,
> Civ. Action No. J89-0562(L), January 29, 1992.

Debarment

The more drastic remedy, debarment, may be imposed for a conviction of or civil judgment for the following:

(1) Commission of fraud or a criminal offense in connection with—

(i) Obtaining;

(ii) Attempting to obtain; or

(iii) Performing a public contract or subcontract.

(2) Violation of Federal or State antitrust statutes relating to the submission of offers;

(3) Commission of embezzlement, theft, forgery, bribery, falsification or destruction of records, making false statements, tax evasion, or receiving stolen property;

(4) Intentionally affixing a label bearing a "Made in America" inscription (or any inscription having the same meaning) to a product sold in or shipped to the United States or its outlying areas, when the product was not made in the United States or its outlying areas (see Section 202 of the Defense Production Act (Public Law 102-558)); or

(5) Commission of any other offense indicating a lack of business integrity or business honesty that seriously and directly affects the present responsibility of a Government contractor or subcontractor.

FAR 9.406-2(a).

Debarment may also be imposed—even if there has been no conviction or civil judgment against a contractor—if there is a preponderance of evidence of:

(i) Violation of the terms of a Government contract or subcontract so serious as to justify debarment, such as—

(A) Willful failure to perform in accordance with the terms of one or more contracts; or

(B) A history of failure to perform, or of unsatisfactory performance of, one or more contracts.

(ii) Violations of the Drug-Free Workplace Act of 1988 (Public Law 100-690), as indicated by—

(A) Failure to comply with the requirements of the clause at 52.223-6, Drug-Free Workplace; or

(B) Such a number of contractor employees convicted of violations of criminal drug statutes occurring in the workplace as to indicate that the contractor has failed to make a good faith effort to provide a drug-free workplace (see 23.504).

(iii) Intentionally affixing a label bearing a "Made in America" inscription (or any inscription having the same meaning) to a product sold in or shipped to the United States or its outlying areas, when the product was not made in the United States or its outlying areas (see Section 202 of the Defense Production Act (Public Law 102-558)).

(iv) Commission of an unfair trade practice as defined in 9.403 (see Section 201 of the Defense Production Act (Public Law 102-558)).

(v) Delinquent Federal taxes in an amount that exceeds $3,000.

(vi) Knowing failure by a principal, until 3 years after final payment on any Government contract awarded to the contractor, to timely disclose to the Government, in connection with the award, performance, or closeout of the contract or a subcontract thereunder, credible evidence of—

(A) Violation of Federal criminal law involving fraud, conflict of interest, bribery, or gratuity violations found in Title 18 of the United States Code;
(B) Violation of the civil False Claims Act (31 U.S.C. 3729-3733); or
(C) Significant overpayment(s) on the contract, other than overpayments resulting from contract financing payments as defined in 32.001.

FAR 9.406-2(b)(1).

Debarment may also result, regardless of the amount of evidence, from a contractor's violation of the immigration laws. The debarment must be "based on a determination by the Secretary of Homeland Security or the Attorney General of the United States, that the contractor is not in compliance with Immigration and Nationality Act employment provisions (see Executive Order 12989, as amended by Executive Order 13286). Such determination is not reviewable in the debarment proceedings. FAR 9.406-2(b)(2).

Finally, debarment can be based on "any other cause of so serious or compelling a nature that it affects the present responsibility of the contractor or subcontractor." FAR 9.406-2(c).

But a conviction remains the most solid basis for a debarment.

> Kun Chae Bae owned a generic drug company. He was permanently debarred by the Food and Drug Administration (FDA) for providing an unlawful gratuity to an FDA official in exchange for favorable action by that official. He was convicted in 1990 on charges of aiding and abetting interstate travel and racketeering. The Generic Drug Enforcement Act (GDEA), 21 U.S.C. 335 [a], requires the permanent debarment of individuals convicted of a felony related to the development, approval, or regulation of drug products. The courts upheld his permanent debarment.
>
> *Bae v. Shalala*, 44 F.3d 489 (7th Cir. 1995).

A company official cannot be debarred for fraud committed by his company simply because he was a company official at the time. To justify a debarment, there must be substantial proof that the official knew of the wrongdoing.

> Lisbon Contractors had a contract to build a sewer in New Hampshire. The company paid its masons wages and expenses because they would be working away from their homes. The state Department of Labor learned that the masons on the job were being paid as pipe layers and ordered them paid properly as masons. Lisbon reclassified them as masons and raised their wages but reduced their expenses so that the net result to the masons was no net increase in pay. The government later found that the company owed the masons back wages. The vice president of the company, Anthony Differ, had a meeting with the masons, gave them checks for the proper amount, had them sign receipts for the proper amounts, and asked the masons to sign the checks over to the company, threatening to deduct the amounts from future wages if they refused. The federal Department of Labor learned of this and debarred the company, its president, and Differ for alleged violations of the Copeland Anti-Kickback Law. All three appealed to federal court.

> The court found that the federal Department of Labor had properly debarred Differ but said that the company and its president should not have been debarred. The court criticized earlier court decisions that had seemed to allow the debarment of employees simply because they were employees of the company—a so-called strict liability standard. The court said that strict liability is not proper. A company employee cannot be debarred "absent substantial evidence that [the employee] knew of the violations." The court concluded that the president of the company did not know of the actions of Differ and had no reason to suspect that Differ planned to violate the Copeland Anti-Kickback Law. It therefore overturned the debarment of the president.
> *Marquis Enterprises dba Lisbon Contractors, Inc. et al. v. United States Department of Labor,* U.S. District Court for the Eastern District of Pennsylvania, No. 92-5876, June 30, 1993.

Debarment can also result from serious violations of a contract's terms, including willful nonperformance of its terms or a history of failure to perform. For example, in *Andrew Calhoun and Angel Construction Co.*, HUD BCA 82-676-D14, 82-2 BCA ¶ 115,921, the contractor did not make the required home repairs and did not even submit progress reports; for these contract violations, he was debarred. "Failure to perform repairs within the time specified in the contract and failure to obtain a timely extension of the period of performance" provided grounds for debarment in *Wilbert T. Alexander and Alexander Reality Co.* HUD BCA 81-648-D47, 82-1 BCA ¶ 115,649 (1982).

Certain statutes and regulations also provide the debarment remedy if they are violated. These include Executive Order 11246 dealing with equal employment opportunity matters, various labor statutes such as Davis-Bacon, the Buy-American Act, and certain environmental statutes.

The FAR specifies the procedures to be followed in carrying out a debarment. The DoD Inspector General (IG) stated in Indicators of Fraud at 21 that the "government has never had a suspension or debarment action challenged successfully so long as [the FAR] procedures are followed." This suggests that contractors should look closely at the due process promised by the FAR and the due process provided by the agency.

Agencies must consider any "mitigating factors" bearing on debarment. These factors must take current facts and circumstances into account. Failure to consider mitigating factors may be fatal to a debarment.

In one case, DoD had a debarment overturned when it failed to consider that a vendor pled guilty to a misdemeanor because he wanted to end the matter and get his business back together.

> Joseph Silverman sold cleaning products to the government as a sole proprietor. In 1986, when he could no longer produce the products himself, he arranged for another company to make the products solely for him. Silverman remained involved in the everyday operations of the business and, on a government form, indicated that he was a "manufacturer or producer" of the product. He came under investigation by the government because the government believed that this was a false statement, that he was not the producer since another company was making the products for him. Although Silverman believed that he had filled out the form properly, he pled guilty to a misdemeanor, was fined $250, and got a year's unsupervised probation. DoD investigated the case and in 1992 debarred him for three years. He challenged the debarment in federal court and won.
>
> The court said that debarment can only be based on a contractor's "present responsibility for government contracting." Before debarring anyone, an agency must carefully consider any favorable evidence of responsibility to ensure that all findings of responsibility are based on the presence of a "real and articulable threat of harm to the government's proprietary interest." Here, the government failed to consider mitigating factors. The decision to debar Silverman was made six years after he made the statement his conviction was based on. Moreover, he pled simply to end the matter and rebuild his business. The government in this case failed to consider why Silverman pled guilty. This made its decision arbitrary and capricious. The court ordered the debarment terminated immediately.
> *Joseph Silverman et al. v. United States Department of Defense,* U.S. District Court for the Southern District of California, No. 92-1009-G (BTM), April 2, 1993

The Treasury Department also had a debarment overturned because it did not consider mitigating factors. Nor did the Treasury Department accurately decide the case.

> Maria Canales was an employee of the Treasury Department who received several emerald chips from an individual she later helped get a Treasury contract. When investigated, she signed an affidavit that she later pled guilty to misdemeanor false statement. The government specifically stated at her probation sentencing that there was "no allegation that Canales broke any of the bribery or gratuity laws or corruption offenses" and that her sole offense was making a "false written statement to the Inspector General." After leaving the Treasury and starting her own company, the Treasury debarred her. She challenged the debarment and won for two reasons.
>
> First, the Treasury did not consider mitigating factors, stated by the court as her "spotless record before" her criminal offense, the fact that five years had passed without incident since that offense, and her "extensive business" with several other federal agencies in the interim, all of which were aware of her misdemeanor conviction when they chose to contract with her. . . ." The government's "failure to address in any detail the mitigating factors Canales raised, or to explain why he gave them so little weight, makes it impossible to evaluate whether there was a 'rational connection' between the facts of her case and his decision to impose debarment."
>
> Second, the government's debarment notice was dead wrong. It said that Canales was subject to debarment because she has been "convicted of violating U.S.C. § 1018, making a false writing in connection with an ongoing procurement" which to the government showed a lack of business integrity or honesty. This statement, however, "is incorrect on its face. Canales pleaded guilty to making a false writing during an official investigation, which is illegal under 18 U.S.C. § 1018. She was neither charged with, nor convicted of, doing anything improper 'in connection with an ongoing procurement.' As a result, Sharpe [the debarring official] appears to have based his decision to debar her on a conviction that never occurred."
>
> *Canales v. Paulson,* Civ. A. No. 06-1330 (GK), D.D.C., July 16, 2007.

Debarment may also be imposed on the rather vague basis of "[a]ny other cause of so serious or compelling nature that it affects the present responsibilities" of a contractor. This basis was used in *Robert C. Gennaro*

(HUD BCA 81-632-D37, 83-1 BCA ¶ 16,141) after the contractor testified at trial that he conspired to pay, but did not actually pay, for political influence. The Department of Housing and Urban Development considered his participation in the corruption of the rent subsidy system an indication of his lack of present responsibility.

A recent trend finds the government using this vague debarment authority to debar companies on the basis of conduct unrelated to government contracts. An excellent article on the current state of debarment summarizes the situation:

> Recently, responding to the headline-grabbing scandals at companies such as Enron, agencies have shown increased willingness to suspend or debar companies that have engaged in corporate malfeasance unrelated to any Government contract activity. For example, in 2003, the General Services Administration, relying on the FAR's "catch-all" provision allowing debarment for any other cause so serious or compelling in nature that it affects an entity's "present responsibility," proposed for debarment MCI WorldCom after it was revealed that MCI had "committed the most massive fraud in U.S. history when it overstated its earnings to the [Securities and Exchange Commission]." Similarly, the GSA suspended both Arthur Anderson and Enron in the wake of their well-publicized scandals. In none of these instances was the underlying conduct directly related to contracts with the Government. This means that today's Government contractor or program participant must give serious consideration to potential suspension and debarment implications of any adverse conduct by its officers or employees, as well as to the resolution of any civil or criminal charges resulting from that conduct.

Suspension & Debarment, Joseph D. West, Timothy J. Hatch, Christyne K. Brennan, and Lawrence J.C. VanDyke, 06-9 Briefing Papers 1 at 5.

As all this material in Chapter 4 shows, the government has more than enough weapons to deal with contractors who are not following the rules. Again, however, the focus of this book is not to help contractors avoid breaking the rules. The focus is to have contractors administering a government contract so fairly and ethically that none of these weapons become remotely applicable.

PART III
Federal Statutes and Rules Affecting Procurement

Having looked at the types of ethics compliance programs that a contractor has set up, and then the FAR rules that procurement personnel, either from the contractor side or the government side, must comply with, the next question becomes: What rules and regulations other than the FAR must the contractor and contracting officer abide by? To answer this question we explore the wide range of rules and regulations applicable to any government employee or contractor, regardless of whether that employee or contractor is involved in the procurement process.

The FAR briefly discusses a number of federal laws and nonprocurement regulations that apply to procurement personnel. In this part, we discuss in greater detail the many federal statutes and regulations that procurement personnel—like all government employees and contractor personnel—must follow, such as the federal laws against bribery. Chapter 5 focuses on the statutes and regulations governing federal employee conduct, and Chapter 6 focuses on federal contractor conduct.

5 Federal Employee Conduct

People working in the government—both government employees and federal contractors—are generally concerned with the federal laws dealing with procurement integrity and procurement fraud. These procurement-specific laws, however, are just the tip of the iceberg. Procurement specialists must also comply with the more general ethics laws that apply government-wide. Something a contractor or government employee does might not violate any procurement integrity laws but could still violate another generally applicable federal ethics law.

How complex this process is can be seen from a decision handed down by the United States Supreme Court in 1999 in the case of *United States v. Sun-Diamond Growers*, 526 U.S. 398 (1999). The case involved a company convicted of giving Agriculture Secretary Espy a gift that a Federal District Court jury concluded was an illegal gratuity. The Supreme Court reversed, holding that the government in that case had not shown that a specific official act was involved. Otherwise it would make harmless acts into criminal acts: "e.g., token gifts to the President based on his official position and not linked to any identifiable act—such as the replica jerseys given by championship sports teams each year during ceremonial White House visits."

Following this decision, the Office of Government Ethics (OGE) warned federal employees against misunderstanding how limited the Supreme Court decision was and how many other ethics rules and regulations were actually involved. First, OGE pointed out the noncriminal *statutory* prohibitions at play:

> The Supreme Court's decision does not disturb the noncriminal prohibitions on gifts found at 5 U.S.C. § 7353.

Second, OGE pointed out the noncriminal administrative regulations that prohibited similar conduct:

> The administrative standards of conduct contained in 5 C.F.R. part 2635, Standards of Ethical Conduct for Employees of the Executive Branch (Standards of Conduct), which, in part, implement those authorities, were not in issue in the Sun-Diamond Growers case. They continue to be fully effective as to executive branch employees. In particular, subpart B of the Standards of Conduct, which contains prohibitions on the acceptance of gifts from outside sources, continues to be fully applicable to the conduct of executive branch employees. Section 2635.202(a)(1) bars an executive branch employee from accepting gifts from prohibited sources. Prohibited sources, as defined at 5 C.F.R. § 2635.203(d), are persons who have interests that may be affected by some official agency action. Section 2635.202(a)(2) prohibits an employee from accepting a gift that is given because of the employee's official position. Section 2635.203(e) defines when a gift is solicited or accepted because of an employee's official position.

Third, OGE pointed out that a specific agency may have supplemental rules that apply:

It is also important that employees be aware of any additional agency-specific prohibitions on the acceptance of gifts. Employees should also be aware of any additional gift exceptions in their agency supplemental regulations and appreciate the significance in terms of the rules on gifts of the division of an agency or department into separate components.

OGE Inf. Ltr. 99 x 13 (May 19, 1999).

Many laws and agency implementing regulations set forth personal behavioral requirements for government employees, whether program managers, contracting officers, contracting officer's technical representative (COTRs), contract specialists, or others involved in the acquisition process. These include federal laws and regulations, as well as agency regulations, dealing with:

- Conflicts of interest
- Bribes and gratuities
- Standards of conduct.

CONFLICTS OF INTEREST

Conflicts of interest deal with a wide range of activities in which the government employee engages in activities that create a conflict between the employee's personal interests and the employee's duty to serve the government's interests. Conflicts of interest are prohibited by 18 U.S.C. 208.

The most notorious example of a personal conflict of interest involved Darlene Druyun who, in 2004, pled guilty to violating 18 U.S.C. 208(a). That law prohibits a government employee from "participating personally and substantially as a government officer or employee in a contract in which to his knowledge an organization with whom he is negotiating or has any arrangement concerning prospective employment, has a financial interest." Druyun was negotiating for a job with Boeing while she was also negotiating on behalf of the Air Force for the lease of 100 Boeing KC 767A tanker aircraft. See *Lockheed Martin Corp.*, B-295402, February 18, 2005.

The conflict of interest law (18 U.S.C. 208) prohibits the following:

Government employees cannot:

1. Participating personally and substantially
2. In a particular matter
3. Which, to their knowledge
4. A government employee, their spouse, minor child, partner

    or

    An organization in which they are serving as Officer, Director, trustee, General partner, or employee

    or

    A person or organization with which they are negotiating for prospective employment

5. Has a financial interest.

18 U.S.C. 208.

Let's look at some of the key phrases. (An excellent guide to the meaning of all these phrases is found in Appendix D of the Advisory Opinion of the Office of Government Ethics, 06 x 9, October 4)

▮ "Participate personally and substantially"

This is broadly defined to include things like approving, disapproving, recommending, giving advice, investigating, or "otherwise." The catch-all language ("participates ... through decision, approval ... or otherwise ...") was designed to allow prosecution on the basis of any type of action taken to execute or carry to completion a contract.

> A Health and Human Services (HHS) budget officer was convicted of "otherwise" participating in a matter in which he had a financial interest. He did not get involved in the awarding of the contract, but he did get involved in its execution because he arranged for the government to pick up contracted-for equipment at his home.
> *United States v. Irons*, 640 F.2d 872 (7th Cir. 1981).

"Particular matter"

This includes contracts, claims, and controversies. In one case the court observed that:

> Courts have consistently treated a series of actions taken by a defendant in connection with a particular matter as a single instance of participation in the matter.... [For example] Assistant U.S. Attorney charged with one count of participating extensively in the case in which he had financial interest; ... several actions on one proposal prosecuted as one count of participation in matter in which defendant had a financial interest.

United States v. Jewell, 827 F.2d 586 (9th Cir.1987).

The OGE adds a significant point:

> It is important to emphasize that the term "particular matter" is not so broad as to include every matter involving Government action. Particular matter does not cover the "consideration or adoption of broad policy options directed to the interests of a large and diverse group of persons." 5 C.F.R. § 2640.103(a)(1). For example, health and safety regulations applicable to all employers

would not be a particular matter, nor would a comprehensive legislative proposal for health care reform. 5 C.F.R. § 2640.103(a)(1). See also OGE Informal Advisory Letter 05 x 1 (report of panel on tax reform addressing broad range of tax policy issues). Although such actions are too broadly focused to be particular matters, they still are deemed 'matters' for purposes of the restrictions described below that use that term.

OGE Advisory Opinion 06 x 9, October 4, 2006 (Appendix D).

"Negotiating for employment"

This includes any arrangement concerning prospective employment. The U.S. Court of Appeals for the Federal Circuit made this observation on "negotiating":

> [Government employees'] discussions [with a company] were only preliminary exploratory talks directed to possibilities that never materialized, not negotiations. . . . The statute does not bar government employees from participating in contract discussions, negotiations, or evaluations merely because, at an earlier time, they had some general discussions with some of the bidders about possible employment. Government officials often are approached about possible private employment. To bar them from participation months later in decisions involving a company that raised the possibility could cause serious problems for the effective functioning of the government. As the Senate Committee Report on the Ethics in Government Act explained: "Conflict of interest standards must be balanced with the government's objective in attracting experienced and qualified persons to public service. . . . There can be no doubt that overly stringent restrictions have a decidedly adverse impact on the government's ability to attract and retain able and experienced persons in federal office." [Citations omitted.]

> *CACI-Federal Inc. v. United States*, 719 F.2d 1567, 1578 (Fed. Cir. 1983).

In *United States v. Conlon*, 628 F.2d 150 (D.C. Cir. 1980), the government claimed that the Director of the Bureau of Engraving and Printing was involved in the Bureau's decision to award a contract to a company with whom the Director had a prospective employment arrangement but could produce no written employment agreement. The Director admitted only that he had "discussed" employment with the company while on the Bureau's payroll. The court said that the government did not have to prove that there were any "specific bilateral arrangements or acts of arranging" to prove a conflict of interest. The court broadly interpreted the words "arrangements for prospective employment."

Federal law provides the following exceptions:

- Recusal of the employee by the agency based on the interest not being significant
- Exempted by regulations issued by the Office of Government Ethics
- A financial interest that would affect a matter of a Native American tribe or nation.

Violations of the law are punishable by imprisonment of up to one year or, if the violation is willful, five years; and a fine of up to $50,000. The U.S. Sentencing Commission has set up to a six-month sentence for conflicts of interest.

> An Air Force officer was working on a government project to sell surplus C-130 airplanes to friendly nations. While he was working on the project, he submitted an application and had an employment interview with Teledyne Brown Engineering (TBE), a contractor for part of the project. After he left active duty he was employed by TBE on a project to maintain C-130 airplanes sold by the United States government to Mexico. The government brought conflict of interest charges alleging that he violated the prohibition against negotiating for prospective employment in a matter in which he was personally and substantially involved.

> The former Air Force officer argued that submitting an application and having an employment interview is not "negotiating" for a job, because merely applying for a job does not bind a person to accept employment if it is offered. Furthermore, the former officer said that no offer was made by TBE until after he had completed his government work.
>
> The former officer was convicted by a federal district court and the conviction was upheld by the court of appeals. The appeals court found that the former officer's activity was negotiation. "The whole purpose of negotiation is for each side to present its position to the other party in hopes that it can attract the other party to eventually submit to a binding agreement."
>
> United States v. Schaltenbrand, 930 F. 2d 1554 (11th Cir. 1991).

Here are some examples of how the conflict of interest law can be violated. Spouses can create a conflict of interest. In many communities, it's a small world. Often, government employees have spouses who work for government contractors. Invariably, conflicts of interest arise. A GAO decision involved a wife/boss who had a conflict with her husband contractor.

> The Army needed Stinger missiles. One of the companies that bid on the procurement was Applied Research Corporation (ARC). The president of ARC was married to the supervisor of the contracting officer who was going to make the award decision. ARC made the low bid. The contracting officer thought there might be an appearance of a conflict of interest, even though his supervisor had done nothing improper. The contracting officer referred the matter to the agency ethics officer, who recommended that ARC not be considered for the award because, among other reasons, the wife had access to the government estimate prior to the bid closing date. The contracting officer followed the recommendation and ruled that ARC was ineligible for award.
>
> ARC protested to GAO. GAO agreed with the contracting officer. FAR 1.602 gives the contracting officer authority to safeguard the government's interests. In doing so, contracting officers can take a number of actions not explicitly provided for in the regulations, including disqualifying bidders. Such actions must be based on facts, not mere innuendo and suspicion.

> GAO said that the agency ethics officer's recommendation showed that the agency had the necessary basis for disqualifying ARC. The wife "failed to disclose her financial interest in ARC and failed to disqualify herself from any participation in this solicitation, thus creating a conflict of interest. Her access to the government estimate warranted" ARC's exclusion from the competition.
> *Applied Resources Corp.*, B-249258, October 22, 1992.

A GAO report explored cases of alleged conflict of interest by those involved with Army and Marine Corps contracts, illustrating how those working on government contracts need to maintain the integrity of their information.

> Ms. B, the wife of a retired Army officer who works for CSC, is a career federal employee who served as the Project Manager and JRTC Team Leader for the JRTC Interim Instrumentation System between December 1988 and September 1991. She also served as the COTR for Task order 32/Subtask 16 (JRTC Interim Instrumentation System) between September 1990 and September 1991. Her duties as the COTR included preparing contract statements of work and task orders, certifying the Independent Government Cost Estimates, and reviewing CSC's monthly labor-hour charges.
>
> During our investigation, a former U.S. Army officer who had been assigned to work for Ms. B admitted that he had "padded" travel and other costs on what was supposed to be an Independent Government Cost Estimate on work for CSC. He told us that Ms. B had given him CSC's cost estimate and told him to "make the numbers come out." He examined the estimate and discovered that the costs were approximately three times what they should have been.
>
> When he brought this to the COTR's attention, he was told to "quit making waves" and maximize the contractor's cost by adding such items as extra days and extra rental cars. He recalled that the final government cost estimate was approximately twice the actual cost of the services.
>
> Ms. B's husband retired from the Army as a Lieutenant Colonel in July 1989. CSC interviewed him for employment in October 1989 and hired him in September 1990—during the same time that his wife was the COTR for the JRTC Interim Instrumentation System—as an Information Systems Designer. His compensation package included a salary and ownership in CSC stock.

We were told by an officer at the Combined Arms Command at Fort Leavenworth that he had heard a rumor that Mr. B was working for CSC while Ms. B was the COTR on the JRTC Interim Instrumentation System. The officer stated that he then advised the Deputy Commanding General for Training that Ms. B had a potential conflict of interest. The officer told us that he was present when the General phoned the CTIES Director and discussed the matter with him. According to the Combined Arms Command officer, the CTIES director subsequently transferred Ms. B.

Neither the General nor the former CTIES director recalled discussing the matter. The former CTIES director, who supervised Ms. B when she worked at CTIES, told us that Ms. B and her husband had advised him of her husband's negotiations with CSC for employment. The former CTIES director acknowledged that there were "appearance" problems, but stated that he had no one else to assign as the COTR. He said that he had asked his legal staff if this would present a conflict of interest and was advised that it was not a problem. However, he did not obtain a written opinion to this effect, and he could not recall who had provided this verbal opinion.

The General, who subsequently ordered the internal audit of the CTIES Directorate contracts, told us that he was unaware of Ms. B's potential conflict of interest until our investigation.

In September 1991, Ms. B was promoted to GS-13 and transferred to the TRADOC office of the Deputy Chief of Staff for Base Operations Support at Fort Monroe, Virginia, where she is currently a Requirements Acquisition Management officer. This is the TRADOC office that grants offload approvals. After she was transferred to Fort Monroe, CSC assigned her husband to the JRTC Interim Instrumentation System project.

During our investigation, we were told that at a late 1992 meeting between TRADOC Contracting Activity officials, Ms. B was introduced as the point of contact for the Army's training needs. A TRADOC Contracting Activity Legal Advisor subsequently questioned whether this presented a conflict of interest, since Ms. B's husband was working for CSC on the JRTC Instrumentation System and was a potential bidder on other Army work. The attorney told us that she was advised that Ms. B had been given ethics counseling and told not to discuss her work with her husband.

U.S. Army and Marine Corps: Allegations of Contracting Irregularities and Conflicts of Interest (GAO, November 1993).

BRIBES AND GRATUITIES

Bribery is defined in 18 U.S.C. 201(b) as:

- Directly or indirectly
- Corruptly asking or accepting
- Anything of value
- By a public official.

An illegal "gratuity" is defined by 18 U.S.C. 301(c) as:

- Directly or indirectly
- Asking or accepting
- Anything of value
- By a public official
- For or because of any official act.

A "bribe" differs from a "gratuity" in three ways:

- A bribe requires a quid pro quo. In exchange for something of value, a public official does some official act. A gratuity needs no quid pro quo; it is sufficient that the public official is "rewarded" for doing an official act that he or she would have done anyway.

  For example, the government charged Oliver North with accepting an illegal gratuity, alleging that he allowed a third person to pay for installation of a security system in his house. Establishing bribery would have been more difficult: The government would have had to prove that, in exchange for the security system, Mr. North took a specific official act.

- Bribery requires proof of the specific intent to influence an official act; the gratuities prohibition does not.
- A former public official can be convicted of a gratuity but not of a bribe.

Let's look at some of the common terms:

- "Anything of value": This includes things like money, stock, trips, and promises of a job. Interestingly, the offer of information about a taxpayer defrauding the government is not considered "anything of value." *United States v. Sandoval,* 20 F.3d 134 (5th Cir. 1994). Thus, a taxpayer offering such information in exchange for leniency from an IRS agent was not guilty of bribing that employee.
- "Official act": This can include things like actions on contract awards, claims, contracting officer's decisions, or terminations for convenience.
- A "public official" can be an Army private, *United States v. Kidd,* 734 F.2d 409 (9th Cir. 1984); a local public housing authority employee administering public funds, *United States v. Strissel,* 920 F.2d 1162 (4th Cir. 1992); or a former EPA employee turned government informer, *United States v. Romero,* 879 F.2d 1056 (2d. Cir. 1990).
- A campaign contribution is not a bribe as long as the contribution is not given in exchange for the performance or nonperformance of an official act. *United States v. Dozier,* 672 F.2d 531 (5th Cir. 1982).

These are some obvious exceptions.

The law does not prohibit the:

(1) Payment or receipt of witness fees provided by law

(2) Payment, by the party upon whose behalf a witness is called and receipt by a witness, of the reasonable cost of travel and subsistence incurred and the reasonable value of time lost in attendance at a proceeding

(3) In the case of expert witnesses, payment of a reasonable fee for time spent in the preparation of such opinion, and in appearing and testifying.

18 U.S.C. 201(d).

Both bribes and giving of gratuities are felonies punishable by a fine of not more than three times the monetary equivalent of the item of value or imprisonment for not more than 15 years, or both, and the offender may be disqualified from holding office.

The following are examples of bribery and gratuities:

Bribery. A base laundry, dry cleaning, and clothing repair contractor offered a Quality Assurance Inspector (QAI) a bribe in return for approval of monthly service costs to the Air Force. The QAI notified the Air Force Office of Special Investigations (AFOSI) and cooperated in an undercover investigation during which the contractor provided money, food, hotel accommodations, liquor, and other gifts to the QAI. The contractor was found guilty on two counts of bribery and two counts of false claims. He was sentenced to three years in jail, given three years probation, and fined $3,000.

Gratuities. A GS-12 contracting officer's technical representative (COTR) admitted soliciting and receiving gratuities from a contractor for which he had responsibility. The gratuities consisted of video equipment, meals, and use of an automobile and a beach condominium over the course of one year. There was no evidence that the COTR did anything in return for these gratuities. The COTR was convicted of receiving gratuities in violation of 18 U.S.C.

201 and was sentenced to one year in jail, which was suspended, and two years of probation. He resigned from federal service while removal action was pending.

STANDARDS OF CONDUCT[1]

Not only must federal employees follow federal criminal laws but they must also follow federal ethics regulations issued by the Office of Government Ethics (OGE). Both the FAR and the OGE principles of ethical conduct describe a federal employee's responsibilities. Common problem situations that federal employees can get involved in relate to restrictions on outside activities like teaching and writing, and restrictions on outside employment.

A more detailed explanation and excellent summary of all the OGE regulations are provided in Appendix D.

In addition, Appendix E is an excellent publication by OGE dealing with a wide range of issues between government employees and contractor personnel.

The FAR states:

> Government business shall be conducted in a manner above reproach and, except as authorized by statute or regulation, with complete impartiality and with preferential treatment for none. Transactions relating to the expenditure of public funds require the highest degree of public trust and an impeccable standard of conduct. The general rule is to avoid strictly any conflict of interest or even the appearance of a conflict of interest in Government-contractor relationships. While many Federal laws and regulations place restrictions on the actions of Government personnel, their

official conduct must, in addition, be such that they would have no reluctance to make a full public disclosure of their actions.

FAR 3.101-1.

Most of the statutory guidelines mentioned in this FAR provision appear in Titles 5, 10, 18, and 41 of the United States Code.

The OGE has established standards of conduct for all government employees. Because of their importance in acquisition programs, employees should be familiar with the following OGE principles of ethical conduct:

- Public service is a public trust, requiring employees to place loyalty to the Constitution, the laws and ethical principles above private gain.
- Employees shall not hold financial interests that conflict with the conscientious performance of duty.
- Employees shall not engage in financial transactions using nonpublic Government information or allow the improper use of such information to further any private interest.
- An employee shall not, except pursuant to the limited exceptions, solicit or accept any gift or other item of monetary value from any person or entity seeking official action from, doing business with, or conducting activities regulated by the employee's agency, or whose interests may be substantially affected by the performance or nonperformance of the employee's duties.
- Employees shall put forth honest effort in the performance of their duties.
- Employees shall make no unauthorized commitments or promises of any kind purporting to bind the Government.
- Employees shall not use public office for private gain.

- Employees shall act impartially and not give preferential treatment to any private organization or individual.

- Employees shall protect and conserve Federal property and shall not use it for other than authorized activities.

- Employees shall not engage in outside employment or activities, including seeking or negotiating for employment, that conflict with official Government duties and responsibilities.

- Employees shall disclose waste, fraud, abuse, and corruption to appropriate authorities.

- Employees shall satisfy in good faith their obligations as citizens, including all just financial obligations, especially those—such as Federal, State and local taxes—that are imposed by law.

- Employees shall adhere to all laws and regulations that provide equal opportunity for all Americans regardless of race, color, religion, sex, national origin, age, or handicap.

- Employees shall endeavor to avoid any actions creating the appearance that they are violating the law or the Standards of Ethical Conduct in 5 CFR 2635.

Restrictions on Outside Activities

Why should the government have any right to limit what federal employees do on their own time? Nathaniel Hawthorne and Herman Melville were employed by the Customs Service; Walt Whitman worked for the Departments of Justice and Interior; and Bret Harte was an employee of the mint. *United States v. National Treasury Employees Union,* 115 S. Ct. 1003 (1995).

Regardless of the effect such restrictions might have on future literary giants, federal employees must deal with restrictions on what they do after hours. Federal employees do not have totally "free" speech because OGE regulations have put some limits on what federal employees can do in their spare time.

Generally, federal employees cannot engage in outside employment or any other outside activity that conflicts with their official duties. 5 CFR 2635.802.

OGE gives a good example:

> An employee of the Environmental Protection Agency has just been promoted. His principal duty in his new position is to write regulations relating to the disposal of hazardous waste. The employee may not continue to serve as president of a nonprofit environmental organization that routinely submits comments on such regulations. His service as an officer would require his disqualification from duties critical to the performance of his official duties on a basis so frequent as to materially impair his ability to perform the duties of his position.

5 CFR 2635.802.

With regard to teaching, speaking, and writing, if what federal employees are teaching, speaking, or writing about relates to their official duties, the only paycheck they can get is from the federal government. Any other form of compensation is forbidden.

Compensation is broadly defined:

> Compensation includes any form of consideration, remuneration, or income, including royalties, given for or in connection with the employee's teaching, speaking, or writing activities. Unless accepted under specific statutory authority, it includes transportation, lodging, and meals, whether provided in

kind by purchasing of a ticket, by payment in advance, or by reimbursement after the expense has been incurred.

However, even if the writing, speaking, or teaching relates to their official duties, employees may accept compensation for teaching a course requiring multiple presentations by the employee if the course if offered as part of a school's regularly established curriculum.

5 CFR 2635.807.

"Relates to an employee's official duties" can mean:

1. The activity is undertaken as part of the employee's official duties

2. The circumstances indicate that the invitation to engage in the activity was extended to the employee primarily because of his or her position rather than his or her expertise on the particular subject matter

3. The invitation to engage in the activity or offer of compensation for the activity was extended to the employee, directly or indirectly, by a person who has interests that may be affected substantially by performance or nonperformance of the employee's official duties

4. The information conveyed through the activity draws substantially on ideas or official data that are nonpublic information

5. The subject of the activity deals in significant part with any matter to which the employee presently is assigned or to which the employee had been assigned during the previous one-year period; or ongoing or announced policy, program, or operation of the agency.

5 CFR 2635.807.

OGE gives a number of helpful examples:

> The Director of the Division of Enforcement at the Commodity Futures Trading Commission has a keen interest in stamp collecting and has spent years developing his own collection as well as studying the field generally. He is asked by an international society of philatelists to give a series of four lectures on how to assess the value of American stamps. Because the subject does not relate to his official duties, the Director may accept compensation for the lecture series. He could not, however, accept a similar invitation from a commodities broker.
>
> On his own time, a National Highway Traffic Safety Administration employee prepared a consumer's guide to purchasing a safe automobile that focuses on automobile crash worthiness statistics gathered and made public by NHTSA. He may not receive royalties or any other form of compensation for the guide. The guide deals in significant part with the programs or operations of NHTSA and, therefore, relates to the employee's official duties. On the other hand, the employee could receive royalties from the sale of a consumer's guide to values in used automobiles even though it contains a brief, incidental discussion of automobile safety standards developed by NHTSA.
>
> An employee of the Securities and Exchange Commission may not receive compensation for a book which focuses specifically on the regulation of the securities industry in the United States, since that subject concerns the regulatory programs or operations of the SEC. The employee may, however, write a book about the advantages of investing in various types of securities as long as the book contains only an incidental discussion of any program or operation of the SEC.
>
> 5 CFR 2635.807.

▊▊ Restrictions on Seeking Employment

We have already discussed the procurement integrity requirements on procurement personnel disqualifying themselves from employment overtures. But those provisions deal with only the contract solicitation process. There are other job-hunting restrictions procurement personnel must comply with just like every other federal employee. For example, earlier in this chapter, we talked about Darleen Druyun's violation of the criminal laws (18 U.S.C. 208) against conflicts of interest; that conflict arose out of her job-hunting efforts.

So a job hunt can be considered a conflict of interest. Our earlier focus was on conflicts, job-hunting or otherwise. Our focus now is solely on job-hunting.

How does OGE define "seeking employment?" It gives two definitions: one defining when job hunting begins and another defining when job hunting ends.

When it begins:

> (1) An employee has begun seeking employment if he has directly or indirectly:
>
>> (i) Engaged in negotiations for employment with any person. For these purposes, as for 18 U.S.C. 208(a), the term negotiations means discussion or communication with another person, or such person's agent or intermediary, mutually conducted with a view toward reaching an agreement regarding possible employment with that person. The term is not limited to discussions of specific terms and conditions of employment in a specific position;

(ii) Made an unsolicited communication to any person, or such person's agent or intermediary, regarding possible employment with that person.

(iii) Made a response other than rejection to an unsolicited communication from any person, or such person's agent or intermediary, regarding possible employment with that person.

5 CFR 2635.603(b).

The definition adds two useful exceptions: Asking for a job application or submitting a resume (under certain circumstances) does not start a job hunt.

When it ends:

(i) The employee or the prospective employer rejects the possibility of employment and all discussions of possible employment have terminated; or

(ii) Two months have transpired after the employee's dispatch of an unsolicited resume or employment proposal, provided the employee has received no indication of interest in employment discussions from the prospective employer.

5 CFR 2635.603(b).

Disqualification is the general rule in job-hunting situations:

To ensure that he does not violate 18 U.S.C. 208(a) or the principles of ethical conduct contained in Sec. 2635.101(b), an employee who is seeking employment or who has an arrangement concerning prospective employment shall comply with the applicable disqualification requirements of Sec. 2635.604 and Sec. 2635.606 if particular matters in which the employee will be participating personally and substantially would directly and predictably affect the financial interests of a prospective employer or of a person with whom he has an arrangement concerning prospective employment. 5 CFR 2635.602.

How do employees disqualify themselves?

Disqualification is accomplished by not participating in the particular matter.

5 CFR 2635.604(a).

The employee should also make a "notification."

An employee who becomes aware of the need to disqualify himself from participation in a particular matter to which he has been assigned should notify the person responsible for his assignment. An employee who is responsible for his own assignment should take whatever steps are necessary to ensure that he does not participate in the matter from which he is disqualified. Appropriate oral or written notification of the employee's disqualification may be made to coworkers by the employee or a supervisor to ensure that the employee is not involved in a matter from which he is disqualified.

5 CFR 2635.604(b).

OGE also describes the paperwork required. Although not required in all cases, it's a good idea to err on the side of caution and document the situation:

An employee need not file a written disqualification statement.... However, an employee may elect to create a record of his actions by providing written notice to a supervisor or other appropriate official.

5 CFR 2635.604(c).

OGE gives some good examples of how these job-hunting restrictions work.

> An employee of the Department of Veterans Affairs is participating in the audit of a contract for laboratory support services. Before sending his resume to a lab which is a subcontractor under the VA contract, the employee should disqualify himself from participation in the audit. Since he cannot withdraw from participation in the contract audit without the approval of his supervisor, he should disclose his intentions to his supervisor in order that appropriate adjustments in his work assignments can be made.

> An employee of the Food and Drug Administration is contacted in writing by a pharmaceutical company concerning possible employment with the company. The employee is involved in testing a drug for which the company is seeking FDA approval. Before making a response that is not a rejection, the employee should disqualify himself from further participation in the testing. Where he has authority to ask his colleague to assume his testing responsibilities, he may accomplish his disqualification by transferring the work to that coworker. However, to ensure that his colleague and others with whom he had been working on the recommendations do not seek his advice regarding testing or otherwise involve him in the matter, it may be necessary for him to advise those individuals of his disqualification.

5 CFR 2635.604(c).

NOTES

1. Portions of the following material are reprinted with permission of Management Concepts, Inc., from *Ethics in Federal Contracting.* Copyright 1997.

6 Federal Laws about Contractor Conduct

All contractors have an obligation to their company and to the government to avoid fraud, waste, and abuse. To carry out this obligation, however, you must be able to spot fraud, waste, and abuse when you see them. In this chapter, we first discuss the federal anti-fraud statutes (the False Statements Act and False Claims Act) and then move on to qui tam suits, mail and wire fraud, major procurement fraud, and obstruction of agency proceedings. We end with a discussion of a number of relatively minor laws that contractors must also observe.

FALSE STATEMENTS ACT

The False Statements Act deals with false, fraudulent, or fictitious material. These terms are not synonyms. The term *fraudulent* deals with untrue matters made with the intent to deceive; *false* or *fictitious* matters are untrue matters without regard to whether they were made with the intent to deceive.

In general terms, the statute prohibits three types of crimes:

1. Hiding a material fact

2. Affirmatively making untrue statements

3. Knowingly using a false writing.

Hiding a material fact requires more than mere nondisclosure; the situation must involve nondisclosure where there is a duty to disclose to the government based, generally, upon some statute or regulation. For example, if a bidder that is not a small business fails to complete the small business certification as part of its bid submission, it is violating the False Statements Act.

In addition, the fact that is hidden must be a material one; hiding a minor, inconsequential matter is not a violation of the statute.

It is also a crime to affirmatively make untrue statements, representations, or documents in any dealings with the government. For example, a bidder represents that it is a small business when in fact it is not, submits a resume of a principal investigator that is misstated, or provides an inaccurate product description in a brand-name or equal bidding situation.

The third type of violation deals with using a false document with false statements or entries. For example, if a prime contractor uses subcontractor invoices it knows to be false, this would violate the False Statements Act even though the prime did not make the false document itself.

Some general principles apply to all three types of violations. First, a crime is committed as soon as the false statement is made to the government; the law has been broken regardless of whether the government relied on the statement or believed it in the first place. *Coastal Engineering and Contracting Co.,* 174 F. Supp. 474 (D. Mo. 1959). An example would be if a local division of IBM represented in the bidding process that IBM is a small business.

Second, a contractor cannot avoid liability under the False Statements Act by claiming that it closed its eyes to what was going on; statements made with a deliberate disregard of whether they were true and with a conscious purpose to avoid learning the truth violate the act. *United States v. Precision Medical Labs Inc.*, 593 F.2d 434 (2d Cir. 1978).

Third, statements cover both oral and written statements, and sworn as well as unsworn statements.

In one case, a contractor sent the Defense Contract Audit Agency (DCAA) a letter in which one of its employees misrepresented the extent of his knowledge of inflated pricing practices by the company. After DCAA informed the employee about his company's practices, he told DCAA that he had just learned about such practices when in fact he had known about them for some time. He was convicted under the False Statements Act. 50 FCR 679 (October 24, 1988).

A more recent and more notorious example of a false statement involved the conviction of Martha Stewart. According to news reports, the indictment accused her of making false statements:

> On or about February 4, 2002 . . . in an interview with the SEC, the FBI, and the U.S. Attorney's Office for the Southern District of New York in New York, New York, in which she made the following false statements and concealed and covered up facts that were material to the investigations. . . . Stewart falsely stated that in a conversation that had occurred at a time when ImClone was trading at $74 per share, Stewart and Bacanovic decided that Stewart would sell her shares when ImClone started trading at $60 per share. Stewart falsely stated that on December 27, 2001, at approximately 1:30 p.m. (EST), Stewart spoke to Bacanovic, who told Stewart that ImClone was trading a little below $60 per share and that he asked Stewart if she wanted to sell, and then Stewart

told Bacanovic to sell her shares. Stewart falsely stated that she did not recall speaking to Bacanovic's assistant on December 27, 2001. Stewart falsely stated that she decided to sell her ImClone stock on December 27, 2001, because she did not want to be bothered over her vacation.[1]

FALSE CLAIMS ACT

The False Claims Act provides both civil and criminal penalties for knowingly making or presenting fraudulent, false, or fictitious claims to the government.

One big difference between civil and criminal is that a criminal violation can send someone to jail. Another difference is that violation of the criminal False Claims Act must be proven "beyond a reasonable doubt" while a civil False Claims Act violation must be proven only by "a preponderance of the evidence."

Criminal False Claims

The federal criminal law at 18 U.S.C. 287 states:

> Whoever makes or presents to any person or officer in the civil, military or naval service of the United States, or to any department or agency thereof, any claim upon or against the United States, or any department or agency thereof, knowing such claim to be false, fictitious, or fraudulent, shall be imprisoned not more than five years.

Civil False Claims

For our purposes, we will focus on the civil False Claims Act for two reasons: (1) the civil False Claims Act is one law that employees of some government contractors must be trained in, according to the 2008 FAR changes discussed previously in Parts I and II; and (2) that law seems to be the primary weapon of the Department of Justice (DOJ). One reason for DOJ's fondness for the civil False Claims Act may be the fact that the standard of proof for a civil False Claims Act violation, preponderance of the evidence, is lower than the standard of proof for criminal False Claims Act violations, beyond a reasonable doubt.

The CFC gave a good summary of the "civil" part of the False Claims Act.

> Anyone who knowingly presents, or causes to be presented . . . a false or fraudulent claim for payment or approval shall be liable for a civil penalty . . . plus 3 times the amount of damages which the Government sustains because of the act of that person. In order to recover damages for a violation of the False Claims Act, the Government must establish that: (1) the contractor presented or caused to be presented to an agent of the United States a claim for payment; (2) the claim was false or fraudulent; (3) the contractor knew the claim was false or fraudulent; and (4) the United States suffered damages as a result of the false or fraudulent claim. A contractor will be deemed to have "knowingly" presented a false claim when that individual either has actual knowledge that the claim is false, or acts in "deliberate ignorance" or "reckless disregard" of the truth or falsity of the claim. The Government does not have to prove specific intent to defraud. "Reckless disregard" has been defined as an "aggravated form of gross negligence." At a minimum, a contractor is required to examine records to ensure they are consistent with the submitted claim [internal citations omitted].
>
> *Trafalgar House Const., Inc. v. United States*, 77 Fed.Cl. 48, 52-53 (2007).

Criminal Conviction Does Not Bar Civil Fines for Fraud

The government gets a double shot against a contractor that defrauds the government. It can get the contractor sent to jail and fined as part of the criminal process, and it can also get the contractor to pay damages under the civil process.

> Gerald Kress was the president of Educational Development Network (EDN), a company that had two contracts with the Department of Defense. Both Kress and his company pled guilty to submitting false claims to the government with the contracts. Kress did four months in jail and agreed to pay the government $300,000 in restitution. EDN was fined $100,000. The government then filed a civil lawsuit against Kress and EDN seeking $2.3 million in damages.
>
> Kress and EDN asked the court to deny the government's claim on the basis that the second suit violated the constitutional protections against double jeopardy. Alternatively, they asked the court to reduce the damage amount to $200,000, an amount that gave them credit for the $300,000 in restitution they paid under the criminal case. They lost on both counts.
>
> The court agreed with the government that the criminal and civil suits did not violate double jeopardy. The reason for conducting a criminal case is to punish wrongdoers; the reason for conducting a civil case is to provide compensation to the government for the damage the fraud caused the government. As long as the civil damage claim was not so large as to constitute a punishment, double jeopardy was not violated.
>
> Here the government suffered more damage than the $300,000 covered by the restitution, so there was no double jeopardy violation. Moreover, the $2.3 million damage figure was accurate. The government overpaid more than $500,000 over the four years the fraud continued. The False Claims Act allows the government to treble its damages, so the court trebled that amount to over $1.5 million. The law also allows the court to assess $5,000 for each false claim, in this case $1.07 million for the 214 false claims. The court, however, did allow Kress to deduct the $300,000 he paid in restitution, leaving an amount in excess of $2.3 million, the figure the government asked for.
>
> *United States v. Educational Development Network, Inc.,*
> U.S. District Court for the Eastern District of Pennsylvania,
> Civil Action No. 89-7780, December 20, 1993.

In addition, a contractor who violates the Anti-Kickback Act can be made to pay penalties under that act as well as penalties under the False Claims Act.

> Morse Diesel had almost $300 million worth of construction contracts with GSA. The contracts eventually led to contractor claims. The government responded to these claims by charging that Morse Diesel had made kickbacks to sureties on some of the projects. The CFC agreed and concluded that the contractor had to pay penalties under both the Anti-Kickback Act and the False Claims Act.
>
> The amount at stake was $219,457.04, plus $40,000 for all four kickbacks under the Anti-Kickback Act, a total of $259,547.04; and under the False Claims Act, the treble damages and penalties came to $7,022,666. The court concluded that the contractor had to pay under both laws: the history of the Anti-Kickback Act evidences that Congress intended to use both statutes to compensate the government fully and deter the same kind of conduct at issue in this case.
>
> *Morse Diesel International Inc. D/b/a/Amec Construction Management Inc., v. United States,* 79 Fed.Cl. 116 (2007).

Note that the False Claims Act covers a narrower range of fraudulent statements because it covers only claims for money or property. Thus, a false statement that is not a claim violates the False Statements Act but not the False Claims Act.

The two key concepts of the False Claims Act are (1) making or presenting and (2) claim. For example, a prime contractor changes a subcontractor's invoice and submits an inflated claim. The prime is "making" a false claim. Or, a sub inflates its actual expenses and submits a false invoice to the prime. The prime doesn't know the sub's invoice is inflated. The prime (not the sub) submits the inflated claim to the government. The sub violates the False Claims Act even though it does not actually submit it directly to the government for payment.

In 2009 amendments to the False Claims Act, Congress closed a loophole that some courts had used to let subcontractors escape responsibility for proven frauds. If a subcontractor submitted a false claim to a prime Government contractor, the sub could violate the False Claims Act only if the government could prove the sub intended to defraud both the prime and the government. In addition, prime contractors had been beyond the reach of the False Claims Act if they defrauded an entity that used some government funds like Amtrak or government grantees, for example.

Under the 2009 amendments, liability under the False Claims Act "attaches whenever a person knowingly makes a false claim to obtain money or property, any part of which is provided by the Government without regard to whether the wrongdoer deals directly with the Federal Government; with an agent acting on the Government's behalf; or with a third party contractor, grantee, or other recipient of such money or property." 31 U.S.C. 3729. 123 STAT. 1622, PUBLIC LAW 111–21, MAY 20, 2009.

These amendments made several other changes to the way the civil FCIA affects government contractors.

Government property. Previously, if the government had not first given someone a receipt for government property, that person could not violate the False Claims Act for later failing to return the government property. Now, where knowing conversion of government property occurs, it makes no difference whether the person receives a valid receipt from the government.

Overpayments. If a government contractor failed to return an overpayment under a government contract, courts were not always finding this to be a violation of the False Claims Act although it could be a cause for debarment or suspension or a finding that the contractor was not responsible.

The reason was that courts did not consider retention of an overpayment to be retention of a government "obligation."

Now, not returning overpayments on government contracts may be a False Claims Act violation. According to Congress:

> The new definition of "obligation" includes an express statement that an obligation under the False Claims Act includes "the retention of an overpayment." This new definition will be useful to prevent Government contractors and others who receive money from the Government incrementally based upon cost estimates from retaining any Government money that is overpaid during the estimate process. Senate Report 111-10, p. 15.

What about contractors using "provisional" rates for costs such as overhead or G&A that will later be set at actual rates following audits? The False Claims Act is not violated by "a simple retention of an overpayment that is permitted by a statutory or regulatory process for reconciliation, provided the receipt of the overpayment is not based upon any willful act of a recipient to increase the payments from the Government when the recipient is not entitled to such Government money or property." Senate Report 111-10, p. 15.

"Claim" has been broadly construed by the courts. A contractor seeking an equitable adjustment could not avoid the False Claims Act by arguing that a submission for a change order was merely an estimate presented to the government as the opening position in negotiations:

> determining the exact cost of changes is difficult . . . and negotiations over these costs must take place. However, a contractor may not invoke the terms "estimates" and "negotiation" to justify a willful attempt to fleece the system. There is a line between estimates which reflect reasonably incurred expenses

and estimates which are so grossly inflated when compared to actual costs that they are by their very nature fraudulent ... the contractor's cost proposals were consistently over-inflated, at times by 100 percent or more. All final submissions of the cost proposal were made after the changed work was completed.

United States v. White, 765 F.2d 1469 (11th Cir. 1985).

Also, claims can be:

- ▶ The submission of sales slips submitted to the government for payment.
  United States v. John Bernard Industries Inc., 589 F.2d 1353 (8th Cir. 1979).

- ▶ Inflated overhead submissions.
  United States v. Systems Architects, Inc., 757 F.2d 373 (1985).

- ▶ Invoices falsely certifying that products furnished to the government satisfied the Buy American Act.
  United States v. Rule Industries, 878 F.2d 535 (1st Cir. 1989).

- ▶ Cost backup data submitted by a company to the government that incorporated the costs of kickbacks paid to a company employee by a subcontractor.
  United States v. General Dynamics, 19 F.3d 770 (2nd Cir. 1994).

- ▶ A contractor billing the government for subcontractor costs that had not been incurred.
  United States v. Thomas Ewing, 957 F.2d 115 (2nd Cir. 1992).

- ▶ A contractor knowingly putting the wrong national stock number on an excess property inventory sheet.
  United States v. Pemco Aeroplex, Inc., 195 F.3d 1234 (11th Cir. 1999).

CHAPTER 6 | Federal Laws about Contractor Conduct

> In an inventory schedule associated with declaring property excess to its government contract, Pemco told the government that it had in its possession wings from C-130s. The wings were identified by national stock numbers on the inventory form. The stock numbers used, however, were not accurate. The numbers used were for obsolete wings valued at a total of $1,875. The government sold the wings to Pemco for that amount. The lawsuit claims that Pemco sold two of the wings for $1.5 million and that all five wings had a value of more than $2 million.
>
> The False Claims Act's use of the word obligation was the heart of the issue. The issue for the court was whether Pemco's conduct involved, in part, a false record or statement to conceal, avoid, or decrease an obligation to pay or transmit money or property to the government. Pemco argued that it had no such existing obligation to pay for the wings or return them to the government at the time it completed the inventory form since the contract was not yet over. It also argued that the inventory sheet was simply an offer to sell the wings to the government, not an obligation to do so.
>
> The court did not agree. Pemco had government property in its possession and a contractual obligation to account for the full value of any excess government property by returning that property or otherwise disposing of it in accordance with the government's instructions. This legal obligation was a specific, ongoing obligation during the life of the contract and did not begin or end at any one point in time.
>
> *United States v. Pemco Aeroplex, Inc.*, 195 F.3d 1234 (11th Cir. 1999).

Information given to the government on DD form 250 when that form is being used not as an invoice but as notice that the goods have been received and accepted by a government official, is not a claim. *United States ex rel. Butler v. Hughes Helicopter, Inc.*, 71 F.3d. 321 (9th Cir. 1995).

However, a claim cannot be false if the government knows the "true" facts. There can be no "false" claim because government knowledge about problems a contractor was having eliminated the false aspect of any information.

Jerome Butler was a reliability engineer for Hughes and its successor McDonnell Douglas Helicopter Company (MDHC). Butler filed a whistleblower action claiming that Hughes and MDHC submitted false statements to the government and misrepresented compliance with the specifications. The case was thrown out because the court learned the information which Butler based his case on was available to the Army and, in fact, in its possession. Since the government had actually known about and agreed to the testing modifications and limitations, there was no false statement or false claim.

United States ex rel. Butler v. Hughes Helicopter, Inc.,
71 F.3d 321 (9th Cir. 1995).

The Veterans Administration was affiliated with the University of Southern California School of Medicine (U.S.C.SM) in staffing an outpatient medical clinic in Los Angeles. Two employees of the clinic, both doctors, filed False Claims Act actions against administrators and physicians of the clinic, claiming that they improperly charged the government for time that the physicians did not spend at the clinic. The plaintiff doctors claimed that the defendants were liable for various types of alleged misconduct. One of the allegations against the clinic was that it hired unnecessary employees. Specifically, the plaintiffs believed that the clinic hired an unnecessary anesthesiologist and two new surgeons.

The court refused to find any liability because the plaintiffs could not show that the decisions were made with the actual knowledge that the expenditures were unnecessary or with reckless disregard of or deliberate indifference to that knowledge. The court noted that the plaintiffs showed only innocent mistake or mere negligence, neither of which can form the basis for False Claims Act liability.

The plaintiffs also claimed that the clinic overpaid physicians and residents, arguing that they were paid for time that they were not physically present at the clinic. The defendants argued that the agreement between the Veterans Administration and the medical school allowed clinic employees to spend time outside the clinic at the U.S.C.SM medical facility teaching residents and performing research.

The court pointed out that the defendants believed that the affiliation agreement between the clinic and U.S.C.SM authorized their time outside the clinic. Because there was no evidence that the defendants believed they were interpreting the affiliation agreement incorrectly, the court denied the plaintiff's claims.

United States ex rel. Robert A. Hochman et al., U.S. Court of Appeals for the Ninth Circuit, No. 96-56790, May 27, 1998.

> The Department of Energy (DOE) had a contract with Westinghouse Savannah River Co. to operate a federally owned nuclear facility in South Carolina. Money to run the facility came from Congress. But the money came from at least two separate congressional appropriations. One of the appropriations funded the Office of Defense Programs and specifically the construction of three buildings. The Defense Programs account had $12 million in it when the construction was done. A second appropriation funded DOE's Office of Environmental Management. When a DOE reorganization transferred the Defense Program's work to Environmental Management, the question arose, could the Defense Program's money, $12 million, be transferred as well? The answer, apparently, was not without Congress' approval. And although DOE asked Congress to approve it, DOE was unclear whether approval by Congress was actually given.
>
> In any event, DOE transferred the $12 million and told Westinghouse to make the $12 million part of the environmental Management account. Westinghouse went along with the DOE direction, even though Westinghouse knew that DOE was uncertain about the requirement of congressional approval.
>
> A taxpayer named Martin Becker tried to be a bounty hunter and went to court claiming that Westinghouse violated the False Claims Act by creating false records to conceal the transfer. An appeals court concluded that Westinghouse was simply following orders so the court focused on what DOE knew. DOE had at least as much knowledge as Westinghouse regarding congressional authority for the transfer and nonetheless directed Westinghouse to change the codes. The appeals court noted that at least three other circuits recognize that prior government knowledge of an allegedly false claim can negate the scienter required for False Claims Act violation. . . . DOE's full knowledge of the material facts underlying any representations implicit in Westinghouse's conduct negates any knowledge that Westinghouse had regarding the truth or falsity of those representations.
>
> *United States of America, ex rel. Martin Becker v. Westinghouse Savannah River Co.*, United States Court of Appeals for the Fourth Circuit, No. 01-2452, September 27, 2002.

The False Claims Act is also violated by the use of exaggerated resumes.

> Payments to a sub were based upon a sliding scale according to the education and experience of the employees of the sub working on a particular task. Blecker had the employees "embellish" the resumes which were then submitted along with invoices based upon the rates to which such "inflated" employees would be entitled. The Court found that this violated the False Claims Act. (False resumes could also support a False Statements Act violation.)
>
> *United States v. Blecker*, 657 F. 629 (4th Cir. 1981).

Amendments to the False Claims Act provide contractors with a strong inducement to cooperate with the government. These amendments state that the government is entitled to treble damages unless the court finds that the contractor (1) furnished the government all information known to it about the false claims violation within 30 days after learning of the violation, and (2) fully cooperated with the government's investigation. These amendments were designed to encourage contractors to voluntarily come forward with information on false claims so that they could avoid the treble damages.

Penalties are significant: treble damages or the possibility of a $5,000 fine for each incident of fraud. Where there is fraud throughout the contract, with many items fraudulently provided the government and many fraudulent invoices submitted, the damages can get very high. On occasion, however, a court will find these damages to be too high.

> GSA had a contract with Advanced Tool Company and its President, William R. McGillivray. Under the contract, Advanced Tool was to provide various types of tools which were described by a particular "brand name" on the FSS. Rather than provide specific brand named tools made by certain manufacturers, McGillivray reverse engineered each of these tools. He got either a sample of the tool or the manufacturer's drawing for the tool and then either reverse-engineered from the tool sample or ordered tools from machine shops in Michigan. These tools were then shipped by McGillivray to fill the GSA purchase orders for these "brand name" items. McGillivray delivered 1,301 tools under this process and submitted 688 invoices to GSA.

> Upon learning that the tools were not brand name, the government filed a False Claims Act seeking for each of the 688 invoices a $5,000 civil penalty. The court concluded that there was fraud in this instance but concluded that the civil penalty based on the number of invoices was too high. The Court set the damages at $5,000 for each of the 73 different tools that were not of the type or quality requested by GSA for a total damage amount of $365,000, down from $3.4 million.
>
> *United States of America v. Advance Tool Company and William R. McGillivray*, U.S.District Court for the Western District of Missouri, Western Division, #94-0062-CV-W-1, July 14, 1995.

Implied Certifications

A contractor can violate the False Claims Act by submitting a valid, non-fraudulent invoice that is accompanied by a certification from the contractor that the contractor is complying with the specific laws when it is not.

Some courts have found an implied certification of contract compliance attached to requests for payment made by a contractor to the government. The result is that a perfectly valid invoice can become a false claim as a result of the false implied certification. The theory is based in part on the legislative history of the False Claims Act.

The Senate Judiciary Committee said that the False Claims Act applied to a claim for goods not provided or provided in violation of contract terms, specification, statute, or regulation. For example, the CFC found that an 8(a) firm had made a false implied certification when it submitted perfectly valid invoices to the government after signing a prohibited co-management agreement with a subcontractor that made the 8(a) firm no longer an 8(a) firm. In another case, a court found a violation of an implied certification when a Medicare provider submitted invoices for payments knowing that it was not complying with all Medicare requirements. In a third case, another appeals court found a violation of the False Claims Act when a contractor knowingly omitted from progress reports vital information concerning non-compliance with the program it was to implement.

What makes the implied certification rule applicable is if payment is conditioned on that certification.

> AAA Engineering and Drafting, Inc. had a contract to do photography for Tinker Air Force Base. The contract included developing pictures. To develop pictures, AAA used a solution containing silver. Environmental Protection Agency (EPA) regulations require the silver to be properly disposed of. The contract AAA had with the Air Force required AAA to comply with these EPA regulations. AAA did not comply with these regulations. It simply poured the silver down the drain. Moreover, the president of the company knew the company was not complying.
>
> Knowing that the company was not complying with EPA regulations, the company submitted routine invoices. There was no express certification on the invoices that the company was complying with the EPA regulations or any other regulations.
>
> The government took the company to court and a jury found that the company had violated the False Claims Act. The company appealed, arguing among other things that the invoices were correct and contained no lies or anything false. The appeals court focused not on what the invoices said but what was implied: that the contractor was complying with the contract. And the contractor was not complying with the contract's requirement to follow EPA regulations. The court stressed the knowing requirement. Inadvertent violations are different. What the court in this case used was a standard that the contractor knew, or recklessly disregarded the risk, that its implied certification of compliance was false.
>
> *Debra A. Shaw v. AAA Engineering & Drafting, Inc et al.*, 213 F.3d 519 (10th Cir. 2000).

Not all courts, however, have bought into the implied certification theory. The Fifth Circuit Court of Appeals is one of them. The appeals court refused to find a False Claims Act violation when a contractor submitted progress payment requests and other documents to the government even though the products provided to the government were not meeting the corrosion standards in the contract.

> The government contracted with S and S Services Inc. to build a variety of military trucks with enclosed cabs. A subcontractor would make the cabs. The prime invoiced the government for progress payments on an SF 1443, which included a certification by the contractor only that the costs were actually incurred. After the government accepted a vehicle, government inspectors signed a DD250 (a material inspection and receiving report), which was then converted by the contractor into an invoice and submitted by the contractor to the government for final payment. Significantly, the DD250 had no express certifications that the contractor was complying with the contract.
>
> The cabs provided by the subcontractor had problems with corrosion believed to be caused by the sub using products and procedures that did not comply with the contract's requirements. An employee of the prime filed a False Claims Act suit, arguing that both the prime and the sub made false certifications under the False Claims Act. The Federal District Court threw the case out and the appeals court threw out the appeal. Both refused to find that the progress payments and the DD250s had any implied certifications. Neither expressly certified compliance with every provision of the overall contract. "Our court has not adopted an implied theory of certification. Even if we were to do so, False Claims Act liability would not attach in this action. The government had been involved in the design, had worked closely with the prime, and knew about the cab's corrosion problems." The appeals court didn't think that the sub caused the prime contractor to submit a false claim to the government.
>
> *United States of America ex rel. Werner Stegner v. Stewart and Stevenson Services Inc.,* United States Court of Appeals, Fifth Circuit, No. 04-20209, August 8, 2005.

The Fifth Circuit is not the only appeals court that has not accepted the implied certification theory. The Fourth Circuit has termed the implied certification theory to be questionable in that circuit.

> A former employee, Jose Herrera, trying to be a bounty hunter sharing in any fraud recovery the government received, argued that Danka, the company he used to work for, did not disclose to government buyers the fee-for-service of one half of one percent it had to pay GSA under its FSS contract for photocopiers. Herrera argued that every invoice Danka submitted to a government customer acted as an implied certification that Danka would comply with the fee-for-service provision.
>
> In throwing Herrera's case out, the Fourth Circuit noted that the implied certification theory requires a showing at least that the certification was a prerequisite to the government action sought. "In this case, the agreement the company had with the government does not condition payment of invoices on a certification that Danka will remit the FSS. Thus, Herrera's theory of implied certification fails. . . ."
>
> United States ex rel. Jose Herrera v. Danka Office Imaging Co.,
91 Fed. Appx. 863 (4th Cir. 2004).

Finally, the D.C. Circuit also requires a connection with the payment requested.

> A former employee of Jamieson Science and Engineering, Inc., Joseph Siewick, filed a False Claims Act action against his former employer and two of its employees. He claimed that one of the employees violated the revolving door provisions of federal law. These provisions generally prohibit a former government employee from "switching sides" and becoming an employee of a contractor that does business with the government and, more importantly, did government business with that very employee. Siewick claimed that the former government employee broke the False Claims Act because the company submitted invoices to the government while this former government employee was violating the revolving door provisions and serving as an employee of the company.

> The court endorsed the rule adopted "by all courts of appeals to have addressed the matter, that a false certification of compliance with a statute or regulation cannot serve as the basis for a qui tam action under the False Claims Act unless payment is conditioned on that certification." Here, Siewick could not prove that the company was required to certify compliance with the revolving door statute as a condition of its contract. As a result, there was no violation of implied certification.
>
> *United States ex rel. Joseph Siewick v. Jamieson Science and Engineering, Inc. et al.*, U.S. Court of Appeals for the D.C. Circuit, No. 99-7090, June 30, 2000.

QUI TAM SUITS

A qui tam lawsuit is a bounty-hunting suit in which a taxpayer suspecting fraud against the government sues on behalf of the government to recover lost tax dollars. *Qui tam* is shortened from the Latin phrase meaning "who on behalf of the king too" indicating the derivative nature of these suits. If the government decides to join in the suit, the qui tam "relator" or original plaintiff can recover a maximum of 25 percent of the recovery; if the government decides not to join in and the taxpayer is successful by himself, he can get up to a maximum of 30 percent of any recovery.

Now this is one government program that really works! By 2003, more than 100 people had collected more than $1 million as bounty hunters. (A qui tam suit in July 1992 netted the qui tam relator $8.7 million.) Between 1986 and 2004 the government recovered more than $8 billion in qui tam suits.[2]

The idea behind qui tam suits is to encourage taxpayers to disclose fraud that would not otherwise be disclosed. To make sure that qui tam suits are not based on information already in the public domain, a qui tam suit can be brought only by the "original source" of the information. Determining whether someone is the original source is difficult.

If the whistleblower's information plays only "some part" in uncovering the fraud, the whistleblower is still entitled to compensation as a bounty hunter.

> A Northrop Corporation employee, Leocadio Barajas, told the government that Northrop was performing false testing of a component in the air launched cruise missile guidance system. As a result of his disclosures, Northrop was indicted on a number of charges. This disclosure led to the disclosure of other fraud: the fraudulent testing charges led to the government making changes in how the transmitters involved were tested. This changed procedure then, in turn, disclosed additional fraud.
>
> Barajas filed a qui tam suit seeking to recover a share of the government's recovery from Northrop. The court concluded that Barajas could be a whistleblower for the subsequent fraud because his original charges of fraud in testing played "some part" in the discovery of this additional type of fraud.
>
> *U.S. ex rel. Barajas v. Northrop Corp.,*
> District Court for Central California No. CV87-7288, May 9, 1995.

Other qui tam plaintiffs find recovery difficult.

> Harold Fine was a civilian employee of the DOE's Office of Inspector General, where his duties included auditing DOE facilities, including Sandia National Laboratory. Sandia is owned by the government and operated by private or University contractors under DOE Administrative Oversight. In 1990 GAO issued a report about improper use of nuclear waste funds at Sandia during fiscal years 1988 and 1989. In March 1991, Congress held hearings that also discussed this improper use of DOE money at its laboratories. In July 1991 Mr. Fine retired from DOE and later filed a qui tam action under the False Claims Act alleging that he should receive a bounty hunters award for disclosing improper use of nuclear waste funds at Sandia during fiscal years 1991 and 1992.
>
> The court denied his qui tam suit: he was not the original source of the information; the original source was GAO and Congressional Reports.
>
> *Harold R. Fine, United States of America ex rel. v. Sandia Corporation,*
> United States Court of Appeals for the Tenth Circuit, #94-2121,
> November 21, 1995.

One possible consequence of a qui tam suit is that a current employee blowing the whistle will be fired. The qui tam law provides employment protections for fired employees. The mere fact of getting fired for blowing the whistle will not, however, entitle the whistleblower to protection.

> Denise Childree testified at a Department of Agriculture hearing and claimed that her employer and one of her employer's customers tried to circumvent a government limit on reimbursable claims. Earlier, she had copied certain documents of her employer which she kept in a box at home until they were subpoenaed by the Department of Agriculture. She was eventually fired for removing confidential customer files without authorization. She filed a suit under the Whistleblower Protection Act (31 U.S.C. 3730(h)). She argued that she was fired in furtherance of a False Claim Act violation. She admitted that no false claims actions had been brought against her former employer, nor did she even know about the False Claims Act and never intended to begin any false claims action.
>
> The Federal District Court in Georgia refused to give Childree the protections of the Whistleblower Protection Act. The law protects those who can show retaliation in connection with a false claims action. She could not show this. Moreover, she performed no affirmative act to help expose the alleged fraud on the government. She did not have any contacts with the Agriculture Stabilization and Conservation Service. Nor did she complain internally or get in touch with any government official to tell them that she suspected the government was being defrauded. All she did was copy documents she thought to be evidence of fraud and store them in her home for four years. The court said the protection was designed for those who come forward with evidence of fraud against the government; that was not the case here. The court refused to bring her under the Whistleblower Protection Law.
>
> *Childree v. UAPGA AgChem Inc.,* U.S. District Court for the Northern District of Georgia, No. 1:94-cv-1312 June 20, 1995.

MAIL FRAUD AND WIRE FRAUD

Statutes dealing with mail fraud (18 U.S.C. 1341) and wire fraud (18 U.S.C. 1343) make it illegal to engage in any scheme to defraud in which the mails or wire communication are used; this includes sending or receiving any matter (including government checks) through the use of these media.

In addition to proving fraudulent intent and the use of the mails, the government must prove a fraudulent act. The Mail Fraud Statute is broader than other statutes, combining elements of the False Statements and False Claims Acts. It covers schemes to defraud as well as to obtain money or property by fraudulent means. In addition, it covers false promises, which traditionally were not covered by fraud statutes at common law.

The Mail Fraud Statute was well summarized by the Court in *United States v. Contenti*, 735 F.2d 628, 631 (1st Cir. 1984):

> It is settled law that an accused causes a letter to be delivered by mail when he does an act with knowledge that the use of the mails will follow in the ordinary course of business, or where he could reasonably foresee that the use of the mails would result. It is not necessary to prove that the accused mailed anything himself, or personally received anything through the mails himself, or actually intended the mail be used . . . The mailed letter need not itself disclose any intent to defraud. It is only necessary that the mailed letter be a part of or incident to some essential step in the execution of the scheme. . . . The fact that the scheme ultimately does not succeed does not render the mailings any less violative of the statute.

The use of the mails in even indirect ways to defraud the government may violate federal law.

> A sub hand delivered its (false) invoice to the prime's Rosslyn office, the prime used its computer to send the data to its accounting department in California, the prime used the mails to send its invoices to its Rosslyn office, and the Rosslyn office hand-delivered the prime's invoice to GSA in Washington. The sub claimed that the Mail Fraud Statute was not violated because (1) no mailing was involved in the defrauding sub's submission of false invoices to the prime (they had been sent by computer) and (2) no mailing was involved in the prime's use of the data in those invoices to in turn prepare invoices to GSA for the services performed by the sub (the prime's invoices were hand-carried from the prime's Rosslyn offices to GSA offices in Washington). The court found, however, that the prime had used the mails to send its bills from its accounting department in California to its Rosslyn office and that the sub could reasonably foresee that the mails would be used by others in the execution of its scheme to defraud; therefore, the law had been broken.
>
> *United States v. Blecker*, 657 F. 629 (4th Cir. 1981).

MAJOR PROCUREMENT FRAUD

In 1988, Congress created a new crime called *procurement fraud* against the United States (18 U.S.C. 1031). It is applicable to contracts, subcontracts, or any constituent part thereof in excess of $1 million. The legislation and legislative history do not further define what are to be considered constituent parts. In view of the complexity of major fraud cases, a statute of limitations of seven years was authorized.

Procurement fraud is committed by someone who knowingly executes or attempts to execute, any scheme or artifice with the intent to (1) defraud the United States; or (2) obtain money or property by means of false or fraudulent pretenses, representations, or promises in procurement. For example, a company official orders his company's proposal writers to put in the company's proposal to the government language stating that the company will dedicate certain specified company experts to the contract effort. The official knows that these individuals have already resigned from the company, effective the month the contract will be awarded.

Heavy fines and prison terms are authorized by the statute: a $1 million fine and 10 years in prison or both for violations of the statute. The statute sets a limit of $10 million for multiple-count violations of the statute.

This law can be broken by someone who does not have a contract with the government. For example, vendors intentionally scheming with a prime contractor to defraud the government can violate this law. Regardless of its privity with the United States, any contractor or supplier involved with a prime contract with the United States who commits fraud with requisite intent is guilty under the major fraud statute so long as a prime contract, subcontract, supply agreement, or any constituent part of such contract is valued at the statute's jurisdictional amount of $1 million or more. *United States v. Brooks*, 111 F.3d 365 (4th Cir. 1997).

Unlike the False Claims Act, there is no requirement that a claim be filed against the government. Simply restructuring a contract to include inflated costs can violate the act. *United States v. Frequency Electronics*, 862 F.Supp. 834 (E.D.N.Y. 1994).

▌ OBSTRUCTION OF AGENCY PROCEEDINGS

Any endeavor to interfere with an agency proceeding is prohibited by 18 U.S.C. 1505 as the obstruction of justice. The two key words are *endeavor* and *proceeding*. Both have been broadly construed.

The term *endeavor* means any effort or act to obstruct or interfere with a proceeding. Because the endeavor is prohibited, success at the endeavor is not an issue; just trying to obstruct a proceeding is illegal regardless of whether the proceeding is actually impeded by the endeavor. Examples include giving blatantly evasive testimony at an agency proceeding (*United States v. Alo*, 439 F.2d 751 (2nd Cir. 1970)) and concealing documents (*United States v. Prosser*, 187 F. Supp 64 (N.D. Ohio 1960)).

Moreover, *endeavor* is broader than the term *attempt*, which is used often in criminal law because endeavor connotes a somewhat lesser threshold of purposeful activity than attempt does. An endeavor was found, for example, when a person suggested, five times, that his listener convey a message to her sister, who was a juror, that the defendant was a good person, and the hearer actually spoke to the sister once. *United States v. Lazzerini*, 611 F.2d 940 (1st Cir. 1979).

The term *proceeding* has also been broadly construed to include all the steps and stages in the performance by an agency of its governmental functions. See *Rice v. United States*, 356 F. 2d 709, 712 (8th Cir. 1966). This includes all the procedures prescribed for conducting business before an agency, both investigative and administrative. No formal stage need have been reached. For example, a contractor conceals pertinent records from DCAA and makes false representations to DCAA in connection with the agency's audit of the contractor's Navy contracts. *United States v. Fisher*, unreported, CA 3, No. 88-1174, September 6, 1988; see 50 FCR 679. See also *United States v. Leo*, 941 F.2d 181 (3rd Cir. 1991).

Other procurement steps and stages are potentially covered by the law. Steps in the procurement process, such as claims and debarment proceedings, would probably be covered by the law; also, a contractor's request for a change order or a contractor's proposal in response to the government's request for a change order could be covered by the act so that concealment and misrepresentations in these processes would be prohibited by the obstruction of justice statutes.

MISCELLANEOUS LAWS

Contractors should also be aware of other laws that, although of more general applicability, could bear on procurement issues.

Trade Secrets Act

The Trade Secrets Act prohibits the unauthorized release of any information relating to trade secrets or confidential business data by a federal employee who receives such information in the course of his or her employment. Such information includes advance procurement information, prices, technical proposals, and proprietary information. Conviction of a federal employee on such charges results in loss of employment in addition to criminal penalties.

Conspiracy

The general conspiracy statute (18 U.S.C. 371) prohibits any agreement between two or more persons to defraud the government or violate any federal law or regulation when at least one act is taken in furtherance of the agreement.

One example is a case where the defendant was found guilty of conspiracy even though he did not profit from the conspiracy. The individual knew of the conspiracy to defraud the government and told one of the conspirators to get receipts in order to back up the bogus checks that were being submitted. The court found that, because the defendant helped perpetuate the conspiracy by telling of ways to prevent detection, he was guilty of conspiracy even though he did not profit personally from it. *United States v. Alford*, No. 87-5627, (4th Cir. 1988).

Theft of Government Property

This statute (18 U.S.C 641) prohibits the intentional and unauthorized taking, destruction, or use of government property. It also prohibits the receiving or concealing of government property.

Restrictions on Lobbying and Consultants

Congress has long been concerned about the improper influence consultants and lobbyists have on awarding a government contract. Not only does this type of influence improperly skew the contract selection process; it costs the government more money because the cost of the contract must go up to pay for the consultant or lobbyist.

Covenant against Contingent Fees

The impartiality and fairness of the contract award process could be seriously compromised if a company paid a consultant only if the consultant brought in a government contract. In addition, the cost of government contracts would needlessly increase.

Companies are not supposed to use a contingent fee to get new contracts. FAR 3.401 defines a continent fee as "any commission, percentage, brokerage, or other fee that is contingent upon the success that a person or concern has in securing a Government contract."

The FAR refers to the various statutes (10 U.S.C. 2306(b) and 41 U.S.C. 254(a)) Congress has passed:

> These statutes—
>
> (a) Require in every negotiated contract a warranty by the contractor against contingent fees;
>
> (b) Permit, as an exception to the warranty, contingent fee arrangements between contractors and bona fide employees or bona fide agencies; and
>
> (c) Provide that, for breach or violation of the warranty by the contractor, the Government may annul the contract without

liability or deduct from the contract price or consideration, or otherwise recover, the full amount of the contingent fee.

FAR 3.402.

FAR 3.403 adds that these statutes have been extended by the FAR to sealed bids as well.

Not all contingent fees are prohibited. Many businesspeople traditionally work on a contingent-fee basis. For example, lawyers working on a contingent-fee basis do not get paid unless they achieve a win for their client.

Since salespeople often work on a commission basis, salespeople selling to the government would be breaking the law with every sale they make to the government unless Congress made exceptions. The FAR makes these commissions for a sales company or salesperson allowable and not a violation of these statutes:

> "Bona fide agency" means an established commercial or selling agency, maintained by a contractor for the purpose of securing business, that neither exerts nor proposes to exert improper influence to solicit or obtain Government contracts nor holds itself out as being able to obtain any Government contract or contracts through improper influence.
>
> "Bona fide employee" means a person, employed by a contractor and subject to the contractor's supervision and control as to time, place, and manner of performance, who neither exerts nor proposes to exert improper influence to solicit or obtain Government contracts nor holds out as being able to obtain any Government contract or contracts through improper influence.
>
> FAR 3.401.

This policy is reflected in FAR 52.203-5, Covenant against Contingent Fees, which must be included in every contract over the simplified acquisition threshold except for commercial items.

The Byrd Amendment

This law, 31 U.S.C. 1352, prohibits recipients of federal grants, contracts, loans, or cooperative agreements from using federal (appropriated) funds to pay persons to influence or to attempt to influence executive or legislative decision making in connection with the awarding of any contract, grant, loan, or cooperative agreement. Key elements of the law include:

- In the case of a payment, or progress payment, received by a contractor for performance of a contract, the portion of the payment properly allocable to the contractor's profit is not appropriated funds.

- The law does not include claims and settlements against the federal government. Activities related to such actions are not prohibited.

- The section also requires that any person requesting or receiving a federal grant, contract, cooperative agreement, loan, loan guarantee, or loan insurance must report to the relevant agency the name of any lobbyists or consultants paid with non-federal funds, the amounts such lobbyists or consultants were paid, and the purpose for which they were paid. The passage of the Lobbying Disclosure Act of 1995, however, makes it unnecessary to submit detailed data on each contact. Only the name of the contact is required.

FAR 3.802 implements the Byrd Amendment and describes a number of restrictions on the use of federal money to lobby for contracts and grants. The FAR requires:

> ... offerors to furnish a declaration consisting of both a certification and a disclosure. These requirements are contained in the

provision at 52.203-11, Certification and Disclosure Regarding Payments to Influence Certain Federal Transactions, and the clause at 52.203-12, Limitation on Payments to Influence Certain Federal Transactions.

FAR 3.802(b).

Specifically, when an offeror submits its offer, it "certifies that no appropriated funds have been paid or will be paid in violation of the prohibitions" in 31 U.S.C. 1352, prohibitions generally described by the FAR. In addition, an offeror "shall identify if any funds other than Federal appropriated funds (including profit or fee received under a covered Federal action) have been paid, or will be paid, to any person for influencing or attempting to influence an officer or employee of any agency, a Member of Congress, an officer or employee of Congress, or an employee of a Member of Congress in connection with a Federal contract, grant, loan, or cooperative agreement." FAR 3.802(b)(2).

There are exceptions:

> (1) Agency and legislative liaison by own employees.
>
> (2) Professional and technical services "rendered directly in the preparation, submission, or negotiation of any bid, proposal, or application for that Federal action or for meeting requirements imposed by or pursuant to law as a condition for receiving that Federal action."
>
> FAR 3.803(a)

The FAR helpfully provides some examples of allowable exceptions:

> For example, drafting of a legal document accompanying a bid or proposal by a lawyer is allowable. Similarly, technical advice provided by an engineer on the performance or operational

capability of a piece of equipment rendered directly in the negotiation of a contract is allowable. However, communications with the intent to influence made by a professional (such as a licensed lawyer) or a technical person (such as a licensed accountant) are not allowable under this section unless they provide advice and analysis directly applying their professional or technical expertise and unless the advice or analysis is rendered directly and solely in the preparation, submission or negotiation of a covered Federal action. Thus, for example, communications with the intent to influence made by a lawyer that do not provide legal advice or analysis directly and solely related to the legal aspects of his or her client's proposal, but generally advocate one proposal over another are not allowable under this section because the lawyer is not providing professional legal services. Similarly, communications with the intent to influence made by an engineer providing an engineering analysis prior to the preparation or submission of a bid or proposal are not allowable under this section since the engineer is providing technical services but not directly in the preparation, submission or negotiation of a covered Federal action.

FAR 3.802(c)(2)(ii).

Contracts over $100,000 must comply with FAR 52.203-11, Certification and Disclosure Regarding Payments to Influence Certain Federal Transactions. This clause requires an offeror to include with its offer the certification and disclosure required by that clause.

In addition, a contractor must tell the contracting officer via a disclosure statement "at the end of each calendar quarter in which there occurs any event that materially affects the accuracy of the information in any disclosure form. . . . "

The FAR says that "an event that materially affects the accuracy of the information reported includes—

> (1) A cumulative increase of $25,000 or more in the amount paid or expected to be paid for influencing or attempting to influence a covered Federal action; or
>
> (2) A change in the person(s) or individual(s) influencing or attempting to influence a covered Federal action; or
>
> (3) A change in the officer(s), employee(s), or Member(s) of Congress contacted to influence or attempt to influence a covered Federal action."
>
> FAR 3.803(b).

A certification and disclosure form might have to be submitted by subcontractors with subcontracts over $100,000.

Reported cases dealing with the Byrd Amendment and lobbying restrictions are rare. In one protest before GAO, a protester, Helmets Unlimited, argued that the winning vendor, Gentex, should have been disqualified from a procurement because an employee of the winner and a government engineer violated the Byrd Amendment. GAO disagreed.

> The Byrd Amendment generally prohibits a contractor receiving appropriated funds from using those funds to pay any person for "influencing or attempting to influence" an agency employee in connection with the award of a federal contract. The record does not support the assertion that Gentex's phone conversation regarding the BAJ fitting kit and BAJ's address with the government engineer influenced or was an attempt to influence the award of the contract. This conversation neither had an impact

on the Navy's review of responsiveness of the bids submitted, nor did it provide the Navy with a basis for canceling the IFB. Moreover, contrary to Helmet's unsubstantiated allegation, there is no indication that appropriated funds were used to pay the Gentex employee's salary for his telephone call on this fixed-price competition. Finally, even assuming the phone call was intended to influence the award, it was not a payment to a person to influence a contract that was required to be disclosed in Gentex's step two bid, since the communication to the agency was by a "regularly employed" Gentex employee. Thus, there is no merit to Helmet's contention that a Byrd Amendment violation occurred.

Helmet's Unlimited, 71 Comp. Gen. 281, 287 1992 WL 52430.

The law's prohibitions on lobbying are limited; only consultants, and not regular employees, are covered by the prohibition.

> The Air Force needed maintenance services for F-15 fighter jets in Europe. It issued a solicitation requiring the provider of the services to be located within the European theatre, which was defined to include a number of European countries. The definition did not include Israel. Israel Aircraft Industries (IAI), which was wholly owned by the Israeli government, submitted an offer which called for the work to be done in Israel, even though the solicitation did not include Israel in the European theatre. One month later, Congress passed a law which in effect eliminated the geographic restriction by providing that Israel was to be considered to be in the European theatre. Several months later, the Air Force amended the solicitation by making Israel an accepted site of work under the contract.
>
> The Air Force eventually awarded the contract to IAI. A disappointed offeror, Construcciones Aeronauticas, S.A., protested. It argued that IAI had violated the Byrd Amendment by not disclosing that IAI had made lobbying expenditures. IAI conceded that representatives of the Israeli government contacted representatives of the U.S. government to get their support for the law making Israel part of the European theatre. But it denied that it or the Israel government paid any consultants or third-parties to lobby for the bill.

> GAO dismissed the protest. It recognized that this solicitation "may well have been the one that Congress had in mind" in declaring Israel part of the European theatre. It also acknowledged that the government of Israel may have influenced the passage of that law. But GAO pointed out that the Byrd Amendment applies only to payments to consultants or nonemployees. Regularly employed officers or employees are not covered by the law. Since IAI did not employ any consultants to lobby for the European theatre law, it did not violate the Byrd Amendment.
> Construcciones Aeronauticas, S.A., Comp. Gen. Dec. B-244717, B-244717.2, November 14, 1991.

NOTES

1. Online at http://news.findlaw.com/cnn/docs/mstewart/usmspb10504sind.html (accessed June 2008).
2. Online at http://www.allaboutquitam.org/DOJstats.fy2004.pdf (accessed June 2008).

PART IV
Preventing and Uncovering Fraud

Having looked at contractor ethics compliance programs, the FAR rules applicable to contract solicitation and administration, and the federal statutes and nonprocurement regulations that govern federal employee and government contractor conduct, we now turn in Part IV to ways procurement personnel can become more skilled at identifying fraudulent activities.

Chapter 7 addresses indicators of fraud and describes in detail what procurement personnel should look for in identifying possible fraudulent activities. As a basis for identifying these activities, procurement personnel need to be familiar with a wide range of rules and regulations that are applicable to all federal employees regardless of whether they are involved in the procurement process.

7 Fighting Fraud: Common Fraudulent Activities

Knowing which contract activities indicate fraud is one of a contracting officer's or contractor's most difficult jobs. Fortunately, the government offers some guidance.

Years ago, the Department of Defense published *Principles of Federal Appropriations Law,* commonly known as "The Red Book," to help DoD personnel identify fraud. In 2001, USAID published a similar book titled *Fraud Indicators.*[1] Much of the information in this chapter is drawn from those publications.

Key areas where procurement-related fraud may occur include:

- Defective pricing
- Antitrust violations
- Cost mischarging
- Product substitution
- Progress payment fraud
- Fast pay fraud.

This chapter concludes with a summary of potential areas for fraud in each phase of the procurement process.

DEFECTIVE PRICING

In September 1983, the Director of the Defense Contract Audit Agency (DCAA) issued a memorandum to DCAA auditors providing guidance related to finding indicators of fraud in the area of defective pricing. Auditors are instructed to refer the case to the proper investigative agency when they find the following significant indicators of fraud:

- Falsification or alteration of supporting data
- Failure to update cost or pricing data even though it is known that past activity showed that costs or prices have decreased
- Failure to make complete disclosure of data known to responsible contractor personnel
- Distortion of the overhead accounts or baseline information by transferring changes or accounts that have a material impact on government contracts
- Failure to correct known system deficiencies which lead to defective pricing
- Protracted delay in release of data to the government to preclude possible price reductions
- Repeated denial by the responsible contractor employees of the existence of historical records that are subsequently found.

ANTITRUST VIOLATIONS

Collusive bidding, price fixing, or bid rigging are commonly used interchangeable terms that describe many forms of illegal anticompetitive activity. The common thread throughout the anticompetitive activities is that they involve agreements or informal arrangements among independent competitors that limit competition. Schemes that allocate contracts and limit competition can take many forms, seemingly limited only by the imaginations of the parties involved. Common schemes include bid suppression, complementary bidding, bid rotation, and market division.

The essential elements of a criminal antitrust offense are (1) the formulation of a contract, combination, agreement, or conspiracy, and (2) the restraint of trade or commerce among the several states.

With regard to the first element, the agreement must be between two or more real competitors. The evidence must establish that the competitors had a common plan, understanding, arrangement, or agreement to fix or stabilize prices, allocate customers, or allocate territories or markets.

With regard to the second element, the evidence must establish that the conspiracy involved goods or funds traveling in the flow of interstate commerce (e.g., materials shipped by common carrier interstate) or affected interstate commerce (e.g., federal funds involved in the procurement).

Certain agreements or business practices are by statute *per se* violations. These agreements or practices, because of their previous effect on competition and lack of any redeeming virtue, are conclusively presumed to be unreasonable and thus illegal. These types of agreements among competitors that would violate the law include, but are not limited to, the following:

- ▶ Agreements to adhere to published price lists
- ▶ Agreements to raise prices by a specified increment
- ▶ Agreements to establish, adhere to, or eliminate discounts
- ▶ Agreements to maintain specified price differentials based on quantity, type, or size of product.

Indicators of Collusive Bidding and Price Fixing

Practices or events that may indicate collusive bidding or price fixing include the following:

- ▶ Certain bidders are qualified and capable of performing but fail to bid, for no apparent reason. A situation where fewer competitors than normal submit bids typifies this situation. (This could indicate a deliberate scheme to withhold bids.)
- ▶ Certain contractors always bid against each other or, conversely, certain contractors do not bid against one another.
- ▶ The successful bidder repeatedly subcontracts work to companies that submitted higher bids or to companies that picked up bid packages and could have bid as prime contractors but did not.
- ▶ Different groups of contractors appear to specialize in federal, state, or local jobs exclusively. (This might indicate a market division by class of customer.)
- ▶ There is an apparent pattern of low bids regularly recurring, such as corporation x always being the low bidder in a certain geographical area or in a fixed rotation with other bidders.

- Original bidders fail to rebid, or bidders are ranked identically upon rebidding, even though the original bids were rejected as being too far over the government estimate.
- A certain company appears to be bidding substantially higher on some bids than on other bids with no logical cost difference to account for the increase.
- Bidders that ship their product a short distance bid more than those who must incur greater expense by shipping their product long distances.
- Two or more contractors submit identical bid amounts on a contract line item. Some instances of identical line item bids are explainable, as suppliers often quote the same prices to several bidders. But a large number of identical bids on any service-related item should be viewed critically.
- Bidders frequently change prices at about the same time and to the same extent.
- Joint venture bids are submitted where either contractor could have bid individually as a prime. (Both had technical capability and production capacity.)
- Incidents suggest direct collusion among competitors, such as the appearance of identical calculation or spelling errors in two or more competitive bids, or the submission by one firm of bids for other firms.
- Competitors regularly socialize or appear to hold meetings, or otherwise get together in the vicinity of procurement offices shortly before bid filing deadlines.
- Employees, former employees, or competitors assert that an agreement to fix bids and prices or otherwise restrain trade exists.

- Bid prices appear to drop whenever a new or infrequent bidder submits a bid.

- Competitors exchange any form of price information among themselves. This may result from the existence of an industry price list or price agreement to which contractors refer in formulating their bids, or it may take other subtler forms such as discussions of the right price.

- Bidders refer to association price schedules, industry-suggested prices, industry-wide prices, or market-wide prices.

- A bidder's justification for a bid price or terms, offered because they follow the industry or industry leader's pricing or terms, may include a reference to following a named competitor's pricing or terms.

- A representative of a contractor states that his company does not sell in a particular area or that only a particular firm sells in that area.

- A bidder states that it is not its turn to receive a job or, conversely, that it is another bidders' turn.

A word of caution: These indicators do not prove that illegal anticompetitive activity is occurring. They are, however, sufficient to warrant referral to appropriate authorities for investigation. Use of indicators such as these to identify possible anticompetitive activity is important because schemes to restrict competition are by their very nature secret and their exact nature is not readily apparent.

Examples of Collusive Bidding and Price Fixing

Common collusive bidding and price fixing schemes often relate to one another and overlap. Frequently, an agreement by competitors to rig bids will involve more than one of the following schemes:

- *Bid suppression or limiting.* In this type of scheme, one or more competitors agree with at least one other competitor to refrain from bidding or agree to withdraw a previously submitted bid so that another competitor's bid will be accepted. Other forms of this activity involve agreements by competitors to fabricate bid protests or to coerce suppliers and subcontractors not to deal with nonconspirators who submit bids.

- *Complementary bidding.* Complementary bidding (also know as protective or shadow bidding) occurs when competitors submit token bids that are too high to be accepted (or if competitive in price, then on special terms that will not be acceptable). Such bids are not intended to secure the buyer's acceptance, but are merely designed to give the appearance of genuine bidding.

- *Bid rotation.* In bid rotation, all vendors participating in the scheme submit bids, but by agreement take turns being the low bidder. In its most basic form, bid rotation will consist of a cyclical pattern for submitting the low bid on certain contracts. The rotation may not be as obvious as might be expected if it is coupled with a scheme to award subcontracts to losing bidders, to take turns according to the size of the contract, or to use one of the other market division schemes explained below.

- *Market division.* Market division schemes are agreements to refrain from competing in a designated portion of a market. Division of a market for this purpose may be accomplished based on the customer or geographic area involved. The result of such a division is that competing firms will not bid or will submit only complementary bids when a solicitation for bids is made by a customer or is in an area not assigned to them.

COST MISCHARGING

One of the most common of abuses found in the procurement system is cost mischarging. This results in large part from the fact that most high-dollar government research and development and production contracts are awarded as cost-type contracts. Because such contracts are paid on the basis of incurred costs, the contractor may increase profits by mischarging. It is important to recognize that the impact of such mischarging is almost always far greater than the basic costs that were falsified. For example, a single hour of labor that is mischarged may result in payments of as much as three times the labor hour rate due to the indirect cost allowances that are added based on that hour.

Mischarging can occur in a number of situations, with a variety of results. It can involve charging labor hours from one contract to another, charging at higher than allowed rates, charging to indirect accounts those charges which should be direct, or vice versa, as well as other schemes. In all cases, mischarging is a serious matter. Even when unintentional or without a fraudulent motive, it undermines confidence in the contractor's accounting and control systems and should raise questions as to the validity of other submissions.

The issue of whether a mischarge was a mistake or a crime usually turns on the intent of the maker. Investigators should examine the issue of intent. Because intentional false submissions themselves are criminal, prosecutors may pursue those cases even though no substantial loss occurs, particularly where the contractor has actively sought to conceal costs. Additionally, to overlook situations such as mischarging from one government contract to another on the theory that it is merely a case of robbing Peter to pay Paul is to ignore the serious consequences of such a scheme. Because cost estimates for future procurements rely in large part on accurate historical cost figures from similar work, the estimates for later work will be tainted by false accounting. Further, moving costs from a government job that is "fat" could prevent an overrun in the case of the former and thus make the contractor appear more efficient than it actually is. This could result in awarding incentive fees or follow-on contracts that would not be appropriate if the true costs were known.

Under cost-type contracts, the government reimburses the contractor's costs that are allowable, reasonable, and allocable to the contract. Those types of contracts include cost-plus-fixed-fee, cost-plus-incentive-fee, cost-plus-award-fee, cost-reimbursable, and cost-sharing contracts. In addition, contract changes and equitable adjustments to contracts are reimbursed on the basis of incurred costs even on fixed-price contracts. Cost mischarging occurs whenever the contractor charges the government for costs that are not allowable, are not reasonable, or cannot be directly or indirectly allocated to the contract.

Allowable Costs

FAR 31-205 identifies costs that are allowable and those that cannot be charged to government contracts. Such costs may be direct costs, such as labor and materials used on one contract and no other, or indirect costs, which contribute to a number of different contracts. Indirect costs are placed in cost pools which are then allocated to contracts on some agreed basis (such as total cost or labor hours).

Unallowable costs include:

- Advertising costs (except to obtain workers or scarce materials for a contract, or to sell surplus or by-product materials)
- Bid and proposal costs in excess of a set limit
- Stock options and some forms of deferred compensation

- Contingencies
- Contributions and donations
- Entertainment costs
- Costs of idle facilities except in limited circumstances
- Interest
- Losses on other contracts
- Long-term leases of property or equipment and leases from related parties are limited to the costs of ownership
- Independent research and development costs beyond set limits
- Legal costs related to a contractor's defense of any civil or criminal fraud proceeding or similar proceeding (including false certifications) brought by the government
- Payments of fines and penalties resulting from violations of, or failure to comply with, federal, state, local, or foreign laws and regulations, except in cases where authorized in writing by the contracting officer or by adherence to contract specifications
- Costs incurred to influence (directly or indirectly) legislative action on any matter pending before Congress or a state legislature
- Costs of membership in any social, dining, or country club or organization
- Costs of alcoholic beverages
- Costs of promotional items and memorabilia, including models, gifts, and souvenirs
- Costs for travel by commercial aircraft which exceed the amount of the standard commercial fare.

Accounting Mischarges

The mischarging most frequently encountered by auditors is called an accounting mischarge. A fraudulent accounting mischarge involves knowingly charging unallowable costs to the government, concealing or misrepresenting them as allowable costs, or hiding them in accounts (such as office supplies) which are not audited closely. Another common fraud variation invoices intentionally charging types of costs which have reached their limits (such as bid and proposal costs or independent research and development costs) to other cost categories.

Material Cost Mischarges

Material is physical inventory and component deliverables. Material includes raw material, purchased parts, as well as subcontractor and intercompany transfers. Labor and material costs are sometimes mischarged with respect to both their reasonableness and their allocability. Numerous cases have been discovered where government-owned material was used on a similar commercial contract but the material accountability records showed that the material was used on a government contract. There have also been cases where government-owned materials were stolen and the thefts were concealed by showing the materials as being issued to and used on government contracts.

Mischarges of materials are usually confined to situations involving raw material or interchangeable parts. Specialized material, such as a certain type of gyroscope, cannot be easily mischarged and go undetected due to its character. For example, a gyroscope for a C-130 aircraft just will not fit on a KC-135 aircraft and would be easily detected as an improper billing.

Labor Mischarges

Labor costs are more susceptible to mischarging than material costs because employees' labor can be readily shifted to any contract with the stroke of a pen on their time cards. The only absolute way to ensure that labor costs are charged to the correct contract is to observe the actual work of each employee to determine which contract he or she is working on and then determine from the accounting records that the employee's cost is charged to the proper contract.

Contractors have devised a number of ways to mischarge labor costs. Common methods of mischarging include the following:

- *Transfer of labor cost.* This mischarge is usually made after the contractor realizes that he has suffered a loss on a fixed-priced contract. To eliminate the loss, a journal entry is made to remove the labor cost from the fixed-priced contract and put it on the cost-type contract. This type of mischarge is very easy to detect but is difficult to prove. The contractor will contend that the labor charges to the fixed-price contract were in error and the journal entry, transferring the cost to the cost-type contract, was made to correct that error. Frequently the dollar amount of the transfer is estimated.

- *Time and charges do not agree with contractor billing to the government.* This accounting mischarge method is probably the easiest to detect and prove. It is a simple matter of totaling the time and hours expended on the cost-type contract and comparing them to the hours billed. For example, the time cards may show that 1,000 hours have been expended on the cost-type contract when, in fact, the contractor has billed the government for 2,000 hours of labor. The difference is obvious and the accounting records (time cards) will not support the billings.

▶ *Contractor labor billings to the government are normally supported by two accounting records.* The source record is the individual employee time card. The other record is the labor distribution. The labor distribution is usually a computer printout that summarizes by contract the individual time card entries. Contractors commonly use the labor distribution to support their government billings. It is relatively easy to falsify a labor distribution, but it is necessary to corrupt the entire workforce to falsify the time cards. Hence, the individual time cards should be totaled and reconciled to the labor distribution at least on a test basis.

▶ *Original time cards are destroyed or hidden and new time cards are prepared for the auditor's benefit.* This is a very successful method of concealing a labor mischarge. Mischarges of this nature are very difficult to detect. They are detected when:

- The hidden time cards are inadvertently given to the auditor.
- Not all the old time cards are destroyed and the auditor finds them.
- Employee signatures on the time cards are carbon copies because the employee's original signature has been traced.
- Time card entries are compared to time records maintained by individual employees (copies of time cards, logs, etc.).

▶ *Changes are made to individual time cards.* A frequent labor fraud encountered by the auditor involves improper changes to the original contract charge numbers on employee time cards. Some of the changes are so well done that it is difficult to tell that a change has been made. In one instance, the change was made so expertly that the auditor could not tell that a change had been made just from looking at the time sheet. The auditor detected the change by running his finger across the entry and noticing a difference in the feel.

Under magnification, the correction fluid used to cover the original entry could be seen. The auditors used a light box to determine what the original charge had been; i.e., by placing a light underneath the time sheet, the auditor could read through the correction fluid to determine the original charge. Making changes on time cards does not necessarily mean that a fraud is being perpetrated. Many times innocent errors are made and corrected. In determining the possibility of fraudulent activity, one should:

- Determine the magnitude of the changes. If only a few changes have been made, then in all probability the changes were made to correct errors. However, if a significant percentage of the charges have been changed, the probability of fraudulent activity is increased.

- Compare the original charge number to the revised charge number. If the net effect of the changes is to increase the charges to cost-reimbursable contracts, the likelihood of fraud is further increased.

- Review the sequence of events. For example, in one case the tail number of the aircraft that the employee worked on was posted to the time card in addition to the contract charge number. The following discrepancies were noted:

    ○ The original contract charge number corresponded to the contract for which work was to be accomplished on a specified aircraft. The changed contract charge number was for work on another contract for an entirely different type of aircraft; i.e., the original charge was to the C-130 aircraft and the tail number was that of a C-130 aircraft, but the new charge was made to the KC-135 aircraft.

- Based on the changed charge numbers, a ridiculous number of employees were working on the same aircraft during the same labor shift.
  - Identify the employee who made the changes, find out why the changes were made and what the employee's source of information was for the changed charge number.

▶ *Time card charges are made by supervisors.* One should be especially skeptical of timekeeping systems where time card labor charges are posted by supervisors. Management can exert pressure and influence on supervisors to accomplish certain goals. The pressure may influence the supervisor to falsify time charges in order to keep higher level management satisfied with his or her performance. An even more serious situation occurs when senior-level management requires the supervisor to record time charges in a manner most profitable to the company. Management might even go so far as to provide supervisors with budgets of how to charge the time for each job. However, if individual employees post their time cards, it would be difficult to corrupt the entire workforce.

When a labor cost is mischarged, so are the associated overhead and general and administrative (G&A) expenses. Overhead costs are allocated to labor costs based on an overhead rate or percentage. Overhead costs usually exceed 100 percent of the labor cost. Therefore, any mischarging on labor rates also affects overhead charges, which ultimately results in a greater-than-double loss to the government. The same is true for G&A rates. In computing the dollar amount of the fraud, the overhead and G&A cost must be added because applied overhead and G&A will probably be more than the labor cost involved.

Examples of Cost Mischarging

An overhead audit conducted by DCAA disclosed substantial cost mischarging by a DoD acoustical research contractor. The mischarging principally involved shifting costs on both commercial and DoD contracts to the overhead category and then allocating the overhead to those contracts (principally DoD) which provided the best overhead rate. A thorough review of the audit work papers disclosed numerous examples of time sheets that had been altered by correction fluid. As a result of the audit and investigation, two senior company vice presidents were found guilty of violations of the federal conspiracy statute and making false statements. Furthermore, the company was fined $706,000 and ordered to make restitution of approximately $2 million; the two senior vice presidents were fined $20,000 each and given six-month sentences.

A major DoD contractor was found to have improperly shifted individual research and development costs (IR&D) to cost-type contracts. The corporation was convicted and fined $30,000. An accompanying civil and administrative settlement resulted in the company paying an additional $720,000 to DoD. The corporation also agreed to major revisions in corporate contracting practices and to increased DoD audit access to contractor records. Additionally, $300,000 in legal costs were disallowed.

PRODUCT SUBSTITUTION

The term *product substitution* generally refers to attempts by contractors to deliver to the government goods or services which do not conform to contract requirements without informing the government of the deficiency, while seeking reimbursement based on alleged delivery of conforming products or services.

When a contract calls for delivery of an item produced by the original equipment manufacturer (OEM), the contractor must furnish that item. The rule excludes even items that may be identical in all respects but are not produced by the OEM. If the contract requires the delivery of end products produced in the United States, then the contractor is obligated to supply items manufactured in the United States. This is required even though comparable or identical items are available from foreign sources at lower costs to the contractor. Further, if the contract requires that certain tests be conducted to ensure that an item is suitable for its intended use and can be relied upon to perform as expected, those tests must be conducted. The contractor's ability to produce an item that will perform within acceptable limits regardless of whether actually tested is not relevant.

Contractors frequently argue that substituted goods or services delivered to the government were just as good as what was contracted for, even if specifications were not met, and that, therefore, no harm was done to the government. There are several important fallacies to be noted when considering this argument. First and foremost, the substitution is usually not as good as what was contracted for. Second, while the immediate harm that the substitute might cause or may have, in fact, caused is sometimes difficult to determine, its introduction into supply channels undermines the reliability of the entire supply system. If, for example, a microchip were in use in larger components that failed, the cause of the failure might not be directly traceable to the inferior quality of the microchip. Third, even if the item is useable, there is harm to the integrity of the competitive procurement system, which is based on all competitors offering to furnish the item precisely described in specifications.

Indicators of Product Substitution Fraud

A wide variety of fraudulent schemes may involve product substitution. Many of the recent product substitution fraud allegations involve consumable or off-the-shelf items. Government employees should be aware of similar problems that have arisen in component parts and materials used in weapon systems, ships, aircraft, and vehicles. Cases have included:

- The provision of inferior quality raw materials
- Materials that have not been tested as required by the contract specifications
- Providing foreign-made products where domestic products were required
- Providing untrained workers when skilled technicians were required.

Product substitution cases sometimes involve government employees. For example, gratuities and bribes have been paid to government inspection personnel to accept items that do not conform to contract requirements.

The potential for a product substitution case is greatest where the government relies on contractor integrity to ensure that the government gets what it has paid for. For example, fast pay procedures apply to small purchases. The government pays contractors for goods based on certification of shipment. Quality assurance is frequently limited in scope and is performed after payment has been made. Thus, small purchases are particularly susceptible to unscrupulous contractors.

In large-dollar-value procurements, government quality personnel often rely on testing performed by the contractor. Falsification of the test documents may conceal the fact that a piece of equipment has not passed all the tests required by contract or has not been tested at all. False entries may also conceal the substitution of inferior or substandard materials in a product. When government personnel actually witness or perform tests themselves, there is always the possibility that what they are seeing is a specifically prepared sample not representative of the contractor's actual production.

Examples of Product Substitution Fraud

A DoD contractor provided false certifications of quality testing for coating on aluminum troop backpack frames. The backpacks were intended for use by military ground troops, and the anodized coating on the frames was dyed light fast olive drab to avoid enemy detection. Inferior anodizing could endanger the lives of U.S. military personnel through the exposure of reflective metal. Investigation disclosed that no testing had been performed and a sample of completed units failed at a rate of 70 percent. The owner of the company, who entered a plea of guilty to false statements, was sentenced to 3 years of supervised probation, fined $6,000, and required to perform 500 hours of community service.

A complainant alleged that a product manufacturer of parts for Army howitzers was submitting defective items which, if installed, could produce significant safety hazards. An investigation revealed that the testing certificates being submitted by the contractor were false. The investigation kept the defective parts from being installed in Army howitzers and kept howitzers from being sold under the Foreign Military Sales program. The corporate president pled guilty to making false statements to the U.S. government and was sentenced to one year of supervised probation; the company and its president have also been debarred from contracting with the government.

▍ PROGRESS PAYMENT FRAUD

Progress payments are payments made as work progresses under a contract, based on the costs incurred, the percentage of work accomplished, or the attainment of a particular stage of completion. They do not include payments for partial deliveries accepted by the government.

Fraud in progress payments occurs when a contractor submits a progress payment request based on falsified direct labor charges, on material costs for items not actually purchased, or on falsified certification of a stage of completion attained/work accomplished.

Requests for progress payments are made on Standard Form 1443 (FAR 53.301-1443). On the form, the contractor identifies its contract costs and certifies that the statement of costs has been prepared from the contractor's books and records and is correct. In addition, the contractor also makes a certification concerning encumbrances against the materials acquired for the contract.

The purpose of progress payments is to provide contractors with a continuing source of revenue throughout contract performance, and to ensure that a contractor will have the necessary financial resources to meet its contractual obligations. Although some progress payment requests are audited before payment, for the most part the government relies solely on a contractor's integrity in making the payments. When a contractor requests payments for costs not actually incurred, the government is harmed in the following ways:

- ▶ The contractor has the interest-free use of money to which it is not entitled and which the government itself may have had to borrow from the public.

- The government may lose the progress payment it advances if the contractor goes out of business and there are no materials or completed products against which the government may assert an interest.

- Honest contractors lose their faith in the system and others, who are less scrupulous, are encouraged to take advantage of the system.

Indicators of Progress Payment Fraud

Firms with cash flow problems are the most likely to request funds in advance of being entitled to them. Progress payments that do not appear to coincide with the contractor's plan and capability to perform the contract are suspicious. They could indicate the contractor is claiming payment for work not yet done.

Another type of contractor fraud in this area is to submit a progress payment claim for materials that have not been purchased. The contractor may be issuing a check to the supplier, then holding it until the government progress payment arrives. Once way to confirm the irregularity is to check the cancellation dates on the contractor's checks. If the bank received the check about the same time or later than the contractor received the progress payment, the check was probably held.

Examples of Progress Payment Fraud

A contractor entered into an agreement with the government to refurbish/overhaul heavy equipment vehicles. The contractor instructed its employees to work on the company's private commercial projects but to use a United States government time card and punch that project. The contractor received large prepayment amounts from the government to support its lagging private business. The government's monies were then used for purposes other than to repair government vehicles. Consequently, the government vehicles either were not repaired or received a few repairs but not of the extent indicated on the government repair documents and were returned to the government as totally overhauled or refurbished equipment. The company president pled guilty to one count of making false statements, was placed on probation for two years, and was fined $5,000. The company was fined $1,000. The company and its president were debarred from future business with the government.

A contractor was awarded a contract to manufacture locking devices for trigger mechanisms valued at $87,000. The former president of the company allegedly submitted false invoices as proof of costs incurred, thus receiving progress payments. The president subsequently pled guilty and was sentenced to 5 years of probation, fined $10,000, ordered to make restitution of $11,000, and ordered to serve 200 hours of community service. The president and the company were debarred from bidding on government contracts during his period of probation.

▌ FAST PAY FRAUD

Fast pay is a procedure that allows certain contractors to be paid for contract work prior to receipt and inspection of the product by the government. In general, the fast pay procedure is limited to contract orders that do not exceed $30,000. The fast payment procedure set forth in FAR 13.4 is designed to reduce delivery times and to improve government relations with certain suppliers by expediting contract payments. The procedure provides for payment based on the contractor's submission of an invoice. That invoice is a representation by the contractor that the supplies have been delivered to a post office, common carrier, or point of first receipt.

Fraud in fast pay occurs when a contractor submits an invoice requesting payment for supplies that have not been shipped or delivered to the government. If the supplies are not in transit or actually delivered at the time the contractor submits his invoice, a criminal violation has occurred because the contractor submitted a false statement. It does not matter if the supplies are subsequently delivered to the government.

Indicators of Fast Pay Fraud

How can government personnel dealing with fast pay identify possible fraud? The most obvious, and sometime most difficult, thing to do is check for the correlation between the claim for payment and the delivery of goods. Since the claim for payment and receipt of goods occur at different locations, communication between the paying and receiving points is required. An employee who becomes suspicious should check with the receiving points to verify that the goods have arrived. Some important things to check for include not receiving the goods at all, receiving the goods later than would be expected if they were mailed when claimed, and receiving nonconforming goods. The last sometimes occurs because the contractor has lost the incentive to perform fully to contract specifications after it has been paid.

Personnel should also be alert for indications that the invoice submitted by the contractor is forged or altered in some way to make it appear that the goods were sent. Information on the invoice such as shipment on a weekend or holiday may raise questions.

Example of Fast Pay Fraud

A GSA supply center received a shipment of bricks instead of several electronic connection plugs allegedly shipped by the contractor. A review of 13 other contracts held by the contractor identified 8 for which payment had been made but shipments were not received at various supply centers across the country. The value of the eight undelivered shipments was over $45,000. The contractor provided alleged proof of shipment and tracer documents which, on further investigation, were determined to be forgeries. The president of the company pled guilty to three counts each of mail fraud and false claims. He was sentenced to concurrent three-year prison terms, ordered to pay $35,915 plus interest as restitution, and fined $3,000.

SUMMARY OF POTENTIAL AREAS FOR FRAUD IN THE GOVERNMENT PROCUREMENT PROCESS

Each phase of the procurement process involves the potential for fraud. The following examples have been taken from a number of sources, including the Federal Contracts Report (FCR), the DoD publication *Indicators of Fraud in DoD Procurement,* and news sources.

Contract Formation

Fraud can occur at many steps during the contract formation stage.

Fraud in Identifying the Government's Need for Goods and Services

Fraud at this stage may be indicated by:

- ▶ A conclusion that the government needs specified goods or services when in fact it does not. For example, stocks of the good are already sufficient or, the other extreme, the good has been declared excess or surplus so no need exists.

- ▶ Intentionally writing the spec around a particular good without regard to whether other suppliers could provide the same product at a lower price.

Fraud in the Pre-Solicitation Phase

Fraud at this stage may consist of the release of insider information to a bidder. In one case, ITT pleaded guilty to conspiracy to defraud the government because one of its marketing representatives had obtained government price estimates prior to bids being solicited; the employee had given procurement officials illegal gratuities, including lunches and golf and tickets to sport events. 50 FCR 732 (1988).

Fraud in the pre-solicitation stage may be indicated by:

- Splitting requirements so that competing contractors can get their fair share

- Collusion between a potential bidder and procurement personnel to write a vague spec so that after award the collusive bidder can seek an increase in contract price to provide the government what it really needs; the DoD IG report describes how one bidder had prepared pre-award a cost-enhancement plan identifying all the changes he would make in order to double the price of the contract

- Unnecessary sole source/non-competitive solicitations

- Providing bidders with any inside information

- Overly restrictive specifications.

Fraud in the Solicitation Phase

In *Creative Systems Electronics, Inc.*, GSBCA No. 8833-P, (1987), 87-2 BCA, ¶ 19,819, the Board dismissed the protest for fraud in the bidding process upon learning of the alteration in the descriptive literature by the protester, who submitted the altered material in an attempt to show that his bid was responsive.

Fraud at the solicitation stage may be indicated by:

- Exclusion of qualified bidders
- Failure to amend a solicitation to include necessary changes or clarifications; telling one bidder that changes can be made after award
- Use of obscure publications to publicize procurement or publishing notice during holiday periods
- Referring bidders to a specific subcontractor, expert, or source of supply
- Withdrawal of the low bidder, who later becomes a subcontractor to the higher bidder, who gets the contract
- Falsification of documents to make a late bid appear timely.

Fraud in the Award of the Contract

Fraud was found where two companies concealed the fact that they were ineligible for small business set-aside contracts yet bid on them nonetheless. They admitted that they had formed a joint venture one day before the bids on the set-aside were submitted. They paid the government $750,000 to settle the case. 50 FCR 440 (1988).

Fraud at this stage may be indicated by:

- Losing the proposal of an outsider seeking to get involved in a specific line of work
- Accepting non-responsive bids from preferred contractors
- Allowing low bidders to withdraw without justification
- Failure to forfeit bid bonds when a contractor withdraws improperly
- Awards made that include items not in the solicitation.

Fraud in the Negotiation of a Contract

Fraud may be indicated by:

- Failure to get certified cost and pricing data
- Failure to get current information on the bidder's record of business ethics and integrity
- Back-dated or after-the-fact justifications in the contract file
- Approval of less than full and open competition by an unauthorized person or for an improper reason
- Release to bidder(s) of government price estimate.

Contract Administration

Likewise, fraud can occur in many aspects of contract administration.

Fraud in Defective Pricing

Fraud was found where one contractor submitted false and fraudulent cost data in representing to the government that the company had paid more for material than the company actually had paid. It would use blank quotation forms from material vendors and also would quote catalog or book prices when it actually paid less than those amounts. The company agreed to pay $15 million in fines and restitution to the government.

Fraud in pricing may be indicated by:

- Indications of falsification or alteration of supporting documentation
- Distortion of overhead accounts by transferring accounts that have an impact on government contracts

- Protracted delay in release of data to the government to preclude possible price reductions.

Fraud in Cost Mischarging

Contractors sometimes mischarge labor and materials or unallowable costs to government contracts. A company official tried to cut his losses on fixed-price contracts by shifting costs to cost-reimbursement contracts. He ultimately received a 25-year suspended sentence and was fined $7,500. *Government Contract Fraud*, Elmer, Swennen, and Beizer, 23-10 (1985).

Fraud may be indicated by:

- Charging costs that have reached their limits (B&P costs, IR&D costs) to other cost categories
- Time card charges that are made by supervisors
- Time and charges that do not agree with billings to the government.

Fraud in Product Substitution

A DoD contractor had a contract with the Army to provide rifle barrels for the M-14. He provided acceptable barrels to the DoD inspectors but then shipped non-conforming barrels to DoD depots. The company was fined $400,000 and suspended.

Fraud may be indicated by:

- Use of inferior-quality raw materials
- Use of materials that have not been tested as required by contract provisions
- Providing untrained workers where skilled workers were required.

Fraud in Progress Payments

A contractor agreed to overhaul government heavy equipment. He told his employees to work on the company's lagging private commercial projects and charge the time to the government project for purposes of receiving progress payments. He pled guilty and received 2 years probation and a $5,000 fine.

Fraud may be indicated by:

- Firms with cash flow problems requesting progress payments
- Progress payments that do not appear to coincide with the contractor's plan and capacity
- Submitting a progress payment claim for materials that have not yet been purchased.

Fraud in Fast Pay Procedure

A DoD supply center received a shipment of bricks instead of electrical connectors allegedly shipped by the contractor. A review of records indicated that he had received payment for a number of shipments which had in actuality not been made. The contractor received concurrent three-year prison terms, was ordered to pay $35,915 as restitution, and was fined $3,000.

Fraud may be indicated by:

- Receiving the goods later than would be expected if they were mailed when the contractor claimed they were
- Forgeries or alterations in shipping records.

NOTES

1. Online at http://www.usaid.gov/oig/hotline/fraud_awareness_handbook_052201.pdf (accessed June 2008).

APPENDIX A

Final Rules: Federal Acquisition Regulation and FAR Case 2006-007, Contractor Code of Business Ethics and Conduct

RULES and REGULATIONS

DEPARTMENT OF DEFENSE

GENERAL SERVICES ADMINISTRATION

NATIONAL AERONAUTICS AND SPACE ADMINISTRATION

48 CFR Parts 2, 3, and 52

[FAC 2005-22; FAR Case 2006-007; Item II; Docket 2007-0001; Sequence 1]

RIN 9000-AK67

Federal Acquisition Regulation; FAR Case 2006-007, Contractor Code of Business Ethics and Conduct

Friday, November 23, 2007

AGENCIES: Department of Defense (DoD), General Services Administration (GSA), and National Aeronautics and Space Administration (NASA).

*65873 ACTION: Final rule.

SUMMARY: The Civilian Agency Acquisition Council and the Defense Acquisition Regulations Council (Councils) have agreed on a final rule amending the Federal Acquisition Regulation (FAR) to address the requirements for a contractor code of business ethics and conduct and the display of Federal agency Office of the Inspector General (OIG) Fraud Hotline Posters.

DATES: Effective Date: December 24, 2007

FOR FURTHER INFORMATION CONTACT: Mr. Ernest Woodson, Procurement Analyst, at (202) 501-3775 for clarification of content. For information pertaining to status or publication schedules, contact the FAR Secretariat at (202) 501-4755. Please cite FAC 2005-22, FAR case 2006-007.

SUPPLEMENTARY INFORMATION:

A. Background

DoD, GSA, and NASA published a proposed rule in the Federal Register at 72 FR 7588, February 16, 2007, to address the requirements for a contractor code of business ethics and conduct and the display of Federal agency Office of the Inspector General (OIG) Fraud Hotline Posters. The original comment period closed on April 17, 2007, but on April 23, 2007, the comment period was reopened and

APPENDIX A

extended to May 23, 2007. We received comments from 42 respondents plus an additional late comment from one of the initial respondents. However, 15 of the respondents were only requesting extension of the comment period. The remaining 27 public comments are addressed in the following analysis.

The most significant changes, which will be addressed, are--

• The clause requirement for a formal training program and internal control system has been made inapplicable to small businesses (see paragraph 5.c.v. and 11. of this section);

• The contracting officer has been given authority to increase the 30 day time period for preparation of a code of business ethics and conduct and the 90 day time period for establishment of an ethics awareness and compliance program and internal control system, upon request of the contractor (see paragraph 6.c. of this section);

• The requirements in the internal control system relating to "disclosure" and "full cooperation" have been deleted, and moved to FAR Case 2007-006 for further consideration (see paragraphs 2.e. and 6.d. of this section);

• The clause 52.203-XX with 3 alternates has been separated into 2 clauses, one to address the contractor code of business ethics and conduct, and one to address the requirements for hotline posters (see paragraphs 3.h. and 10.b. of this section); and

• A contractor does not need to display Government fraud hotline posters if it has established a mechanism by which employees may *65874 report suspected instances of improper conduct, and instructions that encourage employees to make such reports (see paragraph 7.a. of this section).

1. General support for the rule.

Comments: The majority of respondents expressed general support for the rule. These included consultants, industry associations, a non-profit contractor, a construction contractor, inspectors general and interagency IG working groups, other Government agencies, and individuals. Many respondents were laudatory of the rule in general. For example, one respondent considered the proposed rule to be a "good attempt" and another considered it to be "an outstanding, well thought-out and needed policy change." Others identified particular benefits of the proposed rule, such as--

• Reduce contract fraud;

• Reduce waste, fraud, abuse and mismanagement of taxpayers' resources;

• Enhance integrity in the procurement system by strengthening the requirements for corporate compliance systems; and

• Promote clarity and Government-wide consistency in agency requirements.

Response: None required.

2. General disagreement with the rule as a whole.

Although all respondents agree that contractors should conduct themselves with the highest degree of integrity and honesty, not all agree that the proposed rule is taking the right approach to achieve that goal.

a. Ineffective.

Comment: One respondent considers that this rule will not effectively correct the ethics and business conduct improprieties. Other respondents note that a written code of ethics does not ensure a commitment to compliance with its provisions.

Response: There is no law, regulation, or ethics code that ensures compliance. Laws, regulations, and ethics codes provide a standard against which to measure actions, and identify consequences upon violation of the law, regulation, or ethics code.

b. Unnecessary or duplicative, potentially conflicting.

Comment: One respondent views the rule as unnecessary, because it adds "a further level of compliance and enforcement obligations where contractors already are or may be contractually or statutorily obliged to comply." Another respondent comments that the rule is duplicative of other similar requirements. Furthermore, meeting multiple requirements for the same purpose can cause conflicts.

Response: This rule is not duplicative of existing requirements known to the Councils. The rule requires basic codes of ethics and training for companies doing business with the Government. Although many companies have voluntarily adopted codes of business ethics, there is no current Government-wide regulatory requirement for such a code. For DoD contracts, the Defense Federal Acquisition Regulation Supplement (DFARS) recommends such a code, but does not make it mandatory.

Legislation such as the Sarbanes-Oxley Act of 2002 (Pub. L. 107-204), cited by some of the respondents, applies only to accounting firms and publicly traded companies. Sarbanes-Oxley focuses on auditor independence, corporate governance, internal control assessment, and enhanced financial disclosure. Sarbanes-Oxley provides broad definition of a "code of ethics" but does not specify every detail that should be addressed. It only requires publicly-traded companies to either adopt a code of ethics or disclose why they have not done so.

The respondents did not identify any specific points of conflict between this rule and other existing requirements. Since this requirement is broad and flexible, capturing the common essence of good ethics and standards of conduct, the Councils consider that it should reinforce or enhance any existing requirements rather than conflict with them.

c. Negative effect on current compliance efforts.

Comment: According to one respondent, the rule may have a "chilling effect" on

APPENDIX A

current compliance efforts and may create a fragmented approach to standards of conduct.

Response: As stated in the prior response, this rule should enhance current compliance efforts.

d. Vague and too broad.

Comment: Several respondents consider the rule too vague and broad, so that it is open to different interpretations.

Response: The rule is intended to allow broad discretion. The specific requirements of the rule will be further addressed under paragraph 6. of this section.

e. Change in role of Government.

Comment: One respondent fears that the rule will "fundamentally change the Government's role in the design and implementation of contractor codes and programs" because it moves from "the well-established principles of self-governance and voluntary disclosure" to "contractual prescriptions and potentially mandatory disclosure." This respondent states that the proposed rule is not just a minor modification of existing policy. Rather, it "would change far more than the FAR Councils have acknowledged."

Response: This rule does constitute a change. The Councils are requiring that contractors establish minimum standards of conduct for themselves. However, the rule still allows for flexibility and, where appropriate, contractor discretion. The Councils have deleted any clause requirement relating to mandatory disclosure but it will be considered as part of the new FAR Case 2007-006 (72 FR 64019, November 14, 2007).

f. Unduly burdensome and expensive for contractors.

Comment: One respondent thinks that this rule imposes significant new requirements on contractors. Other respondents consider the requirement unduly burdensome for the contractors. They think the rule will be a disincentive to doing business with the Government.

Response: Most companies already have some type of ethics code. The mandatory aspects of this rule do not apply to commercial items, either at the prime or subcontract level. The rule has been changed to lessen the impact on small businesses (see paragraph 11. of this section).

g. Impact on small business.

Comment: Several respondents note the impact on small businesses.

Response: See detailed discussion of impact on small business at paragraph 11. of this section and changes to the rule to lessen that impact.

h. Difficult to administer for Government.

Comment: Several respondents consider the rule expensive and impractical to administer for the Government. One respondent comments on the further paperwork burdens on contracting officials, and that it cannot be effectively administered.

Response: There are no particularly burdensome requirements imposed on the Government by this rule. Review of contractors' compliance would be incorporated into normal contract administration. The Government will not be reviewing plans unless a problem arises.

i. Rule should be withdrawn or issue 2nd proposed rule.

Comment: One respondent requests that the rule be withdrawn. Several respondents recommend significant redrafting of the proposed rule and an opportunity to comment on a second proposed rule that makes important revisions.

*65875 Response: Although the Councils have made significant revisions to the proposed rule to address the concerns of the public, the revisions do not go beyond what could be anticipated from the text of the proposed rule and the preamble to the proposed rule. The changes are in response to the public comments. They do not rise to the level of needing republication under 41 U.S.C. 418b. However, the Councils published a new proposed rule on mandatory disclosure under FAR case 2007-006.

3. Broad recommendations.

a. Should not cover ethics.

Comment: One respondent recommends not using the term "ethics" throughout the rule. Contractors can and should develop and train employees on appropriate standards of business conduct and compliance for its officers, employees and others doing (or seeking to do) business with the Federal Government. However, contractors typically do not teach "ethics" to their employees.

Response: The term "ethics" is a term currently used throughout the FAR (reference FAR 3.104 and 9.104-1(d)) and is not considered to be an unfamiliar term to the professional business world. However, the Councils have modified the term to "business ethics," consistent with usage in other FAR parts.

b. 2005 Federal Sentencing Guidelines.

Comments: Several respondents comment that the requirements of an internal control system should be like the United States Sentencing Commission 2005 Federal Sentencing Guidelines (Ch. 8 section 8B2.1), either by direct incorporation into the FAR or by reference. The proposed rule already included 8B2.1(b)(2) and (b)(3). One respondent is concerned that if they are not identical, businesses (especially small businesses) will believe they have met the compliance requirements of the U.S. Government by following the FAR; this will create a false sense of security. This respondent believes that the FAR requirements fall short when compared to the corporate sentencing guidelines. The respondent also points out that there are no clauses applying to smaller contracts, or to commercial item contracts, although

APPENDIX A | **211**

companies with these contracts are still subject to the sentencing guidelines. Key requirements of the guidelines are omitted from the rule, such as knowledgeable leadership, exclusion of risky personnel, and individuals with day-to-day responsibility for implementing compliance systems.

Several respondents ask for a specific reference to be made in the rule to the U.S. Sentencing Guidelines.

• First, in this area of corporate compliance, it could be confusing if it appeared that the FAR was setting a different standard than the Sentencing Commission and the Federal courts, which implement the Guidelines.

• Second, the Sentencing Guidelines are subject to routine reexamination and revision by both the Sentencing Commission after substantial study and public comment, and the Federal courts in specific cases, allowing for adjustments to this proposed rule without having to open a new FAR case.

Therefore, the respondent believes that the Guidelines should serve as the baseline standard for a contractor's code of ethics and business conduct. By referencing the Guidelines, we would be able to ensure that the Federal Government speaks with one voice on corporate compliance.

Response: The initiators of the case asked that the FAR mirror the DFARS. The DFARS provisions are very similar to the Sentencing Guidelines and are adequate for this final rule. It would require public comment to include additional requirements from the Sentencing Guidelines as requirements in the FAR. The request to more closely mirror the Sentencing Guidelines is being considered as part of a separate case, FAR 2007-006.

c. Make pre-award requirement.

Comments: One respondent suggests making the rule a pre-award requirement, to ensure that only contracts are awarded to firms electing to conduct business in an ethical manner, consistent with FAR Part 9. The respondent believes that once contractors choose to implement the program with employees acknowledging the consequences of violations, it becomes a self-perpetuating program, requiring no additional actions by the contractor other than certification for new awards.

Response: FAR Part 9 (9.104-1(d)) already provides that a prospective contractor must have a satisfactory record in integrity and business ethics as a standard for determining a prospective contractor responsible as a pre-award requirement. The Councils believe that the respondent's suggestion would encumber or circumvent new contract awards which the Government wishes to encourage. Therefore, no change to the rule has been made.

d. Hire certified management consultants (CMCs).

Comments: One respondent recommends that the rule be amended to encourage Government agencies that are hiring consultants to hire Certified Management Consultants or those who ascribe or commit to a code of ethics from an acceptable professional organization such as the Institute of Management Consultants for all Government contracts, including consulting and/or advisory services.

Response: It is the contractors' responsibility to comply with the rule and establish a code of business ethics. The Government cannot endorse any particular business or organization as an appropriate contractor. Therefore, the Councils have not changed the rule in response to this comment.

e. Use quality assurance systems.

Comments: One respondent states that the rule does not lead to future improvements in compliance methods. The respondent recommends that, where possible, corporate compliance systems might be bolstered by drawing on and meshing compliance with existing quality assurance systems. Traditional quality assurance systems, used to capture errors, may be applied to corporate compliance systems to catch and root out ethical and legal failures.

Response: The cost of additional controls may or may not balance with the benefit received and should be carefully considered prior to implementation. While a contractor may elect to draw on existing systems as an additional internal control, the Councils have left the rule unchanged in this regard and do not specifically require use of existing quality assurance systems.

f. Establish rewards rather than punishments.

Comments: One respondent states that the regulation offers an opportunity to establish a regulation that rewards contractors who behave appropriately, contradicting the Federal Government's ". . . mindset to penalize the wrong doer rather than rewarding the desired behavior."

Response: The Councils do not agree that this regulation should include a special "reward" for contractors who behave ethically. The Government "rewards" contractors who perform satisfactorily through payment of profit on the contract, favorable past performance evaluations, and the potential award of additional contracts.

g. Should not be mandatory - be more like the DFARS.

Comments: Several respondents expressed the view that the FAR rule should be modeled on the DFARS rule at Subpart 203.70, which is discretionary rather than mandatory. It states that contractors should have standards of conduct and internal *65876 control systems. One of these respondents believes that the proposal to impose contractual mandates is misguided.

Response: The discretionary rule in the DFARS is no longer strong enough in view of the trend (U.S. Sentencing Guidelines and the Sarbanes-Oxley Act) to increase contractor compliance with ethical rules of conduct. According to the Army Suspension and Debarment Official, the majority of small businesses that he encounters in review of Army contractor misconduct, have not implemented contractor compliance programs, despite the discretionary DFARS rule.

However, with regard to the requirement for posters when the contractor has established an adequate internal reporting mechanism, see paragraph 7. of this section.

APPENDIX A

h. More logical sequence for procedures and clause, and delete opening paragraph of procedures.

Comment: One respondent recommends that the proposed changes at 3.1003 be rewritten in a logical sequence. This respondent also recommended that the clause paragraphs should be rewritten in logical sequence with the alternate versions sequentially deleting the last paragraphs instead of creating the delete and renumber provisions.

Another respondent recommends deletion of the opening paragraph at 3.1003 because following the procedures does not ensure that the policies are implemented.

Response: The procedures section has been completely rewritten to reduce redundancy and inconsistencies. The Councils have separated the clause into two clauses, which makes the second point about logical order in the clause moot. The opening paragraph at 3.1003 has been deleted.

4. Policy.

a. "Should" vs. "shall."

Comment: At least four respondents comment on an inconsistency between "should" in the policy and "shall" elsewhere. Section 3.1002, Policy, states that contractors "should" have a written code of ethics, etc, while the Section 3.1003, Procedures, and the contract clause at 52.203-13 makes the programs mandatory unless the contract meets one of several exceptions.

Response: The inconsistency was deliberate. The policy applies to all contractors but the specific mandatory requirements of the clause apply only if the contract exceeds $5 million and meets certain other criteria. Section 3.1003 has been rewritten as "Mandatory requirements" to clearly distinguish it from the policy, which applies to all Government contractors.

b. "Suitable to" vs. "commensurate with."

Comment: One respondent comments that the policy uses the phrase "suitable to" the size of the business whereas the clause uses the term "Commensurate with."

Response: The phrase "commensurate with" has been deleted from the clause.

5. Exceptions--general.

Comments: Two respondents commented on the exceptions to the rule in general.

- The rule be revised to list exceptions separately.

- The key exceptions to the rule in subpart 3.1003(a) and 3.1004(a)(1) are not consistent. 3.1003(a) exempts contracts awarded under FAR Part 12 from the required employee ethics and compliance-training program and internal control system, or displaying the fraud poster, but it does not list the exemption from having a written code of business ethics. 3.1004(a)(1) clearly exempts contracts awarded under FAR Part 12 from all of the clause requirements.

Response: The Councils partially concur with the respondents' recommendations. The Councils have revised the final rule to--

- Move the exceptions into the clause prescription; and

- Delete the conflicting wording in the proposed rule at 3.1003(a).

a. Commercial items.

i. Concur with exception for commercial items.

Comment: Two respondents agree that the rule should exclude contracts awarded under FAR Part 12. One respondent agrees with the intent of the rule concerning consistent standards of ethics and business conduct for Federal contracts, and the exclusion FAR 12. Another respondent agrees that all contractors should have written codes of conduct as a good business practice code of, but believes the FAR Part 12 exemption should be from the full coverage of the rule, including the written code of conduct requirement.

Response: The Councils note that the FAR Part 12 exemption does include exemption from the requirement for a written code of conduct (see introductory paragraph at beginning of this Section 5.)

ii. Disagree with exception for commercial items.

Comments: Three respondents comment that the rule should apply to commercial contracts. They note that although other Federal agencies currently maintain polices similar to the rule, none of the agencies exclude contracts for commercial services. One respondent recommends that the rule apply to commercial item contracts or require that such contractors should have compliance systems in place, especially since such firms fall under the Sentencing Commission's general expectation that corporations will put appropriate compliance systems in place. Another respondent is concerned that the "errant behavior of contractors" will not stop at contracts awarded under FAR Part 12 and by carving out a major segment of acquisitions to which the rule will not apply, the rule sub-optimizes its intended effect of reducing unethical behavior.

Response: The Councils do not agree the clause should be included in contracts awarded under Part 12. Requiring commercial item contractors to comply with the mandatory aspects of the rule would not be consistent with Public Law 103-355 that requires the acquisition of commercial items to resemble customarily commercial marketplace practices to the maximum extent practicable. Commercial practice encourages, but does not require, contractor codes of business ethics and conduct. In particular, the intent of FAR Part 12 is to minimize the number of Government-unique provisions and clauses. The policy at 3.1002 of the rule does apply to commercial contracts. All Government contractors must conduct themselves with the highest degree of integrity and honesty. However, consistent with the intent of Pub. L. 103-355 and FAR Part 12, the clause mandating specific requirements is not required to be included in commercial contracts.

APPENDIX A

iii. Disagree with exception for commercial items if contract is for advisory and assistance services.

Comment: One respondent believes that the rule should apply to all advisory and assistance services, some of which are commercial items.

Response: The Councils have not agreed to make further distinctions between the types of contracts to which the rule should apply. For the same reasons stated in answer to the prior comment, the Councils do not agree to application of this rule to advisory and assistance services that are commercial items.

b. Outside U.S.

Comment: Two respondents comment on the exception for contracts to be performed outside the United States, mostly from a definitional perspective.

i. Supporting office in the U.S.

Comment: One respondent suggests that the meaning of "work currently performed outside the United States" needs to be better defined. The *65877 proposed rule is unclear whether offices in the United States supporting the foreign project would be required to comply.

Response: The term "performed outside the United States" is used throughout the FAR several dozen times. There is never any explanation regarding possible application to offices in the United States supporting the foreign project. If part of a contract is performed in the United States and part of it is performed outside the United States, then the part performed in the United States is subject to whatever conditions apply to work performed in the United States.

ii. Outlying areas.

Comments: One respondent specifically endorses the exception for contracts performed outside the United States. However, the respondent requests clarification of the term "outlying areas."

Response: This term is defined in FAR 2.101.

c. Dollar threshold.

Eight respondents commented on the rule's $5 million threshold.

i. Should not allow agencies to require posters below $5 million.

Comments: One respondent does not support the requirement at the 3.1003(c) that authorizes agencies to establish policies and procedures for the display of the agency fraud hotline poster for contracts below $5 million.

Response: Federal agency budgets and missions vary and are distinct. Some agencies already require display of the hotline posters below the $5 million threshold. For this reason, agencies that desire to have contractors display the hotline poster should be allowed to implement the program in a way that meets their needs. Therefore, the Councils have not made any change to the rule in response to this comment.

  ii. There should be no threshold.

  Comment: Three respondents suggest removing the $5 million threshold and requiring all contractors to comply with the rule.

  In addition, the late supplemental comment received from the U.S. Government Office of Ethics expressed concern that a specific instance of conflict of interest problems occurred with two contracts that would not meet the $5 million threshold.

  Response: The Councils do not agree with removal of the threshold. Removing the $5 million dollar threshold and requiring all contractors to comply with the rule is not practical. At lower dollar thresholds, the costs may outweigh the benefits of enforcing a mandatory program. Nevertheless, the policy at 3.1002 applies to all contractors.

  The Councils note with regard to the OIG audit report ED-OIG/A03F0022 of March 2007, that the contractor in question did not include the required conflict of interest clauses in its subcontracts and consulting agreements. This is the essence of the problem rather than the lack of a contractor code of ethics and compliance and internal control systems in contracts less than $5 million.

  iii. How is application of the threshold determined?

  Comment: One respondent is concerned that the rule fails to state how the $5 million threshold for the application of the clause is to be determined and questions if the threshold should apply to contracts with multi-years as the option years for such contracts may not be awarded, thereby impacting the total value of the contract award. The respondent recommends that the threshold apply to contracts with one term and only to the base year in contracts with options.

  Response: FAR 1.108(c) provides uniform guidance for application of thresholds throughout the FAR.

  iv. $5 million threshold is too low.

  Comments: One respondent is concerned that many companies have not implemented programs that would adequately meet the rule and that the $5 million threshold is too low. It will therefore serve as a disincentive for many small and medium--sized companies who may not be willing or able to comply with the requirement to implement training and control systems.

  Response: The $5 million threshold is consistent with the threshold established by the U.S. Department of Defense (DoD) for contractor ethics. DoD contracts with the largest number of Federal contractors. Therefore, the Councils have not made any change to the threshold for application of the clause. For revisions made to lessen the impact on small business see paragraph 11. of this section.

  v. Alternate standards.

APPENDIX A

Comment: One respondent recommends that the rule focus on the size of the firm and its volume of Federal work over a more significant period of time, and that SBA size standards and some proportion of the work the contractor performs be used as determining factors.

Response: The Councils have revised the final rule to limit the requirement for formal awareness programs and internal control systems to large businesses, while retaining the $5 million threshold for application of the clause. The clause needs to be included, because it might flow down from a small business to a large business, from whom full compliance would be required. Although the proposed rule allowed contractors to determine the simplicity or complexity and cost of their programs "suitable to the size of the company and extent of its involvement in Government contracting," this left many respondents unsure as to what would be acceptable (see also paragraph 11. of this section).

Comment: One respondent is concerned that the rule does not adequately identify which contractors should be covered by the requirements and suggests that the kind of work and responsibilities of the contractor is a better indicator of the need for ethics rules than the size of the contract award.

Response: As a practical matter, all contractors doing business with the Government should have a satisfactory of integrity and business ethics, irrespective of the work the contractor is performing or the dollar amount of the contract. However, given the volume and complexities of work contractors perform for the Government, it is not practical to apply the rule on the basis of a contractor's work or responsibilities. It is more realistic for the Government to establish monetary thresholds and/or size standards to ensure its widest impact and viability.

d. Performance period.

Comments: Five respondents commented on the 120-day performance period, considering that 120 days is too short, because it takes longer than that to implement a compliance program, including an internal control system. Even if the compliance programs can be implemented in the required timeframe, that leaves as little as 30 days between implementation of the program and completion of the contract. The 120-day performance period operates as a disincentive to small and medium size companies. Some respondents recommend using a minimum of one year for the period of performance.

Response: The Councils do not concur that 120 days is too short. Although on an initial contract it may take some time to get the program established, on follow-on contracts the program will already be in operation. Many contracts responding to emergency situations are of short duration, and are the very type of contract that needs to be covered. The contracting officer is given leeway in the final rule to expand the 90-day period (See paragraph 6.c. of this section).

e. Other exceptions.

Comment: Two respondents submitted comments suggesting an expansion to the list of exceptions.

*65878 One respondent recommends two additional exceptions to the language at 3.1003, to make it clear that the new subpart is only applicable for new, open market, contract awards or agreements. Additional exceptions would include "delivery or task orders placed against GSA Federal Supply Contracts, using Part 8 procedures," and "orders placed against task order and delivery order contracts entered into pursuant to Subpart 16.5, Indefinite Delivery Contracts."

Another respondent recommends that research and development contracts issued to universities and other nonprofit organizations be exempt from the rule. Research institutions uniformly have business codes of conduct and internal controls to enable the reporting of improper conduct as well as disciplinary mechanisms (reference OMB Circular A-110). In addition, the National Science and Technology Council's Committee on Science is currently developing voluntary compliance guidelines for recipients of Federal research funding from all agencies across the Federal Government, to help recipients address the prudent management and stewardship of research funds and promote common policies and procedures among the agencies.

Response: The rule is not applicable to existing contracts. Therefore, an exception for delivery or task orders placed against GSA Federal Supply Contracts or issued under existing Indefinite Delivery Contracts is not necessary.

While universities and other nonprofit organizations may have existing guidelines, policies and procedures for business codes of conduct, there are many benefits of including a clause in new solicitations and contracts. The rule will strengthen the requirements for corporate compliance systems and will promote a policy that is consistent throughout the Government. Therefore, the Councils have not made any changes to the rule in this regard, although the burden on small businesses has been reduced (see 52.203-13(c)).

6. Contractor program requirement.

a. Lack of specific guidelines.

Comments: Various respondents express the view that the rule should be more specific about the required programs.

• Some provided examples of what should be included.

• One was concerned that contractors have increased risk of False Claims Act because when seeking payments under fixed-price construction contracts, they would have to certify that they sought compensation "only for performance in accordance with the specifications, terms, and conditions of the contract", including the new and highly subjective requirements in the proposed rule.

• One recommended that the FAR rule should be held until GAO finishes its study of contractor ethics at DoD.

• Another recommended that the Councils should establish a Government-industry panel to develop a minimum suggested code of ethics and business conduct based upon the best practices many contractors already employ.

APPENDIX A

Response: This rule gives businesses flexibility to design programs. Many sample codes of business ethics are available on-line. The specific issues that should be addressed may vary depending on the type of business. To provide more specific requirements would require public comment. The new FAR Case 2007-006 will propose the imposition of a set of mandatory standards for an internal control system. The Councils will welcome suggestions for further FAR revisions when the GAO finishes its study.

b. Compliance.

Comment: Several respondents questions how the contracting officer would verify compliance with the requirements. There is no requirement for submission to the Government. The internal control system states what should be included. Are these mandatory requirements or is it the judgment of the contracting officer?

Response: The contracting officer is not required to verify compliance, but may inquire at his or her discretion as part of contract administrative duties. Review of contractors' compliance would be incorporated into normal contract administration. The Government will not be routinely reviewing plans unless a problem arises. The Government does not need the code of ethics as a deliverable. What is important is that the Contractor develops the code and promotes compliance of its employees.

"Should" provides guidance and examples, rather than a mandatory requirement. The contracting officer does not judge the internal control system, but only verifies its existence.

c. Time limits.

Various suggestions were made about the time allotted to develop a code of ethics.

- One respondent recommends 180 days for the code.

- Another recommended an extension to 60 days after contract award.

- One respondent states that it takes significantly longer than 30 days to put a written code of conduct in place. In order to be successful, the process should include an analysis of what should be in the code, drafting the code, stakeholder input, publication, and communication of the resulting code. This is difficult to accomplish in less than 6 months and usually requires at least a year to do well.

The same respondents also commented about whether 90 days is sufficient to develop a training program and internal control systems. For example, one respondent comments that compliance training programs must be well designed and relevant to be effective. Establishing an internal-control system also takes significantly more than 90 days. According to the respondent, the rule would yield "cookie-cutter" compliance, devoid of any real commitment to ethics and compliance.

Response: Although the Councils consider that the specified time periods are generally adequate, the Councils have revised the clause so that companies needing more time can request an extension from the contracting officer. The Councils also note that an initial code and program can be subject to further development over time, as experience with it suggests areas for improvement.

d. Internal Control Systems--mandatory disclosure and full cooperation.

Comments: Six respondents consider the requirements for the internal control system regarding disclosure to the Government and full cooperation with the Government to be problematic. Reporting suspected violations of law is troubling and requested more information on the trigger to the requirement. One respondent expresses concern with possible violations of constitutional rights associated with the disclosures.

Other respondents are concerned that "full cooperation" can force companies to relinquish or waive the attorney-client privilege. One respondent requests that the preamble state that full cooperation does not waive attorney-client privilege or attorney work product immunity.

Another respondent recommends expansion of the full cooperation requirement to cover audits. Information received by the OIG may precipitate an audit, rather than a criminal investigation.

Response: The Councils note that the most controversial paragraphs (paragraphs (c)(2)(v) and (vi) in the proposed rule) were not mandatory, but were listed as examples of what a contractor internal control system should include. The mandatory *65879 disclosure requirement in paragraph (c)(1)(i) of the proposed rule was not clear about disclosure to whom. The Councils have removed the disclosure requirement at paragraph (c)(1)(i) of the proposed clause and the examples at (c)(2)(v) and (vi) from this final rule. These issues were included for further consideration in the proposed rule issued for public comment under FAR Case 2007-006.

7. Display of posters.

a. Agency posters.

i. Government posters are unnecessary, if the contractor has internal reporting mechanisms.

Comments: Several respondents do not agree that Government hotline posters should need to be displayed if the contractor has its own code of ethics and business conduct policy and processes already in place to conform to the DFARS rule.

One respondent cites DFARS 203.7001(b), which recognizes and permits companies to post their own internal hotline poster, in lieu of an agency Inspector General (IG) hotline poster, for employees to have an outlet to raise any issues of concern. The respondent believes this coverage is adequate and there is no need to impose an additional requirement to display agency IG hotline posters.

Another respondent states that the rule that requires all Federal contractors to post agency hotlines would deny such contractors the opportunity to funnel problems through their internal control systems and frustrate at least much of the purpose of establishing such systems. One respondent states that companies want an

APPENDIX A | **221**

opportunity to learn about internal matters first and to be in the best position to take corrective action.

Another states that while the agencies currently all mandate that their contractors display a fraud hotline, none mandate that their contractors display a Government hotline. DoD, Veterans Administration, and Environmental Protection Agency currently require their contractors to post their agency hotlines unless they have "established a mechanism, such as a hotline, by which employees may report suspected instances of improper conduct, and instruction that encourage employees to make such reports." Several other respondents recommend that the FAR Councils take the same approach.

Response: Although the proposed rule did not prevent contractors from posting their own hotline posters, the Councils have determined that it will fulfill the objective of the case to mirror DFARS 252.203-7002, Display of DoD Hotline Poster, i.e., display of the Government posters is not required if the contractor has established an internal reporting mechanism by which employees may report suspected instances of improper conduct along with instructions that encourage employees to make such reports.

   ii. Too many posters are unnecessary and potentially confusing.

Comments: Several respondents believe that requiring all contractors to display the hotlines for all Federal agencies for which they are working-- without regard to the number of such agencies, or the contractors' own efforts to encourage their employees to report any evidence of improper conduct--would have several negative and unintended consequences. Rather than facilitate reporting, multiple postings could confuse employees. To which agency should they report a particular problem? Adding agency-specific requirements to existing compliance programs dilutes the impact and message of the existing program and will likely lead to confusion among professionals. A bulletin board with myriad compliance references will be confusing at best.

Response: Each agency's IG may require specific requirements and information for posters. There is no central telephone number or website that serves as the hotline for all agency IGs. However, under the final rule, if the company has its own internal reporting mechanism by which employees may report suspected instances of improper conduct along with instructions that encourage employees to make such reports, there is no need to hang multiple agency posters.

   iii. Responsibility for determining the need for displaying an agency IG Fraud Hotline Poster?

Comment: Several respondents note that the Inspector General Act of 1978 gives the agency's IG (not the agency) the responsibility for determining the need for, and the contents of, the fraud hotline poster.

Response: The Councils agree that it is not the agency that decides the need for the poster, but the agency IG. The Councils have made the requested change at FAR 3.1003(b).

   b. Department of Homeland Security (DHS) Posters.

i. Only when requested by DHS?

Comment: One respondent states that in the Federal Register background and in the proposed language at 3.1003(d)(2) the guidance seems to imply that the display of the DHS poster is required for contracts funded with disaster assistance funds, when and only when so requested by DHS.

Response: This interpretation is correct. The final rule clarifies that it is the DHS Inspector General that requests use of the posters.

ii. Different poster for each event is not best approach.

Comment: One respondent believes that the contractor's own hotline, if one exists, is better suited to providing a mechanism for employees to report concerns than a different poster for each event.

Response: DHS Inspector General must determine whether to use event-specific or broad posters to cover multiple events. However, the Councils have revised the final rule to permit use of the Contractor's own hotline poster if the contractor has an adequate internal control system.

8. Remedies.

Comments: Four comments concerning proposed remedies were received. In general, two of the respondents questioned consistency in application, consistency, and due process, and two were generally opposed to the remedies.

• One respondent asks whether there "should be remedies for non-compliance when the contractor is not required to affirm or otherwise prove compliance, and when there is no adequate guidance for the CO regarding a determination of compliance?" Without guidance, contracting officers in different agencies may make different assessments of the same contractor.

• One respondent "cannot find any rational relationship between the proposed "remedies" and any damages or other losses that the Government might suffer from any breach of the new contractual requirements ethics codes and compliance programs." This respondent strongly recommends that the contractual remedies be limited to such equitable measures as may be necessary to bring the contractor into compliance with its contract obligations to implement certain procedures, and omit any monetary penalties.

• One respondent expressed a similar concern that the remedies "are improper, excessive and unwarranted."

• One respondent requests provision of due process with a proposal to include the following text; "Prior to taking action as described in this clause, the Contracting Officer will notify the Contractor and offer an opportunity to respond."

Response: The Councils have decided that remedies should not be specified in the

APPENDIX A

clause. The FAR already provides sufficient remedies for breach of contract requirements.

9. Flowdown.

*65880 a. Objections to rule also apply to flowdown.

Naturally, those respondents that oppose the rule in general or in particular, will also oppose its flowdown in general or in particular. For example,

• Comment: One respondent recommends exempting this requirement for subcontracts less than one year in length, rather than 120 days.

Response: See discussion in paragraph 5.d. of this section.

• Comment: Another respondent states that this requirement will negatively impact universities, especially given the flow-down requirements for prime contracts. This respondent recommends that research and development contracts issued to universities and other nonprofit organizations should be exempt from this proposed rule.

Response: See discussion at paragraph 5.e. of this section.

• Comment: Another respondent states that the rule has not estimated the number of small business subcontractors that will be adversely impacted by this requirement.

Response: See discussion at paragraph 11. of this section.

b. Rationale for the flowdown.

Comment: One respondent states that there is no rationale provided for this troubling and perplexing flowdown requirement and would like it to be deleted from the rule. None of the agencies currently require any flowdown to subcontractors.

Response: The same rationale that supports application of the rule to prime contractors, supports application to subcontractors. Meeting minimum ethical standards is a requirement of doing business with the Government, whether dealing directly or indirectly with the Government. The rule does not apply to contracts/subcontracts less than $5 million, exempts all commercial contracts/subcontracts, and the final rule reduces the burden on small business, whether prime or subcontractor.

c. Implementation.

Comment: One respondent has questions about the implementation of the flowdown. What is a subcontract--does it include purchase orders? The Government and the construction industry have a different concept of "subcontract." They are concerned that the meaning of "subcontract" is therefore far from clear to general construction contractors and their subcontractors. Are prime contractors expected to distinguish subcontracts for commercial items from subcontracts for other goods and services?

Response: This issue is not specific to this case. Sometimes construction firms think that "subcontract" does not include purchase orders. The FAR does not make this distinction. The intent is that the flowdown applies to all subcontracts, including purchase orders. Prime contractors are expected to distinguish subcontracts for commercial items from subcontractors for other goods and services, not only for this rule but for many other FAR requirements (see FAR clause 52.244-6, Subcontracts for Commercial Items, which is included in all solicitation and contracts other than those for commercial items).

d. Enforcement.

Comment: Several respondents are concerned with how the flowdown requirement will be enforced. One respondent is concerned that prime contractors should not be responsible for subcontractors' compliance with this requirement. Monitoring of subcontracts would impose a significant new cost on prime contractors. Another respondent requests that the rule be revised to clarify that primes are not responsible for monitoring subcontractor compliance. This respondent is particularly concerned about the impracticality of a small or medium-sized business supervising the compliance of major subcontractors.

Response: The contractor is not required to judge or monitor the ethics awareness program and internal control systems of the subcontractors--just check for existence. The difficulty of a small business concern monitoring a large business subcontractor is true with regard to many contract requirements, not just this one. The Councils plan to further address the issue of disclosure by the subcontractor under the new FAR Case 2007-006.

10. Clause prescriptions.

a. Extraneous phrase.

Comment: Several respondents note that something is wrong with the following phrase in 3.1004(a)(1)(i): " ...or to address Contractor Code of Ethics and Business Conduct and the display of Federal agency Office of the Inspector General (OIG) Fraud Hotline Poster".

Response: The extraneous phrase has been removed from the final rule.

b. Alternates.

Comment: One respondent says that what "triggers the insertion of Alternate I or II clause language is ambiguous in the text of the Policy and Procedures sections of the rule and the confusion is compounded when read with the language used in the clause."

One respondent comments that if the contract period of performance is less than 120 days and the agency has not established a requirement for posting at a lower dollar level, there is no requirement to include the clause; in this case Alternate II is never invoked. Another respondent recommends at 3.1004(c)(2) changing "at a lesser amount" to "for contracts valued at $5 million or less".

APPENDIX A | 225

Response: The Councils have decided to use two separate clauses, rather than one clause with alternates. The conditions for use of the alternates were so diverse, that it was impossible to comply with the FAR drafting conventions that the prescription for the clause should include both the requirements for the basic clause and any alternates. Although the Councils do not agree with the respondent (because the conditions are connected by "or" rather than "and"), any ambiguity in the prescription for Alternate II has been eliminated by the use of two clauses. The language at 3.1004(c)(2)(now 3.1004(b)(3)(ii)) has been clarified.

11. Regulatory Flexibility Analysis.

a. Impact on small business requires regulatory flexibility analysis.

Comment: Several respondents note that the rule will have a substantial impact on small business. The SBA Chief Counsel for Advocacy commented that the Councils should therefore publish an Initial Regulatory Flexibility Analysis. The SBA Chief Counsel for Advocacy points out that the minimal set-up cost for the ethics program and internal control system would be $10,000, according to one established professional organization; there would be further costs for maintaining the system, periodic training, and other compliance costs.

Another respondent asks how the finding that "ethics programs and hotline posters are not standard commercial practice" squares with the claim that the proposed rule "will not have a significant impact on a substantial number of small entities". The respondent notes the absence of any cost estimate, or impact on competition for contracts and subcontracts. Mid-sized and small construction contractors would find the cost and complexity of restructuring their internal systems, and continuously providing the necessary training to employees scattered across multiple sites, to be very substantial, and might well exceed benefits of pursuing Federal work. (Another respondent echoes this.) The respondent recommends the Councils undertake a fresh data-driven analysis of how severely such mandates are likely to impact small businesses, including the level of small business participation in Federal work.

*65881 Another respondent comments that the rule may have an unduly burdensome impact on Government contractors, particularly smaller contractors. It may deter small and minority owned businesses from entering the Federal marketplace and from competing for certain contracts.

b. Alternatives. Several alternatives were presented for small business compliance with the regulation.

• Since small business size standards for the construction industry are well over $5 million in annual revenue, the exclusion of contracts under $5 million is not likely to insulate small business from the cost of compliance. Federal construction contracts typically exceed $5 million, and small construction contractors regularly perform them. Instead of $5 million, the requirements should be linked to the size standards the SBA established, and some proportion of the work that the contractor performs for the Federal Government. The construction industry size standard for general contractors is $31 million in average annual revenue. The requirements should be imposed on only the firms that both exceed the standard and derive a large proportion of their revenue from Federal contracts.

- Delay the flow down requirement to small business subcontractors, pending review of data on impact on small business subcontractors (SBA Chief Counsel for Advocacy).

- Provide additional guidance for small businesses on a code of ethics commensurate with their size.

Response:

Exclusion of commercial items. The original Regulatory Flexibility Act statement as published did not identify the rule's exclusion for commercial items. The burdens of the clauses will not be imposed on Part 12 acquisitions of commercial items. This is of great benefit to small businesses.

Reduced burden for small businesses. The Councils acknowledge the difficulty and great expense for a small business to have a formal training program, and formal internal controls. The Councils also acknowledge that the public was confused about the proposed rule's flexible language for small business: "Such program shall be suitable to the size of the company."

The Councils have maintained the clause requirement for small businesses to have a business code of ethics and provide copies of this code to each employee. There are many available sources to obtain sample codes of ethics.

However, the Councils have made the clause requirements for a formal training program and internal control system inapplicable to small businesses (see also paragraph 5.c.v. of this section).

Because the clause 52.203-13 is still included in the contract with small businesses, the requirements for formal training program and internal control systems will flow down to large business subcontractors, but not apply to small businesses.

The Councils note that if a small business subsequently finds itself in trouble ethically, the need for a training program and internal controls will likely be addressed by the Federal Government at that time, during a criminal or civil lawsuit or debarment or suspension.

This is not a significant regulatory action and, therefore, was not subject to review under Section 6(b) of Executive Order 12866, Regulatory Planning and Review, dated September 30, 1993. This rule is not a major rule under 5 U.S.C. 804.

B. Regulatory Flexibility Act

The Department of Defense, the General Services Administration, and the National Aeronautics and Space Administration certify that this final rule will not have a significant economic impact on a substantial number of small entities within the meaning of the Regulatory Flexibility Act, 5 U.S.C. 601, et seq., because the rule does not require use of the clause requiring contractors to have a written code of business ethics and conduct if the contract is--

APPENDIX A

- Valued at $5 million or less;
- Has a performance period less than 120 days;
- Was awarded under Part 12; or
- Will be performed outside the United States.

Furthermore, after discussions with the Small Business Administration (SBA) Office of Advocacy, the Councils have made inapplicable to small businesses the clause requirement for a formal compliance awareness program and internal control system.

C. Paperwork Reduction Act

The Paperwork Reduction Act does not apply because the changes to the FAR do not impose information collection requirements that require the approval of the Office of Management and Budget under 44 U.S.C. 3501, et seq.

List of Subjects in 48 CFR Parts 2, 3, and 52

Government procurement.

Dated: November 16, 2007.

Al Matera,

Director, Office of Acquisition Policy.

Therefore, DoD, GSA, and NASA amend 48 CFR parts 2, 3, and 52 as set forth below:

1. The authority citation for 48 CFR parts 2, 3, and 52 continues to read as follows:

Authority: 40 U.S.C. 121(c); 10 U.S.C. chapter 137; and 42 U.S.C. 2473(c).

PART 2--DEFINITIONS OF WORDS AND TERMS

48 CFR 2.101

2. Amend section 2.101 in paragraph (b), in the definition "United States" by redesignating paragraphs (1) through (7) as paragraphs (2) through (8), respectively, and adding a new paragraph (1) to read as follows:

48 CFR 2.101

2.101 Definitions.

(b) * * *

United States * * *

(1) For use in Subpart 3.10, see the definition at 3.1001.

* * * * *

PART 3--IMPROPER BUSINESS PRACTICES AND PERSONAL CONFLICTS OF INTEREST

48 CFR 3.10

3. Add Subpart 3.10 to read as follows:

Subpart 3.10--Contractor Code of Business Ethics and Conduct

Sec.

3.1000 Scope of subpart.

3.1001 Definitions.

3.1002 Policy.

3.1003 Mandatory requirements.

3.1004 Contract clauses.

Subpart 3.10--Contractor Code of Business Ethics and Conduct

48 CFR 3.1000

3.1000 Scope of subpart.

This subpart prescribes policies and procedures for the establishment of contractor codes of business ethics and conduct, and display of agency Office of Inspector General (OIG) fraud hotline posters.

48 CFR 3.1001

3.1001 Definitions.

United States, as used in this subpart, means the 50 States, the District of Columbia, and outlying areas.

48 CFR 3.1002

3.1002 Policy.

(a) Government contractors must conduct themselves with the highest degree of

APPENDIX A | **229**

integrity and honesty.

(b) Contractors should have a written code of business ethics and conduct. To promote compliance with such code of business ethics and conduct, contractors should have an employee business *65882 ethics and compliance training program and an internal control system that--

(1) Are suitable to the size of the company and extent of its involvement in Government contracting;

(2) Facilitate timely discovery and disclosure of improper conduct in connection with Government contracts; and

(3) Ensure corrective measures are promptly instituted and carried out.

48 CFR 3.1003

3.1003 Mandatory requirements.

(a) Requirements. Although the policy in section 3.1002 applies as guidance to all Government contractors, the contractual requirements set forth in the clauses at 52.203-13, Code of Business Ethics and Conduct, and 52.203-14, Display of Hotline Poster(s), are mandatory if the contracts meet the conditions specified in the clause prescriptions at 3.1004.

(b) Fraud Hotline Poster. (1) Agency OIGs are responsible for determining the need for, and content of, their respective agency OIG fraud hotline poster(s).

(2) When requested by the Department of Homeland Security, agencies shall ensure that contracts funded with disaster assistance funds require display of any fraud hotline poster applicable to the specific contract. As established by the agency OIG, such posters may be displayed in lieu of, or in addition to, the agency's standard poster.

48 CFR 3.1004

3.1004 Contract clauses.

Unless the contract is for the acquisition of a commercial item under part 12 or will be performed entirely outside the United States--

(a) Insert the clause at FAR 52.203-13, Contractor Code of Business Ethics and Conduct, in solicitations and contracts if the value of the contract is expected to exceed $5,000,000 and the performance period is 120 days or more.

(b)(1) Insert the clause at FAR 52.203-14, Display of Hotline Poster(s), if--

(i) The contract exceeds $5,000,000 or a lesser amount established by the agency; and

(ii)(A) The agency has a fraud hotline poster; or

(B) The contract is funded with disaster assistance funds.

(2) In paragraph (b)(3) of the clause, the contracting officer shall--

(i) Identify the applicable posters; and

(ii) Insert the website link(s) or other contact information for obtaining the agency and/or Department of Homeland Security poster.

(3) In paragraph (d) of the clause, if the agency has established policies and procedures for display of the OIG fraud hotline poster at a lesser amount, the contracting officer shall replace "$5,000,000" with the lesser amount that the agency has established.

PART 52--SOLICITATION PROVISIONS AND CONTRACT CLAUSES

48 CFR 52.203-13

48 CFR 52.203-14

4. Add sections 52.203-13 and 52.203-14 to read as follows:

48 CFR 52.203-13

52.203-13 Contractor Code of Business Ethics and Conduct.

As prescribed in 3.1004(a), insert the following clause:

CONTRACTOR CODE OF BUSINESS ETHICS AND CONDUCT (DEC 2007)

(a) Definition.

United States, as used in this clause, means the 50 States, the District of Columbia, and outlying areas.

(b) Code of business ethics and conduct. (1) Within 30 days after contract award, unless the Contracting Officer establishes a longer time period, the Contractor shall--

(i) Have a written code of business ethics and conduct; and

(ii) Provide a copy of the code to each employee engaged in performance of the contract.

(2) The Contractor shall promote compliance with its code of business ethics and conduct.

(c) Awareness program and internal control system for other than small businesses. This paragraph (c) does not apply if the Contractor has represented itself as a

APPENDIX A | **231**

small business concern pursuant to the award of this contract. The Contractor shall establish within 90 days after contract award, unless the Contracting Officer establishes a longer time period--

(1) An ongoing business ethics and business conduct awareness program; and

(2) An internal control system.

(i) The Contractor's internal control system shall--

(A) Facilitate timely discovery of improper conduct in connection with Government contracts; and

(B) Ensure corrective measures are promptly instituted and carried out.

(ii) For example, the Contractor's internal control system should provide for--

(A) Periodic reviews of company business practices, procedures, policies, and internal controls for compliance with the Contractor's code of business ethics and conduct and the special requirements of Government contracting;

(B) An internal reporting mechanism, such as a hotline, by which employees may report suspected instances of improper conduct, and instructions that encourage employees to make such reports;

(C) Internal and/or external audits, as appropriate; and

(D) Disciplinary action for improper conduct.

(d) Subcontracts. The Contractor shall include the substance of this clause, including this paragraph (d), in subcontracts that have a value in excess of $5,000,000 and a performance period of more than 120 days, except when the subcontract--

(1) Is for the acquisition of a commercial item; or

(2) Is performed entirely outside the United States.

(End of clause)

                          48 CFR 52.203-14

52.203-14 Display of Hotline Poster(s).

As prescribed in 3.1004(b), insert the following clause:

DISPLAY OF HOTLINE POSTER(S) (DEC 2007)

(a) Definition.

United States, as used in this clause, means the 50 States, the District of Columbia, and outlying areas.

(b) Display of fraud hotline poster(s). Except as provided in paragraph (c)--

(1) During contract performance in the United States, the Contractor shall prominently display in common work areas within business segments performing work under this contract and at contract work sites--

(i) Any agency fraud hotline poster or Department of Homeland Security (DHS) fraud hotline poster identified in paragraph (b)(3) of this clause; and

(ii) Any DHS fraud hotline poster subsequently identified by the Contracting Officer.

(2) Additionally, if the Contractor maintains a company website as a method of providing information to employees, the Contractor shall display an electronic version of the poster(s) at the website.

(3) Any required posters may be obtained as follows:

Poster(s)   Obtain from

------------------   ------------------
------------------   ------------------
(Contracting Officer shall insert-- (i) Appropriate agency name(s) and/or title of applicable Department of Homeland Security fraud hotline poster); and

(ii) The website(s) or other contact information for obtaining the poster(s).)

(c) If the Contractor has implemented a business ethics and conduct awareness program, including a reporting mechanism, such as a hotline poster, then the Contractor need not display any agency fraud hotline posters as required in paragraph (b) of this clause, other than any required DHS posters.

(d) Subcontracts. The Contractor shall include the substance of this clause, including this paragraph (d), in all subcontracts that exceed $5,000,000, except when the subcontract--

(1) Is for the acquisition of a commercial item; or

(2) Is performed entirely outside the United States.

(End of clause)

[FR Doc. 07-5800 Filed 11-21-07; 8:45 am]

BILLING CODE 6820-EP-S

72 FR 65873-01, 2007 WL 4139114 (F.R.)

APPENDIX B

Proposed Rules: Federal Acquisition Regulation and FAR Case 2006-007, Contractor Compliance Program and Integrity Reporting

RULES and REGULATIONS

DEPARTMENT OF DEFENSE

GENERAL SERVICES ADMINISTRATION

NATIONAL AERONAUTICS AND SPACE ADMINISTRATION

48 CFR Parts 2, 3, 9, 42 and 52

[FAC 2005-28; FAR Case 2007-006; Item I; Docket 2007-001; Sequence 11]

RIN 9000-AK80

Federal Acquisition Regulation; FAR Case 2007-006, Contractor Business Ethics Compliance Program and Disclosure Requirements

Wednesday, November 12, 2008

AGENCIES: Department of Defense (DoD), General Services Administration (GSA), and National Aeronautics and Space Administration (NASA).

67064 ACTION: Final rule.

SUMMARY: The Civilian Agency Acquisition Council and the Defense Acquisition Regulations Council (Councils) have agreed on a final rule amending the Federal Acquisition Regulation (FAR) to amplify the requirements for a contractor code of business ethics and conduct, an internal control system, and disclosure to the Government of certain violations of criminal law, violations of the civil False Claims Act, or significant overpayments. This final rule implements Pub. L. 110-252, Title VI, Chapter 1.

DATES: Effective Date: December 12, 2008.

  Applicability: The Contractor's Internal Control System shall be established within 90 days after contract award, unless the Contracting Officer establishes a longer time period (See FAR 52.203-13(c)). The Internal Control System is not required for small businesses or for commercial item contracts.

FOR FURTHER INFORMATION CONTACT: Mr. Ernest Woodson, Procurement Analyst, at (202) 501-3775 for clarification of content. For information pertaining to status or publication schedules, contact the FAR Secretariat at (202) 501-4755. Please cite FAC 2005-28, FAR case 2007-006.

SUPPLEMENTARY INFORMATION:

Table of Contents

A. Background

B. Discussion and Analysis

1. Interrelationship of previous final rule, first proposed rule, second proposed rule, and new statute.

APPENDIX B

2. Mandatory standards for internal control system.

3. Mandatory disclosure to the OIG.

4. Full Cooperation.

5. Suspension/Debarment.

6. Extend to violation of civil False Claims Act.

7. Application to acquisition of commercial items.

8. Application to contracts to be performed outside the United States.

9. Other applicability issues.

10. Additional recommendations.

11. Regulatory Flexibility Act concerns.

12. Paperwork Reduction Act (PRA).

13. E.O. 12866.

C. Regulatory Flexibility Act

D. Paperwork Reduction Act

67065 A. Background

This case is in response to a request to the Office of Federal Procurement Policy from the Department of Justice, dated May 23, 2007, and the Close the Contractor Fraud Loophole Act, Public Law 110-252, Title VI, Chapter 1. This final rule amends the Federal Acquisition Regulation to require Government contractors to--

• Establish and maintain specific internal controls to detect and prevent improper conduct in connection with the award or performance of any Government contract or subcontract; and

• Timely disclose to the agency Office of the Inspector General, with a copy to the contracting officer, whenever, in connection with the award, performance, or closeout of a Government contract performed by the contractor or a subcontract awarded thereunder, the contractor has credible evidence of a violation of Federal criminal law involving fraud, conflict of interest, bribery, or gratuity violations found in Title 18 of the United States Code; or a violation of the civil False Claims Act (31 U.S.C. 3729-3733).

• The rule also provides as cause for suspension or debarment, knowing failure by a principal, until 3 years after final payment on any Government contract awarded to the contractor, to timely disclose to the Government, in connection with the award, performance, or closeout of the contract or a subcontract thereunder, credible evidence of--

A. Violation of Federal criminal law involving fraud, conflict of interest, bribery, or gratuity violations found in Title 18 of the United States Code;

B. Violation of the civil False Claims Act; or

C. Significant overpayment(s) on the contract, other than overpayments resulting from contract financing payments as defined in FAR 32.001, Definitions.

DoD, GSA, and NASA published a proposed rule in the Federal Register at 72 FR 64019, November 14, 2007, entitled "Contractor Compliance Program and Integrity Reporting." The public comment period closed on January 14, 2008. (This was a follow-on case to the final rule under FAC 2005-22, FAR case 2006- 007 that was published in the Federal Register at 72 FR 65868, November 23, 2007, effective December 24, 2007.) A second proposed rule was published in the Federal Register at 73 FR 28407, May 16, 2008, entitled "Contractor Compliance Program and Integrity Reporting." The public comment period on the second proposed rule closed on July 15, 2008.

On June 30, 2008, the Close the Contractor Fraud Loophole Act (Pub. L. 110-252, Title VI, Chapter 1) was enacted as part of the Supplemental Appropriations Act, 2008. This Act requires revision to the FAR within 180 days of enactment, pursuant to 2007-006, "or any follow-on FAR case to include provisions that require timely notification by Federal contractors of violations of Federal criminal law or overpayments in connection with the award or performance of covered contracts or subcontracts, including those performed outside the United States and those for commercial items." The statute also defines a covered contract to mean "any contract in an amount greater than $5,000,000 and more than 120 days in duration."

First proposed rule. The first proposed rule, published in the Federal Register on November 14, 2007, proposed the following:

1. New causes for suspension/debarment. A contractor may be suspended and/or debarred for knowing failure to timely disclose--

- An overpayment on a Government contract; or

- A violation of Federal criminal law in connection with the award or performance of any Government contract or subcontract.

2. Changes to the requirement for a code of business ethics and conduct (52.203-XX).

- Amplify the requirement to promote compliance with the code of business ethics.

- Require timely disclosure to the agency Office of the Inspector General (OIG), with a copy to the contracting officer, whenever the contractor has reasonable grounds to suspect a violation of criminal law in connection with the award or performance of the contract or any subcontract thereunder.

APPENDIX B

3. Mandatory requirements for internal control system based on U.S. Sentencing Guidelines (USSG).

- Provide more detail with regard to the ongoing business ethics awareness and compliance program (see 52.203-XX paragraph(c)(1)).

- Make all the stated elements of the internal control system mandatory, rather than examples (see 52.203-XX (c)(2)(ii)).

A. Add a new paragraph requiring assignment of responsibility within the organization for the ethics awareness and compliance program and internal control system.

B. Require reasonable efforts not to include as principals individuals who have engaged in illegal conduct or conduct otherwise in conflict with the contractor's code of business ethics and conduct.

C. Provide additional detail with regard to the requirement for periodic reviews.

D. Require that the internal reporting mechanism or hotline must allow for anonymity or confidentiality.

E. Provide that disciplinary action will be taken not only for improper conduct, but also for failing to take reasonable steps to prevent or detect improper conduct.

F. Require timely disclosure, in writing, to the agency OIG, with a copy to the contracting officer, whenever the contractor has reasonable grounds to believe that a violation of Federal criminal law has been committed in connection with the award or performance of any Government contract performed by the contractor or the award or performance of a subcontract thereunder.

G. Require full cooperation with any Government agencies responsible for audit, investigation, or corrective actions.

Second proposed rule. The second proposed rule, published in the Federal Register on May 16, 2008, proposed the following:

1. Require inclusion of the clause at FAR 52.203-13 in contracts and subcontracts that will be performed outside the United States.

2. Require inclusion of the clause at FAR 52.203-13 in contracts (and subcontracts) for all acquisitions of a commercial item. However, similar to small businesses, a formal business ethics awareness and compliance program and internal control system are not required in contracts and subcontracts for the acquisition of commercial items.

3. Add a new cause for suspension and/or debarment, i.e., knowing failure to timely disclose the violation of the civil False Claims Act (civil FCA) in connection with the award or performance of any Government contract or subcontract.

The first two of these three proposed changes are now required by statute

(Pub. L. 110-252, Title VI, Chapter 1). (As pointed out by one of the respondents, there was an error in the amendatory language in the Federal Register. At FAR 3.1004, the introductory text should have been deleted, rather than showing 5 asterisks, indicating that the introductory text is still present. However, the preamble made our intent very clear and this will be clarified in the final rule).

Rule on Contract Debts. DoD, GSA, and NASA published a proposed rule, **67066**FAR case 2005-018, in the Federal Register at 71 FR 62230, October 24, 2006, regarding contract debts. The final rule was published in the Federal Register at 73 FR 53997, September 17, 2008, as part of Federal Acquisition Circular 2005-27. The intent of this rule is to evaluate existing controls and procedures for ensuring that contract debts are identified and recovered in a timely manner, properly accounted for in each agency's books and records, and properly coordinated with the appropriate Government officials.

One of the following payment clauses should be included in each Government solicitation and contract:

--52.212-4, Contract Terms and Conditions--Commercial Items, basic clause and Alternate I.

--52.232-25, Prompt Payment.

--52.232-26, Prompt Payment for Fixed-Price Architect-Engineer Contracts.

--52.232-27, Prompt Payment for Construction Contracts.

These Payment clauses for years have contained the requirement to immediately notify the contracting officer if the contractor becomes aware of any overpayment on a contract financing or invoice payment. Compliance with this requirement fulfills the statutory requirement of Pub. L. 110-252 for timely notification of overpayments.

In addition, under the Contract Debts rule, these Payment clauses were modified to require that if the contractor becomes aware of a duplicate contract financing or invoice payment or if the contractor becomes aware that the Government has otherwise overpaid on a contract financing or invoice payment, the contractor shall--

• Remit the overpayment amount to the payment office cited in the contract along with a description of the overpayment; and

• Provide a copy of the remittance and supporting documentation to the contracting officer.

Because issues of overpayment were addressed in FAR case 2005-018, the Councils did not include additional coverage on contract debt in the subject FAR Case, except for adding--

• Knowing failure to timely disclose significant overpayment as a cause for debarment/suspension as stated at Subpart 9.4 Debarment, Suspension, and Ineligibility; and

APPENDIX B | **239**

- A cross reference at 3.1003(a)(3) to this new cause of suspension/debarment at Subpart 9.4.

B. Discussion and Analysis

The FAR Secretariat received 43 responses to the first proposed rule. The FAR Secretariat received comments on the second proposed rule from 25 respondents of which 15 respondents had also submitted comments on the first proposed rule and 10 respondents were submitting comments for the first time. Overall, 18 of the 53 respondents were from Government agencies, including many responses from agency Offices of the Inspector General (OIG).

In the second proposed rule the Councils specifically requested comments on three issues:

- Elimination of the exemption from inclusion of the clause FAR 52.203-13 for contracts and subcontracts that will be performed entirely outside the United States.

- Elimination of the exemption from inclusion of the clause FAR 52.203-13 for contracts (and subcontracts) for all acquisitions of a commercial item under FAR Part 12.

- Requirement for mandatory disclosure of violations of the civil FCA (31 U.S.C. 3729-3733) (in the clause, in the internal control system required by the clause, and as a cause for suspension or debarment).

Comments on the second proposed rule that do not relate to these three issues, unless presenting a new and pertinent perspective, have not been separately addressed in this preamble.

1. Interrelationship of Previous Final Rule, First Proposed Rule, Second Proposed Rule, and New Statute

a. Previous Final Rule, FAR Case 2006-007

The first proposed rule under FAR case 2007-006 ("first proposed rule"), proposed increases to the requirements introduced by final rule, FAR case 2006-007 ("previous final rule"), in the ways enumerated in the Background section above. Thirteen respondents remarked on the relationship to the previous final rule, some suggesting changes to the previous final rule as well as the first proposed rule.

i. Like the previous final rule under 2006-007.

- No further change needed. One respondent expressed the belief that the previous final rule is adequate to protect the Government's interest. Several other respondents supported the previous final rule's voluntary disclosure. One respondent questioned the need for the first proposed rule in light of the recent implementation of "more expansive contractor compliance standards in the FAR."

- The first and second proposed rules enhance the previous rule. One Government agency explicitly supported the major provisions of both rules as sound business practices, highlighting their contribution to cost control as well as mission safety.

Response: No response necessary.

ii. Ethics code. With regard to the requirement for a code of conduct, one respondent considered that just having a code is meaningless. Several other respondents also objected to the requirement for a code of business ethics and conduct in the previous final rule under FAR case 2006-007, stating that existing contractor ethics standards work well and that these contractual requirements are redundant, add costs and other burdens, and are likely to generate additional uncertainties.

Several respondents objected to the outdated method of communicating the code, requiring a copy to each employee engaged in the contract. One respondent recommended that it may be more effective to refer employees to Web sites or provide tutorials in person, on-line, or through other means. This suggestion could minimize burdens through the use of information technology, as requested in the preamble to the proposed rule for this case.

Another respondent also objected that many institutions have more than a single code of conduct, each addressing different aspects of conduct that together cover all aspects of conduct that the FAR rule requires.

Response: The Councils do not agree that a code of conduct is meaningless. It can serve several related purposes. For a firm's business partners, including the Government, it provides a basis for evaluating the firm's responsibility, including special standards of responsibility when appropriate. It also provides a basis for internal policy development, for example human resources policies. And when something goes wrong, the code is meaningful for enforcement and for understanding and perhaps incorporating lessons learned.

While requiring establishment of a code will add costs and require effort on the part of entities that do not have them already, the Councils agree with several respondents that those resources are reasonable and justified to mitigate other and larger risks to the success and efficiency of Government projects. Because many entities already have made the investment, the rule will level the playing field in competitive environments.

The Councils agree that flexibility in the method of communicating the code to employees is appropriate, and the rule has been changed to require that it be made available to each employee engaged in performance of the contract. The Councils note that the rule does not preclude having multiple codes of **67067** conduct applicable to different segments of contractors' business lines.

iii. Training.

- Training requirement is too burdensome. One respondent was concerned that the requirements for training could take substantial time away from performing on their contracts to train staff on an unknown scope of Federal criminal law. The Government would incur costs from this activity through delays in the fulfillment of contracts and increased contractor expenses that will be passed along to customers.

Response: The Councils recognize that contract costs are reflected in prices, but do not consider schedules to be impacted by this requirement. By identifying the scope of violations of the Federal criminal law as those involving fraud, conflict of interest, bribery, or gratuity violations found in Title 18 of the United States Code, the Councils believe that the training requirements have been more clearly defined and the contractor's training requirement has been reduced.

- Require training on civil FCA. Several respondents proposed that Government contractors be required to educate their employees about the protections available under the civil FCA. The Department of Justice, Criminal Division (DoJ) suggested that contractors should also be required to include in their "business ethics awareness" obligation, reflected in the proposed rule at FAR 52.203-13(c)(2)(ii)(F), training on the civil FCA.

Response: The Councils do not agree that it is necessary under this case to dictate to contractors what they need to cover in business ethics training. If we highlight education on the civil FCA, or other specific areas, the contractors may place undue emphasis only on those areas mentioned in the regulations. The business ethics training courses may cover appropriate education on the civil FCA, as well as many other areas such as conflict of interest and procurement integrity and other areas determined to be appropriate by the contractor, considering the relevant risks and controls.

iv. Hotline posters. One respondent commented that the physical display of multiple hotline posters in common work areas is impractical and wasteful. Another respondent also objects to using hotline posters on the walls of the institution as being the most effective way of communication at every institution.

Response: The issue of multiple hotline posters was resolved under the final rule 2006-007. The requirement for hotline posters is outside the scope of this case.

b. Relationship of Second Proposed Rule to First Proposed Rule

One respondent questioned whether certain requirements of the first proposed rule that did not appear in the second proposed rule had been deleted.

Response: The preamble of the second proposed rule specified that it included only the sections of the rule affected by the three changes; it was only addressing three issues, not providing a completely revised proposed rule. Therefore, the fact that language in the first proposed rule that would not be affected by the 3 issues of concern was not repeated in the second proposed rule does not imply that that language was being deleted.

c. Relationship of Second Proposed Rule to New Statute

One respondent recommends that any disclosure requirement be limited to violations of the types specified in the "Closing the Contractor Fraud Loophole Act (Pub. L. 110-252, Title VI, Chapter 1)" (i.e., exclude violations of the civil FCA). This respondent also states that the statute does not require the disclosure to the OIG and the penalties of debarment/suspension are not required by the new statute, so should be eliminated.

Another respondent also makes the point that since the new law does not address disclosure of violations of the civil FCA, that requirement should not be included in the final rule under this case.

One respondent notes particularly that the new law does not require the "reasonable grounds to believe" standard, reporting to the Inspector General, or failure to report as an independent basis for suspension or debarment.

Response: This rule was initiated as a matter of policy. Although the new statute reinforces and provides a statutory basis for some aspects of the rule, the fact that any part of the rule is not required by statute does not alter the rationale that provided the underpinning for those aspects of the rule. Each aspect of the rule not required by statute must be considered on its own merits.

2. Mandatory Standards for Internal Control System

a. Minimum Requirements for the Internal Control System

One respondent considered that the previously recommended, now mandatory, internal control practices will be inadequate if they are considered to be maximum as well as minimum requirements. Another respondent considered the establishment of an internal control system that satisfies a laundry list of mandates will be overly burdensome. Another respondent would prefer that contractors be left free to choose to implement the USSG "in the prudent exercise of their business discretion," rather than being required to do so. Likewise, another respondent stated that contractors may want to consider the USSG in designing compliance programs but, absent a statute or Executive order, they should not be made mandatory in the regulations.

Response: The rule does reflect minimum expectations. Competing firms are free to establish the highest ethical standards they consider to be appropriate to the business at hand. This case establishes a framework for institutional ethics management and disclosure and does not prescribe specific ethical requirements.

b. Relation of Rule to the USSG

i. Rule is consistent with the USSG. An agency OIG stated that the proposed rule should benefit Federal contractors. It provides guidance for contractors consistent with U.S. Sentencing Commission guidance on effective compliance and ethics programs for organizations. Compliance with the rule should assist contractors subject to the Sarbanes-Oxley Act of 2002 in fulfilling their responsibilities under the Act.

Response: None needed.

ii. USSG should be incorporated by reference. Several respondents commented that rather than using the ad hoc form of the USSG standards for compliance and ethics program, the actual USSG standards should simply be incorporated by reference. Conformity with the USSG will prevent contractors unknowingly failing to comply with all the USSG although complying with the FAR. Formal adoption of the USSG will create uniform criteria. A respondent recommended that all the descriptive paragraphs in (ii) be deleted, instead inserting: "The Contractor's internal control system shall provide for a compliance and ethics program that meets the standards of the Federal Organizational Sentencing Guidelines, as amended from time to time, United States Sentencing Commission Guidelines Manual: Sentencing of Organizations, section 8B2.1.

Response: These respondents would use the USSG Guidelines, in place of the FAR spelling out the required elements of internal control systems. However, **67068** the Councils prefer to spell out the elements. This lets the contractors know what is expected. The USSG are the source of the FAR text, but the FAR text is intentionally not adopting them verbatim. The procurement regulations are not the USSG; the contractor setting up an internal control system is in a different situation than a company accused of a crime. Some elements of the USSG are not appropriate for a procurement regulation. However, by making the minimum requirements generally consistent with the USSG, the Councils believe that a contractor should be in a better position if accused of a crime.

iii. Essential parts of the USSG are missing. One respondent commented that essential parts of the USSG are missing. One example is the reference to the use of an incentive system in compliance programs that encourages and rewards companies for implementing effective programs, following the model of the Organizational Sentencing Guidelines. The respondent recommends modifying 52.203-13(c)(1)(ii)(E) by inserting after "detect improper conduct" the words "and appropriate incentives to perform in accordance with the compliance and ethics program".

Another example the respondent uses is the standard for effectively responding to violations, and taking steps to prevent recurrence. Without these, a company's program would not be considered effective under the USSG.

Response: The Councils note that the respondent must have intended to cite FAR 52.203-13(c)(2)(ii)(E). The Councils do not want to require incentives for employees within contractors' internal control systems. This is within companies' discretion. The mitigating factors for debarment (9.406-1(a)) already include consideration of remedial action (e.g., (6), (7), and (8)) taken by the contractor.

The FAR does cover responding to violations, and preventing recurrence, in FAR 52.203-13(c)(2)(i), and throughout (c)(2)(ii).

c. Principals

Several respondents asked for interpretation of the clause paragraph (c)(2)(ii)(B) requirement that the internal control system provide for reasonable efforts not to include within the organization principals whom due diligence would have exposed as having engaged in conduct that is illegal or otherwise in conflict with the Contractor's code of business ethics and conduct."

- Is the "organization" the entire contractor, instead of the organization responsible for the code?

- Is the code retroactive to catch criminal behavior in the past?

- Is it only Federal crimes, or state and local as well?

• What about non-criminal behavior that did not violate the Contractor's code at the time?

• What kind of due diligence is necessary--a simple pre-employment questionnaire, or instead a costly background check with interviews of friends and neighbors?

Response:

• The Councils have revised the draft final rule (paragraphs (c)(2)(ii)(A), (B), and (C) of the clause 52.203-13) to eliminate use of the term "organization". This term was a carryover from the USSG. This rule is addressed to the contractor--the entity that signed the contract, and subcontractors thereunder.

• The code of conduct is not itself retroactive. However, it is necessary to distinguish conduct of an employee during his/her employment, from past conduct uncovered during a background check of a prospective hire. That past conduct need not be disclosed to the Government, but should be part of the decision whether to hire the individual.

• Past criminal behavior of any type, even criminal behavior unrelated to contracting, calls into question whether the individual at the present time has integrity and is a proper role model for company staff. This is not a mandate to fire the individual, but to determine whether the individual is currently trustworthy to serve as a principal of the company.

• Behavior that was not criminal and did not violate a business's code as it existed at the time, is not the subject of this rule. In response to this comment, the Councils have revised paragraph (c)(2)(ii)(B) to delete the words "illegal or otherwise." The term "illegal" is too broad and could include even a traffic violation. The Contractor's code of business ethics and conduct should cover the types of behavior that this requirement is intended to address.

• The level of background check required depends on the circumstances. This is a business decision, requiring judgment by the contractor.

The source of the FAR clause paragraph (c)(2)(ii)(B) is the USSG Manual paragraph 8B2.1.(b)(3). The Commentary on this paragraph includes this statement: "With respect to the hiring or promotion of principals, an organization shall consider the relatedness of the individual's illegal activities and other misconduct (i.e., other conduct inconsistent with an effective compliance and ethics program) to the specific responsibilities the individual is anticipated to be assigned and other factors such as: (i) the recency of the individual's illegal activities and other misconduct; and (ii) whether the individual has engaged in other such illegal activities and other such misconduct."

d. Periodic Review

One respondent asked for an interpretation of the clause paragraph (c)(2)(ii)(C) requirement for periodic review of business practices. For

APPENDIX B

"monitoring and auditing", is standard business practice and generally acceptable accounting principals sufficient? What system for assessing the "risk of criminal conduct" would be sufficient? Is there a Government program that is an acceptable process?

Response: Standard business practice for "monitoring and auditing to detect criminal conduct" which conforms to generally accepted accounting principles should be sufficient. The "monitoring and auditing" is amplification of the current FAR requirement for periodic review and auditing, from the FAR case 2006-007 published in November 2007.

One respondent stated that annual audits of research processes may already review compliance with policies for ethical conduct of research funded under Federal contracts. The FAR can acknowledge, through an Alternate to the clause, that duplication of review is not required where reviews under other rules already cover the necessary subjects.

Response: The FAR is not requiring wasted duplication of effort. No change to the regulation is necessary.

3. Mandatory Disclosure to the OIG

Of the 43 respondents that commented on the first proposed rule, 36 commented specifically on sub-paragraph (b)(3) of the clause 52.203-13, Contractor Code of Business Ethics and Conduct, which requires mandatory disclosure, in writing, to the agency OIG, with a copy to the contracting officer, whenever the contractor has reasonable grounds to believe that a principal, employee, agent, or subcontractor of the contractor has committed a violation of Federal criminal law in connection with the award or performance of the contract or any subcontract thereunder.

Six agency OIGs, as well as several Government agencies all specifically concurred with the mandatory disclosure of violations by contractors.

67069 Other respondents, including agency OIGs, while concurring with mandatory disclosure, suggested improvements in the way this requirement is implemented in the rule.

The other 17 respondents that commented specifically on the mandatory disclosure disagreed with this approach and recommended voluntary disclosure.

a. Need for Mandatory Disclosure

Note that the following comments in this section all preceded the enactment of the statute that requires mandatory disclosure, so that the issues are now primarily moot.

i. Major departure from long-standing policy. One respondent stated that this rule is a major departure from long-standing and proven Federal policies that encourage voluntary disclosures. Likewise, another respondent stated that mandatory disclosure runs counter to many established Government processes. One respondent considered the proposed regulation to be a "sea change" in the fundamental approach to compliance followed by the Government. Another respondent noted that in 1986 a proposal from DoD to make fraud disclosures mandatory foundered on "state action" grounds. In 1988, then Secretary of Defense Richard Cheney withdrew a proposed rule that would have governed such programs on the grounds that "to be meaningful, corporate codes of conduct must be adopted by contractors voluntarily, not mandated in procurement regulations (54 FR 30911)". Another respondent also cited a 1996 GAO report on the DoD Voluntary Disclosure Program (GAO/NSIAD-96-21) in which the GAO quotes the DoJ as praising the DoD Voluntary Disclosure Program.

Several respondents cited the DFARS regulations as being a model for voluntary disclosure. Several other respondents stated that many Federal agencies that have considered mandatory disclosure rules have declined to adopt them in favor of voluntary disclosure programs (e.g., Department of Health and Human Services in 2000 (65 FR 40170) and in 2004 (69 FR 46866)).

Response: There is no doubt that mandatory disclosure is a "sea change" and "major departure" from voluntary disclosure, but DoJ and the OIGs point out that the policy of voluntary disclosure has been largely ignored by contractors for the past 10 years. In addition, in that same time period mandatory disclosure has been adopted for banks and public companies and stressed by the U.S. Sentencing Commission and DoJ, as further discussed in the following sections.

   ii. Is voluntary disclosure working? Various respondents stated that the proposed rule fails to demonstrate that there is a need for change based on failure of voluntary disclosure. According to these respondents, neither DoJ nor the Councils have cited data supporting the claim that voluntary disclosure is not effective. One respondent stated that a purported paucity of participants in the DoD IG Voluntary Disclosure Program does not establish a decline in contractor disclosures to the Government sufficient to justify a mandatory disclosure requirement. Another respondent stated that DoJ is comparing the last few years to data from 20 years ago. One respondent cited disclosures for FY 2005-2007 that are relatively level. Another respondent cited the December 2006 issue of Corporate Counsel that voluntary disclosures are increasing rather than decreasing, citing Mr. Mark Mendelsohn of DoJ and a recent report by Sherman & Sterling. Even if there is a decline in disclosure under the DoD Voluntary Disclosure Program, another respondent found that the leap to mandatory disclosure "gives rise to a perverse implication that justification for mandating regulations can be asserted simply because no one has shown that the activity to be regulated is not happening."

One respondent stated that the assumptions about the reason for the decrease are misplaced. Another respondent firmly believed that there is need for analysis of the reasons for any decline in voluntary disclosures. Even if mandatory disclosures to the DoD IG Voluntary Disclosure Program are decreasing, several respondents suggested the following possible explanations:

 • Less emphasis by DoD.

 • Fewer reportable violations.

 • More instances resolved as contract matters, with reports to contracting officers or heads of contracting activities or to audit agencies like DCAA and DCMA.

 • Perception that the Government is slow in processing voluntary disclo-

APPENDIX B

sures.

- Lack of restrictions on use of disclosure reports in criminal or civil actions or in administrative actions against individuals.

One respondent elaborated that there may be fewer voluntary disclosures because self-governance is working to prevent and detect contract formation and contract performance issues before they result in criminality or civil fraud. Reduction in the rate of voluntary disclosures would be an expected byproduct of improved internal processes, enhanced training, better internal controls, and an improved culture of ethics and compliance.

One respondent stated that a number of companies have commented that delays in processing disclosures to the OIG are a significant factor in their decision to report problems to the contracting officer instead of to the DoD Voluntary Disclosure Program.

One respondent suggested other avenues for disclosure that are more relevant to the kinds of illegal activity being found these days, such as--

- The DoJ Antitrust Division. Voluntary disclosures to DoJ have increased as disclosures to the DoD IG program have decreased (see http://www/usdoj.gov/atr/public/speeches/232716.htm#N--1--);

- The Department of State Directorate of Defense Trade Controls. This program has been very successful at inducing voluntary disclosures (see GAO-05-234 (Feb 2005)); and

- Foreign Corrupt Practices Act. Enforcement actions for violations of the FCPA have also grown, again largely due to voluntary disclosures made by corporations (see "U.S. Targets Bribery Overseas Globalization; Reforms Give Rise to Spike in Prosecutions," The Washington Post (Dec 5, 2007)).

One respondent suggested that mandatory reporting should be replaced with a strong voluntary disclosure program modeled after the DoJ Antitrust Division's Corporate Leniency Programs.

Another respondent noted that it is DoJ, not DoD, that apparently believed that the mandatory disclosure provisions were necessary. This respondent interpreted this to mean that DoD is satisfied with the number and types of disclosures being made.

One respondent stated that DoJ should be required to demonstrate that there is an upward trend of criminal prosecutions of the top 100 Government contractors where it was established that contractor principals were aware of violations of the law and made a conscious decision not to disclose those violations to the Government. Similarly, another respondent suggested that DoJ should offer factual support for its thesis that crimes are occurring and being found and yet not being reported voluntarily. One respondent also wanted DoJ to explain why other less burdensome changes, such as improving the existing voluntary disclosure programs, cannot be used to achieve the desired result.

On the other hand, in the DoJ letter of May 23, 2007, DoJ stated that its

67070 experience suggests that few corporations have actually responded to the invitation of DoD that they report or voluntarily disclose suspected instances of fraud. An agency OIG stated that the vast majority of crimes involving contractors that it investigates are not reported by the contractor. Another agency OIG stated that Government contractors are coming forward significantly less frequently with voluntary disclosures. It considered that this mandatory requirement may be the most effective way for the Government to monitor its vendors.

Response: In the DoJ letter dated May 23, 2007, which requested the Administrator of the Office of Federal Procurement Policy, Mr. Paul Denett, to open this case, DoJ states that its experience suggests that few companies have actually responded to the invitation of DoD to report or voluntarily disclose suspected instance of fraud. The respondents do not dispute that relatively few contractors are using the DoD Voluntary Disclosure Program. The contractor groups, in their public comments on the rule, implicitly concede that the Voluntary Disclosure program is not being used and blame DoJ and the OIG. Some claim that informal disclosures are being made to the contracting officers but offer no specific evidence.

Even if it is true that there are comparatively fewer violations now than 20 years ago or that some situations are resolved administratively, there are still significant numbers of violations occurring and being prosecuted that have not been self-disclosed.

Importantly, the incentive to self-disclose Antitrust violations is not applicable. Antitrust deals with the Sherman Act and the Clayton Act, which prohibit conspiracy in restraint of interstate or foreign trade and regulate practices that may be potentially detrimental to competition (price discrimination, exclusive dealing contracts, etc.). Under the Antitrust Division's Corporate Leniency Program, the first company that reports the violation receives immunity from prosecution. That type of circumstance does not apply here.

iii. Existing legal requirements and regulations as models for the rule.

In the DoJ letter of May 23, 2007, DoJ stated that--

• Unlike healthcare providers or financial institutions, there is at present no general requirement that contractors alert the Government immediately as a matter of routine when fraud is discovered;

• DoJ has been careful not to ask contractors to do anything that is not already expected of their counterparts in other industries;

• Our Government's expectations of its contractors has not kept pace with the reforms in self-governance in industries such as banking, securities, and healthcare. Several respondents all considered that for far too long contractors have played by different rules than their counterparts in other industries, such as health care providers and research grant recipients. A Government agency commented that healthcare providers and banks have had such a requirement for many years. An agency OIG commented that in the past 15 years there have been significant reforms in industries such as banking, securities, and healthcare, yet we have not asked the same of Government contractors.

APPENDIX B

In the DoJ letter of May 23, 2007, DoJ stated that the requested changes are modeled on existing requirements found in other areas of corporate compliance such as the Sarbanes-Oxley Act of 2002 and expand slightly on the Contractor Standards of Conduct in DFARS 203.7000. DoJ also noted that the National Reconnaissance Office (NRO) has begun requiring its contractors to disclose contract fraud and other illegal activities.

a. More far-reaching. However, one respondent stated that the proposed rule imposes substantially more far-reaching and draconian disclosure obligations on Government contractors than those presently made applicable to financial institutions by submission of Suspicious Activity Reports (12 CFR 21.11). The financial institution has to report a crime if the financial institution is an actual or potential victim of the criminal activity. Where a contractor is a victim of a crime committed by an employee or another person, the employee's conduct is not imputed to the contractor. Therefore, the corporation does not incur the risk of criminal liability when it reports an employee violation and is not incriminating itself.

According to another respondent, the current laws and regulations are not sweeping and burdensome, but are specific and narrowly focused. The respondent pointed out that the Anti-Kickback Act and Foreign Corrupt Practices Act limit their mandatory disclosure to a very limited class of activity. The respondent also pointed out that Sarbanes-Oxley contemplates internal reporting mechanisms and review mechanisms at the highest levels before any reporting occurs. The other respondent also addressed the internal control certification required by the Sarbanes-Oxley Act of 2002. Sarbanes-Oxley applies to a contractor that is a public company. Section 302 of Sarbanes-Oxley does not require that a public company disclose to the Government conduct it believes may be a violation of criminal law.

Response: Many of the public comments reveal a basic misunderstanding of the existing mandatory disclosure requirements found in the healthcare, banking, and securities areas. Each requirement effectively mandates disclosure of fraud as broad as the particular regulatory issue being addressed can reach. Beyond that limitation, these other requirements are no more limited than the proposed rule, particularly with the further changes in the final rule with regard to the types of Federal crimes covered.

In particular, the Councils do not agree with the interpretation of 12 CFR 21.11. 12 CFR 21.11 requires financial institutions to report suspicious activities committed or attempted against the bank or involving a transaction or transactions conducted through the bank, where the bank was used to facilitate a criminal transaction.

Even though Section 302 of Sarbanes-Oxley does not require a public company to disclose to the Government conduct it believes may be a violation of criminal law, there are pre-existing securities laws and regulations that require disclosure to the SEC. Sarbanes-Oxley does not provide immunity from prosecution for wrong-doing but provides protection against third-party liability with regard to a lawsuit by the persons accused of wrongdoing.

b. Conforming the FAR? One respondent stated that if the FAR Council is relying on conforming the FAR to regulations applicable to other industries as a justification, the Council should state this explicitly and provide a detailed analysis of the regulations in other areas on which it is relying.

Response: The Councils did not rely on conforming the FAR to regulations applicable to other industries as a justification, but merely cited some parallels. The FAR regulations are designed to suit the particular circumstances of acquisition.

c. Particular public need/statutory basis? One respondent stated that current disclosure programs are not instructive. The respondent also stated that these programs are targeted towards a particular public need, and in most cases are the product of legislation that was enacted in response to a particular public scandal or important national need. In enacting statutory schemes, Congress saw a particular need and targeted legislation to address the particular need (Sarbanes-Oxley, the **67071** Anti-Kickback Act, the Foreign Corrupt Practices Act, and banking laws).

Several respondents were concerned that the same justification does not exist for this proposed rule as the cited statutes and regulations. One respondent stated that the Council has not provided a rational basis to explain why such a significant change to the FAR is necessary. The respondent asserted that the proposed rule could be challenged under the Administrative Procedure Act (APA) because the FAR Council has not provided a "rational basis" to justify the mandatory disclosure requirement, nor is there statutory authority behind the FAR Council to issue a regulation providing for mandatory disclosure of criminal acts. The respondent therefore concluded that the FAR Council lacks the authority to issue the regulation (See AFL/CIO v. Kahn, 472 F. Supp. 99 (D.D.C. 1979), rev'd, 618 F. 2d 784 (D.C.Cir. 1979)). One respondent saw this as particularly important in light of DoJ's reliance upon the example of other statutorily-mandated disclosure programs (Sarbanes-Oxley, Foreign Corrupt Practices Act, etc.) as justification for this regulatory initiative. The respondent stated that the mandatory disclosure provisions in the proposed rule are neither the product of specific findings or legislation, nor any perceived critical national need, and thus are not appropriately compared to other existing mandatory disclosure programs.

Response: The DoJ proposed a mandatory disclosure program in order to emphasize the critical importance of integrity in contracting. The public demands honesty and integrity in corporations with which the Government does business. If there is concern that there is not a current public need warranting proceeding with this case, the Councils cite the public outcry over the overseas exemption in the first proposed rule and the recent enactment of the Close the Contractor Fraud Loophole Act (Pub. L. 110-252, Title VI, Chapter 1). The Act requires exactly what the first rule proposed, except that the overseas and commercial item exemptions have been eliminated. However, the rule did not require this legislation in order to have the authority to proceed in this case. The Councils issue rules under the authority of the Office of Federal Procurement Policy Act as well as 40 U.S.C. 121(c), 10 U.S.C. chapter 137, and 42 U.S.C. 2473(c). The Administrator for Federal Procurement Policy may prescribe Governmentwide procurement policies to be implemented in the FAR (41 U.S.C. 405). This case was opened at the request of OFPP. This case is making clear what was already expected. It is not unreasonable or "capricious" to require contractors doing business with the Government to disclose violations of the civil False Claims Act (civil FCA) or a violation of Federal criminal law involving fraud, conflict of interest, bribery, or gratuity violations found in Title 18 of the United States Code that have occurred in connection with the award, performance, or closeout of any Government contract performed by the contractor or a subcontract thereunder. Existing DoJ guidelines addressing corporate prosecution standards, while certainly not providing amnesty, suggest that if a company discloses such violations, the prosecution will be of the individuals responsible for the violation, not the entire organization.

d. Empirical support that mandatory disclosure will achieve the Councils' objective. One respondent stated that mandating disclosure without empirical support to show that it will achieve the Councils' objectives will be susceptible to challenge. The APA requires courts to strike down rules devoid of factual support. Another respondent also cited the APA, and that a rule may be set aside if it is arbitrary or capricious (5 U.S.C. 706).

Response: The Councils point to the testimony from DoJ and various OIGs that the experience with the NRO mandatory disclosure clause has been positive (see next paragraph). The Councils further cite the enactment of the Close the Contractor Fraud Loophole Act (see prior section), which now mandates many of these revisions to the FAR.

e. The NRO requirement. An agency OIG noted that similar contractually imposed disclosure requirements have been successfully implemented by the NRO. According to DoJ, the NRO reports that this requirement has improved its relationships with its contractors and enhanced its ability to prevent and detect procurement fraud. Another agency OIG stated that adoption of the NRO clause resulted in increased and earlier disclosure of wrongdoing and better working relationships built upon greater sharing of information and trust. It also led to the conclusion that it is more effective for a contractor to mandatorily disclose information pursuant to a requirement, than it is for a contractor to be in a position of offering up information that it could be criticized, or even sued, for providing.

One respondent, however, stated that the NRO requirement is not an appropriate model for all Government contractors because it requires disclosure of potential illegal activity related to the conduct of intelligence operations in the interest of national security and thus is not instructive. In fact, according to another respondent, the unique nature of the NRO and its responsibilities are major reasons cited as justification for its disclosure program. Similarly, the other respondent stated that, while the NRO's mandatory disclosure program was not the product of legislation, it was the direct product of an obvious and public awareness that we live in a different world after September 11, 2001.

Furthermore, several respondents cited problems with the NRO disclosure program. One respondent stated that "it is far from clear at this point whether the NRO mandatory disclosure program is or will be productive", citing anecdotal reports from the contractor community suggesting that the program is not as effective as the NRO claims. One respondent cited problems experienced by contractors subject to the NRO OIG reporting clause, claiming that the NRO OIG has inserted itself in the administration of contracts by using the clause as the basis to become involved in all aspects of the contractor ethics functions and corporate investigations. For example, the respondent stated that the OIG has used this clause to investigate, as a Federal offense, matters as mundane as employees who have been disciplined for leaving work early while reporting they were present. The respondent does not believe that OIG agents should be routinely involved in company internal ethics functions and contract administration. The respondent quoted Mr. Paul Denett, Administrator of the Office of Federal Procurement Policy: "The IG serves a purpose, but it needs to be limited to core areas."

However, the response from the National Procurement Fraud Task Force (NPFTF), signed by the IG of the NRO, stated that the requirement for mandatory reporting has worked very well at NRO: The reporting of wrongdoing has increased, comes earlier, and has led to a good working relationship. NPFTF considers that this model can have a similar impact across the Federal Government, and that the situation at NRO is not unique.

Response: Almost all the agency OIGs submitting public comments cite the success of the clause initiated by the NRO OIG as a reason for supporting this rule for their agency procurements.

As to limiting the role of the OIG to its core area, the core area of the OIG is to investigate fraud, conflict of interest, bribery, and gratuity violations. OIG agents will not be routinely involved in company internal ethics functions and **67072** contract administration unless violations are disclosed. The final rule has been revised to more closely focus the situations that must be disclosed by limiting violations of criminal law to violations involving fraud, conflict of interest, bribery, or gratuity violations found in Title 18 of the United States Code (see B.3.b.iii.).

iv. Will mandatory disclosure make reporting easier or better? In the DoJ letter of May 23, 2007, DoJ stated that if the FAR were more explicit in requiring such notification, it would serve to emphasize the critical importance of integrity in contracting. An agency OIG stated that the requirement will simplify the contractors' decision on whether to disclose suspected violations. Likewise, another agency OIG stated that the contractor is in a stronger position when reporting for the purpose of complying with a mandatory requirement than if voluntarily disclosing information, for which it could be criticized, or even sued. Another agency OIG commented that making self-reporting a requirement gives the honest contractor employees necessary leverage over those who may seek to shield the employer when wrongdoing is noticed or suspected.

On the other hand, some other respondents believed that if employees know that everything they report will be passed on to the Government, this may result in less reporting up the chain of the company rather than more. One respondent saw substantial potential to decrease rather than enhance cooperation with company compliance efforts.

The respondent was concerned that the likelihood of severe consequences will necessarily change the relationship of the company and its employees. Every interview will have the potential of resulting in employees being reported. It may be that investigative targets may not only be entitled to counsel, but to Miranda warnings, if the company is deemed to be acting on behalf of the Government. Further, another respondent was concerned that mandatory reporting may violate existing contracts with a labor union and may be an unfair labor practice if imposed without bargaining, citing American Elec. Power Co., 302 NLRB 161(1991). Resistance by the employees can undercut the entire compliance program. A respondent also believed that employees may be reluctant to come forward if they are aware that the contractor will be required to report their co-workers, or report the company itself, to the OIG. This respondent cited studies by the framers of the USSG who undertook significant research addressing these issues.

Response: The Councils believe that by mandating disclosure, contractor executives and their counsel will be more inclined to make the required disclosure to the OIG, as opposed to either not disclosing or informally alerting the contracting officer, who is not in a position to evaluate the criminal behavior of individual employees. By mandating disclosure to the OIG, the rule will add weight to the arguments inside a corporation that good business practices in the long run favor compliance and disclosure. Nothing in the proposed rule requires administration of "Miranda" warnings. The rule does not place contractors in the role of law enforcement officers. With regard to the concerns about labor agreements, contractors can find ways to disclose without violating labor union provisions that protect individual privacy of workers.

v. Cooperative atmosphere more effective. According to one respondent, voluntary disclosure fosters a cooperative environment and rewards contractors that adopt effective internal controls. Another respondent considered that it is a key principle to promote self-governance as the preferred model to ensure compliance. This respondent quoted the Packard Commission findings in June 1986 that self-governance is the most promising mechanism to foster improved contract compliance. Self-governance makes the difference between responsibility for compliance and a mere facade of compliance. This respondent concluded that, based on 20 years of experience, both scholars and industry leaders believe that the current system of voluntary disclosure encourages companies to develop a stronger culture while still affording the Government broad remedies to protect the Government's interests. Under mandatory disclosure, contractors may focus on the ambiguities of the letter of the rule rather than the spirit of mutual commitment. One respondent expressed long standing support for and experience with voluntary self-reporting. It is concerned that mandatory self-reporting could discourage partnerships with the Government. One respondent cited the "fundamental principle" that contractor compliance programs resulting from internal company commitments to ethical behavior are more likely to be effective in preventing illegal behavior than programs imposed by "overbearing regulations."

Response: The Councils disagree. See "Is voluntary disclosure working?" at paragraph B.3.a.ii.

vi. Incentives. Several respondents contended that existing Government programs and contractor initiatives offer ample incentives for contractors to voluntarily report procurement violations.

- Several respondents pointed out that contractors may receive favorable consideration in debarment proceedings if they have voluntarily disclosed the conduct in question.

- Several respondents cited the civil FCA, which provides contractors with an incentive to report potentially fraudulent behavior. Organizations will voluntarily disclose to avoid lengthy and costly whistleblower litigation (qui tam actions). According to several respondents, voluntary disclosure can undermine a court's jurisdiction to entertain future qui tam cases and can mean the difference between maximum and reduced penalties.

- Several respondents also addressed the reduced penalties under the guidelines of the USSG, adopted in 1991, which are predicated on a model of rewarding voluntary reports. Two respondents stated that the proposed rule is inconsistent with the favorable treatment of voluntary disclosures under the USSG.

* Respondents cited the Deputy Attorney General's January 20, 2003, memorandum, "Principles of Federal Prosecution of Business Organizations," which provides to Federal prosecutors guidance governing charging decisions with respect to corporations and sentencing. Several respondents also cited Deputy Attorney General Paul J. McNulty's memorandum of December 12, 2006, which demonstrated that the DoJ considers an organization's voluntary disclosure and cooperation in determining whether to bring charges.

Various respondents were concerned that the proposed rule may eliminate the ability of a contractor to claim the benefit of "timely and voluntary disclosure" to the Government. One respondent recommended that, if the rule is finalized, a contractor should not be precluded from seeking and receiving leniency because a disclosure is made in compliance with the rule. One respondent stated that the proposed rule is not more consistent with the USSG, but actually contradicts them.

One respondent stated that the Councils must consider these concerns and evaluate the extent to which eliminating incentives to voluntary disclosure will affect a contractor's decision to disclose underlying behavior. The respondent believed that **67073** eliminating incentives could cause contractors to adopt a protective posture in the face of evidence of potential criminal behavior.

Another respondent suggested that, instead of mandating compliance and ethics programs, the Councils should open a new FAR case to develop an incentive-based approach. This respondent was concerned that the logic of penalizing contractors for failure to disclose a crime, rather than offering incentives, will not work. The disclosure obligation applies only if a crime has already occurred. If there is already a crime, then the company is already subject to punishment. Failure to disclose will only be an aggravating factor. So, if a company fails to disclose, it may escape punishment, but if it discloses, it will likely still be subject to punishment for the crime committed. Therefore, punishment for failure to disclose may not be sufficient incentive to disclose.

Response: There is nothing in this rule that removes any of the existing incentives. The incentives in the FAR (FAR 9.406-1(a)) and the USSG are not limited to "voluntary" disclosures but to "disclosures." Even if disclosure is "mandatory," incentives will still be offered to promote compliance.

b. Vagueness of Rule

i. "Reasonable grounds to believe." Numerous respondents were concerned that the rule does not specify what constitutes "reasonable grounds." One respondent stated that "reasonable grounds" is subject to varying interpretations, and may be viewed as an even lower standard than "probable cause." Should the contractor report based on mere suspicion or based on evidence that criminal activity has occurred? Because of this lack of clarity, several respondents were concerned that companies may tie up Government resources with a mountain of meaningless legal trivia. Numerous respondents stated that there will be

APPENDIX B

substantial over-reporting because contractors may report even remotely possible criminal conduct out of an abundance of caution. One respondent considered that this will raise company costs through the investigation of baseless claims and incidents. Several other respondents stated that there will be an enormous amount of time spent sorting out the true criminal activity and truly significant problems.

One respondent suggested that the proposed rule will potentially subject an employer to civil actions brought by an employee when the reports forwarded by the employer to the Federal Government (because conceivably "reasonable grounds" existed) ultimately are determined to lack merit.

Response: The Councils have replaced "reasonable grounds to believe" with "credible evidence." DoJ Criminal Division recommended use of this standard after discussions with industry representatives. This term indicates a higher standard, implying that the contractor will have the opportunity to take some time for preliminary examination of the evidence to determine its credibility before deciding to disclose to the Government. See also the following discussion of "timely disclosure."

ii. Timely disclosure.

There are 3 aspects of timely disclosure that are of concern to the respondents:

• To which violations/contracts does timely disclosure apply?

• How much time does a contractor have to disclose a possible violation after first hearing something about it?

• How do we transition into this rule? How is timeliness measured for violations that the contractor may already know about and did not disclose prior to becoming subject to this rule?

Further, in analyzing these issues, there are 3 separate requirements for timely disclosure in this rule which may affect the response to the above questions:

• The contract clause requirement to disclose (paragraph (b)(3)).

• The contract clause requirement for an internal control system (paragraph (c)(2)(ii)(F)).

• Failure to timely disclose as a cause for suspension/debarment regardless of requirement for contract clause or internal control system (Subpart 9.4).

a. To which violations/contracts does timely disclosure apply?

Various respondents were concerned about whether the rule can apply to violations that occurred before the effective date of the rule, the date of the bid, or the date the clause is incorporated into the contract.

• Effective date of the rule. Numerous respondents recommended that the rule be made applicable only to conduct occurring on or after the date the rule is effective. The respondents argued that there is presently no requirement in the FAR for a contractor to disclose to the Government criminal violations committed by its employees. The respondents cited case law to support the argument that application of the rule to conduct occurring before the rule effective date would be impermissible. One respondent stated that the reporting requirement should be "prospective only". Otherwise this requirement may impose an unreasonable burden.

• Date the clause is incorporated. Another respondent questions whether the rule is meant to cover past acts, or only acts going forward from the date the clause is incorporated into a contract. According to one respondent, to punish entities for past acts would violate constitutional ex post facto prohibitions.

• Date of the bid. One respondent suggested that the violation would have to occur after the date of the bid.

Several respondents also looked at the end of the period during which violations that occur must be reported. One respondent suggested that completion of performance would be appropriate.

DoJ suggested limiting the mandatory disclosure of overpayments or criminal violations to matters discovered by the contractor within three years after contract completion.

Response: The first significant point to remember is that in all cases the reportable violations are linked to the performance of Government contracts. In the case of the contract clause direct requirement for contractor disclosure, the reportable violations are limited to the contract containing the clause. So the questions raised by the respondents about occurrence of violations are not an issue with regard to the contract clause disclosure requirement, because violations would necessarily occur during award or performance of the contract, through contract closeout, which would necessarily be after the effective date of the rule and after incorporation of the clause. (Note: The clause will be included in solicitations and resultant contracts after the effective date of the rule, in accordance with FAR 1.108(d)).

However, in the case of internal control systems and suspension/debarment, the proposed rule states that reportable violations could occur in connection with "any Government contract." This could be overly broad in two regards--

• Does it apply to violations on the contracts of other contractors?

• Does it apply to contracts closed out 20 years ago?

The Councils have made clear in the final rule that this disclosure requirement is limited to contracts awarded to the contractor (or subcontracts thereunder). It was not the intent of the proposed rule to require contractors to report on violations of other contractors under contracts unrelated to their own contracts.

The Councils do not agree with the respondents who think that disclosure under the internal control system or as a potential cause for suspension/**67074** debarment should only apply to conduct occurring after the date the rule is effective or the clause is included in the contract, or the internal control

APPENDIX B | 257

system is established. The laws against these violations were already in place before the rule became effective or any of these other occurrences. This rule is not establishing a new rule against theft or embezzlement and making it retroactive. The only thing that was not in place was the requirement to disclose the violation. If violations relating to an ongoing contract occurred prior to the effective date of the rule, then the contractor must disclose such violations, whether or not the clause is in the contract and whether or not an internal control system is in place, because of the cause for suspension and debarment in Subpart 9.4.

However, the Councils agree that this requirement should not stretch back indefinitely into the past (e.g., contracts that were closed 20 years ago). At that point, relevance with regard to present responsibility has diminished, there is less availability of evidence to support an investigation, there is more difficulty locating the responsible parties (who is the contracting officer?), and there should be some reasonable limitation on a contractor's liability after contract closeout.

The Councils considered using contract closeout as the end point for the requirement to disclose fraud, but according to the DoJ, often contract fraud occurs at the time of closeout, and cutting off the obligation to disclose at that point would exempt many of these violations from the obligation to disclose. Three years after final payment is consistent with most of the contractor record retention requirements (see Audit and Records clauses at FAR 52.214-26 and 52.215-2). Therefore, the Councils concur with the DoJ recommendation that the mandatory disclosure of violations should be limited to a period of three years after contract completion, using final payment as the event to mark contract completion.

Therefore, the Councils have added the phrase "Until 3 years after final payment on any Government contract awarded to the contractor" at 9.406-2(b)(1)(vi) and 9.407-2(a)(8), and has added in the clause at paragraph (c)(2)(ii)(F) the statement that "The disclosure requirement for an individual contract continues until at least 3 years after final payment on the contract." To make the applicability during the close-out phase of a contract clearer, the Councils have revised the draft final rule in all applicable places to refer to "award, performance, or closeout."

b. Does "timely" allow sufficient time between first learning of the allegation and the disclosure?

One respondent objected that "timely" is very broad in scope which could permit contracting officers to have inconsistent interpretations of what is timely. One respondent questioned whether "timely" means upon first learning of an allegation or only upon conducting an adequate internal investigation. The respondent recommended that the regulations should include a set period of time (i.e., 90 days) for any reporting requirement. Another respondent recommended that the regulations might allow 60 days to determine if there are reasonable grounds to conclude that the contractor committed a crime. The 60 day period would start when a principal of the company suspects that a crime might have been committed, but lacks reasonable grounds for concluding that a crime has been committed. An agency OIG suggested "timely" should be replaced with "within 30 calendar days."

Another respondent was concerned that when "timely" disclosure must occur is ambiguous because the timing of a violation is troublesome. Contractors often settle cases without any admission of fault or liability. The rise in deferred and non-prosecution agreements in criminal cases brought by the Government against contractors creates confusion regarding disclosure of criminal violations.

According to many respondents, the proposed rule may require premature reporting. One respondent questioned the requirement to notify without delay, whenever the contractor becomes "aware" of violations of Federal criminal law. According to this respondent, the rule does not clarify what constitutes "awareness." Several other respondents were concerned that the proposed amendment does not appear to allow a contractor to complete an internal investigation before notifying the OIG and contracting officer. Several respondents considered that an internal investigation could be compromised by premature reporting. One respondent recommended that the rule should allow the contractor the opportunity to comply with its ethics and compliance program and conduct an internal investigation prior to disclosure to the Government. Contractors should be required to report only actual violations of law, not those incidents that have not been confirmed as actual violations.

One respondent pointed out that existing voluntary disclosure protocols allow for internal investigation by the reporting parties before a disclosure is made. Another respondent stated that under the DoD Voluntary Disclosure Program, if the preliminary investigation reveals evidence to suggest that disclosure is warranted, contractors may disclose information sufficient for preliminary acceptance into the DoD Voluntary Disclosure Program, and then have 60 days to complete a fuller investigation. This rule provides no guidance on preliminary steps afforded to a contractor.

One respondent also recommended that the contractor be explicitly provided with a reasonable period of time to internally investigate a potential violation.

DoJ suggested that the preamble to the final rule should make clear that nothing in the rule is intended to preclude a contractor from continuing to investigate after making its initial disclosure to the Government. DoJ would expect that the OIG or the contracting officer will encourage the contractor to complete its internal investigation and make full report of its findings.

In their comment on the second proposed rule, one respondent recommends that the preamble should explain that a contractor, with the contracting officer's approval, may tailor the "timely reporting" provision of its internal control system in order to make meaningful reports to the contracting officer.

Response: First, the Councils note that the new statute uses the term "timely" in setting forth disclosure requirements. The Councils considered, and rejected, adding a set period of time, e.g., 30 days, to the disclosure requirement. It was decided that doing so would be arbitrary and would cause more problems than it would resolve, e.g., how to determine when the 30 days begins.

Further, the Councils believe that using the standard of "credible evidence" rather than "reasonable grounds to believe" will help clarify "timely" because it implies that the contractor will have the opportunity to take some time for preliminary examination of the evidence to determine its credibility before deciding to disclose to the Government. Until the contractor has determined the evidence to be credible, there can be no "knowing failure to timely disclose." This does not impose upon the contractor an obligation to carry out a complex investigation, but only to take reasonable steps that the contractor considers sufficient to determine that the evidence is credible.

67075 The Councils note that there is no rigidity to our proposed requirement to establish an internal control system. The rule just sets forth minimum requirements. The contractor can use its own judgment in the details of setting up a system that meets the minimum requirements. The clause does not require contracting officer approval of this system.

c. Transitioning into the rule. Meaning of "timely" when the knowledge of credible evidence pre-dates the requirements of this rule. One respondent stated that the reporting requirement should be "prospective only". Otherwise this requirement may impose an unreasonable burden.

Response: As just discussed, the disclosure requirement is prospective only. Although violations on the current contract might have occurred during the pre-award phase and violations on other contracts may have already occurred prior to establishment of the internal control system or prior to the effective date of the rule, timely disclosure of the violation can only be measured from the time when the requirement to disclose the violation came into effect, even if credible evidence of the violation was previously known to the contractor.

With regard to the contractual disclosure requirement, the timely disclosure would be measured from the date of determination of credible evidence or the date of contract award, whichever event occurs later.

With regard to the disclosure requirement of the internal control system, it can only become effective upon establishment of the internal control system. The violation can have occurred with regard to any Government contract which is still open or for which final payment was made within the last 3 years, so may predate establishment of the internal control system. Therefore, timely disclosure of credible evidence as required by the internal control system would be measured from the date of determination by the contractor that the evidence is credible, or the date of establishment of the internal control system, whichever event occurs later.

With regard to the knowing failure by a principal to timely disclose credible evidence of a violation or significant overpayments as a cause for suspension or debarment, the violation can have occurred with regard to any Government contract, which is still open or for which final payment was made within the last 3 years, so may predate the effective date of the rule. Therefore, timely disclosure of credible evidence as required by the rule as a cause for suspension or debarment would be measured from the date of determination by the contractor that the evidence is credible, or from the effective date of the rule, whichever event occurs later.

To some extent, the effective date of the rule actually trumps the other events, because the failure to timely disclose as a cause for suspension/debarment is independent of the inclusion of the contract clause in the contract or the establishment of an internal control system. At least in those instances where disclosure was not timely in regard to effective date of the rule, but was reported as soon as the clause was in the contract, or as soon as the control system was in place, then it would not be a violation of the contract or a mark against the control system. It could still be a cause for suspension or debarment, although the Councils consider that suspension or debarment would be unlikely, if the contractor came forward as soon as the clause or the internal control system was in place (before that, the contractor might have been unaware of the requirement to disclose).

iii. "Criminal violation in connection with contract award or performance." Numerous respondents stated that the rule fails to specify what constitutes a "criminal violation" "in connection with contract award or performance". Some of these respondents made the following comments:

• The broad nature of the phrase "violation of Federal criminal law in connection with contract award or performance" places a heavy burden. The Government is in the best position to provide specific guidance to contractors as to the violations that would be considered covered by this new requirement. Otherwise, each contractor will have to develop its own list and explanations to its employees as to what constitutes criminal violations.

• If the FAR Council proceeds with the rule, it should provide a specific list of the criminal violations that the contractor is required to disclose.

• The self-reporting requirements should be revised to provide the specific circumstances under which self-reporting is required.

• The provision is vague in regard to the type of "criminal violation" covered, leaving open application of the rule to non-procurement related offenses. If an employee commits a criminal violation while driving on Federal lands in the course of performing a contract, must the traffic violation be reported to the agency OIG? Also, the agency OIGs may receive reports about violations of Federal tax law or Occupational Safety and Health laws that occur in connection with the performance of the contract, over which the OIGs do not have jurisdiction. This can result in unnecessary or inappropriate reports.

• The proposed rule does not elaborate on the nexus between the perceived criminal conduct and the Federal contract so as to trigger the reporting requirement. A contractor's silence could be alleged to be a false statement where the employer had "reason to believe" that one of its employees, agents, or subcontractors had violated criminal law in connection with a contract.

• The rule should define more clearly what is reportable and when the obligation to report is triggered.

One Government agency suggested adding "potential" to "violation."

DoJ also suggested tightening the standard for disclosure by adding the phrase "involving fraud, conflict of interest, bribery, or gratuity violations found in Title 18 of the United States Code."

Response: The Councils have adopted the more specific description of criminal law suggested by DoJ as responsive to many of the concerns expressed by the respondents.

APPENDIX B

As to nexus with the contract, the clause stipulates in paragraph 52.203-13(b)(3)(i) that the violation should have occurred "in connection with the award, performance, or closeout of this contract, or any subcontract thereunder." With regard to the internal control system disclosure required in paragraph 52.203-13(c)(2)(ii)(F) and the cause for debarment or suspension in Subpart 9.4, the violation must be in connection with the award, performance, or closeout, of any Government contract performed by the contractor, or a subcontract thereunder, and the obligation to disclose information lasts until 3 years after final payment. If there is no connection to a Government contract performed by the contractor, or a subcontract thereunder, then it need not be disclosed.

The Councils do not consider it necessary to add "potential" to "violation" because that preceding language already is in terms of "credible evidence." That does not necessarily mean that a violation has occurred, but the principals are looking for "credible evidence" that a violation has occurred. "Potential violation" would open it even wider and could result in too many unnecessary disclosures.

iv. Level of employee with knowledge. Several respondents wanted the rule to identify the level of contractor employee whose knowledge will be imputed to the contractor, such that the contractor has the requisite **67076** knowledge. Absent such identification, consistent with the doctrine of respondeat superior applied in Federal criminal law, a contractor may be deemed to have requisite knowledge warranting disclosure if any employee at any level is aware of conduct which may constitute a Federal criminal offense. This could cause a contractor to be accused of violating the mandatory disclosure provision before the contractor's management becomes aware of the offense and before the appropriate steps for disclosure may be undertaken. One respondent stated that it is unreasonable to expect all knowledge to be passed up the chain. Several respondents recommended revision of the proposed rule to require that a contractor principal must have the requisite knowledge of a Federal criminal law violation before that knowledge will be imputed to a contractor.

Response: The Councils concur that for debarment and suspension, a principal must have the requisite knowledge in order for mandatory disclosure to be applicable. See response under the heading "Suspension/Debarment", "Who has knowledge?" at paragraph B.5.e.

c. Disclosure to OIG. One respondent considered that the proposed rule would essentially require contractors and subcontractors to become fraud detection and reporting entities. Must contractors become experts in forensic accounting and private investigation? This respondent considered that the proposed rule essentially would "deputize" contractors and subcontractors as agents of the OIG. One respondent also considered that the company is now acting as an agent of the Government.

Is "the agency OIG" the OIG for the agency which awarded the contract under which the action in question took place? One respondent was concerned when contractor is required to disclose to different inspectors general because the proposed rule is silent on what actions and procedural safeguards are to be implemented in the various offices of the Inspectors General. A contractor that deals with a variety of different Federal agencies will unreasonably be faced with significantly increased risk and uncertainty.

Several respondents considered that a likely outcome of the mandatory reporting to the agency OIG will be to remove from a contracting officer or agency the authority or the ability to settle and compromise the issues by a disclosure. One industry association indicated that member companies report that in their experience, the vast majority of potential violations disclosed to a contracting officer or other agency official are quickly resolved as an administrative matter. Once a matter is referred to the DoD OIG as a potential criminal or civil fraud matter, under the Contract Disputes Act the contracting officer loses his or her ability to compromise or settle the issue. One respondent was also concerned about the impact of the proposed rule on the influence and authority of the contracting officer. The respondent considered that disclosure to the OIG passes the leadership role on any subsequent investigation and review to the OIG's office and undercuts the authority and ability of the contracting officer to manage contracts.

One respondent noted that under the DFARS rule, the OIG only needs to be notified when appropriate. One respondent considered that mandatory notification to the OIG defeats the concept of internal audits and correction of possible irregularities. The respondent is concerned that, once the OIG is brought into the process, both the contracting officer and the contractor/subcontractor lose control of the process.

One respondent was concerned with the ability of the OIG to handle an increased level of reports. One respondent stated that their experience with the capability of the OIG's offices to deal with complicated, sophisticated and/or fact-intensive issues is very mixed at best. Current demands have placed substantial strain in the ability of the OIG's offices to support investigations, and delays are commonplace. "According to the respondent, 'competing demands for resources to support overseas investigations and Homeland Security defense have drained whatever experienced resources existed" at the agency OIGs.

An agency OIG suggested replacing "agency Office of the Inspector General" with "A President-selected and Senate-approved Inspector General or designated Federal entity Inspector General." The agency OIG stated that this better describes the correct agency to which the contractor should report potential violations.

Response: There is nothing in the proposed rule that "deputizes" contractors. The Councils have concluded that it is appropriate for contractors to send the reports directly to the OIG, with a copy to the contracting officer, because it is the OIG that is responsible for investigating the disclosure.

The disclosure would be to the OIG of the agency that awarded the subject contract. The Councils have added clarification that if a violation relates to more than one Government contract, the Contractor may make the disclosure to the agency OIG and Contracting Officer responsible for the largest dollar value contract impacted by the violation. If the violation relates to an order against a Governmentwide acquisition contract, a multi-agency contract, a multiple-award schedule contract such as the Federal Supply Schedule, or any other procurement instrument intended for use by multiple agencies, the contractor shall notify the OIG of the ordering agency and the IG of the agency responsible for the basic contract.

APPENDIX B

Whether OIGs can handle an increase in the level of reporting depends on the expected level of increase. The Councils do not anticipate that companies are going to flood the OIG with trivialities, as some respondents fear. The Council also notes that the agency OIGs were all strongly in favor of this rule.

The Councils do not agree with the suggestion of one agency IG that the rule should specify "A President-selected and Senate-approved Inspector General or designated Federal entity Inspector General." Although this is probably accurate, the Councils consider it too complicated for some contractors to determine. It is the opinion of the Councils that, if a contractor submits a report to the wrong OIG, that OIG will forward it to the appropriate OIG.

Throughout the rule, the Councils have used the words "disclose" and "disclosure" for consistency, rather than in some places using the word "notify" or "report".

4. Full Cooperation

The proposed rule states at paragraph (c)(2)(ii)(G) of FAR 52.203-XX (now 52.203-13) that a contractor Code of Business Ethics and Conduct shall, at a minimum, have an internal control system that provides "full cooperation with any Government agencies responsible for audit, investigation, or corrective actions."

a. Waiver of Privileges/Protections/Rights

Many respondents expressed concern that compliance with the rules requiring disclosure and full cooperation would be interpreted to--

• Require contractors waive an otherwise valid claim of attorney-client privilege or protections afforded by the attorney work product doctrine, both protecting attorney-client communications; or

• Interfere with an employee's right under the Fifth Amendment of the U.S. Constitution covering the right of an **67077** individual not to be compelled to incriminate itself.

One respondent recommended addition of strong language to preserve privilege protections.

DoJ and an agency OIG indicated awareness of these concerns in their comments and recommended clarification in the final rule. DoJ proposed that the final rule state explicitly:

"Nothing in this rule is intended to require that a contractor waive its attorney-client privilege, or that any officer, director, owner, or employee of the contractor, including a sole proprietor, waive his or her attorney-client privilege or Fifth Amendment rights."

Response: It is doubtful any regulation or contract clause could legally compel a contractor or its employees to forfeit these rights. However, the Councils have revised the final rule to provide such assurance. To address concern that cooperation might be interpreted to require disclosure of materials covered by the work product doctrine, the Councils have added a definition of "full cooperation" at 52.203-13(a) to make clear that the rule does not mandate disclosure of materials covered by the attorney work product doctrine.

For comparison purposes, it is instructive to refer to the flexible approach adopted in the USSG:

Waiver of attorney-client privilege and of work product protections is not a prerequisite to a reduction * * * unless such waiver is necessary in order to provide timely and thorough disclosure of all pertinent information known to the organization.

It also is worth pointing out the DoD Voluntary Disclosure Program never required waiver as a condition of participation. Contractors in that program routinely found ways to report wrongdoing without waiving the attorney-client privilege or providing their attorney memoranda reflecting their interviews that normally are covered by the work product doctrine.

Any limitation in this rule should not be used as an excuse by a contractor to avoid disclosing facts required by this rule. Facts are never protected by the attorney-client privilege or work product doctrine. Moreover, the Fifth Amendment has no application to corporations, so the only sensitive area is mandatory disclosure or cooperation by individuals or sole proprietors, which is addressed in the clarification.

b. Indemnification of Employees

Several respondents expressed concern that full cooperation will be interpreted as prohibiting a contractor from indemnifying its employees or their individual counsel to the extent permitted or required by state law or the contractor's charter or bylaws. Several respondents expressed concern that the Government may view indemnification of contractor employees as not cooperating. One respondent asked if there was a difference between "cooperation" and "full cooperation" and, more seriously, whether full cooperation restricted a contractor's ability to make counsel available to its employees. Several respondents pointed to the district court opinion in U.S. v. Stein, 435 F.Supp. 2d 330 (SDNY 2006), and 440 F.Supp. 2d 315 (SDNY 2006) that suggests the Government viewed KPMG's practice of paying for employees' legal costs pursuant to indemnification rules was not "cooperation" favored by the prosecutors in that case.

Response: With regard to indemnification of employees for legal costs, State law--not Federal--controls. Just as full cooperation cannot mean a company forfeits its attorney-client privilege, there is no reason to think it means employees forfeit their right to indemnification from their employers. On December 12, 2006, DOJ addressed this issue in a memorandum sent to all DoJ attorneys by Deputy Attorney General Paul McNulty ("McNulty Memorandum"), stating:

Prosecutors generally should not take into account whether a corporation is advancing attorneys' fees to employees or agents under investigation and indictment. Many state indemnification statutes grant corporations the power to advance the legal fees of officers under investigation prior to a formal determination of guilt. As a consequence, many corporations enter into contractual obligations to advance attorneys' fees through provisions contained in

APPENDIX B

their corporate charters, bylaws or employment agreements. Therefore, a corporation's compliance with governing state law and its contractual obligations cannot be considered a failure to cooperate.

c. Requirement to Fire an Employee

One respondent asked that the rule clarify that cooperation does not mean a contractor must fire an employee.

Response: It is inappropriate for the Government to direct a contractor to fire an employee, although the Government may require that an employee be removed from performance of the Government contract. However, most corporate compliance programs assert that violation of law or company policy is grounds for dismissal. Also note the internal control system requirements for principals at paragraph (c)(2)(ii)(B) of the clause.

d. Ability To Conduct a Thorough and Effective Internal Investigation

Several respondents expressed concern that cooperation or disclosure will be interpreted to interfere with a contractor's ability to conduct a thorough and effective internal investigation. Some respondents were concerned that a contractor continuing to investigate a matter after reporting would be deemed not cooperating. One respondent recommended that the rule state explicitly that: "A contractor has a reasonable time to investigate a potential investigation * * * and that nothing in the rule prohibits or restricts a contractor from conducting an internal investigation."

Response: Any interpretation of full cooperation that would suggest a limit on contractors conducting internal investigations would be clearly at odds with the intent of the rule, which encourages compliance program investigations, reporting, and cooperation.

e. Defending a Proceeding or Dispute Arising From or Related to Disclosure

Various respondents expressed concern that full cooperation will be interpreted to preclude a contractor from defending itself in a proceeding or dispute arising from or related to the disclosure. One respondent raised concerns that a rule mandating full cooperation could be interpreted as prohibiting a contractor from "vigorously defending its actions." Another respondent observed that full cooperation might require a contractor to waive its right to appeal the results of an audit.

Response: Nothing in the rule would foreclose a contractor from advancing a defense or an "explanation" for the alleged fraud or corruption arising in a Government contract. This includes being free to use any administrative or legal rights available to resolve any dispute between the Government and the contractor. The rule is intended simply to require the contractor to be forthcoming with its customer, the Government, with regard to credible evidence relating to alleged fraud or corruption in its Government contracts.

f. Expansion of Audit Rights and Access to Records

Various respondents asked to what extent full cooperation overrode the limits on Government audit rights and access to records limitations, giving the

Government "unfettered access" to individuals to conduct interviews, even though the current audit access clauses are limited to documents. Expanding on **67078** that, one respondent also asked if the rule requires contractors to give the Government "full access to their financial and proprietary information, beyond that required by existing contract clauses." Another respondent also observed that the Government may invoke the requirement in connection with disputes before the Board of Contract Appeals or U.S. Court of Federal Claims. One respondent requested clarification that the cooperation requirement applies only to agencies affected by the conduct and not the entire Government.

Response: The proposed rule was not intended to have any application or impact on the Government's exercise of its audit and access to records rights in the routine contract administration context except as the issue arises when a contractor discloses fraud or corruption or the Government independently has evidence sufficient to open an investigation of fraud and solicit the contractor's cooperation. The issue of contractor cooperation in this rule arises primarily in the context of Government investigation of contract fraud and corruption and any application of this rule in any other context by the Government would be clearly overreaching.

g. Inadvertent Failure as Non-Cooperation

One respondent feared that an "inadvertent" failure to provide documents in a routine DCAA audit would be deemed non-cooperative.

Response: The rule has no application to routine DCAA audits.

h. Need for Definition

Many respondents asked for an expanded definition of "full cooperation" in order to reduce the potential for misinterpretation of the rule, resulting in the concerns addressed in the preceding paragraphs.

Response: Contractors are not expected to block Government auditors and investigators' access to information found in documents or through its employees in furtherance of a contract fraud or corruption investigation.

Generally speaking, it is also reasonable for investigators and prosecutors to expect that compliant contractors will encourage employees both to make themselves available and to cooperate with the Government investigation.

That also applies to responding to reasonable Government requests for documents. Ignoring or offering little attention to detail in responding to auditor or investigator requests or subpoenas for documents or information may, in some circumstances, be obstruction of justice and, if established, certainly would not be deemed full cooperation.

According to the USSG, cooperation must be both timely and thorough:

- To be timely, the cooperation must begin essentially at the same time as the organization is officially notified of a criminal investigation.

- To be thorough, the cooperation should include the disclosure of all per-

APPENDIX B

tinent information known by the organization.

--A prime test of whether the organization has disclosed all pertinent information is whether the information is sufficient for law enforcement personnel to identify--

--The nature and extent of the offense; and

--The individual(s) responsible for the criminal conduct.

--However, the cooperation to be measured is the cooperation of the organization itself, not the cooperation of individuals within the organization. If, because of the lack of cooperation of particular individual(s), neither the organization nor law enforcement personnel are able to identify the culpable individual(s) within the organization despite the organization's efforts to cooperate fully, the organization may still be given credit for full cooperation.

The DoD Voluntary Disclosure Program described expected cooperation in some detail in its standard agreement (the "XYZ Agreement"), and it may be a useful reference in this circumstance where the contractor discloses credible evidence of fraud or corruption under this rule. However, the detail found there goes significantly beyond the scope of this rule and is best addressed on a case-by-case basis.

The final rule includes a definition that incorporates some of the concepts in the USSG and the general principle that cooperation must be both timely and thorough. It is intended to make clear that cooperation should include all information requested as well as all pertinent information known by the contractor necessary to complete the investigation, whether the information helps or hurts the contractor. Contractors are expected to make their employees available for Government investigators and auditors investigating contract fraud and corruption and respond in a timely and complete manner to Government requests for documents and other information required to conduct an investigation of contract fraud and corruption. Responding to concerns expressed by the respondents, the Councils have incorporated the following definition into the final rule at 52.203-13(a):

"Full cooperation"--

(1) Means disclosure to the Government of the information sufficient for law enforcement to identify the nature and extent of the offense and the individuals responsible for the conduct. It includes providing timely and complete response to Government auditors' and investigators' requests for documents and access to employees with information;

(2) Does not foreclose any contractor rights arising in law, the FAR, or the terms of the contract. It does not require--

(i) A contractor to waive its attorney-client privilege or the protections afforded by the attorney work product doctrine; or

(ii) Any officer, director, owner, or employee of the contractor, including a sole proprietor, to waive his or her attorney client privilege or Fifth

Amendment rights; and

(3) Does not restrict a contractor from--

(i) Conducting an internal investigation; or

(ii) Defending a proceeding or dispute arising under the contract or related to a potential or disclosed violation.

5. *Suspension/Debarment*

a. New Cause for Suspension or Debarment

Various respondents expressed concern that the proposed rule establishes failure to timely disclose a violation as a new cause for suspension or debarment, rather than suspension or debarment just for the underlying violation.

Response: The requirement for timely disclosure could in some circumstances be considered a new cause for suspension or debarment. However, the question of timely disclosure will not come up unless the Government independently discovers that there has been a significant overpayment, a violation of the civil FCA, or a violation of Federal criminal law to be disclosed, that the Contractor knew about and elected to ignore. It is unlikely that any contractor would be suspended or debarred absent the determination that a violation had actually occurred. Present responsibility is the ultimate basis of suspension or debarment.

b. Unnecessary and Not Good Policy

Many respondents criticized the additional suspension and debarment coverage in the proposed rule as **67079** unnecessary and redundant to existing regulations that--

• Provide strong incentives for contractors to voluntarily disclose criminal behavior;

• Require a prospective contractor to demonstrate a satisfactory record of integrity and business ethics; and

• Provide a "panoply of methods for prosecuting and eliminating those companies that fail to abide by the highest ethical and legal standards."

One respondent stated that the proposed suspension and debarment for "violation of Federal criminal law" simply repeats much of what is contained in FAR 9.406-2 and 9.407-2. Another respondent considered the suspension and debarment regulations punitive.

Response: As addressed in the preceding paragraph, the added causes for suspension/debarment add the requirement to timely disclose the violation and are not duplicative of the violation itself as a cause for suspension/debarment.

APPENDIX B

The suspension and debarment policies and standards are not punitive. The purpose of suspension and debarment is to ensure that the Government does business only with responsible contractors, not to punish. This final rule continues to embrace the responsibility standard.

c. Mitigating Factors

Several respondents were concerned whether the proposed rule maintains the current scheme of ten mitigating factors at FAR 9.406-1(a) or renders it meaningless by establishing failure to disclose itself as a cause for debarment (thus preventing "voluntary" disclosure).

Response: The mitigating factors currently at FAR 9.406-1(a) will continue to be used, and a contractor's timely disclosure to the Government will continue to be a mitigating factor. As stated in the response in paragraph B.3.a.vi. "Incentives", above, the incentives in the FAR and the USSG are not limited to "voluntary" disclosures but to "disclosures."

Even if disclosure is "mandatory," incentives will still be offered to promote compliance. The Councils do not recommend any revision as a result of these comments.

d. Undefined Terms

Many respondents expressed concern that terms such as "knowing," "timely" "reasonable grounds to believe," and "overpayment" are undefined and will thus put contractors at risk. One Government respondent suggested adding "knew, should have known, or" to "had reasonable grounds to believe."

Response: See responses under paragraph B.3.b."Vagueness of rule." for discussions of "timely," and "reasonable grounds to believe."

With regard to the term "knowing failure to disclose" the "knowing" refers to the failure to disclose. "Knowing failure to disclose" was added in the proposed rule to the causes for debarment at FAR 9.406-2(b)(1)(vi) and the causes for suspension at FAR 9.407-2(a)(8). Requiring a "knowledge" element to the cause for action actually provides more protection for contractors. The Councils do not agree with adding "or should have known." The principals are only required to disclose what they know. Further, using the standard of "credible evidence" rather than "reasonable grounds to believe" will help clarify "knowing" (See response at "Vagueness of rule" at paragraph B.3.b.i., "Reasonable grounds to believe").

The term "overpayment" is described in a number of FAR clauses and provisions and does not require a definition with respect to suspension and debarment. For further discussion of overpayments, see response at "Suspension and Debarment", paragraph B.5.f. "Limit or abandon suspension/debarment for failure to disclose overpayment".

e. Who has knowledge?

One respondent stated that a contractor should be suspended or debarred for failing to disclose violations of Federal criminal law only if a "principal" of the company (as defined in the proposed contract clause) has knowledge of the crime. Failure to disclose crime should not be a basis for suspension or debarment if lower-level employees, who are not managers or supervisors, commit a crime and conceal the crime from the contractor's supervisory-level personnel.

Response: Paragraph (a)(2) of the clause at FAR 52.209-5 defines "principals" to mean "officers; directors; owners; partners; and, persons having primary management or supervisory responsibilities within a business entity (e.g., general manager; plant manager; head of a subsidiary, division, or business segment, and similar positions)". The Councils agree with the respondent and have revised 3.1003(a)(2), 9.406-2(b)(1)(vi), and 9.407-2(a)(8) to make disclosure mandatory when a principal of the company has knowledge. The Councils have also added the definition of a principal at FAR 2.101 because it now applies to more than a single FAR part, and revised both definitions to be singular rather than plural.

The Councils note that this definition should be interpreted broadly, and could include compliance officers or directors of internal audit, as well as other positions of responsibility.

f. Limit or Abandon Suspension/Debarment for Failure To Disclose Overpayment

One respondent stated that the proposed ability to suspend or debar for failure to disclose an "overpayment" on a Government contract may create operational difficulties because contracts are subject to reconciliation processes with payments audited and adjusted over time. Likewise, another respondent stated that singling out routine contract payment issues, which are daily events, with errors on both sides, is simply unworkable. The respondent cites a situation where a defense contractor did disclose an overpayment to the payment office, only to be told that it was wrong, yet was later made the subject of a qui tam action. Another respondent likewise objected to making reporting of overpayments grounds for suspension or debarment rather than a matter of contract administration. The respondent stated that the proposed rule does not connect overpayments to the criminal law violations upon which the rest of the proposed rule is focused.

One respondent recommended that the FAR Council should abandon the proposed changes that would make failure to disclose an "overpayment" a new cause for suspension or debarment because a number of current FAR clauses already require the contractor to disclose specific types of overpayments, e.g., 52.232-25, 52.232-26, 52.232-27, and 52.212-4(i)(5). These clauses treat such overpayments as a matter of contract administration and do not treat them as a matter of possible fraud and a basis for suspension or debarment. In addition, the Part 9 provisions should state explicitly that the cause for suspension or debarment is for violation of the requirements in FAR 52.232-25, 52.232- 26, 52.232-27, and 52.212-4(i)(5). The respondent noted that the proposed rule did not demonstrate that the present FAR provisions requiring the disclosure of overpayments are ineffective.

On the other hand, another respondent stated that contractors currently have no obligation to report overpayment.

One respondent was more specifically concerned that overpayments can result from indirect rate variances or similar credits that can occur years after 67 080 contract performance and that can put the contractor in an over-billed

APPENDIX B

situation. The severe sanctions that could inure to contractors so situated seem patently unfair. The respondent suggested either excluding rate variances or applying the section only to payments made during or immediately following contract performance.

Another respondent was concerned that this ethics rule creates potential inconsistency in the treatment of overpayments with the existing regulatory provisions of the FAR, and recommends deletion of the issue of "overpayment" as a basis for suspension and debarment.

DoJ suggested some answers to these concerns. DoJ considers that a duty to disclose an overpayment is just as important as the disclosure of criminal violations, and the requirement to disclose both will save the contractor from having to decide whether a criminal violation has in fact occurred in the case of an overpayment. However, DoJ concedes that a materiality requirement is appropriate to limit the scope of the requirement to disclose overpayments.

Response: The Councils dispute the allegation that "contractors currently have no obligation to report overpayments" and refers the respondent to the payment clauses at FAR 52.232-25, 52.232-26, 52.232-27, and 52.212-4(i)(5). Although other clauses already require reporting of overpayment, this inclusion of the requirement in Subpart 9.4 to disclose significant overpayments is necessary to make it clear that, if a contractor does not meet this condition of the contract, it can be subject to suspension or debarment.

The Councils agree with the suggestion by the DoJ that it is appropriate to limit the application of suspension or debarment to cases in which the unreported overpayment is significant. This will resolve some of the respondents' concerns over routine contract payment issues. The Councils have revised the final rule to address only significant overpayments, which implies more than just dollar value and depends on the circumstances of the overpayment as well as the amount. Since contractors are required by the Payment clauses to report and return overpayments of any amount, it is within the discretion of the suspension and debarment official to determine whether an overpayment is significant and whether suspension or debarment would be the appropriate outcome for failure to report such overpayment.

Rate variances do not need to be specifically excluded by the case because this issue is already taken care of in Part 32 and the Payment clauses. Rate variances are not considered overpayments until the rates are determined. The suggestion to apply the section only to payments made during or immediately following contract performance would not necessarily exempt rate variances, depending on when the rates are determined.

Further, the Councils decided to exclude knowing failure to report overpayments that result from contract financing payments, as defined in FAR 32.001, as grounds for suspension or debarment. Even though such overpayments must be reported and returned under the Payment clauses, these ongoing payments that are not the final payment on a contract are often based on estimates, and are subject to correction as the contract progresses. This rule is aimed at the type of overpayment that the contractor knows will result in unjust enrichment, and yet fails to disclose it.

The Councils have ensured that there is no overlap or inconsistency between this final rule and the current FAR requirements relating to overpayment, as well as the Contract Debt case published as part of Federal Acquisition Circular 2005-27 on September 17, 2008 (73 FR 53997).

g. Blacklisting

One respondent had a different concern, that the proposed changes in Part 42 with regard to past performance would allow "blacklisting" of contractors through consideration of "integrity and business ethics" in the past performance evaluation without due process protections. The respondent stated that the suspension and debarment procedures are the proper means to address responsibility issues.

Response: A contractor's satisfactory record of integrity and business ethics has long been one of the required elements for determining that a prospective contractor is responsible (see FAR 9.104-1(d)). The rules for assessing responsibility at FAR Subpart 9.1 provide for sufficient standards to ensure that offerors are treated fairly. FAR 15.306(b)(1) and (d)(3), and 42.1503(b) give the contractor the opportunity to comment on adverse past performance. The Councils do not recommend any change as a result of this comment.

h. Amendment of the Civil FCA

One respondent believed that the proposed cause for suspension/debarment language effectively amends the civil FCA. The respondent objected to changing contractors' obligations regarding overpayments without using the legislative procedure.

Response: The Councils disagree that the rule intended to, or did, amend the civil FCA outside the legislative process. The civil FCA provides a legal tool to counteract fraudulent billings turned in to the Federal Government by encouraging "whistleblowers" who are not affiliated with the Government to file actions against Federal contractors, claiming fraud against the Government. It also provides incentives to contractors to self-disclose. This does not preclude the Government from imposing an obligation on Federal contractors to themselves disclose to the Government if instances of overpayment are known to the company principals, and to hold them liable for knowing failure to disclose such an overpayment. This rule provides another tool to determine present responsibility of Government contractors.

FAR Subpart 9.4 provides debarment/suspension as a possible consequence for conviction of or civil judgment for commission of fraud or a variety of criminal offenses, although those statutes may already provide criminal or civil penalties for violation thereof. For example, the Sherman Act (15 U.S.C. 1-7) provides statutory penalties, including fines and imprisonment, for violation of the antitrust provisions of the statute. It is not inconsistent with the statute, nor does it require legislative amendment to include in the FAR that violation of the Federal statutes in submission of an offer is cause for debarment or suspension.

i. Technical Corrections

The Councils moved FAR 3.1002(c) to 3.1003(a)(2), because it presents a requirement rather than just policy guidance. In addition, the term "Mandatory"

APPENDIX B

was removed from the phrase "Mandatory requirements" at 3.1003, because it is redundant. The title of paragraph (a)(1) of FAR 3.1003 has been amplified to indicate that this paragraph is describing contractor requirements.

6. Extend to Violation of Civil False Claims Act

a. Support Application to Disclosure of Violations of the Civil FCA

The Department of Justice, Civil Division, which is responsible for the enforcement of the civil FCA, fully supports the extension of the proposed rule to require that contractors report violations of the civil FCA, 31 U.S.C. 3729 et seq., and to provide that the knowing failure to timely disclose such violations may be grounds for **67 081** suspension or debarment. Various respondents, including agency OIGs, express support for these provisions.

Response: Concur.

b. Same Issues as Raised With Regard to Other Mandatory Disclosures

Numerous respondents suggested that certain of their objections to the original proposal to require disclosure of criminal violations and to make a knowing failure to timely disclose such violations grounds for suspension or debarment, also apply to an expanded requirement that contractors disclose civil FCA violations. For example, some commented that disclosure should not be required because the conduct constituting violation of federal criminal law or the civil FCA is potentially broad and subject to varying interpretations by the Government, contractors and courts (and by relators in civil qui tam suits); that the requirement that violations be "timely" disclosed upon "reasonable grounds to believe" a violation has occurred are subject to varying interpretations as to when and under what circumstances a violation must be disclosed; that there is no rational basis for the proposed rule; that the rule would impose an unreasonable burden on contractors; and, that knowing failure to timely disclose should not be cause for suspension or debarment.

Response: These areas of concern common to both criminal and civil violations are addressed in other sections of this report. As discussed more fully elsewhere, the Councils have replaced the "reasonable grounds to believe" standard of the proposed rule with a "credible evidence" standard in the final rule, and to specify that the violation must have a nexus to contract award, performance or close-out, and to clarify that it is the knowledge of the principal that triggers the suspension and debarment cause. See responses under "Vagueness of rule" at paragraph B.3.b.i. (Reasonable grounds to believe); B.3.b.ii.(Timely disclosure); B.3.b.iii. (Criminal violation in connection with contract award or performance); and B.3.b.iv. (Level of employee with knowledge).

c. Issues Particular to the Civil FCA

i. Difficult to determine if violation has occurred. Several respondents urged that contractors should not be required to disclose violations of the civil FCA or be subject to suspension or debarment for a knowing failure to do so on a timely basis because, they suggest, the potential misconduct covered by the Act is broad, and the application of the statute raises many difficult factual and legal issues that the Government, contractors, relators and courts interpret in various ways. For example, one respondent argues that the contractor and the Government are not always aligned on whether a violation of the civil FCA has occurred, and suggests that it is impractical to assume that an average contractor employee will know definitively when a violation of the civil FCA has occurred. Several respondents observe that that there are many difficult legal and factual issues that arise in civil FCA matters, such as whether a submission constitutes a "claim", whether a statement is "false," and whether the person making the statement or submitting the claim acted with the requisite knowledge. Another respondent argues the courts are in conflict over what conduct constitutes a violation of the civil FCA. Another respondent considers it unfair to require contractors to make civil FCA liability determinations given conflicting judicial interpretations of the civil FCA and the contractor's inability to access relevant facts. This respondent argues that certain Federal appellate courts and the United States Supreme Court have read a materiality requirement into the civil FCA even though that element is not stated explicitly in the text. One respondent cites a split in the circuits regarding whether an entity that is subject to complex regulatory requirements can be held liable under the civil FCA when the entity bases its conduct on a reasonable interpretation of an ambiguous statute or regulation. Another respondent states that whereas federal crimes are fairly well-defined, novel and aggressive interpretations of the civil FCA have created an environment in which many claims of breach of a contract might be construed as civil FCA violations.

Based on the premise that violations of the civil FCA are difficult to define, several respondents concluded that contractors will be subject to suspension and debarment if the contractor misinterprets the circumstances and does not report a violation, even if there exists an honest disagreement about whether a violation of the civil FCA has occurred.

Response: The Councils do not agree that the requirements of the civil FCA cannot be reasonably ascertained and understood by contractors, and expects that contractors doing business with the Government are taking appropriate steps to ensure their compliance with that statute and all other applicable laws. The most recent amendments to the statute were made in 1986, and a significant body of case law interpreting the statute, and the 1986 amendments in particular, has developed in that time period. These cases interpret the various elements of a civil FCA violation, including the definition of a claim, falsity, knowledge, and damages.

Although the Councils recognize that some issues concerning the proper application of the civil FCA remain unsettled and subject to further judicial interpretation, this is not unique to the civil FCA.

Moreover, the disclosure requirement applies only where the contractor has "credible evidence" that a violation of the civil FCA has occurred. The contractor is subject to suspension and debarment for failure to timely disclose the violation only where the contractor does so knowingly. Genuine disputes over the proper application of the civil FCA may be considered in evaluating whether the contractor knowingly failed to disclose a violation of the civil FCA.

In this regard, the Councils note that the mere filing of a qui tam action under the civil FCA is not sufficient to establish a violation under the statute, nor does it represent, standing alone, credible evidence of a violation. Similarly, the decision by the Government to decline intervention in a qui tam action is not dispositive of whether the civil FCA has been violated,

APPENDIX B

nor conclusive of whether the contractor has credible evidence of a violation of the civil FCA.

ii. Broad scope of civil FCA. Several respondents suggested that requiring contractors to disclose violations of the civil FCA significantly expands the situations in which disclosure must be considered, and notes that the civil FCA can be violated even in situations where the Government suffers no financial loss. One respondent states that the civil FCA encompasses an "almost limitless universe of activities."

Response: The Councils do not agree that requiring disclosure of civil FCA violations will significantly broaden the situations where disclosure must be considered. Concerning the suggested breadth of the civil FCA, please see response to "Issues particular to the civil FCA", at paragraph B.6.c.i. "Difficult to determine if violation has occurred". The first proposed rule required contractors to disclose significant overpayments and violations of criminal law in connection with a Government contract or subcontract awarded thereunder, and the addition of the civil FCA is a natural extension of the rule. When a claim or payment comes under review, it often is not known at the outset of the investigation whether the matter is an overpayment, or a civil or criminal violation. In many cases, the same investigation must be done to determine the nature of the **67 082** conduct at issue. The same fraud may be actionable under the civil FCA or its criminal analogs, and require proof of the same general elements. See, e.g., 18 U.S.C. 287 (criminal False Claims Act); 18 U.S.C. 1001 (false statements).

Moreover, the fact that a course of conduct can violate the civil FCA even if the Government does not suffer a financial loss does not mean that disclosure is not relevant to the contractor's present responsibility. For example, the Government may avoid a financial loss because a contracting officer alertly catches and declines to pay a false or fraudulent claim, or perhaps because the false claim is disclosed by the contractor.

iii. Mitigation in civil FCA for voluntary disclosure. One respondent argues that there is no need to make failure to timely disclose a civil violation of the civil FCA a basis for suspension and debarment because the civil FCA already provides that damages may be reduced from trebles to doubles where the contractor discloses a violation to the United States. Another respondent suggests that the proposed FAR rule would convert these otherwise voluntary disclosures into mandatory disclosures, thereby preventing contractors from benefiting from the damages reduction provision of the civil FCA. One respondent requests that the final rule clarify that any mandatory reporting obligation is not intended to and does not prevent a contractor from seeking, and the Government from providing, reduced damages as a result of a disclosure made in compliance with the new contract provision.

Response: The Councils do not agree that the reduced damages available to contractors who disclose violations of the civil FCA in accordance with that Act obviates the need for the proposed amendment to make a failure to timely disclose a violation the basis for suspension or debarment. These provisions address two separate Governmental interests. The damages provisions of the civil FCA address the Government's ability to recoup its loss as a result of a violation, and recognize that timely disclosure is an important means for mitigating that loss. Suspension and debarment is concerned with the contractor's present responsibility. Timely disclosure of violations of the civil FCA is an important indicator of the contractor's present responsibility.

The mitigating provisions of the civil FCA apply to any disclosure that meets the requirements set forth in 31 U.S.C. 3729(a)(A). There is nothing in the FAR rule that would preclude a contractor from meeting the actual requirements of the reduced damages provision of the civil FCA. (See response at paragraphs B.3.a.vi. and B.5.c. discussing the mitigating factors in the USSG and in the FAR.) In its comments to the proposed rule, the Civil Division of DOJ, which enforces the civil FCA for the United States, noted that a contractor that meets both the disclosure requirements of the FAR and the civil FCA "would receive the dual benefit of qualifying to seek reduced damages under the civil FCA and avoiding the potential for suspension and debarment under the FAR."

iv. Proposed amendments to the civil FCA. Several respondents suggest that a contractor making a mandatory disclosure of a violation of the federal civil FCA risks prompting a potential relator to file a qui tam suit based on the disclosure, and note that the public disclosure bar under existing law likely would not bar such a suit. These respondents further suggest that this risk is increased if proposed amendments to the civil FCA (S.2041 and H.4854) are enacted because they would eliminate the public disclosure bar as a jurisdictional defense to a qui tam suit.

Response: The Councils recognize that mandatory disclosure of a violation of the civil FCA presents a risk that a qui tam action will follow. This risk is not unique for disclosures of civil FCA violations; the same risk arises from disclosures of overpayments and violations of criminal law. Furthermore, the underlying violation itself presents a risk of a qui tam action. Timely disclosure of a knowing violation offers the contractor an opportunity to demonstrate its present responsibility to avoid suspension or debarment, and to obtain a reduction in damages under the civil FCA.

v. Healthcare and banking. Several respondents disagreed with the view expressed by DOJ that the civil FCA reporting requirement imposes on Government contractors the same disclosure standards as those required of the healthcare and banking industries, and that no law requires disclosure of a civil FCA violation.

Response: See response, in paragraph B.3.a.iii.a. under "Mandatory disclosure to the OIG", "More far-reaching".

vi. Inherently governmental. One respondent objects that requiring contractors to disclose violations of the civil FCA to the Government would force contractors to interpret and enforce Federal law, which epitomizes an inherently governmental function.

Response: The Councils disagree that the mandatory disclosure provisions result in a transfer of an inherently governmental function to contractors. As noted in response B.6.c.i. above, individuals and entities contracting with the Government are subject to the civil FCA, and the Government expects that its contractors will take appropriate steps to ensure their compliance with all applicable laws. Compliance necessarily requires that contractors interpret the law as it may apply to their own circumstances and conduct, and this obligation is no different whether the law is civil or criminal. The Government will continue to exercise its independent judgment as to the proper interpretation of the civil FCA, to enforce the civil FCA consistent with ap-

APPENDIX B 277

plicable law, and to pursue violations of that law where appropriate, irrespective of whether those violations are brought to its attention by a contractor's disclosure or otherwise.

vii. Technical correction. One respondent is concerned that with addition of disclosure of violations of the False Claims Act, it is not entirely clear whether the limiting clause "in connection with the award or performance of this contract or any subcontract thereunder" applies to reporting both violations of Federal criminal law and violations of the civil FCA.

Response: Concur. The Councils have modified the rule accordingly.

7. *Application to Acquisition of Commercial Items*

a. Support Application to Acquisition of Commercial Items

An agency OIG, in commenting on the first proposed rule, believed that the responsibility of the contractor to report potential violations of criminal law or safety issues related to Government contracts or subcontracts should not be based on contract type and should not exclude commercial contracts from the reporting requirement.

In response to the question on the expansion of the second proposed rule to apply to commercial items, various respondents, including many agency OIGs, support application to contracts for the acquisition of commercial items.

Response: Concur.

b. Do Not Support Application to Acquisition of Commercial Items

Several respondents state that the proposed rule is inconsistent with Public Law 103-355 and FAR Part 12.

Another respondent is concerned that application of the proposed rule to commercial acquisitions will be difficult for educational institutions to implement.

Another respondent states that DoJ fails to show any deference to OFPP 67 083 with respect to commercial item policy, asserting without any rationale or elaboration that there would be no reason to exclude so-called commercial item contracts. This respondent states that the rule cannot be applied to commercial items without specific authorization by Executive Order or statute.

One respondent believes that applying Government-unique clauses to commercial suppliers will drive them away from the Government marketplace. Since this respondent recognizes that this is now required by statute, they will continue to seek a repeal of the statute.

Another respondent recommends against requiring commercial item contractors to develop new, Government-only ethics standards that result in a company having two standards of conduct, one for Government business and one for everything else.

Response: The disclosure requirements of the new statute specifically apply to commercial items. Furthermore, the statute includes the words "pursuant to FAR Case 2007-006 or any follow-on FAR case" which the Councils interpret as covering the inclusion of the civil FCA as addressed in the second proposed rule.

c. Application to Commercial Subcontracts

One respondent questions whether application of the proposed rule to the business practices of a commercial vendor that has no direct contractual relationship with the Federal Government has any relevance to assuring proper stewardship of Federal funds.

One respondent is concerned that without a more distinct definition of "subcontractor," the flowdown obligation may be applied more broadly than necessary. The respondent requests additional guidance in order to distinguish actual subcontractors from entities that may be contracted to provide collateral services to the commercial contractor (e.g., service vendors, licensors, corporate subsidiaries).

Further, another respondent states that revision to FAR Subpart 44.4 or FAR clauses 52.212-4 or 52.212-5 and clause 52.244-6 would be necessary before this requirement can be flowed down to commercial item subcontractors, but because the proposed rule has neglected to specify changes, there is no proposed authorization to revise those clauses in the final rule.

Response: "Subcontract" and "subcontractor" are defined at FAR 44.101. To clarify the meaning in this context, the Councils have borrowed from those definitions for use in the text at 3.1001 and in the clause at FAR 52.203-13.

The Councils are authorized to make any revisions to Subpart 44.4, Part 12 and Part 44, necessary to conform changes in the final rule, as long as changes in the final rule are reasonably foreseeable from either the proposed rule text or the discussions in the preamble. This constitutes adequate notice to the public. Both the text and preamble of the May 16, 2008, proposed rule were specific that the rule would apply to subcontracts. The Councils have made appropriate conforming changes to 52.212-5 and 52.244-6.

d. Other Concerns

One respondent questions whether the phrase "if 52.212-4 appears in this contract" (52.203-13(c)) is another way of saying it is a commercial item contract.

Response: Yes, inclusion of clause 52.212-4 in the prime contract would indicate that it is a contract for the acquisition of commercial items. However, now that the final rule requires flow down to commercial subcontracts, this phrase is inadequate for indicating a subcontract for commercial items, and has been revised accordingly.

e. Comments on the First Proposed Rule That Are No Longer Applicable

One respondent was concerned that the opportunity for substantial confusion exists with the rule and recommends additional guidance on how the rule im-

APPENDIX B | **279**

pacts companies selling commercial items under FAR Part 8 acquisitions.

Another respondent was concerned that the proposed language at 3.1004 "awarded under FAR Part 12" is likely to be misunderstood as applying only when the policies of FAR Part 12 are used exclusively and the procedures in Parts 13, 14, and 15 are not used.

Another respondent was concerned that the proposed rule does not properly address the exemption for commercial item vendors.

One respondent was concerned that the proposed rule does not justify imposing the new cause for suspension or debarment based on failure to disclose a "violation", and that will also place restrictions on commercial contractors that are not required by law and not consistent with the commercial market place.

Response: These comments are no longer applicable because the statute now requires application of most of this rule to commercial item contracts.

8. Application to Contracts To Be Performed Outside the United States

a. Support Application Outside the United States

Four respondents to the first proposed rule questioned the exceptions for overseas contacts.

• DoJ disagreed with excluding contracts performed entirely outside the United States from the requirements of the rule. The respondent indicates that the United States is still party to such contracts and potentially a victim when overpayments are made or when fraud occurs in connection with the contacts.

• One respondent was concerned that the rule exempts contracts performed overseas without providing an explanation as to why a basic policy of a code of ethics and business conduct should not apply overseas.

• An agency OIG believed that the responsibility of the contractor to report potential violations of criminal law or safety issues related to Government contracts or subcontracts should not be based on contract type and should not exclude contracts performed outside the United States from the reporting requirements.

• Another agency OIG believed that it is counterproductive to exclude contracts performed entirely outside the United States because the United States is still party to such contracts and may be victimized when overpayments are made or fraud occurs in connection with those contracts. The respondent also argues the contracts require greater vigilance because they are performed overseas where U.S. resources and remedies are more limited; and that the inclusion would reduce the vulnerabilities that often plague overseas programs and increase the effectiveness of those programs.

In response to the proposed expansion overseas in the second proposed rule, various respondents, including several agency OIGs, support making the requirements of this rule applicable to contracts and subcontracts performed outside the United States.

Response: Concur.

b. Do Not Support Application Outside the United States

One respondent raised the concern that if any part of the work is performed outside the United States, labor and privacy laws in Europe would prohibit mandatory reporting by employees.

Another respondent is concerned that extension of the requirements to contracts and subcontracts performed 67 084 outside the U.S. will likely have a significant and negative effect on academic institutions' ability to engage international partners. It is inappropriate and impractical to expect our international partners to do business in the same way as U.S. organizations. Many foreign academic institutions are instrumentalities of foreign governments and are subject to their own laws and regulations. Without flexibility, it will be impossible to pursue the international research and education

One respondent also believes that it is unreasonable and impractical to expect foreign firms to understand and be able to comply with the unique procedural requirements the U.S. imposes on its contractors. This respondent recognizes that this is now required by statute and it will seek a repeal of the statute.

Response: The disclosure requirements of the new statute specifically apply to acquisitions to be performed outside the United States. Furthermore, the statute includes the words "pursuant to FAR Case 2007-006 * * * or any follow-on FAR case" which the Councils interpret as covering the inclusion of the civil FCA as addressed in the second proposed rule.

9. Other Applicability Issues

a. Educational Institutions

i. Exempt educational and research institutions. One respondent requested that educational and research institutions be granted the same exemption afforded small business by making the requirement for a formal training and/or awareness program and internal control systems inapplicable to such institutions.

Response: By passing the "Close the Contractor Fraud Loophole Act," Congress made clear its preference for fewer, rather than more exemptions. The requirements at 3.1002(b) are that the ethics and compliance training program be suitable to the size of the entity and extent of its involvement in Government contracting. Further, this regulation applies only to contracts using appropriated funds, not to grants.

ii. Imposition of procurement requirements on grant recipients. One respondent stated that OMB regulation 2 CFR 215.40 forbids agencies to impose procurement requirements on grant recipients unless required by statute or Executive order or approved by OMB.

Response: This rule is not imposing any requirements on grant recipients.

APPENDIX B

The FAR does not apply to contracts awarded using grant money. Federal Government grant recipients who are also Federal Government contractors must comply with both the grant regulations and the FAR, as applicable.

b. Subcontractors

Various responses were received on the obligations imposed by this rule between contractors and subcontractors and the flow down of this rule to subcontractors.

Response: The Councils note that the same rationale that supports the application of the rule to prime contractors supports the application to subcontractors. The same reasonable efforts the contractor may take to exclude from its organizational structure principals whom due diligence would have exposed as engaging in illegal acts are the same reasonable efforts the contractor should take in selecting its subcontractors. Subcontractors should also use those same reasonable efforts in employment and subcontracting efforts.

i. Obligation to report violations by subcontractors. According to several respondents, prime contractors should not be responsible for oversight of their subcontractors and should not be subject to debarment for failure of a subcontractor to meet the requirement of the rule. The respondents were concerned that the rule renders prime contractors police for their subcontractors which respondents consider unreasonable and burdensome. One respondent was also concerned that rule creates a contractual obligation on the part of the contractor to ensure that its subcontractors perform as required by the rule. Another respondent stated that the rule fails to define the obligation of the contractor to police its subcontractors with regard to the required compliance program and integrity reporting. It is unclear what degree of due diligence the Government expects of the contractor.

Response: There is no requirement for the contractor to review or approve its subcontractors' ethics codes or internal control systems. Verification of the existence of such code and program can be part of the standard oversight that a contractor exercises over its subcontractors. The prime contractor is subject to debarment only if it fails to disclose known violations by the subcontractor. Therefore, a change to the rule is not necessary.

ii. Disclosure through the prime contractor. One respondent was concerned that the rule mandates that the disclosures go directly to the Government and not through the prime contractor. DoJ was concerned that some subcontractors may not be comfortable making disclosure through the prime contractor and suggested that a mechanism through which a subcontractor makes a disclosure be addressed in the final rule.

Response: The clause flow down in paragraph (d)(2) states that in altering the clause to identify the appropriate parties, all disclosures of violations of the civil FCA or of Federal criminal law shall be directed to the agency OIG, with a copy to the contracting officer. The clause does not require disclosure through the prime contractor.

iii. Liability for erroneous disclosure. One respondent was concerned that the rule creates a potential significant liability for the contractor if disclosures concerning subcontractors turn out to be in error. The respondent requested the Councils to consider whether damages assessed against contractors for erroneous reports would be allowable costs. Also, the respondent was concerned that the rule is unclear about the disclosure of criminal violations by subcontractors, and suggests that the Councils revise the rule to make the disclosure requirements for the contractor and the subcontractor parallel.

Response: The Councils revised the rule to require the contractor to disclose credible evidence of a violation of Federal criminal law in connection with the contract or any subcontract under the contract. This revision provides to the contractor sufficient opportunity to take reasonable steps to determine the credibility of any possible disclosure prior to disclosing it to the agency Inspector General and contracting officer. The potential for erroneous disclosure is minimized by requiring the contractor to disclose only credible evidence of violations, thereby reducing the contractor's potential liability for damages associated with erroneously disclosing alleged violations which are not substantiated.

c. Small Businesses (See Also Paragraph 11. "Regulatory Flexibility Act Concerns", for Comments on Initial Regulatory Flexibility Analysis)

i. Support level of applicability to small businesses. An agency OIG supported the application of the basic requirements of the rule to small business because the rule avoids imposing unnecessary burdens on small businesses by creating expensive paperwork requirements. Likewise, another agency OIG considered the exemption for small business contractors (from the requirements for a formal internal control system) reasonable. Another agency OIG also indicated that undesirable results for small business which could have resulted from initial drafts of the rule have been mediated by this rule.

67085 Response: Concur.

ii. Overly burdensome on small business: One respondent believed that the rule is an overly burdensome and unrealistic policing requirement that imposes significant new cost requirements and is particularly burdensome for small businesses; effectively precluding such businesses from competing for prime contract work or as a high-tier subcontractor.

• Response: Although the rule may have a significant economic impact on a substantial number of small entities with respect to the disclosure requirement, the rule is structured to minimize its impact on small business concerns by making the requirement for formal training programs and internal control systems inapplicable to small businesses, and limiting the disclosure requirement of violations of Federal criminal law to those violations involving fraud, conflict of interest, bribery, or gratuity violations found in Title 18 of the United States Code, although the rule did add the reporting of violations of the False Claims Act. The Councils do not believe that a change to the rule is necessary.

d. Dollar Threshold or Minimum 120 Day Performance Period

i. Recommend no threshold and no minimum performance period. One agency OIG commented on the rule's threshold of $5 million and 120-day performance period. The agency OIG believed that the application of the rule should not be determined on the basis of the dollar value or the period of performance of the contract. The respondent was concerned that, at times, contracting offi-

APPENDIX B   283

cers have awarded smaller dollar value contracts or modifications instead of one large dollar contract to circumvent various thresholds that trigger requirements. The respondent believed that the public and members of Congress have similar expectations of all contractors no matter the contract value or type.

Response: The Close the Contractor Fraud Loophole Act (Pub. L. 110-252, Section 6103) now defines a covered contract for application of this regulation as any contract in an amount greater than $5 million and more than 120 days in duration. The Councils also note that, regardless of whether the clause is included in the contract, the suspension and debarment provisions in Subpart 9.4 apply to all contractors, regardless of contract value or duration.

ii. Applicability of thresholds to Federal Supply Schedule (FSS) contracts and Blanket Purchase Agreements (BPA). One respondent requests explanation of the applicability of the thresholds to FSS contracts. The respondent does not believe that FAR 1.108(c) adequately clarifies the issue. Are the thresholds based on each individual order?

Response: According to FAR 1.108(c), unless otherwise specified, if the action establishes a maximum quantity of supplies or services to be acquired, the final anticipated dollar value must be the highest final priced alternative to the Government, including the dollar value of all options. That is, if it is anticipated that the dollar value of orders on an FSS contract will exceed $5 million, then this clause is included in the basic contract against which orders are placed.

e. Single Government Standard Also Applicable to Grants

One respondent was concerned that multiple Federal agencies already have compliance guidelines and regulations in place, or in development, and believes the rule may be inconsistent with other Federal agency requirements. The respondent requested that a single Federal Government-wide standard be created to foster integrity and honesty that applies to both Government contracts and Federal grants.

Response: The Councils acknowledge the respondent's concern. However, this rule establishes a Government-wide standard for contractor compliance programs and integrity reporting with respect to Government contract awards. Under the rule, all Federal agencies will be required to implement the same requirements in the same manner consistent with the award of Federal contracts. However, the rule does not and is not intended to address contractor compliance programs and integrity reporting with respect to agency grant-making procedures. Given the legal differences between a grant and a contract that concern performance and termination for default, the creation of a single Government standard addressing contractor compliance programs and integrity reporting is not practical and is outside the scope of the rule.

10. Additional Recommendations

a. Defer Final Rule Until

i. More experience with 2006-007. One respondent suggested that the FAR Council evaluate experience with the final rule, before proposing changes. The FAR Council should withdraw the proposed rule in favor of allowing covered contractors to implement the November 23, 2007, final rule.

ii. Completion of the National Science and Technology Council initiative. Several respondents urged the FAR Council to defer further action on proposed FAR Case 2007-006 pending completion of the National Science and Technology Council (NSTC) initiative to develop compliance guidance for recipients of Federal research funding from all agencies across the Federal Government.

iii. Further action on related legislation that would expand the scope of the civil FCA. One respondent requests postponement until after enactment of pending legislation on the civil FCA.

iv. Public hearings. One respondent alternatively suggests additional public comment in light of the pertinent intervening legislation and public hearings.

Response: The intervening legislation requires implementation of this rule in the FAR within 180 days of enactment of Pub. L. 110-252 (by December 26, 2008). Therefore, the Councils will proceed with this rule without delay.

At the time of publishing the final rule (2006-007), the proposed rule (2007-006) under this case had already been published. The preamble of the final rule under 2006-007 stated the intent to address mandatory disclosure and full cooperation under the follow-on rule.

It is unknown when the NSTC initiative to develop compliance guidance for recipients of Federal research funding from all agencies across the Federal Government will be completed. The Councils do not agree to delay the FAR rule pending the outcome of this particular initiative. Often the regulations for grants use the FAR as a model.

b. Expand Policy and Clause to Cover Overpayments

DoJ and an agency IG commented that the drafters of the proposed rule neglected to incorporate "knowing failure to timely disclose an overpayment" in the first reference at 3.1002(c).

Several respondents proposed that the language in the proposed FAR clause be expanded to also include instances of overpayment. More inclusive language removes any ambiguity (and loopholes) about what should be revealed to the Government. By expanding the scope to include overpayments, contractors are no longer asked to label (or mislabel) their activity as "criminal". In the opinion of the respondents, the proposed rule does not match the stated objective of encouraging Government notification of fraud and overpayments.

Response: The mandatory reporting of overpayments is addressed in the **67 086** Payments clauses. However, to aid in clarity, we have added a cross reference at FAR 3.1003 to the Payment clauses and the knowing failure to timely disclose significant overpayments as a cause for suspension/debarment in FAR Subpart 9.4.

c. Create a Contractor Integrity and Business Ethics Information Section in FAR Part 42

APPENDIX B | **285**

One respondent urged the FAR Councils to create a contractor integrity and business ethics section in FAR Part 42 that would require Government officials to record and maintain integrity and business ethics information that can be shared with Government officials. Although contractor performance and responsibility are part of FAR Subpart 9.1, the respondent requests that distinctive data and information be collected on each.

Another respondent, on the other hand, is very satisfied that the rule only proposed one change to the contractor past performance information in FAR 42.1501, and properly reinforces the existing emphasis on contractor cooperation across a broad range of contract administration matters, including cooperation with investigations.

Response: The proposed rule has added a cross reference in Part 42 to promote the inclusion of business integrity in past performance. The request to collect distinctive data and information on contractor responsibility is outside the scope of this rule. The past performance databases are controlled by the agencies. (See also response to "Suspension/Debarment", paragraph B.5.g. "Blacklisting")

d. Add Safety Issues

An agency IG suggested that safety issues should be included in the mandatory disclosure requirement.

Response: Adding explicit coverage of safety issues is outside the scope of this case.

e. Protection of Contractor Disclosures

The proposed rule states at 3.1002 (Policy) that contractors should have an internal control system that facilitates timely discovery of improper conduct in connection with Government contracts. A contractor may be suspended or debarred for knowing failure to timely disclose a violation of Federal criminal law in connection with the award or performance of any Government contract performed by the contractor.

DoJ suggested that, in order to encourage contractors to submit information, the Councils may wish to recommend to agencies that the submitted information be maintained confidentially to the extent permitted by law and that any disclosure of the information under FOIA should only be made after full consideration of institutional, commercial, and personal privacy interests that could be implicated by such a disclosure. In particular, agencies should be mindful that the Trade Secrets Act operates as a prohibition on the discretionary disclosure of any information covered by Exemption 4 of the FOIA, unless disclosure is otherwise authorized by law.

Response: The Councils have added the following provision to the final rule, similar to the provision employed by the DoD Voluntary Disclosure Program (DoD Directive 5106.01, April 23, 2006) in "XYZ" agreements with contractors pursuant to DoD Voluntary Disclosure Program Guidance (IGD 5505.50, CIPO, April 1990) (see http://www.dodig.mil/Inspections/vdprogram.htm): "The Government, to the extent permitted by law and regulation, will safeguard and treat information obtained pursuant to the contractor's disclosure as confidential where the information has been marked "confidential" or "proprietary" by the company. To the extent permitted by law and regulation, such information will not be released by the Government to the public pursuant to a Freedom of Information Act request, 5 U.S.C. section 552, et. seq., without prior notification to the contractor. The Government may transfer documents provided by the contractor to any department or agency within the Executive Branch if the information relates to matters within the organization's jurisdiction."

The addition of the above provision will provide appropriate assurance to contractors about the Government's protection afforded to disclosures.

11. *Regulatory Flexibility Act concerns*

a. IRFA Does Not Identify a Rational Basis for the Rule

Several respondents criticized the Initial Regulatory Flexibility Analysis (IRFA) as deficient because they believe that it does not identify a rational basis for the rule. They claim that there is no empirical or anecdotal evidence to explain why the mandatory disclosure requirement is required for the proper functioning of the procurement system.

Response: See response to "Mandatory disclosure to the OIG", "Empirical support that mandatory disclosure will achieve the Councils' objective", at paragraph B.3.a.iii.d.

b. The IRFA Underestimates the Number of Small Businesses Affected and the Associated Costs

Several respondents also considered that the IRFA underestimates the number of small businesses affected, as it only describes the estimated 28 small businesses which conclude that disclosure is required, rather than the larger number which will have to conduct internal investigations before concluding that disclosure is not required. One respondent pointed out the costs to run a compliance program. Another respondent pointed out that the IRFA does not ascertain the costs when a company chooses to retain outside counsel to investigate, which could range from $1 million to $20 million. The rule will cost small businesses over $1 billion a year (calculation--for each report there would be 5 internal investigations at a cost of $5 million per contractor and $2.5 million per subcontractor.)

Response: First, the IRFA estimated an impact on 45 small businesses, not just the 28 covered by the clause.

Second, an ethical company that learns that an employee may have committed a violation of Federal criminal law would not ignore this information. A company would normally investigate allegations of wrongdoing within the company as a sound business practice. If there was clearly no violation, the investigation would be short. Although the rule allows contractors time to take reasonable steps to determine that evidence of wrongdoing is credible, it does not direct contractors to carry out any particular level of internal investigation. The IRFA focused on the effort which results from this rule-- disclosure to the Government--although there are other incentives outside this rule which could cause a contractor to voluntarily disclose violations to the Government, such as the U.S. Sentencing Guidelines. Although the IRFA does not include the cost of the investigation in its calculations, the FAR

APPENDIX B   **287**

does not require or envision a small business paying millions of dollars for an investigation. The respondent's calculated cost estimates are not supported or credible.

The FAR did give relief for the costs of running a compliance program by leaving it to the discretion of the small business and paragraph (c) of the clause is not mandatory for small businesses.

67087 c. Imposition of Suspension and Debarment Will Disproportionately Damage Small Businesses

One respondent stated that small businesses do not have the resources that large businesses do. They do not have the resources to institute compliance programs. They are more likely to be caught in the suspension and debarment process. They lack the leverage to negotiate agreements in lieu of debarment. Therefore, the rule's reliance on suspension and debarment as an enforcement mechanism will disproportionately damage small businesses.

Response: The Councils agree that small businesses often have fewer resources than other than small business. Nonetheless, the Councils cannot give further flexibility here. The Councils have already eliminated the requirement for the internal control system for small businesses. The Councils cannot establish a different suspension or debarment standard for small businesses.

d. Estimate of Small Businesses That Would Disclose if No Mandatory Requirement

One respondent quoted the IRFA as estimating that, in the absence of the proposed disclosure requirement, 1 percent of small business contractors that are aware of a violation would voluntarily report it. This suggests, according to the respondent, that the FAR Council believes that mandatory disclosure would lead to a 100-fold increase in the number of reported violations. The respondent states that there is no support for this estimate and no rational basis to support a claim that this disclosure requirement is needed for the effective functioning of the procurement system.

Response: The respondent has drawn an unwarranted conclusion about the estimated impact of mandatory disclosure. The estimated 1% disclosure rate in the IRFA is for small businesses that do not have the clause in their contract (i.e., small dollar value or short performance period). There was no estimate in the IRFA about what percentage of this population would disclose if the clause were included. Further, any estimates about this segment of the population cannot be extrapolated to a conclusion about the effect of mandatory disclosure requirements on higher dollar value, noncommercial contracts or contracts with large businesses.

e. Recordkeeping Requirements

One respondent objected that the IRFA did not provide a full discussion of the projected recordkeeping and compliance requirements. Good business sense will require a contractor to develop and keep more records for the purpose of documenting its investigation.

Response: The Councils agree that recordkeeping would be wise, but the rule does not require recordkeeping beyond the recordkeeping that would be part of the contractor's normal business practices. Under 5 U.S.C. 601, the term "recordkeeping requirement" is defined as a requirement imposed by an agency on persons to maintain specified records.

f. Duplication, Overlap, or Conflict

Several respondents criticized the statement in the IRFA that the rule does not duplicate, overlap, or conflict with any other Federal rules. The respondents state that the IRFA--

• Ignored the obvious interrelationship with the civil Federal civil FCA and its qui tam provisions;

• Did not address the inconsistency between the proposed rule and the Federal Sentencing Guidelines; and

• Did not address that the rule is inconsistent with a voluntary disclosure being a mitigation consideration in the FAR debarment and suspension proceedings and under the civil FCA because disclosure would be mandatory rather than voluntary.

Response: Under 5 U.S.C. 601, "rule" is defined as meaning "any rule for which the agency publishes a general notice of proposed rulemaking pursuant to section 553(b) of this title or any other law * * * ". Codified laws are not a rule. The Sentencing Guidelines are, strictly speaking, also not a rule. However, the Councils disagree that this rule is duplicative of the civil FCA. Any inadvertent inconsistency with the Guidelines has been considered in formulating this final rule.

Regarding mitigation and voluntary disclosure, see "Mandatory disclosure to the OIG", "Incentives" at paragraph B.3.a.vi.

12. Paperwork Reduction Act (PRA)

a. Burden Underestimated

One respondent stated that the Councils' Paperwork Reduction Act analysis is inadequate. The estimates are so conservative as to be unrealistic. If it only takes 20 hours to conduct pre-disclosure review and draft a corresponding report, why does it take the Government a year to decide whether to intervene in a traditional qui tam case? The respondent points out that "burden" includes all aspects of the reporting process, including the separation of reportable events from non-reportable events.

Another respondent also considers the estimated burden of 3 hours per report woefully inadequate, considering the time needed by respondents to investigate and determine whether a civil FCA violation or criminal violation occurred.

Response: Burden includes estimated hours only for those actions which a company would not undertake in the normal course of business. The Government does not direct companies to investigate. In the normal course of business, a company that is concerned about ethical behavior will take reasonable steps

APPENDIX B | **289**

to determine the credibility of allegations of misconduct within the firm. It is left to the discretion of the company what these reasonable steps may entail. The Government has added the requirement to disclose to the Government when credible evidence of misconduct is obtained, which would not necessarily otherwise occur. The estimated hours in the regulatory flexibility analysis and the paperwork burden act analysis are to cover the hours required for preparing and reviewing the disclosure to the Government when credible evidence has been obtained. The estimated hours must also be viewed as an average between the hours that a simple disclosure by a very small business might require and the much higher numbers that might be required for a very complex disclosure by a major corporation. However, upon further discussion with subject matter experts, the Councils have revised the estimated hours to 60 hours per response, considering particularly the hours that would be required for review within the company, prior to release to the Government.

b. Recordkeeping and Other Compliance Requirements

One respondent stated that the projected recordkeeping and compliance requirements are far more burdensome than reflected in the IRFA. The contractor must keep and maintain extensive records any time it investigates allegations or suspicions of violations. Even if a company determines that disclosure is not required, the contractor must keep records of its decision-making process in order to defend against possible future accusations of failure to disclose.

Another respondent states that time is required for 1400 covered contractors to establish systems for complying with this regulation.

67 088 Response: See the response in previous section on Regulatory Flexibility Analysis (B.11.).

c. Data and Methodology Should Be Made Part of the Rulemaking Record

Response: The public can request copies of the supporting statements.

13. _Executive Order 12866_

a. Significant Rule

A number of respondents are concerned that this rule is a significant rule in accordance with E.O. 12866 section 3.(f). One respondent is concerned that, by extending the rule to cover commercial acquisitions and overseas contracts, a review requirement as a "major rule" or a significant rule under section 3. (f)(1) may have been unintentionally triggered. Another respondent believes that the rule should have a cost-benefit analysis.

One respondent states that the addition of violations of the civil FCA as a ground for mandatory disclosure is sufficient standing alone to trigger review under Section 6(b) of E.O. 12866.

Another respondent submits that this is a significant regulatory action because it will, among other things, adversely affect in a material way a sector of the economy (Government contractors).

Several respondents also state that the second proposed rule raises important legal and policy issues, another grounds for the Office of Information and Regulatory Affairs (OIRA) to declare a rule significant under E.O. 12866, under section 3.(f)(4).

One respondent suggests that it was a Freudian slip when the FR notice for the first proposed rule stated that the first proposed rule was a significant regulatory action and therefore was not subject to review.

Response: The first proposed rule was declared to be a significant rule by OIRA. The typographical error was in the second half of the sentence, not the first. The rule was subject to review under the Executive order and was so reviewed. OIRA did not declare the second proposed rule to be a significant rule.

All rules are sent through the Office of Information and Regulatory Affairs for determination as to whether the rule is significant. OMB's Office of Information and Regulatory Affairs has determined this is a significant rule, and not a major rule.

b. Violates E.O. 12866

One respondent states that the proposed rule violates the E.O. 12866 requirement that rules be "consistent, sensible, and understandable" and that agencies promulgate only such regulations as are required by law, are necessary to interpret the law, or are made necessary by compelling public need. This respondent submits that just because DoJ wants to make its job easier is not sufficient grounds for rulemaking.

Response: This rule is required by law and by compelling public need. The Councils have made every effort to make the draft final rule consistent, sensible, and understandable.

This is a significant regulatory action and, therefore, was subject to review under Section 6(b) of Executive Order 12866, Regulatory Planning and Review, dated September 30, 1993. This rule is not a major rule under 5 U.S.C. 804.

C. Regulatory Flexibility Act

The Regulatory Flexibility Act, 5 U.S.C. 601, et seq., applies to this final rule. The Councils prepared a Final Regulatory Flexibility Analysis (FRFA), and it is summarized as follows:

1. Statement of the need for, and objectives of, the rule.

This rule amends the Federal Acquisition Regulation to require Government contractors to--

• Establish and maintain specific internal controls to detect and prevent improper conduct in connection with the award or performance of any Government contract or subcontract; and

• Notify without delay the agency Office of the Inspector General, with a copy to the contracting officer, whenever, in connection with the award, performance, or closeout of a Government contract awarded to the contractor or a subcontract awarded thereunder, the contractor has credible evidence of a violation of Federal criminal law involving fraud, conflict of interest, bribery, or gratuity violations found in 18 U.S.C. or a violation of the civil False Claims Act.

This case is in response to a request to the Office of Federal Procurement Policy from the Department of Justice and Public Law 110-252. Based on the requirements of Pub. L. 110-252, the rule was expanded to include the clause 52.203-13 in contracts performed overseas and contracts for the acquisition of commercial items.

The objective of the rule is to emphasize the critical importance of integrity in contracting and reduce the occurrence of improper or criminal conduct in connection with the award and performance of Federal contracts and subcontracts.

2. Summary of the significant issues raised by the public comments in response to the initial regulatory flexibility analysis, a summary of the assessment of the agency of such issues, and a statement of any changes made in the proposed rule as a result of such comments.

a. IRFA does not identify a rational basis for the rule. Several respondents criticized the Initial Regulatory Flexibility Analysis (IRFA) as deficient because they believe that it does not identify a rational basis for the rule. They claim that there is no empirical or anecdotal evidence to explain why the mandatory disclosure requirement is required for the proper functioning of the procurement system.

Response: DoJ and various OIGs provided testimony that the experience with the National Reconnaissance Organization mandatory disclosure clause has been positive. Further, enactment of the Close the Contractor Fraud Loophole Act (Pub. L. 110-252, Sec VI, Chapter 1) now mandates many of these revisions to the FAR.

b. The IRFA underestimates the number of small businesses affected and the associated costs. Some respondents considered that the IRFA underestimates the number of small businesses affected, as it only describes the estimated 28 small businesses which conclude that disclosure is required, rather than the larger number which will have to conduct internal investigations before concluding that disclosure is not required. Respondents pointed out the costs to run a compliance program and that the IRFA does not ascertain the costs when a company chooses to retain outside counsel to investigate, which could range from $1 million to $20 million. The rule will cost small businesses over $1 billion a year (calculation--for each report there would be 5 internal investigations at a cost of $5 million per contractor and $2.5 million per subcontractor).

Response: First, the IRFA estimated an impact on 45 small businesses, not just the 28 covered by the clause. Further, an ethical company that finds out an employee may have committed a violation of Federal criminal law would not ignore this. A company would normally follow up allegations of wrongdoing within the company as a sound business practice. If there was clearly no violation, the investigation would be short. Although the rule allows contractors time to take reasonable steps to determine that evidence of wrongdoing is credible, it does not direct contractors to carry out any particular level of internal investigation. The IRFA focused on the effort which results from this rule--reporting to the Government. Although there are other incentives outside this rule which could cause a contractor to voluntarily disclose violations to the Government, such as the U.S. Sentencing Guidelines. Although the IRFA does not include the cost of the investigation in its calculations, the FAR does not require or envision a small business paying millions of dollars for an investigation. The respondent's calculated cost estimates are not supported or credible.

The FAR did give relief for the costs of running a compliance program by leaving it to the discretion of the small business; paragraph (c) of the clause is not mandatory for small businesses.

c. Imposition of suspension and debarment will disproportionately damage small businesses. A respondent stated that small businesses don't have the resources that large businesses do. They do not have the resources to institute compliance programs. They are more likely to be caught in the suspension and debarment process. They lack the leverage to negotiate agreements in **67089** lieu of debarment. Therefore, the rule's reliance on suspension and debarment as an enforcement mechanism will disproportionately damage small businesses.

Response: The Councils agree that small businesses have fewer resources than other than small businesses. Nonetheless, the Councils cannot give further flexibility here. The Councils have already eliminated the requirement for the internal control system for small businesses. The Councils cannot establish a different suspension or debarment standard for small businesses.

d. Estimate of small businesses that would report if no mandatory requirement. One respondent quoted the IRFA as estimating that, in the absence of the proposed disclosure requirement, 1% of small business contractors that are aware of a violation would voluntarily report it. This suggests, according to the respondent, that the FAR Council believes that mandatory disclosure would lead to a 100 fold increase in the number of reported violations. The respondent states that there is no support for this estimate.

Response: The respondent has drawn an unwarranted conclusion about the estimated impact of mandatory disclosure. The estimated 1% disclosure rate in the IRFA is for small businesses that do not have the clause in their contract (i.e., small dollar value or short performance period). There was no estimate in the IRFA about what percentage of this population would report if the clause were included. Further, any estimates about this segment of the population cannot be extrapolated to a conclusion about the effect of mandatory disclosure requirements on higher dollar value contracts of duration more that 120 days or contracts with large businesses. The number of small businesses affected cannot be known exactly because there is no data at this time on disclosures that will result from this rule, but the numbers represent the best estimate of subject matter experts in the Government.

e. Recordkeeping requirements. One respondent objected that the IRFA did not provide a full discussion of the projected recordkeeping and compliance requirements. Good business sense will require a contractor to develop and keep more records for the purpose of documenting its investigation.

APPENDIX B | 293

Response: Although recordkeeping would be wise, the rule does not require it. Under 5 U.S.C. 601, the term "recordkeeping requirement" is defined as a requirement imposed by an agency on persons to maintain specified records.

f. Duplication, overlap, or conflict. Several respondents criticized the statement in the IRFA that the rule does not duplicate, overlap, or conflict with any other Federal rules. The respondents state that the IRFA ignores the obvious interrelationship with the Federal False Claims Act and its qui tam provisions and it did not address the inconsistency between the proposed rule and the Federal Sentencing Guidelines. The rule is inconsistent with a voluntary disclosure being a mitigation consideration in the FAR debarment and suspension proceedings and under the False Claims Act because disclosure would be mandatory rather than voluntary.

Response: Under 5 U.S.C. 601, "rule" is defined as meaning any rule for which the agency publishes a general notice of proposed rulemaking pursuant to section 553(b) of this title. Codified laws are not a rule. The Sentencing Guidelines are, strictly speaking, also not a rule. However, the Councils disagree that this rule is duplicative of the False Claims Act and any inadvertent inconsistency with the Guidelines has been considered in formulating this final rule. The FAR, the U.S. Sentencing Guidelines, and the civil False Claims Act consider any self-disclosure to constitute a mitigating circumstance, whether voluntary or mandatory.

3. Description and estimate of the number of small entities to which the rule will apply.

The rule imposes a clause in contracts that exceed $5 million and a performance period greater than 120 days. Based on FY 2006 data collected from the Federal Procurement Data System, the Councils estimate that this clause will apply to 2700 prime contractors per year, of which 1050 companies are small business concerns.

The clause also flows down to subcontracts that exceed $5 million, and we estimate that approximately 1050 additional small business concerns will meet these conditions. We calculate the number of small business concerns that will be required by the clause to report violations of Federal criminal law with regard to a Government contract or subcontracts as follows:

1050 prime contractors + 1050 subcontractors = 2100 x 4% = 84.

In addition, although there is no clause required, all contractors will be on notice that they may be suspended or debarred for failure to report known violations of Federal criminal law with regard to a Government contract or subcontract. In FY 2006 there were 144,854 small business concerns listed in FPDS-NG with unique DUNS numbers. We estimate that of the listed small business concerns, approximately 116,000 (80%) will receive contracts in a given fiscal year. Government small business experts guess that at least twice that number of small businesses (232,000) will receive subcontracts. However, the only small business concerns impacted by this cause for suspension or debarment are those that are aware of violation of Federal criminal law with regard to their Government contracts or subcontracts. Subtracting out those contracts and subcontracts covered by the clause (1050 each), we estimate this number as follows: (114,950 + 230,950 = 345,900 x 1% = 3,459). We estimate a lower percentage than used for contracts and subcontracts that contain the clause, because these are lower dollar contracts and subcontracts, including commercial contracts, and there may be less visibility into violations of Federal criminal law. Because there is no contract clause, we estimate that only 1% of those contractors/subcontractors that are aware of a violation of Federal criminal law in regard to the contract or subcontract will voluntarily report such violation to the contracting officer (3459 x 1% = 34). The estimated number of small businesses in the FRFA (119) has increased from the IRFA (45) because of the applicability of the clause to commercial contracts and contracts to be performed outside the United States and because the disclosure requirement now applies to violations of the civil False Claims Act as well as violations of Federal criminal law.

4. Description of projected reporting, recordkeeping, and other compliance requirements of the rule, including an estimate of the classes of small entities which will be subject to the requirement and the type of professional skills necessary for preparation of the report or record.

The rule requires contractors to report to the agency office of the inspector general, with a copy to the contracting officer, violations of Federal criminal law in connection with the award or performance of any Government contract or subcontract for contracts that exceed $5 million with a contract performance period greater than 120 days, and the same criteria for flow down to subcontracts. Such a report would probably be prepared by company management, and would probably involve legal assistance to prepare and careful review at several levels. There are no recordkeeping requirements in the rule.

5. Description of the steps the agency has taken to minimize the significant economic impact on small entities consistent with the state objectives of applicable statute, including a statement of the factual, policy, and legal reasons for selecting the alternative adopted in the final rule and why each one of the other significant alternatives to the rule considered by the agency which affect the impact on small entities was rejected.

The Councils adopted the following alternatives in order to minimize the impact on small business concerns:

• The final rule requires small businesses to "make a copy of the code available" to each employee (rather than "provide a copy"). The Councils rejected the addition of a requirement that small businesses must specifically make each employee aware of the duties and obligations under the code.

• The requirement for formal training programs and internal control systems is inapplicable to small business concerns. Large businesses are still required to have an ongoing business ethics and conduct awareness and compliance program

• Disclosure of violations of criminal law is limited to violations of Federal criminal law involving fraud, conflict of interest, bribery, or gratuity violations found in 18 U.S.C., rather than any violation of criminal law.

• The violations that must be disclosed do not include violations under the contracts of other contractors.

• The period of occurrence of violations that must be disclosed is limited

APPENDIX B

to 3 years after contract closeout, rather than extending indefinitely.

The Councils could not exclude small businesses that provide commercial items, because Pub. L. 110-252 requires application to contracts for the acquisition of commercial items.

The Councils decided to require disclosure of violations of civil False Claims Act (from both large and small businesses), as requested by the Department of Justice, **67090** because to achieve the objectives of this rule, it is crucial to deal with responsible contractors, whether large or small. It is not necessarily evident at the beginning of an investigation whether an incident is simply an overpayment, a civil false claim, or a criminal violation. There is no rational reason to exclude civil false claims from the mandatory disclosure requirement.

Interested parties may obtain a copy of the FRFA from the FAR Secretariat. The FAR Secretariat has submitted a copy of the FRFA to the Chief Counsel for Advocacy of the Small Business Administration.

D. Paperwork Reduction Act

The Paperwork Reduction Act (44 U.S.C. Chapter 35) applies because the final rule contains an information collection requirement (ICR). The clause at 52.203-13 requires the Contractor to disclose "credible evidence of a violation" of Federal criminal law or a violation of the False Claims Act, involving fraud, conflict of interest, bribery, or gratuity violations found in Title 18 of the United States Code. We received one comment from the public on this disclosure requirement. Based on the comment that the Government's estimated burden of 3 hours per response was inadequate, the Councils have revised the estimated burden hours to 60 hours per response. This change particularly considers the hours that would be required for review of the collection within a company, prior to release to the Government. Based on the revised estimated burden of 60 hours per response, the annual reporting burden is revised as follows:

```
-------------------------------------------------
-------------------------------------------------
Respondents: ............................... 284
Responses per respondent: .......... x 1
Total annual responses: ..................... 284
Preparation hours per response: .... x 60
Total response burden hours: .............. 17,040
Averages wages ($75 + 32.85% OH): .. x $100
Estimated cost to the Public: ........ $1,704,000
-------------------------------------------------
```

Accordingly, the FAR Secretariat has forwarded a request for approval of a new information collection requirement concerning 9000-00XX to the Office of Management and Budget under 44 U.S.C. 3501, et seq.

List of Subjects in 48 CFR Parts 2, 3, 9, 42 and 52

Government procurement.

Al Matera,

Director, Office of Acquisition Policy.

Therefore, DoD, GSA, and NASA amend 48 CFR parts 2, 3, 9, 42 and 52 as set forth below:

1. The authority citation for 48 CFR parts 2, 3, 9, 42 and 52 continues to read as follows:

Authority: 40 U.S.C. 121(c); 10 U.S.C. chapter 137; and 42 U.S.C. 2473(c).

PART 2--DEFINITIONS OF WORDS AND TERMS

48 CFR 2.101

2. Amend section 2.101 in paragraph (b)(2) by adding, in alphabetical order, the definition "Principal" to read as follows:

48 CFR 2.101

2.101 Definitions.

* * * * *
(b) * * *

(2) * * *

Principal means an officer, director, owner, partner, or a person having primary management or supervisory responsibilities within a business entity (e.g., general manager; plant manager; head of a subsidiary, division, or business segment; and similar positions).

* * * * *

PART 3--IMPROPER BUSINESS PRACTICES AND PERSONAL CONFLICTS OF INTEREST

48 CFR 3.1001

3. Revise section 3.1001 to read as follows:

48 CFR 3.1001

3.1001 Definitions.

As used in this subpart--

Subcontract means any contract entered into by a subcontractor to furnish supplies or services for performance of a prime contract or a subcontract.

Subcontractor means any supplier, distributor, vendor, or firm that furnished supplies or services to or for a prime contractor or another subcon-

APPENDIX B

tractor.

United States means the 50 States, the District of Columbia, and outlying areas.

48 CFR 3.1003

4. Amend section 3.1003 by revising the section heading and paragraph (a); redesignating paragraph (b) as paragraph (c), and adding a new paragraph (b) to read as follows:

48 CFR 3.1003

3.1003 Requirements.

(a) Contractor requirements. (1) Although the policy at 3.1002 applies as guidance to all Government contractors, the contractual requirements set forth in the clauses at 52.203-13, Contractor Code of Business Ethics and Conduct, and 52.203-14, Display of Hotline Poster(s), are mandatory if the contracts meet the conditions specified in the clause prescriptions at 3.1004.

(2) Whether or not the clause at 52.203-13 is applicable, a contractor may be suspended and/or debarred for knowing failure by a principal to timely disclose to the Government, in connection with the award, performance, or closeout of a Government contract performed by the contractor or a subcontract awarded thereunder, credible evidence of a violation of Federal criminal law involving fraud, conflict of interest, bribery, or gratuity violations found in Title 18 of the United States Code or a violation of the civil False Claims Act. Knowing failure to timely disclose credible evidence of any of the above violations remains a cause for suspension and/or debarment until 3 years after final payment on a contract (see 9.406-2(b)(1)(vi) and 9.407-2(a)(8)).

(3) The Payment clauses at FAR 52.212-4(i)(5), 52.232-25(d), 52.232-26(c), and 52.232-27(l) require that, if the contractor becomes aware that the Government has overpaid on a contract financing or invoice payment, the contractor shall remit the overpayment amount to the Government. A contractor may be suspended and/or debarred for knowing failure by a principal to timely disclose credible evidence of a significant overpayment, other than overpayments resulting from contract financing payments as defined in 32.001 (see 9.406-2(b)(1)(vi) and 9.407-2(a)(8)).

(b) Notification of possible contractor violation. If the contracting officer is notified of possible contractor violation of Federal criminal law involving fraud, conflict of interest, bribery, or gratuity violations found in Title 18 U.S.C.; or a violation of the civil False Claims Act, the contracting officer shall--

(1) Coordinate the matter with the agency Office of the Inspector General; or

(2) Take action in accordance with agency procedures.

* * * * *

48 CFR 3.1004

5. Amend section 3.1004 by removing the introductory text and revising the introductory text of paragraph (b)(1) to read as follows:

48 CFR 3.1004

3.1004 Contract clauses.

* * * * *
(b)(1) Unless the contract is for the acquisition of a commercial item or will be performed entirely outside the United States, insert the clause at **67 091**FAR 52.203-14, Display of Hotline Poster(s), if--

* * * * *

PART 9--CONTRACTOR QUALIFICATIONS

48 CFR 9.104-1

6. Amend section 9.104-1 by revising paragraph (d) to read as follows:

48 CFR 9.104-1

9.104-1 General standards.

* * * * *
(d) Have a satisfactory record of integrity and business ethics (for example, see Subpart 42.15).

* * * * *

48 CFR 9.406-2

7. Amend section 9.406-2 by revising the introductory text of paragraph (b)(1) and adding paragraph (b)(1)(vi) to read as follows:

48 CFR 9.406-2

9.406-2 Causes for debarment.

(b)(1) A contractor, based upon a preponderance of the evidence, for any of the following--

* * * * *
(vi) Knowing failure by a principal, until 3 years after final payment on any Government contract awarded to the contractor, to timely disclose to the Government, in connection with the award, performance, or closeout of the contract or a subcontract thereunder, credible evidence of--

(A) Violation of Federal criminal law involving fraud, conflict of interest, bribery, or gratuity violations found in Title 18 of the United States Code;

APPENDIX B

(B) Violation of the civil False Claims Act (31 U.S.C. 3729-3733); or

(C) Significant overpayment(s) on the contract, other than overpayments resulting from contract financing payments as defined in 32.001.

* * * * *

48 CFR 9.407-2

8. Revise section 9.407-2 by redesignating paragraph (a)(8) as paragraph (a)(9) and adding a new paragraph (a)(8); to read as follows:

48 CFR 9.407-2

9.407-2 Causes for suspension.

(a) * * *

(8) Knowing failure by a principal, until 3 years after final payment on any Government contract awarded to the contractor, to timely disclose to the Government, in connection with the award, performance, or closeout of the contract or a subcontract thereunder, credible evidence of--

(i) Violation of Federal criminal law involving fraud, conflict of interest, bribery, or gratuity violations found in Title 18 of the United States Code;

(ii) Violation of the civil False Claims Act (31 U.S.C. 3729-3733); or

(iii) Significant overpayment(s) on the contract, other than overpayments resulting from contract financing payments as defined in 32.001; or

* * * * *

PART 42--CONTRACT ADMINISTRATION AND AUDIT SERVICES

48 CFR 42.1501

9. Amend section 42.1501 by revising the last sentence to read as follows:

48 CFR 42.1501

42.1501 General.

* * * It includes, for example, the contractor's record of conforming to contract requirements and to standards of good workmanship; the contractor's record of forecasting and controlling costs; the contractor's adherence to contract schedules, including the administrative aspects of performance; the contractor's history of reasonable and cooperative behavior and commitment to customer satisfaction; the contractor's record of integrity and business ethics, and generally, the contractor's business-like concern for the interest of the customer.

PART 52--SOLICITATION PROVISIONS AND CONTRACT CLAUSES

48 CFR 52.203-13

10. Amend section 52.203-13 by--

a. Revising the date of clause;

b. Revising paragraph (a);

c. Revising paragraphs (b)(1)(i), (b)(1)(ii), (b)(2) and adding paragraph (b)(3); and

d. Revising paragraphs (c) and (d).

The revised text reads as follows:

48 CFR 52.203-13

52.203-13 Contractor Code of Business Ethics and Conduct.

* * * * *

Contractor Code of Business Ethics and Conduct

(Dec 2008)

(a) Definitions. As used in this clause--

Agent means any individual, including a director, an officer, an employee, or an independent Contractor, authorized to act on behalf of the organization.

Full cooperation--(1) Means disclosure to the Government of the information sufficient for law enforcement to identify the nature and extent of the offense and the individuals responsible for the conduct. It includes providing timely and complete response to Government auditors' and investigators' request for documents and access to employees with information;

(2) Does not foreclose any Contractor rights arising in law, the FAR, or the terms of the contract. It does not require--

(i) A Contractor to waive its attorney-client privilege or the protections afforded by the attorney work product doctrine; or

(ii) Any officer, director, owner, or employee of the Contractor, including a sole proprietor, to waive his or her attorney client privilege or Fifth Amendment rights; and

(3) Does not restrict a Contractor from--

(i) Conducting an internal investigation; or

(ii) Defending a proceeding or dispute arising under the contract or related to a potential or disclosed violation.

Principal means an officer, director, owner, partner, or a person having primary management or supervisory responsibilities within a business entity (e.g., general manager; plant manager; head of a subsidiary, division, or business segment; and similar positions).

Subcontract means any contract entered into by a subcontractor to furnish supplies or services for performance of a prime contract or a subcontract.

Subcontractor means any supplier, distributor, vendor, or firm that furnished supplies or services to or for a prime contractor or another subcontractor.

United States means the 50 States, the District of Columbia, and outlying areas.

(b) * * *

(1) * * *

(i) Have a written code of business ethics and conduct;

(ii) Make a copy of the code available to each employee engaged in performance of the contract.

(2) The Contractor shall—

(i) Exercise due diligence to prevent and detect criminal conduct; and

(ii) Otherwise promote an organizational culture that encourages ethical conduct and a commitment to compliance with the law.

(3)(i) The Contractor shall timely disclose, in writing, to the agency Office of the Inspector General (OIG), with a copy to the Contracting Officer, whenever, in connection with the award, performance, or closeout of this contract or any subcontract thereunder, the Contractor has credible evidence that a principal, employee, agent, or subcontractor of the Contractor has committed—

(A) A violation of Federal criminal law involving fraud, conflict of interest, bribery, or gratuity violations found in Title 18 of the United States Code; or

(B) A violation of the civil False Claims Act (31 U.S.C. 3729-3733).

(ii) The Government, to the extent permitted by law and regulation, will safeguard and treat information obtained pursuant to the Contractor's disclosure as confidential where the information has been marked "confidential" or "proprietary" by the company. To the extent permitted by law and regulation, such information will not be released by the Government to the public pursuant to a Freedom of Information Act request, 5 U.S.C. Section 552, without prior notification to the Contractor. The Government may transfer documents provided by the Contractor to any department or agency within the Executive Branch if the information relates to matters within the organization's jurisdiction.

(iii) If the violation relates to an order against a Governmentwide acquisition contract, a multi-agency contract, a multiple-award schedule contract such as the Federal Supply Schedule, or any other procurement instrument intended for use by multiple agencies, the Contractor shall notify the OIG of the ordering agency and the IG of the agency responsible for the basic contract.

(c) Business ethics awareness and compliance program and internal control **67 092** system. This paragraph (c) does not apply if the Contractor has represented itself as a small business concern pursuant to the award of this contract or if this contract is for the acquisition of a commercial item as defined at FAR 2.101. The Contractor shall establish the following within 90 days after contract award, unless the Contracting Officer establishes a longer time period:

(1) An ongoing business ethics awareness and compliance program.

(i) This program shall include reasonable steps to communicate periodically and in a practical manner the Contractor's standards and procedures and other aspects of the Contractor's business ethics awareness and compliance program and internal control system, by conducting effective training programs and otherwise disseminating information appropriate to an individual's respective roles and responsibilities.

(ii) The training conducted under this program shall be provided to the Contractor's principals and employees, and as appropriate, the Contractor's agents and subcontractors.

(2) An internal control system.

(i) The Contractor's internal control system shall--

(A) Establish standards and procedures to facilitate timely discovery of improper conduct in connection with Government contracts; and

(B) Ensure corrective measures are promptly instituted and carried out.

(ii) At a minimum, the Contractor's internal control system shall provide for the following:

(A) Assignment of responsibility at a sufficiently high level and adequate resources to ensure effectiveness of the business ethics awareness and compliance program and internal control system.

(B) Reasonable efforts not to include an individual as a principal, whom due diligence would have exposed as having engaged in conduct that is in conflict with the Contractor's code of business ethics and conduct.

(C) Periodic reviews of company business practices, procedures, policies,

APPENDIX B | 303

and internal controls for compliance with the Contractor's code of business ethics and conduct and the special requirements of Government contracting, including--

(1) Monitoring and auditing to detect criminal conduct;

(2) Periodic evaluation of the effectiveness of the business ethics awareness and compliance program and internal control system, especially if criminal conduct has been detected; and

(3) Periodic assessment of the risk of criminal conduct, with appropriate steps to design, implement, or modify the business ethics awareness and compliance program and the internal control system as necessary to reduce the risk of criminal conduct identified through this process.

(D) An internal reporting mechanism, such as a hotline, which allows for anonymity or confidentiality, by which employees may report suspected instances of improper conduct, and instructions that encourage employees to make such reports.

(E) Disciplinary action for improper conduct or for failing to take reasonable steps to prevent or detect improper conduct.

(F) Timely disclosure, in writing, to the agency OIG, with a copy to the Contracting Officer, whenever, in connection with the award, performance, or closeout of any Government contract performed by the Contractor or a subcontractor thereunder, the Contractor has credible evidence that a principal, employee, agent, or subcontractor of the Contractor has committed a violation of Federal criminal law involving fraud, conflict of interest, bribery, or gratuity violations found in Title 18 U.S.C. or a violation of the civil False Claims Act (31 U.S.C. 3729-3733).

(1) If a violation relates to more than one Government contract, the Contractor may make the disclosure to the agency OIG and Contracting Officer responsible for the largest dollar value contract impacted by the violation.

(2) If the violation relates to an order against a Governmentwide acquisition contract, a multi-agency contract, a multiple-award schedule contract such as the Federal Supply Schedule, or any other procurement instrument intended for use by multiple agencies, the contractor shall notify the OIG of the ordering agency and the IG of the agency responsible for the basic contract, and the respective agencies' contracting officers.

(3) The disclosure requirement for an individual contract continues until at least 3 years after final payment on the contract.

(4) The Government will safeguard such disclosures in accordance with paragraph (b)(3)(ii) of this clause.

(G) Full cooperation with any Government agencies responsible for audits, investigations, or corrective actions.

(d) Subcontracts. (1) The Contractor shall include the substance of this clause, including this paragraph (d), in subcontracts that have a value in excess of $5,000,000 and a performance period of more than 120 days.

(2) In altering this clause to identify the appropriate parties, all disclosures of violation of the civil False Claims Act or of Federal criminal law shall be directed to the agency Office of the Inspector General, with a copy to the Contracting Officer.

(End of clause)

48 CFR 52.209-5

11. Amend section 52.209-5 by revising the date of clause; and paragraph (a)(2) to read as follows:

48 CFR 52.209-5

52.209-5 Certification Regarding Responsibility Matters.

* * * * *

Certification Regarding Responsibility Matters

(Dec 2008)

* * * * *
(a) * * *

(2) Principal, for the purposes of this certification, means an officer, director, owner, partner, or a person having primary management or supervisory responsibilities within a business entity (e.g., general manager; plant manager; head of a subsidiary, division, or business segment; and similar positions).

* * * * *

48 CFR 52.212-5

12. Amend section 52.212-5 by--

a. Revising the date of the clause;

b. Redesignating paragraphs (b)(2) through (b)(40) as (b)(3) through (b)(41), respectively, and adding a new paragraph (b)(2);

c. Removing from paragraph (e)(1) "paragraphs (i) through (vii)" and adding "paragraphs (e)(1)(i) through (xi)" in its place; and.

d. Redesignating paragraphs (e)(1)(i) through (e)(1)(x) as paragraphs (e)(1)(ii) through (e)(1)(xi), respectively, and adding a new paragraph (e)(1)(i).

The added and revised text reads as follows:

APPENDIX B

48 CFR 52.212-5

52.212-5 Contract Terms and Conditions Required To Implement Statutes or Executive Orders--Commercial Items.

* * * * *

Contract Terms and Conditions Required To Implement Statutes or Executive Orders--Commercial Items

(Dec 2008)

* * * * *
 (b) * * *

 (2) 52.203-13, Contractor Code of Business Ethics and Conduct (DEC 2008) (Pub. L. 110-252, Title VI, Chapter 1 (41 U.S.C. 251 note)).

* * * * *
 (e) * * *

 (1) * * *

 (i) 52.203-13, Contractor Code of Business Ethics and Conduct (DEC 2008) (Pub. L. 110-252, Title VI, Chapter 1 (41 U.S.C. 251 note)).

* * * * *

48 CFR 52.213-4

52.213-4 [Amended]

48 CFR 52.213-4

 13. Amend section 52.213-4 by--

a. Revising the date of the clause to read (DEC 2008); and

b. Removing from paragraph (a)(2)(vi) "(MAR 2007)" and adding "(DEC 2008)" in its place.

48 CFR 52.244-6

 14. Amend section 52.244-6 by--

a. Revising the date of the clause;

b. Redesignating paragraphs (c)(1)(i) through (c)(1)(vi) as paragraphs (c)(1)(ii) through (c)(1)(vii), respectively, and adding a new paragraph (c)(1)(1).

The added and revised text reads as follows:

48 CFR 52.244-6

52.244-6 Subcontracts for Commercial Items.

* * * * *

Subcontracts for Commercial Items

(Dec 2008)

* * * * *
 (c)(1) * * *

 67 093 (i) 52.203-13, Contractor Code of Business Ethics and Conduct (DEC 2008) (Pub. L. 110-252, Title VI, Chapter 1 (41 U.S.C. 251 note).

* * * * *

[FR Doc. E8-26953 Filed 11-10-08; 8:45 am]

BILLING CODE 6820-EP-P

 73 FR 67064-02, 2008 WL 4861443 (F.R.)

END OF DOCUMENT

Code of Ethics Guide

U.S. Department of Transportation
Federal Highway Administration

Search | Feedback

Construction

FHWA > Engineering > Construction > Contract Administration > Construction Guide > Code Of Ethics Guide

Code Of Ethics Guide

A Sample Guide Developed by the USDOT/ AGC / ARTBA / AASHTO Suspension & Debarment Work Group

Elements of a Code of Business Ethics

A Code of Business Ethics is an open disclosure of the way an organization operates and provides visible guidelines for behavior. It serves as an important communication vehicle to the company's employees, customers, subcontractors, and the community at large that the organization is committed to the highest ethical standards of conduct in its operations. Additionally, a Code of Business Ethics is intended to promote ethical and law-abiding conduct within an organization and clearly communicate to employees what is expected of them and the consequences for violations. The following are a few of the elements an effective Code of Business Ethics should have:

- Commitment by the organization's directors and top management to abiding by the Code and also ensuring that all employees are aware of and abide by the Code
- Applicability to all levels of the organization
- A letter from the President or Chief Executive of the organization communicating what the Code is and the organization's commitment to following the Code
- A table of contents so that employees will be able to easily find the organization's policy for a specific issue
- A statement of policy concerning the Code and the general rules that apply to the Code
- Standards of Conduct that communicate what issues employees should be aware of and what to do whenever confronted with any such issue
- A statement requiring employees to report suspected violations and to cooperate with the implementation of the Code

More Information

- Contract Administration

Contact

Jerry Yakowenko
Office of Program Administration
202-366-1562
E-mail

APPENDIX C

- A statement that clearly communicates the consequences for Code violations

This page last modified on 03/29/07

FHWA Home | Engineering | Construction

United States Department of Transportation - **Federal Highway Administration**

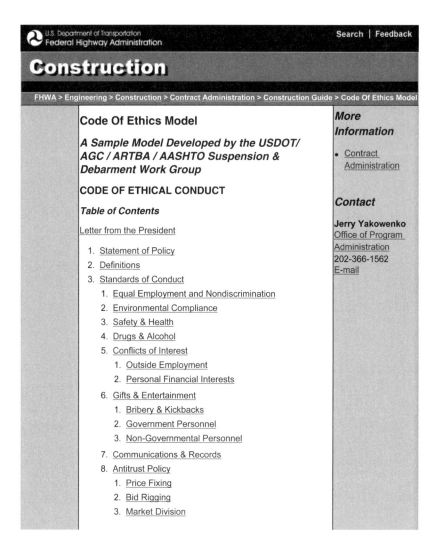

9. Claims
10. Statements & Certifications
11. Commitment to Disadvantaged Business Enterprises
4. Obligation to Report Violations & Cooperation
5. Consequences for Violations

Acknowledgement

Letter from the President

Dear employees:

X Company has a long reputation for honesty and integrity in business dealings and lawful and ethical behavior. This reputation is a source of pride for us as well as one of our greatest assets because it instills the necessary trust and confidence in us by our customers, subcontractors, suppliers, and the overall community in which we live. Here at X Company, we are committed to the highest standards of business ethics.

In order to maintain our commitment to integrity, we have established a Code of Ethical Conduct and Corporate Compliance Program. The Code of Ethical Conduct is intended to identify the our employees are expected follow whenever conducting business at this company and the Corporate Compliance Program is intended to ensure that all employees are abiding by the Code. an employee, you are expected to read both the Code and the Program and certify annually your commitment to complying fully with them.

To administer this Program, I have appointed John/Jane Doe as the corporate compliance officer. Among other things, s/he will be responsible for implementing appropriate procedures and policies the Program, ensuring that each of you receive a copy of the Program, providing regular training on compliance with the Program, and ensuring effective and appropriate enforcement of the Program. Mrs./Ms./ Doe reports directly to me and has my full support and attention. I expect our officers and managers will ensure that this Program and Mr./Mrs./Ms. Doe receives full attention and fully in the program's implementation. Also, even though I have appointed Mr./Mrs./Ms. Doe corporate compliance officer, please know that I maintain an open door policy for any employee who has concerns Company or employee practices.

I cannot stress strongly enough that X Company does not, and will not, tolerate any form of unlawful or unethical behavior by any person or entity associated with it. At the very least, X Company that each of its employees conducts himself or herself in accordance with the laws and regulations that apply to our business and not condone criminal or unethical behavior by others. Each of you is expected to alert Mr./Mrs./Ms. Doe of any information you may have of any unlawful or unethical behavior by any of our employees, prime contractors, subcontractors, suppliers, or customers. violation of this program, including failure to report a violation or other unlawful or unethical behavior, can be grounds for discipline, including termination.

Our continued success depends on all of us doing the right thing at all times and maintaining the highest ethical standards. Only in this way, can we continue to earn the trust and confidence of our customers and the community in which we live.

Sincerely,

President

I. Statement of Policy

It is X Company's policy to maintain the highest ethical standards and comply with all applicable laws, rules, and regulations. We believe that adherence to this policy will ensure our continued success as well as earn and maintain the confidence of our customers and the community in which we live. In order to ensure X Company operates pursuant to this policy, we have established this Code of Ethical Conduct. The following general rules apply to the implementation of this Code of Ethical Conduct:

1. All employees must comply this Code of Conduct. Any officer, director, or employee violating this Code is subject to discipline, which may include demotion or dismissal.
2. All employees have a duty to report all suspected violations of the Code or other potentially unethical behavior by anyone, including officers, directors, employees, agents, customers, subcontractors, suppliers, and prime contractors, to the Corporate Compliance Officer.
3. Employees in management positions are personally accountable for their own conduct and the conduct of those reporting to them. Each management employee is

expected to inform those reporting to them about this Code of Conduct and take all necessary steps to ensure compliance with this Code.
4. No employee has the authority to direct, participate in, approve, or tolerate any violation of this Code by anyone.
5. Any employee who has questions about the application of this Code should consult with the designated Corporate Compliance Officer.

II. Definitions

Code of Ethical Conduct: The written statement of acceptable behavior by X Company's officers, directors, and employees that ensures X Company operates according to the highest ethical standards.

Code: The Code of Ethical Conduct.

Corporate Compliance Officer: The company official designated by the President to be responsible for implementing and administering the Code of Ethical Conduct. In the case where there is no Corporate Compliance Officer, or the Corporate Compliance Officer is not available, the Company President will be responsible for implementing and administering the Code of Ethical Conduct.

Corporate Compliance Program: The written procedures and policies used by X Company that are designed to ensure that all officers, directors, and employees are aware of the Code of Ethical Conduct and adhere to its standards. The Corporate Compliance Program is implemented and administered by the Corporate Compliance Officer.

Employee: Any person employed by X Company, including employees, foremen, managers, officers, directors, and persons authorized to act on behalf of the Company.

Program: Corporate Compliance Program.

III. Standards of Conduct

A. Equal Employment and Nondiscrimination

The continued success of our company is dependant upon employing the most qualified people and establishing a work environment that is free of discrimination, harassment, intimidation or coercion related to race, color, religion, sex, age, national origin, disability, or sexual orientation. This policy extends to all phases of employment, including hiring, placement, promotion, transfer, compensation, benefits, training and the use of facilities. X Company is committed to complying with all applicable laws related to equal employment opportunities and to ensure that there is no unlawful discrimination by any officer, director, or employee. X Company is committed to a work environment in which everyone is treated with respect, trust, honesty, fairness, and dignity.

B. Environmental Compliance

X Company is committed to full compliance with all federal, state and local environmental laws, standards, and guidelines. Not only is environmental compliance legally necessary, but it is also an important component of our obligation to the community and our good reputation. It is essential that each employee involved with regulated air emissions, water discharges, hazardous materials, or other regulated pollutants know and comply with all applicable environmental laws and guidelines. No one at X Company may participate in concealing an improper discharge, disposal, or storage of hazardous materials or other pollutants. Any person who has reason to believe that there may have been violations of any aspect of X Company's environmental compliance policy shall report immediately to the Company's environmental compliance officer or Corporate Compliance Officer. Moreover, in addition to compliance with all environmental laws and guidelines, X Company is also committed to utilizing energy and materials in a manner that will minimize the impact on the environment. X Company will also consider using recycled materials whenever feasible.

C. Safety & Health

X Company considers employee safety and health as one of the highest priorities. Many of the job activities, products, and materials handles by our employees require strict adherence to safety procedures, rules and regulations. Each employee must be aware of the Company's safety program that incorporates all of the applicable health and safety laws and guidelines and follow all applicable procedures. Also, supervisors are responsible for ensuring that all reasonable safeguards and precautions are taken in the workplace including ensuring compliance with the Company's procedures and guidelines, promoting safe work practices, and the use of personal protective equipment. If any employee has any safety related concerns, he or she should report these concerns to the Company's safety compliance officer.

APPENDIX C

D. Drugs and Alcohol

X Company is firmly committed to providing its employees with a safe and productive work environment to the extent possible and promoting high standards of employee health. Accordingly, X Company expects all of its employees to report to work and be able to perform his or her duties productively and safely. Drug and alcohol abuse by employees is regarded as unsafe by creating an increased risk to the safety of themselves, their fellow employees, and the general public and contrary to the Company's interests in maximizing its productivity. Therefore, drug and alcohol abuse in X Company will not be tolerated and the company will take appropriate action to ensure compliance with this policy. Additionally, anyone caught using drugs or alcohol in the workplace will be subject to discipline, including termination.

E. Conflicts of Interest

Employees must avoid situations in which their personal interests could conflict with, or even appear to conflict with, the interests of the Company. Conflicts of interest arise when an individual's position or responsibilities with the Company present an opportunity for personal gain of profit separate and apart from that individual's earnings from the Company or where the employee's interests are otherwise inconsistent with the interests of the Company. A conflict of interest may arise in any number of situations and it is impossible to describe each and every instance. As a general matter, if you think that any situation may be a potential conflict of interest, you should consult with the Corporate Compliance Officer. However, the following situations have a great potential for conflicts of interest:

1. Outside Employment

As a matter of company policy, employees may pursue outside employment opportunities. However, such opportunities must not interfere with the employee's job responsibilities with the Company. Any outside employment that interferes with the employee's job responsibilities or conscientious performance of his or her duties are deemed to be a conflict of interest is not permitted. Likewise, an employee's participation in civic, charitable, or professional organizations or activities that interferes with the employee's job responsibilities or conscientious performance of his or her job is deemed to be an impermissible conflict of interest. Additionally, employees may not use company time or resources to further non-company business. Employees also may not use the Company's name to lend weight or prestige to an outside activity without prior approval from authorized management. Prior to engaging in any outside employment activity or participating in any civic, charitable, or professional organization or activity that may give rise to an actual or potential conflict of interest, the employee must consult with the Corporate Compliance Officer and obtain express written approval.

2. Personal Financial Interests

Employees should avoid personal financial interests that might be in conflict with the interests of the Company. Such interests may include, but are not limited to, the following: obtaining a financial or other beneficial interest in a supplier, customer, or competitor of the Company; directly or indirectly having a personal financial interest in any business transaction that may be adverse to the Company; acquiring real estate or other property that the employee knows, or reasonably should know, that is of interest to the Company. Such personal financial interests include those interests of not only the individual employee, but also those of the employee's spouse, children, parents, grandparents, siblings and family in-law. If the employee knows, or reasonably should know, that a personal financial interest may be in conflict with the interests with the Company, the employee must first consult with the Corporate Compliance Officer and obtain express written approval.

F. Gifts and Entertainment

1. Bribery and Kickbacks

All forms of bribery and kickbacks are illegal and expressly prohibited. Any employee caught participating in such activity will be promptly terminated. Any employee who knows about, or reasonably should know about, any such activity and fails to report it to the Corporate Compliance Officer will be disciplined.

2. Government Personnel

All forms of gifts and entertainment to or from government personnel (Federal, State, and local), including persons that may be acting for or on behalf of the government, are expressly prohibited. However, the Corporate Compliance Officer may authorize an exception where a familial or personal relationship exists outside of the employee's business relationship with the government employee.

3. Non-Governmental Personnel

Receiving or accepting gifts or entertainment in the business context is a particularly sensitive area and can be inappropriate, or even illegal, depending on the circumstances. For this reason, it is important that all employees be extra sensitive when it comes to giving or receiving gifts and entertainment from non-governmental personnel (as stated above, the giving or receiving of gifts from government personnel is prohibited). Therefore, regardless of the circumstances, the following rules apply:

- The Corporate Compliance Officer must approve the giving or receiving of all forms of gifts and entertainment.
- Money, in any form, is never given, offered, solicited, or accepted.
- No gift or entertainment may be given or received if it is, or could reasonably be construed to be, intended to influence an employee's behavior.
- No employee may encourage or solicit gifts or entertainment of any kind from any individual or entity with whom the Company conducts business.
- The Corporate Compliance Officer may authorize the expenditure of a non-monetary gift or entertainment with a value equal to or less than $500 in the aggregate for any calendar year to an individual or entity with whom the Company conducts business only if it is for a legitimate and identifiable business purpose.
- Employees may receive a non-monetary gift or entertainment from an individual or entity with whom the Company conducts business with a value equal to or less than $500 in the aggregate for any calendar year, provided that such gifts or entertainment are reported to and approved by the Corporate Compliance Officer and is for a legitimate and identifiable business purpose.
- The Corporate Compliance Officer may authorize an exception where a familial or personal relationship exists outside of the employee's business relationship with the non-governmental employee.

G. Communications and Records

All employees are expected to be familiar with, and conform to, the Company's document retention policy as well as the Company's recordkeeping and reporting procedures. Additionally, all Company and employee communications, correspondence, and records must be accurate, complete, and timely. The contents of any written communication must be legible and unambiguous. If, after making any communication, correspondence, or record, the employee discovers that s/he has made a mistake, then the employee must take all steps as may be reasonably necessary to correct such mistake. Any employee who knowingly makes a false or misleading communication, correspondence, or record will be terminated.

H. Antitrust Policy

X Company is fully committed to compliance with the antitrust laws, which are designed to promote free and open competition in the marketplace. Not only does the customer benefit by getting the best product at the lowest price, but the Company also benefits by being able to compete on a fair level playing field with competitors. The antitrust laws are complex and must be complied with strictly. Routine business decisions involving prices, terms and conditions or sale, dealings with competitors, and many other matters present problems of great sensitivity. It is therefore essential that every employee be generally aware of the antitrust laws and that all employees that are actively involved in the bidding process participate in the Company's Antitrust Program. Below is a general overview of the antitrust laws: The Sherman Act is the primary federal antitrust statute. The Sherman Act prohibits any agreement among competitors to fix prices, rig bids, or engage in other anticompetitive activity. Violation of the Sherman Act is a felony punishable by a fine of up to $10 million for corporations, and a fine of up to $350,000 or 3 years imprisonment (or both) for individuals and may subject the Company and/or the individual to suspension or debarment. In addition, collusion among competitors may constitute violations of the mail or wire fraud statute, the false statements statute, or other federal felony statutes. In addition to receiving a criminal sentence, a corporation or individual convicted of a Sherman Act violation may be ordered to make restitution to the victims for all overcharges. Victims of bid-rigging and price-fixing conspiracies also may seek civil recovery of up to three times the amount of damages suffered. Most criminal antitrust prosecutions involve price fixing, bid rigging, or market division or allocation schemes. Under the law, price-fixing and bid-rigging schemes are per se violations of the Sherman Act. This means that where such a collusive scheme has been established, it cannot be justified under the law by arguments or evidence that, for example, the agreed-upon prices were reasonable, the agreement was necessary to prevent or eliminate price-cutting or ruinous competition, or the conspirators were merely trying to make sure that each got a fair share of the market.

1. Price-Fixing

Price-fixing is an agreement among competitors to raise, fix, or otherwise maintain the price at which their goods or services are sold. It is not necessary that the competitors agree to charge exactly the same price, or that every competitor in a given industry join the conspiracy. Price-fixing can take many forms, and any agreement that restricts price competition violates the law. Other examples of price-fixing agreements include those to:

- Establish or adhere to price discounts;
- Hold prices firm;
- Eliminate or reduce discounts;
- Adopt a standard formula for computing prices;
- Maintain certain price differentials between different types, sizes, or quantities of products;
- Adhere to a minimum fee or price schedule;
- Fix credit terms; and
- Not advertise prices.

2. Bid-Rigging

Bid-rigging is the way that conspiring competitors effectively raise prices where purchasers - often federal, state, or local governments - acquire goods or services by soliciting competing bids. Essentially, competitors agree in advance who will submit the winning bid on a contract being let through the competitive bidding process. Bid-rigging also takes many forms, but bid-rigging conspiracies usually fall into one or more of the following categories:

1. Bid Suppression: In bid suppression schemes, one or more competitors who otherwise would be expected to bid, or who have previously bid, agree to refrain from bidding or withdraw a previously submitted bid so that the designated winning competitor's bid will be accepted.
2. Complementary Bidding: Complementary bidding (also known as "cover" or "courtesy" bidding) occurs when some competitors agree to submit bids that either are too high to be accepted or contain special terms that will not be acceptable to the buyer. Such bids are not intended to secure the buyer's acceptance, but are merely designed to give the appearance of genuine competitive bidding. Complementary bidding schemes are the most frequently occurring forms of bid rigging, and they defraud purchasers

by creating the appearance of competition to conceal secretly inflated prices.

3. Bid Rotation: In bid rotation schemes, all conspirators submit bids but take turns being the low bidder. The terms of the rotation may vary; for example, competitors may take turns on contracts according to the size of the contract, allocating equal amounts to each conspirator or allocating volumes that correspond to the size of each conspirator company. A strict bid rotation pattern defies the law of chance and suggests collusion is taking place.

4. Subcontracting: Subcontracting arrangements can be part of a bid-rigging scheme. Competitors who agree not to bid or to submit a losing bid frequently receive subcontracts or supply contracts in exchange from the successful low bidder. In some schemes, a low bidder will agree to withdraw its bid in favor of the next low bidder in exchange for a lucrative subcontract that divides the illegally obtained higher price between them.

3. Market Division

Market division or allocation schemes are agreements in which competitors divide markets among themselves. In such schemes, competing firms allocate specific customers or types of customers, products, or territories among themselves. For example, one competitor will be allowed to sell to, or bid on contracts let by, certain customers or types of customers. In return, he or she will not sell to, or bid on contracts let by, customers allocated to the other competitors. In other schemes, competitors agree to sell only to customers in certain geographic areas and refuse to sell to, or quote intentionally high prices to, customers in geographic areas allocated to conspirator companies.

Compliance with the antitrust laws is a serious matter and, as explained above, violations could subject the Company substantial civil and criminal liability. Accordingly, any employee who violates antitrust laws shall be terminated. Additionally, any employee who knows, or reasonably should know, that an antitrust violation has been, or will be, committed and fails to report it to the Corporate Compliance Officer will be subject to discipline, which may include termination.

I. Claims

All requests or demands for payment made on behalf of X Company pursuant to any contract or business agreement shall truthfully and accurately reflect the value of the goods or services provided. Under no circumstances may an employee make a false claim. Examples of false claims include billing extra time not spent working on a project, charging for materials not used in a project, or artificially inflating a claim in order to negotiate additional compensation from the customer. Any claims that are false, fraudulent or otherwise deceitful may subject the company, and/or the individual making the claim, to civil liability up to 3 times the amount false claim for payment, criminal liability punishable by up to 5 years imprisonment, a fine, and restitution, and administrative liability through suspension or debarment. Accordingly, any employee who knowingly makes false claims shall be terminated. Additionally, any employee who knows, or reasonably should know, that another employee has submitted, or intends to submit, a false claim and fails to report it to the Corporate Compliance Officer, will be subject to discipline, which may include termination.

J. Statements & Certifications

All statements, representations, and certifications made on behalf of X Company, whether written or oral, shall be accurate, truthful, and timely. Under no circumstances may an employee make a false or misleading statement, representation, or certification. Any statements that are false, fictitious, or fraudulent or contain materially false, fictitious, or fraudulent statements or entries, may subject the Company, and/or the individual making the statement, to criminal liability punishable by up to 5 years imprisonment, a fine, and restitution, and administrative liability through suspension and debarment. In addition, if a false statement is used to get a claim paid, then the Company and/or the individual, may be subject to civil liability up to 3 times the amount claimed for payment.

Additionally, employees are routinely required to certify that they and the Company are in compliance with various contractual provisions and regulatory requirements. Examples of common certifications include certifications pertaining to environmental, safety, personnel, and health matters, product quality and material certifications, and quality control and quality assurance testing certifications. Employees must be aware of the requirements applicable to their jobs and ensure that all certifications are accurate and that there is neither a material omission of fact or materially misleading statements.

K. Commitment to Disadvantaged Business Enterprises

X Company is committed to full compliance with government

sponsored opportunity programs, such as the disadvantaged business enterprise (DBE) program, and maximizing the opportunities of DBEs. As such, X Company will not discriminate on the basis of race, color, national origin, or sex in the hiring of suppliers or subcontractors and will foster an environment in which everyone is treated with respect, trust, honesty, fairness, and dignity. For each government-funded contract, X Company will make good faith efforts to maximize the participation of DBEs in subcontracts and ensure that each DBE is performing a commercially useful function. A DBE is deemed to be performing a commercially useful function if the DBE is responsible for executing the work and carrying out their responsibilities by actually performing, managing, and supervising the work.

IV. Obligation to Report Violations and Cooperation

Each employee must promptly report any known or suspected violation of this Code of Ethical Conduct and all other unlawful or unethical conduct to the Corporate Compliance Officer. Employees are obligated to report such known or suspected conduct without regard to the identity or position of the suspected offender. Any report made under this section will be strictly confidential and under no circumstances will any employee who makes a report be subject to any acts of retribution or retaliation or disciplinary action. Additionally, all employees must fully cooperate in any investigation of a suspected violation of this Code and fully cooperate with any request by the Corporate Compliance Monitor.

Any employee found to have violated this Code or engaged in other unlawful or unethical behavior shall be disciplined, including demotion or dismissal. Any employee who fails to report known or suspected violations of this Code or other unlawful or unethical behavior shall be subject to appropriate disciplinary action.

V. Consequences for Violations

Any violation of this Code is cause for disciplinary action that may result in any of the following consequences:

- Reprimand.
- Loss of compensation, seniority, or promotional opportunities.
- Reduction in pay.
- Demotion.
- Suspension with or without pay.

APPENDIX C

- Discharge.

ACKNOWLEDGMENT

I acknowledge that I have received, reviewed and understand X Company's Code of Business Ethics. I agree to strictly comply with the Code and understand that I will be subject to disciplinary action if I violate the Code.

_____
(Signature)

_____
(Print Name)

_____
(Date)

This page last modified on 03/29/07

FHWA Home | Engineering | Construction

FHWA

United States Department of Transportation - **Federal Highway Administration**

U.S. Department of Transportation
Federal Highway Administration

Search | Feedback

FHWA > Engineering > Construction > Contract Administration > Construction Guide > Corporate Compliance Program Guide

Corporate Compliance Program Guide

A Sample Guide Developed by the USDOT/ AGC / ARTBA / AASHTO Suspension & Debarment Work Group

Elements of a Corporate Compliance Program

The Corporate Compliance Program is the mechanism a company uses to implement, administer, and enforce a Code of Ethical Conduct. An effective Corporate Compliance Program is one that is reasonably designed, implemented, and enforced so that the Program is effective in educating and training employees on their ethical and legal responsibilities and in preventing, detecting, and deterring criminal conduct or other unethical behavior. In structuring a Corporate Compliance Program, a company should consider the following general elements:

- The company's governing authority and top management must fully support all elements of the Program. This includes being knowledgeable about the content and operation of the Program and exercising oversight with respect to the implementation and effectiveness of the Program.
- A specific individual within the company is appointed as the Corporate Compliance Officer, who is responsible for the day-to-day administration and implementation of the Program. This position should be a separate, independent position within the company that only reports to the company's top executive officer and board of directors. If a separate position is not created, then the position should be delegated to only high-level management within the company and must have the authority to operate independently and to administer and implement the Program company-wide.
- The Program should include regular training regarding the

More Information

- Contract Administration

Contact

Jerry Yakowenko
Office of Program Administration
202-366-1562
E-mail

APPENDIX C

Program and Code of Ethical Conduct. The Program should also include legal training on compliance with specific regulatory areas that are directly applicable to the company, such as antitrust, claims, and environmental compliance.
- The Program should include procedures for employees and others to confidentially report suspected violations and to safeguard the confidentiality of the source. The Program should also prohibit any form of retaliation for reporting a suspected violation.
- The Program should require investigations of all suspected violations and should include procedures to safeguard the confidentiality of such investigations.
- The Program should include requirements to regularly audit the company's internal accounting controls and other procedures to ensure their effectiveness in safeguarding against inaccuracies, fraud, or other misconduct.
- The Program should commit to providing sufficient resources, including the hiring of consultants and outside auditors, investigators, and legal counsel, in the administration and implementation of the Program.
- The Program should ensure that appropriate steps will be taken whenever a violation occurs or whenever deficiencies are found in the company's control systems or whenever recommendations are otherwise made to improve the company's ethical and legal compliance.

This page last modified on 03/29/07

FHWA Home | Engineering | Construction

FHWA

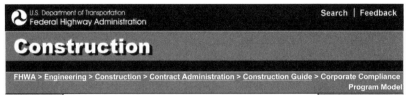

Corporate Compliance Program Model

A Sample Program Model Developed by the USDOT/ AGC / ARTBA / AASHTO Suspension & Debarment Work Group

I. Purpose

The purpose of this Corporate Compliance Program is to assist and ensure that all employees understand and adhere to the Code of Ethical Conduct. The Program is designed to educate employees, ensure compliance with the Code, foster an ethical corporate environment, establish a mechanism to detect and identify violations of the Code or other unethical behavior, and audit the Company's and employees' compliance adherence to the Code.

II. Corporate Structure

[Describe the different management positions and hierarchy, including who reports to whom (an organization chart, either inserted into this section or referenced as an appendix, would be useful, for example: "X Company consists of a Board of Directors, a President, a Chief Financial Officer, a Corporate Compliance Officer, 3 Vice Presidents, and 10 foremen. The President reports to the Board of Directors; the Chief Financial Officer, the Corporate Compliance Officer, and the Vice Presidents report to the President; and the foremen report to the Vice Presidents. Attached is a corporate organization chart showing the corporate structure and the names of the relevant individuals appointed to each position."]

III. Corporate Compliance Officer

The position of Corporate Compliance Officer is established to ensure that all employees are aware of and understand the Code of Ethical Conduct and to administer the Corporate

More Information

- Contract Administration

Contact

Jerry Yakowenko
Office of Program Administration
202-366-1562
E-mail

Compliance Program. The Corporate Compliance Officer reports to the President and, from time to time, to the Board of Directors.

Specifically, the Corporate Compliance Officer has the following responsibilities:

- To designate appropriate supervisory employees and officers to assist in administering the Program;
- To ensure that all employees receive and acknowledge in writing that they have received, reviewed, and understand the Code and will comply with its requirements;
- To develop and facilitate suitable regular and periodic training programs designed to understand the Code, antitrust compliance, environmental requirements, health and safety requirements, and DBE requirements, and obtain (and maintain) necessary technical training and certifications;
- To investigate reports of suspected Code violations and make independent determinations as to whether a violation occurred;
- To recommend to the President disciplinary action for Code violations;
- To ensure that all reports of suspected violations and investigations remain confidential;
- To establish and maintain appropriate systems and internal controls to implement the Code and the Program;
- To conduct both periodical and regular audits of employees (including the President), divisions, departments, or offices of X Company to ensure that they are in compliance with the Code;
- To recommend hiring such consultants, auditors, or other persons as may be necessary to ensure that each employee receives adequate training and to conduct audits and investigations; and
- To make recommendations to the President and Board of Directors of changes that may better facilitate compliance with the Code.

IV. Reports

The Corporate Compliance Officer will report monthly to the President concerning all activities regarding the Code of Ethical Conduct and Corporate Compliance Program. The Corporate Compliance Officer will report quarterly to the Board of Directors all activities regarding the Code of Ethical Conduct and

Corporate Compliance Program.

V. Investigations

The Corporate Compliance Officer shall investigate all reports of suspected Code violations. The reports may either be on the Compliance Officer's own initiative or in response to a compliant. All reports shall be documented, reviewed and evaluated and the Compliance Officer shall safeguard the confidentiality of all reports and investigations. The Compliance Officer shall also institute necessary policies to prohibit any form of retaliation against any person who makes a report. The Compliance Officer may recommend that the Company retain such consultants or auditors as may be necessary to conduct a proper investigation and consult with any outside counsel as may be retained for such purpose. In conducting an investigation, the Compliance Officer shall have access to all corporate documents, including e-mail, and authority to interview any employee. After concluding an investigation, the Compliance Officer shall make a report and submit it to the President with recommendations for appropriate disciplinary action.

VI. Audits

The Corporate Compliance Officer shall regularly (at least annually) and periodically audit the Company's compliance with the Code. Additionally, the Corporate Compliance Officer and the Chief Financial Officer shall jointly audit the effectiveness of, and compliance with, the Company's financial controls and procedures. In conducting such audits, the Corporate Compliance Officer may recommend that the Company retain such consultants or auditors as may be necessary. Such audits may be of any corporate office, division, department, or employee. After concluding such audit, the Compliance Officer and Chief Financial Officer, as appropriate, shall submit a report to the President and make appropriate recommendations for improvement.

VII. Training

The Corporate Compliance Officer shall provide, or arrange to have provided, regular training on the Code of Ethical Conduct and Corporate Compliance Program. Such training must be provided to all employees, including the President and the Board of Directors. For new employees, this training shall be provided as part of new hire orientation. At the conclusion of each training session, the Compliance Officer shall obtain a written

APPENDIX C

acknowledgement from every employee that they have received, reviewed, and understand the Code and will comply with its requirements. Additionally, the Compliance Officer shall provide, or arrange to have provided, training necessary to ensure compliance with antitrust requirements, environmental requirements, health and safety requirements, and DBE requirements, as well as the necessary technical training for certain specialized positions and to obtain (and maintain) necessary certifications. The Compliance Officer will maintain a file of all training sessions, attendance at such training sessions and acknowledgement forms.

VIII. Cooperation & Responsibility

All employees are required to fully cooperate with the Corporate Compliance Officer in administering the Corporate Compliance Program. All supervisory employees are responsible for ensuring that their subordinates cooperate, are aware of and understand the Code, and comply with the Code and the Program.

This page last modified on 03/29/07

FHWA Home | Engineering | Construction

FHWA

United States Department of Transportation - **Federal Highway Administration**

APPENDIX D: Advisory Opinion of the Office of Government Ethics

06 x 9
Memorandum dated October 4, 2006,
from Robert I. Cusick, Director,
to Designated Agency Ethics Officials
Office of Government Ethics Memorandum

Perhaps no subject has generated as many questions from ethics officials over the years as the difference between the phrases "particular matter involving specific parties" and "particular matter." These phrases are used in the various criminal conflict of interest statutes to describe the kinds of Government actions to which certain restrictions apply. Moreover, because these phrases are terms of art with established meanings, the Office of Government Ethics (OGE) has found it useful to include these same terms in various ethics rules. A third term, "matter," also has taken on importance in recent years because certain criminal post-employment restrictions now use that term without the modifiers "particular" or "involving specific parties."

It is crucial that ethics officials understand the differences among these three phrases. OGE's experience has been that confusion and disputes can arise when these terms are used in imprecise ways in ethics agreements, conflict of interest waivers, and oral or written ethics advice. Therefore, we are issuing this memorandum to provide guidance in a single document about the meaning of these terms and the distinctions among them.

Because the three phrases are distinguished mainly in terms of their relative breadth, the discussion below will proceed from the narrowest phrase to the broadest.

PARTICULAR MATTER INVOLVING SPECIFIC PARTIES

The narrowest of these terms is "particular matter involving specific parties." Depending on the grammar and structure of the particular statute or regulation, the wording may appear in slightly different forms, but the meaning remains the same, focusing primarily on the presence of specific parties.

1. Where the Phrase Appears

This language is used in many places in the conflict of interest laws and OGE regulations. In the post-employment statute, the phrase "particular matter . . . which involved a specific party or parties" is used to describe the kinds of Government matters to which the life-time and two-year representational bans apply. 18 U.S.C. § 207(a)(1), (a)(2). Occasionally, ethics officials have raised questions because section 207 includes a definition of the term "particular matter," section 207(i)(3), but not "particular matter involving specific parties"; however, it is important to remember that each time "particular matter" is used in section 207(a), it is modified by the additional "specific party" language.[1]

In addition to section 207(a), similar language is used in 18 U.S.C. §§ 205(c) and 203(c). These provisions describe the limited restrictions on representational activities applicable to special Government employees (SGEs) during their periods of Government service.[2]

As explained below, 18 U.S.C. § 208 generally uses the broader phrase "particular matter" to describe the matters from which employees must recuse themselves because of a financial interest. However, even this statute has one provision, dealing with certain Indian birthright interests, that refers to particular matters involving certain Indian entities as "a specific party or parties." 18 U.S.C. § 208(b)(4); *see* OGE Informal Advisory Letter 00 x 12.

Moreover, OGE has issued certain regulatory exemptions, under section 208(b)(2), that refer to particular matters involving specific parties. 5 C.F.R. § 2640.202(a), (b). Likewise, the distinction between particular matters involving specific parties and broader types of particular matters (i.e., those that have general applicability to an entire class of persons) is crucial to several other regulatory exemptions issued by OGE under section 208(b)(2). 5 C.F.R. §§ 2640.201(c)(2), (d); 2640.202(c); 2640.203(b), (g).

Finally, OGE has used similar language in various other rules. Most notably, the provisions dealing with impartiality and extraordinary payments in subpart E of the Standards of Ethical Conduct for Employees of the Executive Branch (Standards of Conduct) refer to particular matters in which certain persons are specific parties. 5 C.F.R. §§ 2635.502; 2635.503. OGE also uses the phrase to describe a restriction on the compensated speaking, teaching and writing activities of certain SGEs. 5 C.F.R. § 2635.807(a)(2)(i)(4).

2. What the Phrase Means

When this language is used, it reflects "a deliberate effort to impose a more limited ban and to narrow the circumstances in which the ban is to operate." Bayless Manning, *Federal Conflict of Interest Law* 204 (1964). Therefore, OGE has emphasized that the term "typically involves a specific proceeding affecting the legal rights of the parties, or an isolatable transaction or related set of transactions between identified parties." 5 C.F.R. § 2640.102(1).[3] Examples of particular matters involving specific parties include contracts, grants, licenses, product approval applications, investigations, and litigation. It is important to remember that the phrase does not cover particular matters of general applicability, such as rulemaking, legislation, or policy-making of general applicability.[4]

APPENDIX D | 335

Ethics officials sometimes must decide when a particular matter first involves a specific party. Many Government matters evolve, sometimes starting with a broad concept, developing into a discrete program, and eventually involving specific parties. A case-by-case analysis is required to determine at which stage a particular matter has sufficiently progressed to involve specific parties. The Government sometimes identifies a specific party even at a preliminary or informal stage in the development of a matter. *E.g.*, OGE Informal Advisory Letters 99 x 23; 99 x 21; 90 x 3.

In matters involving contracts, grants and other agreements between the Government and outside parties, the general rule is that specific parties are first identified when the Government first receives an expression of interest from a prospective contractor, grantee or other party. As OGE explained recently in Informal Advisory Letter 05 x 6, the Government sometimes may receive expressions of interest from prospective bidders or applicants in advance of a published solicitation or request for proposals. In some cases, such matters may involve specific parties even before the Government receives an expression of interest, if there are sufficient indications that the Government actually has identified a party. *See* OGE Informal Advisory Letter 96 x 21.

PARTICULAR MATTER

Despite the similarity of the phrases "particular matter" and "particular matter involving specific parties," it is necessary to distinguish them. That is because "particular matter" covers a broader range of Government activities than "particular matter involving specific parties." Failure to appreciate this distinction can lead to inadvertent violations of law. For example, the financial conflict of interest statute, 18 U.S.C. § 208, generally refers to particular matters, without the specific party limitation. If an employee is advised incorrectly that section 208 applies only to particular matters that focus on a specific person or company, such as an enforcement action or a contract, then the employee may conclude it is permissible to participate in other particular matters, even though the law prohibits such participation.

1. Where the Phrase Appears

In addition to 18 U.S.C. § 208, several other statutes and regulations use the term "particular matter."[5] The representational restrictions applicable to current employees (other than SGEs), under 18 U.S.C. §§ 203 and 205, apply to particular matters.[6] As mentioned above, section 207 also contains a definition of "particular matter."[7] However, where the phrase is used in the post-employment prohibitions in section 207(a)(1) and (a)(2), it is modified by the "specific parties" limitation.[8]

The phrase "particular matter" is used pervasively in OGE's regulations. Of course, the term appears throughout 5 C.F.R. part 2640, the primary OGE rule interpreting and implementing 18 U.S.C. § 208. Similarly, it is used in 5 C.F.R. § 2635.402, which is the provision in the Standards of Conduct that generally deals with section 208. The phrase also is used throughout subpart F of the Standards of Conduct, which contains the rules governing recusal from particular matters affecting the financial interest of a person with whom an employee is seeking non-Federal employment. 5 C.F.R. §§ 2635.601-2635.606. Moreover, the phrase appears in the "catch-all" provision of OGE's impartiality rule, 5 C.F.R. § 2635.502(a)(2). *See also* 5 C.F.R. 2635.501(a).[9] Various other regulations refer to "particular matter" for miscellaneous purposes. *E.g.*, 5 C.F.R. § 2635.805(a)(restriction on expert witness activities of SGEs); 5 C.F.R. § 2634.802(a)(1)(written recusals pursuant to ethics agreements).

2. What the Phrase Means

Although different conflict of interest statutes use slightly different wording, such as different lists of examples of particular matters, the same standards apply for determining what is a particular matter under each of the relevant statutes and regulations. *See* 18 Op. O.L.C. 212, 217-20 (1994). Particular matter means any matter that involves "deliberation, decision, or action that is focused upon the interests of specific persons, *or* a discrete and identifiable class of persons." 5 C.F.R. § 2640.103(a)(1)(emphasis added). It is clear, then, that particular matter may include matters that do not involve parties and is *not* "limited to adversarial proceedings or formal legal relationships." *Van Ee v. EPA*, 202 F.3d 296, 302 (D.C. Cir. 2000).

Essentially, the term covers two categories of matters: (1) those that involve specific parties (described more fully above), and (2) those that do not involve specific parties but at least focus on the interests of a discrete and identifiable class of persons, such as a particular industry or profession. OGE regulations sometimes refer to the second category as "particular matter of general applicability." 5 C.F.R. § 2640.102(m). This category can include legislation and policymaking, as long as it is narrowly focused on a discrete and identifiable class. Examples provided in OGE rules include a regulation applicable only to meat packing companies or a regulation prescribing safety standards for trucks on interstate highways. 5 C.F.R. §§ 2640.103(a)(1)(example 3); 2635.402(b)(3)(example 2). Other examples may be found in various opinions of OGE and the Office of Legal Counsel, Department of Justice. *E.g.*, OGE Informal Advisory Letter 00 x 4 (recommendations concerning specific limits on commercial use of a particular facility); 18 Op. O.L.C. at 220 (determinations or legislation focused on the compensation and work conditions of the class of Assistant United States Attorneys).

Certain OGE rules recognize that particular matters of general applicability *sometimes* may raise fewer conflict of interest concerns than particular matters involving specific parties.[10] Therefore, while both categories are included in the term "particular matter," it is often necessary to distinguish between these two kinds of particular matters. Of course, in many instances, the relevant prohibitions apply equally to both kinds of particular matters. This is the case, for example, in any application of 18 U.S.C. § 208 where there is no applicable exemption or waiver that distinguishes the two.

It is important to emphasize that the term "particular matter" is not so broad as to include every matter involving Government action. Particular matter does not cover the "consideration or adoption of broad policy options directed to the interests of a large and diverse group of persons." 5 C.F.R. § 2640.103(a)(1). For example, health and safety regulations applicable to all employers would not be a particular matter, nor would a comprehensive legislative proposal for health care reform. 5 C.F.R. § 2640.103(a)(1) (example 4), (example 8). *See also* OGE Informal Advisory Letter 05 x 1 (report of panel on tax reform addressing broad range of tax policy issues). Although such actions are too broadly focused to be particular matters, they still are deemed "matters" for purposes of the restrictions described below that use that term.

A question that sometimes arises is when a matter first becomes a "particular matter." Some matters begin as broad policy deliberations and actions pertaining to diverse interests, but, later, more focused actions may follow. Usually, a particular matter arises when the deliberations turn to specific actions that focus on a certain person or a discrete and identifiable class of persons. For example, although a legislative plan for broad health care reform would not be a particular matter, a particular matter would arise if an agency later issued implementing regulations focused narrowly on the prices that pharmaceutical companies could charge for prescription drugs. 5 C.F.R. § 2640.102(a)(1)(example 8). Similarly, the formulation and implementation of the United States response to the military invasion of an ally would not be a particular matter, but a particular matter would arise once discussions turned to whether to close a particular oil pumping station or pipeline operated by a company in the area where hostilities are taking place. 5 C.F.R. § 2640.102(a)(1) (example 7).

MATTER

The broadest of the three terms is "matter." However, this term is used less frequently than the other two in the various ethics statutes and regulations to describe the kinds of Government actions to which restrictions apply.

1. Where the Phrase Appears

The most important use of this term is in the one-year post-employment restrictions applicable to "senior employees" and "very senior employees." 18 U.S.C. § 207(c), (d). In this context, "matter" is used to describe the kind of Government actions that former senior and very senior employees are prohibited from influencing through contacts with employees of their former agencies (as well as contacts with Executive Schedule officials at other agencies, in the case of very senior employees). The unmodified term "matter" did not appear in these provisions until 1989, when section 207(c) was amended to replace "particular matter" with "matter" and section 207(d) was first enacted. Pub. L. No. 101-194, § 101(a), November 30, 1989. OGE also occasionally uses the term "matter" in ethics regulations, for example, in the description of teaching, speaking and writing that relates to an employee's official duties. 5 C.F.R. § 2635.807(a)(2)(i)(E)(1).

2. What the Phrase Means

It is clear that "matter" is broader than "particular matter." *See* 17 Op. O.L.C. at 41-42. Indeed, the term is virtually all-encompassing with respect to the work of the Government.[11] Unlike "particular matter," the term "matter" covers even the consideration or adoption of broad policy options that are directed to the interests of a large and diverse group of persons. Of course, the term also includes any particular matter or particular matter involving specific parties.

Nevertheless, it is still necessary to understand the context in which the term "matter" is used, as the context itself will provide some limits. In 18 U.S.C. § 207(c) and (d), the post-employment restrictions apply only to matters "on which [the former employee] seeks official action." Therefore, the only matters covered will be those in which the former employee is seeking to induce a current employee to make a decision or otherwise act in an official capacity.

NOTES

1. For a full discussion of the post-employment restrictions, see OGE DAEOgram DO-04-023A [OGE Informal Advisory Memorandum 04 x 11], at http://www.usoge.gov/pages/daeograms/dgr_files/2004/do04023a.pdf .
2. These restrictions on SGEs are discussed in more detail in OGE DAEOgram DO-00-0003A [OGE Informal Advisory Memorandum 00 x 1], at http://www.usoge.gov/pages/daeograms/dgr_files/2000/do00003a.pdf .)
3. This definition, found in OGE's regulations implementing 18 U.S.C. § 208, differs slightly from the definition found in the regulations implementing a now-superseded version of 18 U.S.C. § 207, although this is more a point of clarification than substance. Specifically, the old section 207 regulations referred to "identifiable" parties, 5 C.F.R. § 2637.201(c)(1), whereas the more recent section 208 rule refers to "identified" parties. As explained in the preamble to OGE's proposed new section 207 rule: "The use of 'identified,' rather than 'identifiable,' is intended to distinguish more clearly between particular matters involving specific parties and mere

'particular matters,' which are described elsewhere as including matters of general applicability that focus 'on the interests of a discrete and *identifiable* class of persons' but do not involve specific parties. [citations omitted] The use of the term 'identified,' however, does not mean that a matter will lack specific parties just because the name of a party is not disclosed to the Government, as where an agent represents an unnamed principal." 68 *Federal Register* 7844, 7853-54 (February 18, 2003).

4. Usually, rulemaking and legislation are not covered, unless they focus narrowly on identified parties. *See* OGE Informal Advisory Opinions 96 x 7 ("rare" example of rulemaking that involved specific parties); 83 x 7 (private relief legislation may involve specific parties).
5. The relevant language in 18 U.S.C. § 208(a) is "a judicial or other proceeding, application, request for a ruling or other determination, contract, claim, controversy, charge, accusation, arrest, *or other particular matter*" (emphasis added).
6. The prohibition in 18 U.S.C. § 205(a)(2) actually uses the phrase "covered matter," but that term is in turn defined as "any judicial or other proceeding, application, request for a ruling or other determination, contract, claim, controversy, investigation, charge, accusation, arrest *or other particular matter,*" 18 U.S.C. § 205(h)(emphasis added).
7. The definition in 18 U.S.C. § 207(i)(3) provides: "the term 'particular matter' includes any investigation, application, request for a ruling or determination, rulemaking, contract, controversy, claim, charge, accusation, arrest, or judicial or other proceeding." This language differs slightly from other references to "particular matter" in sections 203, 205 and 208, in part because the list of matters is not followed by the residual phrase "or other particular matter." However, OGE does not believe that the absence of such a general catch-all phrase means that the list of enumerated matters exhausts the meaning of "particular matter" under section 207(i)(3). The list is preceded by the word "includes," which is generally a term of enlargement rather than limitation and indicates that matters other than those enumerated are covered. *See* Norman J. Singer, 2A *Sutherland on Statutory Construction* 231-232 (2000).
8. At one time, the post-employment "cooling-off" restriction for senior employees in 18 U.S.C. § 207(c) applied to particular matters, but the language was amended (and broadened) in 1989 when Congress removed the adjective "particular" that had modified "matter." *See* 17 Op. O.L.C. 37, 41-42 (1993).
9. Generally, section 2635.502 focuses on particular matters involving specific parties, as noted above. However, section 2635.502(a)(2) provides a mechanism for employees to determine whether they should recuse from other "particular matters" that are not described elsewhere in the rule. In appropriate cases, therefore, an agency may require an employee to recuse from particular matters that do not involve specific parties,

based on the concern that the employee's impartiality reasonably may be questioned under the circumstances.
10. As noted above, OGE's impartiality rule generally focuses on particular matters involving specific parties. *See* OGE Informal Advisory Letter 93 x 25 (rulemaking "would not, except in unusual circumstances covered under section 502(a)(2), raise an issue under section 502(a)"). Furthermore, as also discussed above, several of the regulatory exemptions issued by OGE under 18 U.S.C. § 208(b)(2) treat particular matters of general applicability differently than those involving specific parties. The preamble to the original proposed regulatory exemptions in 5 C.F.R. part 2640 explains: "The regulation generally contains more expansive exemptions for participation in 'matters of general applicability not involving specific parties' because it is less likely that an employee's integrity would be compromised by concern for his own financial interests when participating in these broader matters." 60 *Federal Register* 47207, 47210 (September 11, 1995). Of course, Congress itself has limited certain conflict of interest restrictions to the core area of particular matters that involve specific parties. *E.g.*, 18 U.S.C. § 207(a)(1), (a)(2).
11. A now-repealed statute, 18 U.S.C. § 281 (the predecessor of 18 U.S.C. § 203), used the phrase "any proceeding, contract, claim, controversy, charge, accusation, arrest, *or other matter*" (emphasis added). One commentator noted that the term "matter" in section 281 was "so open-ended" that it raised questions as to what limits there might be on the scope. Manning, at 50-51. Manning postulated that some limits might be inferred from the character of the matters listed before the phrase "or other matter." *Id.* at 51. Whatever the force of this reasoning with respect to former section 281, the same could not be said with respect to 18 U.S.C. § 207(c) or (d), as neither of these current provisions contains an exemplary list of covered matters.

APPENDIX E: Office of Government Ethics, Ethics and Working with Contractors

ETHICS AND WORKING WITH CONTRACTORS
QUESTIONS AND ANSWERS

CONTENTS

I. Revolving Door Questions

   A. <u>Seeking Future Employment</u>

      1. What are the criminal restrictions that relate to looking for future employment with a contractor? Page 5

      2. Do the OGE implementing regulations add anything to the criminal restriction? Page 6

      3. Do the OGE regulations require employees to notify anyone that they have begun seeking employment or are recused from certain matters? Page 7

      4. Beyond the criminal law and the OGE regulations, what additional requirements are there under the Procurement Integrity Act concerning employment contacts? Page 7

   B. <u>Post-Employment Restrictions</u>

      5. What are the restrictions under the Procurement Integrity Act for employees who leave Government after working on matters relating to a Government contractor? Page 8

      6. If a former employee did not serve in any of the specific contracting roles or perform any of the specific contracting functions described above, is he free from any post-employment restrictions? Page 9

      7. Which restrictions in 18 U.S.C. § 207 apply most frequently to employees who have been involved in contracting matters or have worked with contractors? Page 10

      8. Does section 207 apply when a former employee is simply performing work under a Government contract? Page 11

APPENDIX E | 345

C. Relationship with Former Private Employer

9. Are there criminal conflict of interest restrictions that especially affect personnel coming into Government after working for a Government contractor? Page 12

10. If an employee has divested all interests in a former employer who is a Government contractor, is that sufficient to comply with all ethical obligations? Page 13

11. May there be impartiality concerns even where it has been more than one year since an employee terminated from a contractor? Page 14

II. Other Financial Conflicts

12. Is an employee always prohibited from participating in a contract if he owns stock in the contractor? Page 15

13. Are interests in subcontractors covered? Page 15

14. Does section 208 affect an employee who "moonlights" for a contractor as an outside activity? Page 15

15. How does section 208 apply if a Government employee is married to an employee of a Government contractor? Page 16

III. Other Impartiality Issues

16. If an employee's spouse works for a contractor, could there be any impartiality concerns, even if 18 U.S.C § 208 does not apply? Page 17

17. What if the Government employee is dating a contractor employee? Page 18

18. May an employee award a contract to a personal friend or a company owned by a personal friend? Page 18

IV. Gifts

19. May an agency employee ever accept a gift from a contractor or an employee of a contractor? Page 19

20. May an employee use the $20 de minimis exception to accept gifts from various employees of the same contractor? Page 19

21. Are there limits on the frequency with which employees can accept gifts from contractors and contractor employees under the gift exceptions? Page 20

22. May an employee use the exception for gifts based on a personal relationship to accept gifts from a contractor employee with whom he has developed a friendship on the job? Page 20

23. If an employee's spouse works for an agency contractor, may the employee accept gifts from the contractor? Page 21

24. May an agency employee accept ground transportation from a contractor or contractor employee? Page 21

25. If agency employees work in the same office with contractor employees, may agency employees solicit contractor employees for voluntary contributions for gifts to be given to certain agency employees on special occasions, such as marriage or retirement? Page 22

26. May an employee accept free attendance at a conference or similar event sponsored by an agency contractor? Page 23

27. May an agency employee accept free attendance at a holiday party sponsored by an agency contractor? Page 23

28. May an employee use an agency contractor to perform personal work? Page 24

APPENDIX E

V. Miscellaneous Ethics Questions

29. May an agency employee raise funds for his favorite charity from a contractor employee with whom he works? Page 25

30. Are there limits on the kinds of official information a Government employee may share with a contractor or contractor employee? Page 26

31. Are there limits on an employee's ability to benefit personally from information pertaining to a contract or potential contract? Page 26

32. May an employee "moonlight" for an agency contractor? Page 27

33. May an employee contract with the Government or own businesses that do? Page 28

34. May an employee provide a letter or other statement discussing the quality of a particular contractor's performance? Page 29

I. Revolving Door Questions

These Q&As begin with a discussion of several aspects of "the revolving door," i.e., the movement of personnel between the Government and Government contractors (and those who represent them). The revolving door in the contracting area has been the subject of a fair amount of attention, both historically and also more recently, for example, with the prosecutions arising from the Druyun matter involving Air Force procurement.

As set out below, the revolving door Questions are divided into three subgroups: current Government employees seeking future employment with contractors; former Government employees working for or on behalf of contractors; and former contractor employees now working in the Government.

A. <u>Seeking Future Employment</u>

Employees who work on contract matters or who have contact with contractor employees sometimes may consider the possibility of going to work for a contractor. There are several laws and rules that govern employees who seek future employment, or receive employment overtures from, contractors: 18 U.S.C. § 208, OGE implementing regulations at 5 C.F.R. §§ 2635.601 - 2635.606, and the Procurement Integrity Act. This is an area that has received considerable attention recently, not only from the media and Congress but also from Federal prosecutors. <u>See</u> OGE DAEOgram DO-04-029, available at http://www.usoge.gov/pages/daeograms/dgr files/2004/do04029.pdf. Employees should be made aware of the seriousness of these issues and encouraged to seek timely advice from agency ethics officials about their own specific situations.

1. What are the criminal restrictions that relate to looking for future employment with a contractor?

Under 18 U.S.C. § 208, an employee may not participate in any particular Government matter that would affect the financial interests of any contractor (or other person) with which the employee is negotiating, or has an arrangement, for future employment. Although it may be possible for an employee to receive a waiver of this prohibition, OGE gives heightened scrutiny to proposed waivers in this situation, and waivers for employment negotiations should be issued only in compelling circumstances. <u>See</u> DAEOgram DO-04-029, at 7-8.

It is important to remember that this criminal prohibition applies to <u>all particular matters</u> that would have a direct and predictable effect on the financial interest of the

APPENDIX E | 349

prospective employer. In contrast, as discussed below, related provisions of the Procurement Integrity Act apply only to certain kinds of procurements and certain specific kinds of official activities in connection with those procurements. The restrictions in section 208 apply whether or not the Procurement Integrity Act applies, as long as the employee is participating in a particular matter.

It is also important to remember that the employee's level of participation in the particular matter need only be "personal and substantial" in order to violate section 208; the employee need not be the final decisionmaker on any contract matter and need not serve in any specifically designated role (such as contracting officer) or perform any specifically designated procurement function (such as preparing specifications and solicitations or evaluating bids). As discussed below, the Procurement Integrity Act uses similar language concerning personal and substantial participation, but that language has a narrower meaning than in section 208.

> <u>Example</u>: A contractor provides engineering support services for an agency program. An agency employee involved in this program periodically provides information to the contracting officer concerning the quality of the contractor's performance. The employee begins discussing the possibility of going to work with the contractor. Under 18 U.S.C. § 208, he must immediately recuse himself from any further participation in the evaluation of this contractor's performance or any other issue arising under the contract.

2. Do the OGE implementing regulations add anything to the criminal restriction?

Yes. The OGE implementing regulations do not cover only employees who are actually negotiating or have an agreement to work for a prospective employer. They also require recusal by those who are merely "seeking" employment by making unsolicited contacts about possible employment, such as sending a resume to a firm on whose contract or bid the employee is working. Likewise, the OGE regulations require recusal if an employee makes any response other than rejection to a contractor's unsolicited overtures about possible employment.

> <u>Example</u>: The employee in the previous example to Question 1 has not actually begun discussions with the contractor, but has simply submitted a resume with a cover letter indicating his interest in working for the company. Even though he has heard no response from the company, he has begun seeking employment under the OGE rule, and must recuse himself from working on matters arising under the contract. If two months elapse and the employee still has received no indication of interest on the part of the contractor, the employee no longer will be deemed to be seeking employment with the contractor. Likewise, if the contractor tells the employee that it is not interested and there

is no further discussion of possible employment, the employee no longer will be deemed to be seeking employment with that contractor.

3. Do the OGE regulations require employees to notify anyone that they have begun seeking employment or are recused from certain matters?

The OGE regulations do not require any particular notification. Employees comply with any recusal obligations under section 208 and the OGE regulations simply by avoiding participation in any particular matter in which the prospective employer has a financial interest. However, the regulations add that an employee "should" notify the person responsible for his assignment of the need to recuse from a particular matter; while this is not a mandatory notification duty, it does point employees in the direction of common sense. Moreover, an agency ethics official may require written documentation of a recusal, and such documentation also may be required as evidence of compliance with an ethics agreement. Note, furthermore, that the Procurement Integrity Act and the Federal Acquisition Regulation do impose certain mandatory notification procedures, as discussed in Question 4 below.

4. Beyond the criminal law and the OGE regulations, what additional requirements are there under the Procurement Integrity Act concerning employment contacts?

The Procurement Integrity Act imposes additional requirements on employees who are participating personally and substantially in a procurement (i.e., the acquisition of goods or services by using competitive procedures and awarding a contract) in excess of the simplified acquisition threshold. 41 U.S.C. § 423(c). For purposes of the Procurement Integrity Act, personal and substantial participation is limited to certain specific functions involving: the specification or statement of work; the solicitation; the evaluation of bids or proposals, or selecting a source; negotiation of price or terms and conditions of the contract; or the review or approval of the award of a contract. 48 C.F.R. § 3.104-1. Employees who are participating in these ways in a covered procurement have the following obligations if they contact, or are contacted by, a bidder or offeror regarding possible employment:

- Promptly report the employment contact, in writing, to both the employee's supervisor and the Designated Agency Ethics Official (or designee); and

APPENDIX E | 351

- Either--

    (a) reject the possibility of employment, or

    (b) recuse from the procurement until the agency has authorized the employee to resume participating (in accordance with 18 U.S.C. § 208 and applicable regulations) on the ground that the prospective employer is no longer a bidder or offeror, or on the ground that all employment discussions have terminated without an agreement or arrangement.

Note additionally that the Federal Acquisition Regulation requires—in addition to the written report on employment contacts discussed above—a written disqualification notice, which must be submitted to the contracting officer, the source selection authority, and the employee's immediate supervisor. 41 C.F.R. § 3.104-5(a).

Also, keep in mind that, even though section 208 and the Procurement Integrity Act use similar language concerning personal and substantial participation, section 208 covers activities and functions beyond those listed in the Federal Acquisition Regulation at 41 C.F.R. § 3.104-1. For purposes of the Procurement Integrity Act, the FAR has interpreted personal and substantial participation more narrowly than OGE interprets the language in section 208 and the OGE implementing regulations.

B. Post-Employment Restrictions

Employees who are involved in contracting matters or who work with contractors and contractor personnel need to be aware that certain restrictions may apply to their activities even after they leave Government. It is also important for employees to remember that the procurement-specific provisions of the Procurement Integrity Act, 41 U.S.C. § 423, are not the only post-employment restrictions about which they must be concerned: the criminal post-employment law, 18 U.S.C. § 207, contains different, and in some respects broader, requirements.

5. What are the restrictions under the Procurement Integrity Act for employees who leave Government after working on matters relating to a Government contractor?

An employee who has served in specific contracting roles, or performed specific contracting functions, on certain contract matters over $10,000,000, generally is prohibited for one year from receiving compensation from the contractor for service as an employee, officer, director, or consultant. The specific contracting roles and functions are as follows:

- serving as program manager, deputy program manager, or administrative contracting officer for a contract over $10,000,000;
- making a decision to award a contract, subcontract, modification of a contract or task or delivery order over $10,000,000;
- making a decision to establish overhead or other rates for a contract or contracts for a particular contractor over $10,000,000;
- making a decision to issue payments over $10,000,000 to a particular contractor;
- making a decision to pay or settle a claim over $10,000,000 with a particular contractor. 41 U.S.C. § 423(d).

This prohibition does not prevent an employee from going to work for a division or affiliate of the contractor that does not produce the same or similar products or services as the entity of the contractor responsible for the contract in which the employee was involved. 41 U.S.C. § 423(d)(2).

Note also that a current or former Government employee may not disclose contractor bid or proposal information or source selection information before the award of the procurement contract. 41 U.S.C. § 423(a).

> *Example*: An agency employee served as administrative contracting officer on a $25,000,000 contract with ABC Company. Shortly after he retired from Government, ABC approached him about working as a consultant on a different contract with a different agency. Even though his duties for the company would not involve any contact with his former agency, the former employee may not accept compensation as a consultant for ABC for one year after he last served as administrative contracting officer on the ABC contract.

6. If a former employee did not serve in any of the specific contracting roles or perform any of the specific contracting functions described above, is he free from any post-employment restrictions?

No. Quite apart from the Procurement Integrity Act, there is a criminal statute, 18 U.S.C. § 207, that imposes several restrictions that could apply to a former employee who worked on contract matters but did not actually serve in any of the contracting roles or perform any of the contracting functions designated in the Procurement Integrity Act.

APPENDIX E | 353

> *Example*: An employee participated in evaluating the performance of a contractor, but did not serve in any of the positions or perform any of the functions or make any of the decisions described in 41 U.S.C. § 423(d). The employee is barred by 18 U.S.C. § 207(a)(1) from representing the contractor (or any other person) before the Government concerning this same contract.

7. Which restrictions in 18 U.S.C. § 207 apply most frequently to employees who have been involved in contracting matters or have worked with contractors?

Although section 207 has seven separate prohibitions applicable to executive branch employees, three provisions tend to come up most frequently. (For a full description of all of the restrictions and exceptions in section 207, see OGE DAEOgram DO-04-023A, available at http://www.usoge.gov/pages/daeograms/dgr_files/2004/do04023a.pdf.) Each of these three applies to representing another person before the Government, i.e., making a communication or appearance with the intent to influence the Government. They do not, however, apply to behind-the-scenes work for a contractor or other person.

A lifetime ban on representing any other person before the Government on the same "particular matter involving specific parties," such as a contract, in which the former employee participated for the Government; the former employee may have participated personally and substantially in a contract, under this provision, without actually serving in any of the specific contracting roles or performing any of the specific functions or decisions designated in the Procurement Integrity Act.

> *Example*: See the Example following Question 6 above.

Section 207 also has a two-year ban on representing another person before the Government on the same contract (or other particular matter involving specific parties) that was pending under the official responsibility of the former employee during his last year of Government service; the former employee need not have participated at all in the contract, so long as the matter was in his chain of supervision.

> *Example*: The head of a division at an agency was not involved in any particular contract. However, every contract that was pending in his division, even if handled by subordinates several levels below the division head, was under his official responsibility. Consequently, for two years after he leaves Government, he could not represent anyone on any contract that was pending in his division during his last year of service.

The third major prohibition is a one-year "cooling-off" period for any matter involving the employee's former agency; this provision is applicable only to senior employees, e.g., commissioned officers at 0-7 and above and civilian employees with a rate of basic pay equivalent to 86.5 % of Executive Level II ($142,898 in 2006); the ban can apply even to new contracts, as well as to broader procurement policy matters that don't even focus on specific contracts.

> *Example*: A member of the Senior Executive Service was paid at a rate of $150,000 in 2006, when he left his agency for a position with a contractor. The contractor wants him to call his former agency about a potential new contract. This matter was not pending in the agency when the former employee was employed there. Nevertheless, the former employee may not represent the contractor before the agency on this (or any other) matter for one year after terminating his senior position with the agency.

8. Does section 207 apply when a former employee is simply performing work under a Government contract?

It depends. If the former employee is able to remain "behind-the-scenes," he will not violate any of the three main prohibitions discussed in Question 7. Note that the less frequently applicable provisions in section 207(b), (f) and (l) do cover certain behind-the-scenes activities.

If the former employee's work under the contract requires communication with the Government, these prohibitions in section 207 may apply. Employees sometimes assume, incorrectly, that section 207 applies only to communications about the award or modification or other major business aspects of a contract. However, section 207 also can apply to communications that a former employee makes while performing work under the contract, even if the contract specifically requires contractor personnel to communicate with the Government. Of course, certain routine or ministerial communications would not be covered, for example, making routine factual statements that are not potentially controversial. However, many communications made while the former employee is performing the contract may involve the intent to influence the Government, because the contractor and the Government have potentially differing views or interests on the matter being discussed. (For further discussion of this issue, see OGE Informal Advisory Letters 99 x 19, 03 x 6, and 05 x 3.)

> *Example*: A Government economist participated personally and substantially in a contract that required the contractor to perform certain econometric studies. The contractor would like to hire him to work on performing further research under the same contract. The job would require the individual to meet frequently with agency personnel to answer any questions concerning the research that has been performed and to obtain instructions for further research. It is expected that these discussions sometimes may involve questions about the adequacy of research already performed or alternative

approaches to performing future research. Such discussions, even though required under the contract, potentially could involve disputes between the contractor and the agency. The employee should be advised that section 207 could prevent him from meeting with agency employees as intended.

C. **Relationship with Former Private Employer**

Ethics questions can arise not only when a Government employee moves to the private sector, but also when a private sector employee moves to the Government.

9. **Are there criminal conflict of interest restrictions that especially affect personnel coming into Government after working for a Government contractor?**

Yes. Although individuals are subject to a number of criminal conflict of interest laws after they leave a contractor and go to work for the Government, issues are most likely to arise under 18 U.S.C. § 208 and, possibly, 18 U.S.C § 209.

Former employees of Government contractors may have continuing financial interests in their former employer. These could include stock, stock options, different types of pensions and deferred compensation arrangements, or other miscellaneous benefits. Depending on the circumstances, any of these interests could give the employee a continuing financial interest in contracts and other particular matters that affect the contractor. Under 18 U.S.C. § 208, a Government employee must recuse himself from any particular matter in which he has a financial interest, absent a waiver or applicable regulatory exemption. Therefore, any continuing interest in a former employer must be examined to determine whether it requires the individual to be recused from contract matters affecting the former employer. In some cases, it may be necessary for the employee to divest the conflicting interest. See 5 C.F.R. § 2635.403.

> *Example*: *An individual worked for many years for a computer company. He has acquired over $100,000 in the company's stock as a result of various profit-sharing benefits. The individual joins the IT office at an agency that does substantial business with the company. Absent a waiver, he may not participate in any contracts involving the company. If the agency does not believe a waiver would be appropriate, and recusal would prevent the employee from performing critical duties, the agency may require the employee to divest the stock.*

Occasionally, issues also may arise under 18 U.S.C. § 209 if payments or other benefits are given to an employee by a former employer who is a Government contractor. Section 209 prohibits employees from receiving any supplementation of their Federal salary as compensation for their services to the Government. Section 209 may apply if a former employer makes a payment to a Government employee and there is an indication that the payment is intended to compensate the employee for doing his Government job, rather than to compensate the person for past services to the former employer or for some other reason unrelated to Government service. For a comprehensive discussion of section 209, see DAEOgram DO-02-016A, available at http://www.usoge.gov/pages/laws_regs_fedreg_stats/lrfs_files/othr_gdnc/og_sum209_02.pdf. Note that section 209 does not apply to a payment made before the individual actually starts as a Government employee; in such cases, however, the employee may be subject to recusal obligations described in Question 10 below.

10. If an employee has divested all interests in a former employer who is a Government contractor, is that sufficient to comply with all ethical obligations?

Not necessarily. There are two provisions in the OGE standards of conduct that may require an employee to recuse, for a certain period of time, from working on contracts and certain other matters involving a former employer.

Under 5 C.F.R. § 2635.502, an employee must recuse, for one year after leaving a former employer, from any contract or other particular matter in which the former employer is a party (or represents a party), if either the employee or an agency designee determines that a reasonable person with knowledge of the circumstances would question the employee's impartiality. This recusal obligation may be lifted only by an authorization from an agency designee.

> *Example*: *An agency, which is responsible for certain emergency management operations, has a contract with a company to provide a range of support services in a particular location. An individual, who had been working as an employee of the contractor, now has been hired directly by the agency. The employee will have a covered relationship with the contractor for one year. Before the employee is assigned to work on any contract involving the company, the employee and the agency need to consider impartiality concerns and determine whether the employee should be recused or authorized to participate in the matter.*

Under 5 C.F.R. § 2635.503, an employee must recuse, for two years after receiving an "extraordinary payment" from a former employer, from any contract or other particular matter in which the former employer is a party (or represents a party). An extraordinary payment means a payment (1) in excess of $10,000, (2) determined after the former employer knew that the individual was being considered for a Government position, and (3) not pursuant to the former employer's established compensation program.

Example: The employee in the previous example was given a $15,000 severance payment after the company learned that he was being considered for a position with the agency. According to the company, the severance payment was intended to honor the individual for his hard work and contribution to the mission of the company. This individual was the first person ever awarded such a payment by the company, and the company had no written policy or contract establishing the benefit. This is an extraordinary payment, and the employee would be recused for two years from working on any contract involving the company, absent a waiver.

11. Can there be impartiality concerns even where it has been more than one year since an employee terminated from a contractor?

Possibly. As noted above, if the employee received an extraordinary payment from a contractor, impartiality concerns are addressed for two years under the recusal requirements of 5 C.F.R. § 2635.503. Even if the employee did not receive an extraordinary payment and more than a year has transpired since the employee left the contractor, there still may be impartiality concerns if the employee is assigned to participate in contracts involving the former employer. Section 2635.502(a)(2) provides a "catch-all" mechanism for employees and agencies to address impartiality concerns arising in circumstances that are not specifically covered in the rule.

Example: An individual was the director of a university laboratory, where he was responsible for the lab's contract with an agency to perform research on a new communications technology for an agency system. Then the agency hired him. Two years later, the lab made a claim for payment, which the agency is considering denying on the ground that the lab has not completely performed certain required work. The program manager would like to use the employee to review the adequacy of the lab's work, in light of his significant expertise with the technology. Given the employee's past level of involvement with this same contract on behalf of the contractor, as well as the sensitivity of the performance dispute, it would be reasonable for the agency and the employee to conclude that the employee should not participate in this decision.

II. Other Financial Conflicts

Questions 1 and 9 above deal with various aspects of 18 U.S.C. § 208, which prohibits employees from working on contracts and other particular matters affecting their personal or imputed financial interests. In addition to those situations discussed above, the following Questions explore some of the more common scenarios involving section 208 and contractors.

12. Is an employee always prohibited from participating in a contract if he owns stock in the contractor?

Not always. OGE has issued regulations exempting certain de minimis amounts of publicly traded securities. An employee can work on a contract as long as he owns no more than $15,000 of publicly traded stock in the contractor. The $15,000 limit applies to the sum of all stock owned by the employee, the employee's spouse and the employee's minor children, in all companies affected by the same contract (including subcontractors and competing offerors). It is important to remember that this exemption applies to publicly traded stock, not to stock or any other ownership interest in a privately held company. (Note that this exemption does not apply to stock that would be a prohibited holding for the employee, for example, under an agency-specific statute or regulation.) Also, in some cases, an agency may grant an employee an individual waiver under 18 U.S.C. § 208(b)(1), to permit participation where the employee owns more than $15,000 in stock.

> *Example:* An employee's spouse owns $10,000 of stock in a private company that has submitted a bid on a small contract with the employee's agency. The de minimis exemption does not apply to this non-publicly traded stock, and the employee may not participate in the procurement, absent an individual waiver. On the other hand, if the company's stock were publicly traded, the employee could participate. However, if the employee also owned another $10,000 in the stock of a competing bidder on the same contract, he would exceed the $15,000 limit and would have to recuse, absent a waiver.

13. Are interests in subcontractors covered?

Yes. Section 208 applies to an employee's financial interest in a subcontractor involved in a Government contract.

> *Example:* An employee's spouse owns a controlling interest in a private company. A bidder on a Government contract plans to use this company as a subcontractor on the contract. The employee may not participate in the procurement.

14. Does section 208 affect an employee who "moonlights" for a contractor as an outside activity?

Yes. Under section 208, an employee may not participate in any contract or other particular matter in which his outside employer has a financial interest. A Government employee who moonlights for a contractor must recuse from particular matters affecting that contractor. Outside employment with a contractor is discussed in more detail in Question 32 below.

Example: An agency has a contract with a medical testing company to provide certain diagnostic services to beneficiaries under an agency health program. An agency doctor orders tests for patients pursuant to the contract. The doctor may not participate in these decisions if he takes an outside job with the company, absent a waiver.

15. How does section 208 apply if a Government employee is married to an employee of a Government contractor?

Section 208 prohibits an employee from working on contracts and other particular matters affecting a spouse's financial interests. The need to recuse could arise in various situations.

Example: An employee works on a contract for his agency. His spouse is hired by the contractor to work on the same contract. The spouse's continued employment and possible advancement with the company depend on the firm's success with this particular contract. Section 208 would apply, even if the Government employee does not personally review the work of the spouse or even participate in the same part of the contract in which the spouse is involved.

Example: An employee's spouse works for an agency contractor. She participates in the company's stock purchase program and also receives periodic cash bonuses tied to firm profitability. Therefore, she has a financial interest in *any* contract that her company has with the agency, even if her own work does not involve the particular contract and she does not work in the same division of the company that is performing the contract. The employee may not participate in any contract with the company, absent a waiver.

Example: The spouse of an employee is a partner at a law firm that is representing a disappointed bidder in a bid protest against the agency. As a partner, the spouse has a financial interest in all particular matters in which her firm is representing a client, including matters in which she herself is not providing services. The employee may not work on the bid protest, without a waiver.

In some cases, however, the spouse will not have any financial interest in a Government contract.

Example: An agency employee is assigned to work on a contract involving his spouse's employer. The contractor is a large company with many different contracts and business operations. The spouse works in an area of the company's business that is unrelated to the contract with the employee's agency. Moreover, the spouse receives a straight salary from the company, without any equity or profit-sharing interests. Section 208 would not prohibit the employee from participating in this contract.

Even if the spouse does not have a financial interest in the contract on which the Government employee is working, there still may be impartiality issues, as described in Question 16.

III. Other Impartiality Issues

OGE's impartiality rule, 5 C.F.R. § 2635.502, is discussed in Questions 10 and 11 above. In addition to the situations described in those Questions, various other relationships and interests can raise concerns about an employee's impartiality. A few of the more common scenarios are described in Questions below.

16. If an employee's spouse works for a contractor, could there be any impartiality concerns, even if 18 U.S.C § 208 does not apply?

Yes. A Government employee has a "covered relationship" with his spouse's employer, under 5 C.F.R. § 2635.502(b) (1) (iii), even if his spouse does not have a financial interest in a particular Government contract. This rule would require an employee to recuse from any contract involving a spouse's employer, if either the employee or an agency designee determines that a reasonable person with knowledge of the circumstances would question the employee's impartiality. In some cases, the agency might authorize the employee to work on the contract in any event.

Example: The employee in the last Example following Question 15 above has a covered relationship with the contractor that employs his spouse. Because of his significant experience in the subject matter, the employee is the most qualified person in his office to work on the particular matter, and it would be difficult to find another employee to perform the same duties. In light of the size of the company, the variety of its business activities, and the fact that the spouse is employed in a totally different area of the company's operations, the agency might determine that a reasonable person would not question the employee's impartiality in this matter. Alternatively, the agency might determine that any impartiality concerns are outweighed by the agency's need for the employee's services on the matter, in which case the employee could participate in the contract pursuant to an authorization under 5 C.F.R. § 2635.502(d). Depending on the circumstances, the agency might want to impose certain conditions, such as limits on the kinds of decisions the employee can make without review or approval by supervisors.

17. What if the Government employee is dating a contractor employee?

Under the impartiality rule, an employee does not have a "covered relationship" with a person he is merely dating or with the employer of a person he is dating. However, the impartiality rule provides a mechanism for employees and agencies to evaluate impartiality concerns, even in situations not involving a covered relationship. See 5 C.F.R. § 2635.502(a) (2).

> Example: An agency employee begins dating a contractor employee with whom he works. One of his duties involves reviewing the work of the contractor, including the contractor employee he has begun dating. The employee's impartiality in reviewing the work could reasonably be questioned under these circumstances, and the employee and the agency should use the procedures in section 2635.502 to determine whether, or under what conditions, he should be permitted to continue participating in the matter.

Note that there would be additional considerations if the Government employee and the contractor employee were residing together. 18 U.S.C. § 208 would prohibit a Government employee from working on a contract that affects the contractor employee's ability to pay any shared living expenses. In any case, the impartiality rule expressly covers situations in which an employee participates in a contract that affects the financial interest of "a member of his household." 5 C.F.R. § 2635.502(a). Similarly, the Government employee would have a covered relationship with a person who is a member of his household. 5 C.F.R. § 2635.502(b)(ii). For all of these reasons, a Government employee should not participate in a contract if a contractor employee, with whom he resides, is working on the same contract, unless the employee and his agency first have resolved any potential financial conflict of interest under section 208 and any impartiality concerns under section 2635.502.

18. Can an employee award a contract to a personal friend or a company owned by a personal friend?

It depends. An employee does not have a covered relationship with someone merely because that person is a personal friend. However, it is clear that employees should consider any potential impartiality questions before participating in a decision to give a contract to a personal friend, and the procedures set out in 5 C.F.R. § 2635.502(a)(2) will facilitate the review of all relevant circumstances. Allegations of favoritism can, and sometimes do, arise when Government contracts are awarded to a friend, so agencies and employees should be particularly alert to any impartiality concerns.

Example: An employee has long been friends with someone who is a healthcare consultant. They periodically meet for lunch and also occasionally get together with their families. The agency needs to acquire healthcare consulting services about a subject on which the employee knows his friend is an expert. Before recommending that his agency consider giving a contract to his friend, the employee should follow the process described in section 2635.502.

IV. Gifts

A common issue, particularly among employees who work closely or share office space with contractor personnel, is how to deal with gift-giving between contractor employees and Government employees. Employees should know that the ethics rules generally forbid them from accepting gifts from "prohibited sources," which clearly includes any contractor working for the employee's agency. 5 C.F.R. § 2635.203(d). It is important to remember that, regardless of the working relationship between Government and contractor personnel, contractor personnel remain employees of the contractor. As such, they are deemed "prohibited sources," under the OGE gift rules, to the same extent as the contractor that employs them. See 5 C.F.R. § 2635.102(k) (definition of person includes not only an entity but also any employee of that entity).

19. May an agency employee ever accept a gift from a contractor or an employee of a contractor?

Yes. The OGE gift rules have several exceptions that would permit gifts from a prohibited source, including an agency contractor or an employee of an agency contractor. See 5 C.F.R. § 2635.204. (In addition, there are certain items that a Government employee may accept from a prohibited source because those items are not considered gifts. See 5 C.F.R. § 2635.203(b)(1)-(9).) Questions 20-27 discuss some of the exceptions that may be applicable in common situations involving contractors and contractor personnel.

20. May an employee use the $20 de minimis exception to accept gifts from various employees of the same contractor?

Possibly. Under 5 C.F.R. § 2635.204(a), an employee may accept noncash gifts from a prohibited source, if the gifts from a particular source have a value of no more than $20 per occasion and $50 per calendar year. A contractor and an employee of a contractor are considered the same source under the OGE rules. Therefore, an agency employee could accept gifts from multiple contractor employees, but such gifts could not exceed the applicable limits for one source.

> *Example*: On his birthday, an agency employee receives a birthday gift valued at $20 from a contractor employee with whom he works in a shared office space. Later in the year, during the holiday season, the same agency employee receives a $15 gift from another employee of the same contractor. The employee could accept these gifts. However, if a third contractor employee offered to pick up a $20 lunch check for the agency employee the next day, the agency employee would have to decline the gift, as this would exceed the $50 annual limit per source.

21. Are there limits on the frequency with which employees can accept gifts from contractors and contractor employees under the gift exceptions?

Yes. An employee may not use any of the gift exceptions, including the de minimis exception, to accept gifts from the same or even different sources so frequently that a reasonable person would believe the employee is using his public office for private gain.

> *Example*: An agency employee works in an office along with personnel from several different support contractors, and she has responsibility for providing feedback on the performance of all of these contracts. She could not make a practice of going to lunch nearly every week at the expense of one or another of these contractors or their employees, even if the gifts from any one contractor fell within the de minimis limits for one source.

22. May an employee use the exception for gifts based on a personal relationship to accept gifts from a contractor employee with whom he has developed a friendship on the job?

Maybe. Under 5 C.F.R. § 2635.204(b), an employee sometimes may accept a gift from a prohibited source with whom the employee has a personal friendship. However, it must be clear from the circumstances that it was the friendship, and not the employee's official position, that motivated the gift. Relevant factors include the history of the relationship and whether the gift was actually paid for by the friend (as opposed to, for example, the contractor who employs the friend). Although it is certainly possible that an agency employee could develop a personal friendship with a contractor employee on the job—especially given the close working conditions in some mixed workplaces today—caution is advised. Particular care should be exercised to evaluate whether the nature of the relationship really justifies a particular gift. Where the relationship developed on the job, a gift rarely would be justified if the Government employee were actually in a position to oversee the work of the contractor employee or to participate in decisions affecting the interests of the contractor.

> *Example*: An employee has a pleasant, but relatively short, job-centered relationship with a contractor employee. The contractor employee offered a free weekend away at his beach house. Based on the history and nature of the relationship, one reasonably would question whether the motive for the offer was related to the Government employee's official position.

23. If an employee's spouse works for an agency contractor, may the employee accept gifts from the contractor?

Possibly. Under 5 C.F.R. § 2635.204(e)(1), an employee may accept gifts from his spouse's employer under certain circumstances. The employee may accept meals, lodgings, transportation, or other benefits that result from his spouse's business or employment activities, but it must be clear that the benefits have not been offered or enhanced because of the employee's official position.

> *Example*: An agency employee could accept free attendance at an annual retreat offered by a contractor to the families of all contractor employees. However, an employee could not accept if the same benefit were not extended to the families of similarly situated contractor employees who were not married to an agency employee.

24. May an agency employee accept ground transportation from a contractor or contractor employee?

It depends. The definition of "gift" in the OGE rules expressly includes "transportation" and "local travel." 5 C.F.R. § 2635.203(b). However, in order to determine whether such a gift would violate the ethics rules, it would be necessary to determine whether the transportation is duty-related or for the personal benefit of the individual.

If the transportation is provided in connection with the performance of the employee's official duties, there would be no gift to the employee personally, but rather a service provided to the agency. As described more fully in OGE Informal Advisory Letter 98 x 8, such benefits must be analyzed under fiscal law considerations, not the OGE ethics rules.

> *Example*: An employee is offered ground transportation by a contractor to travel between two work sites during official site visits. This is a benefit provided to the agency, not the

employee personally, and therefore does not implicate the OGE gift rules. The agency would have to determine whether it has authority to accept this benefit.

However, if the transportation was for the personal benefit of the employee, then it would constitute a gift to the employee under the OGE gift rules.

Example: A contractor offers to allow an employee to use the contractor's shuttle bus as part of his daily commute to the office. This is a gift to the employee personally and may be accepted only if one of the gift exceptions applies. For example, if the employee were only going to use the shuttle service for two days while he was on a special assignment, and it could be determined that the value of the service for that limited time period fell within the $20 de minimis amount, then the employee could accept the offer.

25. If agency employees work in the same office with contractor employees, may agency employees solicit contractor employees for voluntary contributions for gifts to be given to certain agency employees on special occasions, such as marriage or retirement?

No. While the OGE rules permit the solicitation of voluntary contributions for certain gifts to official superiors on special occasions, see 5 C.F.R. § 2635.304(c), the rules allow only solicitation of other Government employees. Therefore, the provisions governing gifts between Government employees do not apply to gifts from contractor employees to Government employees.

Furthermore, there is no exception in the OGE gift rules that would permit an agency employee to solicit a gift from a prohibited source for the benefit of another agency employee. See 5 C.F.R. §§ 2635.202(c)(2)(gift exceptions may not be used to solicit gifts); 2635.203(f)(soliciting indirect gifts for another person). An agency employee may accept an unsolicited gift from a contractor employee, if permitted by any of the gift exceptions, but there is no specific exception focusing on gifts for special occasions, such as marriage or retirement.

Example: An agency employee is organizing a dinner in honor of her supervisor's upcoming retirement and would like to invite several contractor employees who share the same workplace. The agency employee may not solicit a contribution from the contractor personnel for a retirement gift. Any contractor personnel who attend the dinner may contribute their appropriate share for the cost of their own meals, which would not be a gift at all. Moreover, all employees of the same contractor may give the retiree a single, unsolicited gift valued at $20.

26. May an employee accept free attendance at a conference or similar event sponsored by an agency contractor?

It depends. Under 5 C.F.R. § 2635.204(g)(2), an employee may accept free attendance at a widely attended gathering of mutual interest under certain circumstances. The event must be truly widely attended (see the Example following Question 27), and the agency must make a determination that the employee's attendance would be in the agency's interest. If the employee is actually working on matters that affect the particular contractor who made the offer, then the agency would have to make a written determination that the agency's interest outweighs the concern that the gift could improperly influence the employee in the performance of his duties. Note that free attendance, under this rule, does not include travel expenses.

> *Example*: An agency employee is one of several employees who are involved in the ongoing evaluation of work performed by a contractor that provides certain IT services. The contractor is co-sponsoring (along with a university) a one-day conference on security threats to IT systems. The contractor has extended an offer of free attendance to the agency employee. The event will include speakers from academia, industry and government and will not focus on any particular company's own products and services. The agency may authorize the acceptance, in writing, based on a determination that the agency's interest in the employee learning about IT security threats at this substantive event outweighs any concern that the offer of free attendance will affect the performance of the employee's official duties.

In some cases, the agency may choose to send the employee to the event on official duty. In those instances, free attendance would be a gift to the agency, rather than to the employee personally. Such gifts might be accepted under an applicable agency gift acceptance statute or, if the employee would be on official travel, under 31 U.S.C. § 1353. If the contractor were a 501(c)(3) nonprofit organization, the gift also might be accepted under 5 U.S.C. § 4111.

27. May an agency employee accept free attendance at a holiday party sponsored by an agency contractor?

Maybe. The definition of "gift" in the OGE rules covers any item having monetary value, including, among other things, "entertainment," "hospitality" and "meals." Although the definition of gift excludes "modest" refreshments (such as soft drinks, coffee and donuts, as long as they are not part of a meal), most holiday parties are not confined to such items. Accordingly, free attendance at a contractor party would be permitted only pursuant to an applicable gift exception.

Example: A contractor invites agency employees to a holiday party. The party will be attended only by contractor personnel who work in a particular office. If the value of the food and any entertainment were determined to be no more than $20, the employees could accept. However, the employees could not use the widely attended gathering exception to accept this gift, because the event would not be attended by a large number of persons with a diversity of views or interests.

28. May an employee use an agency contractor to perform personal work?

It depends. Certainly, an employee could not have a contractor perform private work under the agency's own contract. At the very minimum, this would violate 5 C.F.R. § 2635.704. However, if the employee entered into an agreement to hire the contractor, and paid the full market value for any goods and services, there would not be a prohibited gift. 5 C.F.R. § 2635.203(b)(9). Nevertheless, the employee should be particularly careful to make sure that he actually pays market value, which is defined as what the employee would have to pay, at retail cost, for similar goods or services of like quality: it must be clear that it is an arm's length transaction, under standard terms. Additionally, if the employee is actually working on an agency contract involving the contractor, the employee needs to be careful not to create the appearance that he is in anyway using his authority over the contractor to induce or coerce the contractor into providing services or favorable treatment. 5 C.F.R. §§ 2635.702(a); 2635.202(c)(2). Furthermore, if the personal work involves anything other than a routine consumer transaction, the employee will have a "covered relationship" with the contractor that could require the employee's recusal from agency matters involving the contractor under 5 C.F.R. § 2635.502(a); other circumstances also could raise impartiality concerns under 5 C.F.R. § 2635.502(a)(2). For all of these reasons, employees should exercise great care if they want to hire an agency contractor for outside personal business.

Example: An agency employee works in a large office that receives IT support under an agency-wide contract. The employee does not place task orders under the contract and does not have any other procurement duties. He occasionally receives support from contractor employees when he reports computer problems to the executive officer for his office. On one occasion, he asks a contractor employee whether his company does any residential work, and the contractor employee gives him a telephone number for the residential services division of the company. The employee calls this number and arranges for a technician to do some private work on the employee's home computer, for which he pays the standard residential rate. This arrangement would not violate 5 C.F.R. 2635, Subpart B, nor does it appear to be impermissible under Subpart G. Moreover, because the relationship with the contractor involves a routine consumer transaction, the employee would not have a "covered relationship" under Subpart E.

Example: In the preceding example, the employee is the contracting officer. He has been having problems with his daughter's laptop computer and brings it into the office. He asks one of the contractor employees with whom he works if he has any time to look at the laptop. The contractor employee takes the laptop home and in a few minutes fixes what he determines to be an easy problem. He says it was "no big deal" and tells the employee not to worry about paying anything. The employee has received a gift from a prohibited source. Moreover, given the contracting officer's authority over the contractor and the circumstances in which he asked for help, there could be an appearance that he used his official position to induce or coerce the contractor employee to provide this service. If the employee had actually used the agency contract to have this personal work done, at a minimum, he would have violated 5 C.F.R. § 2635.704.

V. Miscellaneous Ethics Questions

The Questions below deal with various subjects that can arise in connection with employees who work on contract matters or work closely with contractor personnel.

29. May an agency employee raise funds for his favorite charity from a contractor employee with whom he works?

No. Employees may engage in personal fundraising, with certain limitations. One limitation is that employees may not personally solicit funds or other support for a charity from a prohibited source, including an agency contractor or its employees. See 5 C.F.R. § 2635.808(c). (An employee does not violate this rule, however, if the solicitation is made to a large group through the media, oral remarks, or mass mailings, as long as the solicitation is not targeted at prohibited sources.) The prohibition includes even fundraising on the employee's own time and outside the Federal workplace.

Example: An agency employee is assigned to work at a contractor's site. He has become quite friendly with several contractor employees, with whom he has daily interactions and discusses various personal and professional issues. He is active in a local historic preservation society, which is conducting its annual fund drive. He knows that one contractor employee has a particular interest in historic preservation issues. The agency employee may not ask the contractor employee if he would like to make a donation.

Note that some agencies have authority to engage in "official" fundraising, and there is no general prohibition on official solicitation of prohibited sources by agency employees carrying out their authorized official duties. See 5 C.F.R. § 2635.808(b).

However, individual agencies may have policies or practices limiting official solicitation of prohibited sources.

30. Are there limits on the kinds of official information a Government employee may share with a contractor or contractor employee?

Yes. A Government employee may not allow the improper use of nonpublic information to further the private interest of another person, including a contractor or contractor employee. 5 C.F.R. § 2635.703. This includes any information about a contract that the employee gains through his job and that he reasonably should know has not been made available to the public. Additionally, the Procurement Integrity Act has restrictions covering specific types of procurement information: contractor bid or proposal or source selection information prior to the award of an agency procurement contract; the disclosure of such information is subject to criminal as well as civil penalties, and also can result in various administrative actions. 41 U.S.C. § 423(a), (e). In some situations, other laws may prohibit the disclosure of certain information. E.g., 18 U.S.C. § 1905 (Trade Secrets Act); 5 U.S.C. § 552a (Privacy Act).

> Example: An employee has nonpublic information that his agency is deliberating the termination a particular contract. The employee has become friends with a contractor employee who would be affected if the contract were terminated. The agency employee would like to share this information with the contractor employee so he can start making new career plans. The agency employee is prohibited by 5 C.F.R. § 2635.703 from doing so.

31. Are there limits on an employee's ability to benefit personally from information pertaining to a contract or potential contract?

Yes. A Government employee may not use nonpublic information to engage in any financial transaction or otherwise to further his own private interest. 5 C.F.R. § 2635.703.

> Example: An agency employee has access to nonpublic information concerning the likely award of a large contract to a company. He may not rely on this information to buy stock in the company or advise others (such as family or friends) to do likewise. Apart from the ethics rules, such conduct also could violate Federal securities statutes.

32. May an employee "moonlight" for an agency contractor?

Maybe. As discussed in Question 14 above, an employee may not participate personally and substantially in any contract or other particular matter in which his outside employer has a financial interest. 18 U.S.C. § 208. In some cases, the necessary recusal would impair the employee's ability to do his job or the agency's ability to accomplish its mission. In such cases, the agency may prohibit the outside employment. 5 C.F.R. §§ 2635.802(b); 2635.403(b).

> *Example*: An agency employee is the contracting officer's technical representative (COTR) on a particular contract. Service as COTR on this contract is the primary duty of the employee's position. The employee also happens to be a certified public accountant, and he is always looking for opportunities to stay current with his accounting skills. He learns that the contractor is looking for a part-time accountant to work on a totally different contract involving a private sector client. The agency determines that the employee could not engage in this outside employment because the necessary recusal would make it impossible for him to continue as the COTR.

Even if any employee does not have official duties involving a particular agency contractor, there may be some limitations on his outside activities. Employees may not engage in outside activities that create the appearance that they are using their public office for private gain. 5 C.F.R. §§ 2635.702; 2635.801(c); see OGE DAEOgram DO-04-011, http://www.usoge.gov/pages/daeograms/dgr_files/2004/do04011.pdf.

> *Example*: An employee is an expert on his agency's procurement policies and practices and is generally familiar with the typical procurement needs of various offices. A company would like to hire him as a consultant to help develop a business plan for marketing products to his agency. Even though the employee's official duties do not involve any current contract with this company, he may not accept this offer. The circumstances would create the appearance that the employee obtained this outside employment opportunity because of his official position and would be using his position for the private advantage of the company.

Employees also must be aware that criminal statutes, 18 U.S.C. §§ 203 and 205, prohibit them from representing any contractor in dealings with the Government. For the reasons discussed above in Question 8, these prohibitions can extend even to certain communications made during the course of performing work under the Government contract.

> *Example*: An employee of the Environmental Protection Agency (EPA) has taken a part-time job with a Navy contractor. The outside job does not involve any interaction with

EPA, and it does not even involve the same subject matter as the employee's EPA duties. Nevertheless, the employee may not make any representational contacts with the Navy on behalf of the contractor.

Finally, some agencies have supplemental standards of conduct regulations pertaining to outside employment with certain entities. In some cases, agency supplemental regulations may prohibit certain outside employment with an agency contractor (or potential contractor). E.g., 5 C.F.R. §§ 6901.103(c)(1) (NASA); 5501.106(c)(1)&(2) (HHS). Employees also must follow any agency prior approval requirements for outside activities; even if the agency has no such prior approval requirements, usually it would be prudent for an employee to seek advice from an ethics official prior to engaging in outside employment for an agency contractor.

33. May an employee contract with the Government or own businesses that do?

Generally no. The general policy under the Federal Acquisition Regulation (FAR) prohibits a contracting officer from awarding a contract to a Government employee "or to a business concern or other organization owned or substantially owned or controlled by one or more Government employees." 48 C.F.R. § 3.601. (Somewhat lesser restrictions apply to contracts with special Government employees.) Although this is not an OGE ethics rule, it is clear that the FAR provision is intended to avoid any employee "conflict of interest" as well as "the appearance of favoritism or preferential treatment by the Government toward its employees." Id. An exception may be granted by the agency head or a designee no lower than the head of the contracting activity, "only if there is a most compelling reason to do so, such as when the Government's needs cannot reasonably be otherwise met." 48 C.F.R. § 3.602.

Additionally, it is important to remember that criminal statutes, 18 U.S.C. §§ 203 and 205, may prohibit an employee from communicating with the Government about a contract. These statutes do not prohibit self-representation, so an employee acting strictly as a sole proprietor could freely communicate with the Government about a contract. However, in many cases, an employee may have formed a separate business entity, such as a corporation, partnership or limited liability company (LLC); in such cases, the employee would be prohibited from representing the entity in connection with a Government contract.

Example: A Government employee wants to submit a proposal to another agency to provide certain consulting services. He would be submitting the proposal on his own behalf as an individual. Sections 203 and 205 would not prohibit him from doing so. He is also considering establishing his own consulting company as a corporation. He may not personally submit a proposal to the Government or make any other representational contact on behalf of the corporation. The corporation may communicate with the Government through other persons, such as its employees or an attorney, provided that the communication is not intended to attribute any information to the Government employee. In any case, the Federal Acquisition Regulation may prevent the contracting officer from awarding the contract to the Government employee or his corporation.

34. May an employee provide a letter or other statement discussing the quality of a particular contractor's performance?

Maybe. The OGE rule on endorsements, 5 C.F.R. § 2635.702(c), generally prohibits an employee from using his official position, title or authority to endorse any product, service or enterprise. Therefore, statements commending the performance of a contractor or a contractor's products generally are not permissible. However, the rule does not prohibit an employee from making a simple factual statement that the contractor's work satisfied the Government's requirements. (Note also that OGE does not view its endorsement rule as applying to authorized agency actions; rather, the prohibition generally is focused on the personal, unauthorized conduct of individual employees who abuse their position to make endorsements.) In addition to section 2635.702, there may be other policies or procedures, such as agency procurement or public affairs policies, that limit the situations in which an employee may make statements about a contractor's performance. Therefore, employees should consult with the contracting officer or an agency ethics official.

> *Example*: A contractor asks an employee for a letter stating that the contractor performed all its work under a particular contract. After consulting with the contracting officer, the employee provides a statement indicating that the contractor met all benchmarks, submitted all reports, and delivered a fully operational product to the agency. This would not be a prohibited endorsement, even if it is anticipated that the contractor will share the letter with prospective customers.

Index

A

ACS. *See* American Construction Services
administering contracts
   Aerojet Solid Propulsion Company example, 83
   American Construction Services example, 96
   Armed Services Board of Contract Appeals, 85
   Army example, 99
   Baker School Specialty Co. example, 84
   BASIX example, 102
   contract modifications, 80
   cost or pricing data, 78–79
   current, accurate, and complete, 81–83
   debarment, 98–105
   defective pricing, 78–81
   fraud, 73–75, 88–93, 201–203
   Giuliani Associates Inc. example, 89–90
   government reliance on defective pricing, 86–88
   Human Resources Management example, 95
   inspection clause, government rights under, 93–94
   Medina Construction example, 89
   Morton example, 94–95
   Motorola example, 88
   N.R. Acquisition Corp. example, 91–92
   pricing rules, 79
   Program Fraud Civil Remedies Act, 97–98
   Pro-Mark, Inc. example, 103
   Spread Information Sciences example, 96
   subcontractors, 92
   suspension, 98–102
   termination for default, 94–96
   Truth in Negotiations Act, 80
   UMC Electronics Company example, 92–93
   United Technologies Corporation example, 86–87
advertising costs, 183
Advisory Opinion of the Office of Government Ethics, 331
alcoholic beverages, 184
American Construction Services (ACS), 96
Anti-Kickback Act, 145
antitrust violations
   evidence of collusive bidding and price fixing, 178–180
   examples of collusive bidding and price fixing, 180–181
   overview, 177–178
applicability of new ethics regulations
   compliance, 10
   covered contracts, 19
   exceptions, 19
   Federal Register Responses, 17–18
   should versus shall, 17
   subcontracts, 21–26

three-rule summary, 18–19
Armed Services Board of Contract Appeals (ASBCA), 85–86, 96
award phase, 200

B

BAFO. *See* best and final offer
bait and switch. *See* misrepresentation
BCA. *See* Board of Contract Appeals
best and final offer (BAFO), 86
biased ground rules, 48
bid rotation, 181
bid suppression, 181
Board of Contract Appeals (BCA), 90
bounty hunting. *See* qui tam lawsuit
bribery, 73, 100, 102
Buy American Act, 148
Byrd Amendment, 167–172

C

CAFC. *See* U.S. Court of Appeals for the Federal Circuit
Cancellation, Rescission, and Recovery of Funds for Illegal or Improper Activity, 71–72
CDA. *See* Contract Disputes Act
Civil False Claims Act, 97–98
civil fines, 144–153
claims, 146–147
code of business ethics, 9–14
Code of Ethics Guide, 307
complementary bidding, 181
compliance
  Cancellation, Rescission, and Recovery of Funds for Illegal or Improper Activity, 71–72
  profit reductions, 73–74
  U.S. Court of Appeals for the Federal Circuit, 75
conflicts of interest, 44
conspiracy, 164
consultant restrictions, 165
contingencies, 184
contingent fees, 165–167
contract award phase, 200
Contract Disputes Act (CDA), 74, 90
contract formation stage
  biased ground rules, 48
  conflicts of interest types, 44
  ensuring compliance, 71–75
  fraud, 198
  impaired objectivity, 59–61
  job offers, 38–41
  misrepresentation, 61–64
  organizational conflicts of interest, 47–48
  personal conflicts of interest, 45–46
  procurement integrity regulations overview, 30–32
  protecting procurement information, 32–38
  status of the offeror, 64–70
  unequal access to information, 49–59
  violations, 42–44
contract losses, 184
contract negotiation phase, 201
contractor conduct
  AAA Engineering and Drafting, Inc. example, 154
  Advanced Tool Company example, 152–153
  Air Force example, 171–172
  Anti-Kickback Act, 146
  Byrd Amendment, 167–172
  civil fines, 144–153
  claims, 146–147
  conspiracy, 164
  contingent fees, 165–167
  criminal conviction, 145–153
  criminal false claims, 144–145
  Danka example, 156
  Department of Agriculture example, 159
  Department of Energy example, 151
  Educational Development Network, 145–146
  False Claims Act summary, 143–144
  False Statements Act, 140–143
  implied certifications, 153–157
  Jamieson Science and Engineering, Inc. example, 156–157
  mail fraud and wire fraud, 159–161
  major procurement fraud, 161–162
  McDonnell Douglas Helicopter Company example, 150

INDEX | 375

Morse Diesel example, 146–147
Northrop Corporation example, 158
obstruction of agency proceedings, 162–163
Pemco example, 149
qui tam lawsuit, 157–159
restrictions on lobbying and consultants, 165
Sandia National Laboratory example, 158
S and S Services Inc. example, 155
So-Cal example, 144–145
theft of government property, 165
Trade Secrets Act, 164
Veterans Administration example, 150
contributions, 184
corporate malfeasance, 110
cost backup data, 148
cost mischarging
    accounting mischarges, 185
    allowable costs, 183–184
    examples, 190
    labor mischarges, 186–189
    material cost mischarges, 185
    overview, 182–183
criminal conviction, 144–152
criminal false claims, 143–144
criminal offense, committing, 100

D

debarment
    contract formation stage, 69
    corporate malfeasance, 110
    Food and Drug Administration example, 106
    immigration laws, 106
    Joseph Silverman example, 108
    Lisbon Contractors example, 106
    regulations, 104–106
    Treasury Department example, 109
defective pricing, 78, 176
Defense Federal Acquisition Regulation Supplement (DFARS), 1
Defense Production Act, 104
deferred compensation, 183
Department of Justice, 77
Department of Veterans Affairs (VA), 45

destruction of records, 100, 103
DFARS. *See* Defense Federal Acquisition Regulation Supplement
donations, 184
Drug-Free Workplace Act of 1988, 100, 103

E

embezzlement, 100, 102
entertainment costs, 184
ethics training program, 14–16

F

failure to rebid, 179
false certifications, 155
falsification, 100, 102
FAR. *See* Federal Acquisition Regulation
FAR Case 2006-007, 206
fast pay fraud
    examples, 197–198
    indicators, 197
    overview, 196–197
FDA. *See* Food and Drug Administration
Federal Acquisition Regulation (FAR), 1–3
federal employee conduct
    Applied Research Corporation example, 122–123
    bribes and gratuities, 125–127
    conflicts of interest, 117–118
    CSC example, 123–124
    Health and Human Services example, 119
    illegal gratuity, 115
    negotiating for employment, 120–124
    Office of Government Ethics, 116
    participate personally and substantially, 118–119
    particular matter, 119–120
    restrictions on outside activities, 130–133
    restrictions on seeking employment, 134–137
    standards of conduct, 128–130
    Standards of Ethical Conduct for Employees of the Executive Branch, 116
    Teledyne Brown Engineering example, 121–122

Federal Property and Administrative
 Services Act of 1949, 36
Federal Supply Schedule (FSS) contracts,
 20
Final Rules: Federal Acquisition
 Regulation, 206
fines, 184
Food and Drug Administration (FDA), 106
foreign-made products, 192
forgery, 100, 103
fraud
 administering contracts, 77–78, 88–93
 contract administration phase, 201–203
 contract award phase, 200
 contract formation phase, 198
 contract negotiation phase, 201
 major procurement, 161–162
 pre-solicitation phase, 199
 product substitution, 193
 solicitation phase, 199–200
FSS. *See* Federal Supply Schedule contracts

G

GCAS. *See* Government Contract Advisory
 Services
general and administrative (G&A), 88, 189
General Services Administration (GSA),
 66–67
gifts, gratuities, and bribes, 31
global positioning system (GPS), 60
Government Contract Advisory Services
 (GCAS), 69
GSA. *See* General Services Administration
 (GSA)

H

head of contracting agency (HCA), 42
Health and Human Services (HHS), 119

I

identical bids, 189
idle facility costs, 184
IG. *See* Inspector General
illegal gratuity, 115
Immigration and Nationality Act, 106
impaired objectivity, 60–61
implied certifications, 153–157
IMS. *See* information management
 specialist
independent research, 184
industry-suggested prices, 180
inflated overhead submissions, 145
influencing legislative action, 184
information management specialist (IMS),
 60–61
Inspector General (IG), 107
interest, 186
internal control system
 assignment of responsibility, 12
 company personnel, 9–10
 Contractor Code of Business Ethics and
  Conduct, 9
 criminal conduct, 13
 disciplinary action, 13
 periodic reviews, 1

J

job offers
 competitive procurements, 38–39
 procurement integrity, 30
joint venture bids, 179

K

kickbacks, 148

L

large business government contractor, 19
legal costs, 184
lobbying restrictions, 170
long-term leases, 184
low bids, 178

M

Mail Fraud Statute, 160
major procurement fraud, 161–162
market division, 181
market-wide prices, 180
material testing, 192
memberships, 184

misrepresentation, 61–63
    Air Force example, 62
    Army example, 63
    GAO summary, 62

N

national stock number, 148

O

OEM. *See* original equipment manufacturer
Office of Government Ethics (OGE), 116
Office of Government Ethics, Ethics and Working with Contractors, 343
organizational conflict of interest (OCI)
    Air Force examples, 52, 55
    Army examples, 50, 53, 56–59
    biased ground rules, 48
    Coast Guard example, 54
    Continental Service Company example, 54
    contracting officer role, 47
    Defense Information Systems Agency example, 58
    Department of Agriculture example, 56
    Department of Defense example, 61
    identifying, 46
    impaired objectivity, 59–60
    Ktech Corporation example, 59
    National Aeronautics and Space Administration examples, 53, 55
    Naval Investigative Service example, 51
    types, 47
    unequal access to information, 48–59
original equipment manufacturer (OEM), 191
overhead costs, 189

P

penalties, 184
personal conflicts of interest, 27–28, 41–42
pre-solicitation phase fraud, 199
private employment after federal service, 28
Procurement Integrity Act, 26

procurement integrity regulations, 26–28
product substitution
    fraud, 193
    indicators of, 192
    original equipment manufacturer, 191
    overview, 190
Program Fraud Civil Remedies Act, 93–94
progress payment fraud
    examples, 195
    indicators, 195
    overview, 194
promotional items, 184
Proposed Rules: Federal Acquisition Regulation, 234
protecting procurement information
    anti-leaking laws, 33–34
    bid prices, 34
    competitive procurements, 32
    competitive range determinations, 35
    contractor bid or proposal information, 35, 36
    cost or price evaluations of proposals, 35
    cost or pricing data, 36
    disclosure and use of data, 36–37
    indirect costs and direct labor rates, 36
    leaked information, method obtained, 37
    proposed costs or prices, 34
    proprietary information, 36
    rankings of bids, proposals, or competitors, 35
    reports or evaluation of source selection panels, boards, or advisory councils, 35
    source selection information, 35
    source selection plans, 34
    technical evaluation plans, 35
    technical evaluations of proposals, 35
    time of award, 37–38

Q

qui tam lawsuit, 157–159

R

RAA. *See* Record of Acquisition Action
raw materials, inferior, 192

receiving stolen property, 100, 103
Record of Acquisition Action (RAA), 86
research costs, 184
responsibility determinations, 64–69
restrictions on lobbying and consultants, 165
restrictions on outside activities, 130–133
restrictions on seeking employment, 134–137
resumes, 151
revolving door, 39–41

S

sales slips, 148
shadow bidding, 181
small business government contractor, 19
solicitation phase fraud, 199–200
standards of conduct, 129–130
Standards of Ethical Conduct for Employees of the Executive Branch, 116
status of the offeror
  business integrity, 67
  debarment and suspension, 69–71
  de facto debarment, 67, 69
  General Services Administration example, 66–67
  Government Contract Advisory Services example, 69
  J.B. Kies Construction Co., 71
  responsibility determinations, 64–69
stock options, 183
subcontractors, 91
subcontracts
  compliance with ethics regulations, 21–22
  flow-down requirements, 21
  government hotline posters, 24–26
  purchase orders, 22
  types of, 21–22
suspension
  Army example, 99
  BASIX example, 102
  contract administration, 201
  Pro-Mark, Inc. example, 103
  regulations concerning, 100–101

T

tax evasion, 100, 103
templates, 10
theft, 100, 103, 164
time cards, 186–187
TINA. *See* Truth in Negotiations Act
Trade Secrets Act, 164
transfer of labor cost, 186
travel, 184
Truth in Negotiations Act (TINA), 80

U

unallowable costs, 183
unequal access to information, 48–59
untrained workers, 192
U.S. Attorney, 78
U.S. Court of Appeals for the Federal Circuit (CAFC)
  conflict of interest, 45–46
U.S. Department of Transportation Suspension and Debarment Work Group, 9–10
U.S. Sentencing Commission's guidelines
  importance of, 11
  satisfying, 11

V

VA. *See* Department of Veterans Affairs
violations
  Computer Technology Associates, Inc. example, 44
  impact, 42
  Loral Western Development Lab example, 42–43

W

whistleblower, 158–159
withholding bids, 178

Complement Your Federal Contracting Library with These Additional Resources from
MANAGEMENTCONCEPTS

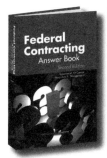

Federal Contracting Answer Book, Second Edition
Terrence M. O'Connor and Mary Ann P. Wangemann

Anyone involved in government contracting—whether a contractor or a federal contracting professional—knows how tough it is to learn the contracting process and stay on top of the ever-changing rules, regulations, and details. *Federal Contracting Answer Book, Second Edition*, provides clear, succinct answers to questions on all aspects of federal government contracting, particularly procedures and regulations. This second edition provides updated information about how the government makes an award decision, the key components required for negotiation, and the increased emphasis on procurement integrity. New chapters on costing and pricing offer insights into what the government looks for in evaluating an offeror's proposal.

ISBN 978-1-56726-245-2 ■ Product Code B452 ■ 558 pages

The COR/COTR Answer Book, Second Edition
Bob Boyd
The BESTSELLING COR/COTR Answer Book—Now Available in an Updated Second Edition with NEW Searchable CD!

Today, many CORs, COTRs, and other members of the acquisition team are taking on additional responsibilities from their contracting officers—including overseeing and monitoring contracts. If you are facing these new challenges, your knowledge of contracting issues is critical to your success. If you lack the knowledge you need, you risk making huge and costly mistakes. Make sure you know the issues, your roles and responsibilities, and common pitfalls in contract oversight. This second edition provides the practical guidance you need to ensure each contract's successful completion. Written in an easy-to-use Q&A style, this comprehensive guide includes answers to 460 common questions on how to monitor and oversee contracts.

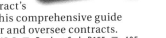

ISBN 978-1-56726-215-5 ■ Product Code B155 ■ 405 pages

Understanding Government Contract Law
Terrence M. O'Connor

A usable, plain-English explanation of the basic legal concepts that procurement officers need to know for their day-to-day procurement work, this book is a must-have resource. Examples and easy-to-understand explanations make procurement law understandable. This book follows the same structure as the Federal Acquisition Regulation, making it especially useful.

ISBN 978-1 56726-187-5 ■ Product Code B875 ■ 264 pages

Federal Acquisition Report

This monthly newsletter is the most thorough and informative way to ensure you stay on top of federal procurement. It is essential for government acquisition officials and private sector contractors to have a finger on the pulse of the federal procurement environment. The *Federal Acquisition Report* captures all of the current news trends, relevant board and court decisions, congressional legislation, rule changes, and public policy driving federal procurement standards and practices today. Expert legal interpretation translates Comptroller General decisions into easy-to-read reviews, informing you exactly how new legal decisions will affect your work. Available in your choice of formats: online, print, or both.

Online: Product Code ONLFA ■ Print: Product Code NLFA
Print and Online Combination: Product Code ONLFAC

Federal Acquisition ActionPacks

Federal Acquisition ActionPacks are designed for busy professionals who need to get a working knowledge of government contracting quickly—without a lot of extraneous detail. This ten-book set covers all phases of the acquisition process, grounds you firmly in each topic area, and outlines practical methods for success, from contracting basics to the latest techniques for improving performance.

Each spiral-bound book contains approximately 160 pages of quick-reading information—simple statements, bulleted lists, questions and answers, charts and graphs, and more. Each topic's most important information is distilled to its essence, arranged graphically for easy comprehension and retention, and presented in a user-friendly format designed for quick look-up.

Order the full set of Federal Acquisition ActionPacks to get a comprehensive knowledge of government contracting today.
Full set: ISBN 978-1-56726-198-1 ■ Product Code B981

Order the full set or order the single titles that are most important to your role in the contracting process. Either way, this is the most effective, affordable way for both buyers and sellers to get a broad-based understanding of government contracting—and proven tools for success.

Earned Value Management
Gregory A. Garrett
ISBN 978-1-56726-188-2 ■ Product Code B882
173 Pages

Best-Value Source Selection
Philip E. Salmeri
ISBN 978-1-56726-193-6 ■ Product Code B936
178 Pages

Performance-Based Contracting
Gregory A. Garrett
ISBN 978-1-56726-189-9 ■ Product Code B899
153 Pages

Government Contract Law Basics
Thomas G. Reid
ISBN 978-1-56726-194-3 ■ Product Code B943
175 Pages

Cost Estimating and Pricing
Gregory A. Garrett
ISBN 978-1-56726-190-5 ■ Product Code B905
161 Pages

Government Contracting Basics
Rene G. Rendon
ISBN 978-1-56726-195-0 ■ Product Code B950
176 Pages

Contract Administration and Closeout
Gregory A. Garrett
ISBN 978-1-56726-191-2 ■ Product Code B912
153 Pages

Performance Work Statements
Philip E. Salmeri
ISBN 978-1-56726-196-7 ■ Product Code B967
151 Pages

Contract Formation
Gregory A. Garrett and William C. Pursch
ISBN 978-1-56726-192-9 ■ Product Code B929
163 Pages

Contract Terminations
Thomas G. Reid
ISBN 978-1-56726-197-4 ■ Product Code B974
166 Pages

Order today for a 30-day risk-free trial!
Visit **www.managementconcepts.com/pubs** or call **703-790-9595**

DEFENSE ACQUISITION UNIVERSITY
DAVID D. ACKER LIBRARY
9820 BELVOIR ROAD
FORT BELVOIR, VA 22060-5565